Environment
of International
Business

Endel-Jakob Kolde
University of Washington

ENVIRONMENT
OF INTERNATIONAL
BUSINESS

KENT PUBLISHING COMPANY
Boston, Massachusetts
A Division of Wadsworth, Inc.

Senior Editor: *Keith O. Nave*
Production Editor/Designer: *Dale Anderson*
Manufacturing Coordinator: *Linda Card*
Cover Designer: *Steve Snider*

 Kent Publishing Company
A Division of Wadsworth, Inc.

Printed in the United States of America
1 2 3 4 5 6 7 8 9——86 85 84 83 82

Library of Congress Cataloging in Publication Data
Kolde, Endel-Jakob, 1917–
    The environment of international business.

    Bibliography: p.
    Includes index.

    1.   International business enterprises.   2.   International economic relations.
    I.   Title.

HD2755.5.K63   337   81–17122
ISBN 0–534–01038–5   AACR2

Preface

When the American Assembly of the Collegiate Schools of Business, the accrediting agency of top business schools in the United States, in 1977 mandated all accredited business schools to add international business to their core requirements, a vigorous debate ensued over how this could best be accomplished. Though marginal disagreements still remain, the central issue has been resolved: a growing consensus of academics and executives has opted for *a core course in international business focused on the environmental complexities that arise when business activities and institutions transcend international borders.*

Placing the focus on environment represents a significant step up from the mixed course format, which attempted to cover not only the environment but also the functional and business policy aspects of international business all in the same course. Such a shotgun approach seemed justified when no international topics were treated in the functional and policy courses of business administration. This is no longer true. Most business professors now cover international aspects of their respective disciplines; moreover, the recent trend has been to establish specialized international courses in the different functional departments.

The growing international capabilities in the functional disciplines (a) render redundant any operations-oriented introductory courses of international business, and (b) expose business schools to the risk of an extensive duplication of basic environmental concepts as each of the specialized courses attempts to establish the international environmental backgrounds and context necessary for their respective discipline.

From these developments within business schools has derived the necessity to focus the core courses on the environmental aspects of international business. Added impetus has come from the continued multiplication of cross-boundary interactions of business and from the quickening pulse of global dynamics in general.

The Environment of International Business was written in response to this newly recognized need. It is the first major text devoted exclusively to the analysis of environmental factors of international business. As such, it presents the most complete, systematic, and balanced treatment of the subject ever published. Its emphasis on the fundamental dynamics—the sources and causes of change in international business conditions—makes the book an uniquely effective means for developing the students' intellectual grasp of international realities. As such, *the book provides an ideal background for courses and seminars in international finance, marketing, management, or any other specialized international course.*

The basic structure of the book is designed according to the primary sources of problems confronting international business: cross-cultural conflicts, trade and payments systems, multinationalization of business enterprises, the issues and ideas of the North-South dialogue, the confrontations and accommodations between the communist East and the capitalist West, international integration and the rise of supranational economic systems, and the assimilation of international expertise into administrative professions. Within this structure the discussion is organized so that what is already familiar serves as a vehicle for understanding subsequent topics.

The interdisciplinary approach is another unique strength of the book. Both its conceptual framework and problem settings are unconstrained by traditional disciplinary boundaries, giving the analysis a refreshing sense of reality and concreteness. The interdisciplinary treatment minimizes the arbitrary exclusion of relevant factors that is characteristic of unidisciplinary works.

The author's research and consultant work embraces over forty countries, including most major business centers of the world. This actual involvement with strategic international issues of numerous industries and governments, it is hoped, should add authoritativeness and a global perspective to the book. It also helps to place U.S. problems and initiatives in their global context.

I would like to acknowledge the following people for the constructive suggestions they offered in reviewing the manuscript: James D. Goodnow, Roosevelt University; Arvind Phatak, Temple University; Howard C. Reed, University of Texas at Austin; and David Ricks, Ohio State University. Of great value to the author was a survey of the leading professionals in the field of international business; the responses helped greatly in shaping the book. I would like to thank the participants for their assistance and Keith O. Nave for organizing the survey and for his other valuable contributions to the creation of this book.

Endel-Jakob Kolde
Seattle, 1982

Contents

18.   The Human Environment in Developing Countries   **322**

19.   North-South Dialogue: Commodity Trade
   and Economic Structure   **343**

20.   North-South Dialogue: Resource Transfers   **359**

About the Author

*E*ndel-Jakob Kolde, Professor at the Graduate School of Business Administration, University of Washington, has been a pioneer of international business as a field of study. A native of Estonia, Dr. Kolde holds four academic degrees, including DHS Stockholm, Sweden, and Ph.D. Washington. His scholarly contributions are recognized the world over: he is an elected Fellow of the Academy of International Business; a winner of the McKinzey prize for his writings on management; an honorary citizen of Hyogo Prefecture, and a holder of the key to the city of Kobe, for his contributions to Japanese business education; and an honorary member of the Institute of Management Research, Seoul, Korea. He has held visiting professorships at Harvard, Lausanne, California (Berkeley), British Columbia, Kobe, Tokyo, and Cranfield (England), and has appeared as guest lecturer at the universities of some forty other nations on all continents.

In industry and government, Dr. Kolde has been valued as a researcher and adviser. Multinational companies, government agencies, and international organizations have sought his expertise to help solve a variety of international problems. Among the organizations he has advised are Boeing, Cross and Blackwell, Crown Zellerbach, Exxon, the Japan Management Association, Mitsubishi, Nestlé, the Pacific Northwest Trade Association, Standard Oil of California, Varian, the Lesotho Development Corporation, the Washington State International Trade Fair, Weyerhaeuser, the European Community, the Organization for Economic Cooperation and Development, the U.S. Departments of State and Commerce, and a number of other public bodies.

Dr. Kolde has published extensively. Several of his works have been translated into other languages.

Part One

THE SCOPE AND CONTEXT OF INTERNATIONAL BUSINESS

*T*he contemporary world is organized into nations. Their territorial boundaries are assumed to denote the partitions between sovereign political realms and separate national economies, each pursuing its own national interest. Though never completely true, this conceptualization no longer corresponds to reality. Businesses, along with many sociocultural organizations, have shown increasing propensities to transcend national boundaries and to create programs that are multinational in scope. As a result, the economic meaning of national boundaries has been changing, and the environment of business taking on new dimensions.

Part One of this book explores the avenues of the increasing intermingling of national business systems and the types of influences that flow from it. Chapter 1 defines the different forms of international business and outlines their purposes and problems. Chapter 2 presents a concise overview of the environmental plurality of international business and the complex relationships it embodies.

1

The Expanding Scope
of International Business

*D*efinitions of *business* are notoriously apt to delude. To some people, business is the pursuit of profits, to others it is private enterprise, and to still others it is any occupation or calling. None of these or similarly limited notions can sustain the burden of the word as used in this volume. For us, business is a comprehensive concept; it includes all productive enterprises organized to supply goods and services for society's material needs. Since business firms in the United States and many other countries are primarily in private control, it is inevitable that in talking of those countries *business* becomes more or less synonymous with *privately owned business*. Conceptually, however, the term *business* as used in this book encompasses also enterprises owned by states, municipalities, and other public bodies. To refer to socialized industries and Soviet enterprises as businesses may clash with ideological stereotypes or strain some latent biases—to the American tycoon it may be outrageous, to the Soviet commissar malicious, and to the Swedish neutralist slanderous. Yet this cannot be helped. Neither the advocacy of one or another business system nor the defense of any particular dogma can enhance the search for truth about a new and little-known subject. Objective analysis demands emotional indifference.

Business, then, is modern society's means of subsistence. In industrial countries it determines not only the material standards of life but also the modes of production, consumption, work, and leisure, and to an increasing degree the influence of individuals on the power structure of the society. Business has replaced the traditional elites—the landed aristocracy, the ecclesiastics, and the military—in the industrial countries, and it is forcing reform in the semi-industrial and even primitive ones. Thus, business is more than the workshop of the society. Besides providing goods and services, it provides the stage on which most of modern life's drama is played; and besides being the main source of wealth and power, it is a source of both economic and social progress. Indeed, modernity in a social sense is synonymous with a business-dependent industrial society, such as is found in the United States, Japan, and Western Europe.

BUSINESS SYSTEMS

A *system* is a set of interrelated elements. In simple systems, the elements are individual components or factors that have cause-and-effect relationships with one another. In complex systems, the elements are interacting subsystems, which themselves may contain several orders of subsystems as well as non-system components. The business system is such a complex hierarchy of subsystems of different order and character.

The National Business System

The components of the national business system are, first, the different enterprises—both private and public—created to produce goods and services. They in turn consist of internal subsystems such as subsidiaries, branches, divisions, departments, cost centers, and work groups. A second category of components of the system consists of industry associations of various kinds; these range from intraindustry trade associations (often with limited purposes) to interindustry and community-wide bodies, such as chambers of commerce, development associations, and industrial planning boards. A third set of components comprises labor, vocational, and professional groups, which are self-explanatory.

A fourth category embraces subsystems that function simultaneously as components in the business system and in one or more of the political, legal, governmental, educational, and other social systems of the country. This includes such organizations as vocational schools and performing arts groups. These elements link the business system functionally to most other important systems of the society. Through such links, the interactions among the business system and the society as a whole, the inputs and the outputs, manifest themselves.

For any one of the subsystems in a complex hierarchy such as the international business system, the next smaller subsystems are its *components*, and the larger systems to which it belongs constitute its *environment*. The impacts of the environment upon the system (effects of the system upon a subsystem) are *inputs*, and the impacts of the system upon its environment (effects of a subsystem upon the system) are *outputs*, positive or negative. The impacts among the components, the interactions within the system, constitute the *behavior* of the system. To give an example, a U.S. company is a subsystem of the U.S. economic system, its environment. A subsidiary is the company's component. Antipollution laws passed by the government are inputs on the company; the goods it produces are outputs affecting the environment.

The International Business System

All the national business systems combine into the international or multinational business system. Its components are the five types on page 6:

1. National business systems of individual countries
2. Various intermediary institutions designed to serve as channels for interaction, such as export and import middlemen, specialized foreign trade service firms, and international banking institutions
3. Multinational enterprises
4. Intergovernmental agencies and agreements, such as GATT (the General Agreement on Tariffs and Trade), UNCTAD (the United Nations Conference on Trade and Development), and OPEC (the Organization of Petroleum Exporting Countries)
5. Supranational entities and bodies, such as the EC (European Community), LAFTA (the Latin American Free Trade Association), and the Andean Pact

The middle three categories are peculiar to international business in the sense that without it they would not exist. They have evolved in response to multinational business requirements. As intercountry links, they transmit and often generate many of the interactions among the different national business systems. For this reason, the study of international business tends to polarize around intercountry links and to treat the internal workings of the national business systems in only a limited way.

The international business system has no fixed geographical boundaries but varies with one's objective. Unlike a national system, which by definition has concrete territorial scope and is composed of relatively easily defined subdivisions (regions, provinces, and municipalities), the international business system covers a geographical range from only two countries up to the entire world. Between these extremes one can conceive, at least in theory, as many different systems as there are combinations of countries. In practice, then, the boundaries of the international system should be chosen in such a way as to facilitate the study or analysis of particular aspects or particular behavior. Thus, different geographical boundaries are appropriate for different purposes.

MAIN TYPES OF INTERNATIONAL BUSINESS

The System of Nation States

The modern world is a mosaic of nation states. Its organization rests on the theory that each nation is the sole source of all the rights and powers to govern human affairs in its territory; its internal affairs are subject only to the values and laws that the sovereign state's authorities establish. Foreign interference and dependence on other countries violate the concept of sovereignty. Thus, as a political ideal, absolute national sovereignty or independence requires an absence of international interdependence.

In reality, no country can completely isolate its internal life from external forces. To be sure, some nations, including Albania, Burma, and China recently, have tried to isolate themselves from the outside world; some other nations, such as Nepal, Bhutan, Chad, and the Mongolian Republic, are geographically isolated by being landlocked. But national borders have never been capable of sealing out all foreign influences and transboundary relationships. Even the most inward-looking regimes must ultimately cope with the limitations of their domestic resources as well as the unsuppressible human curiosity about the world beyond their borders.

In the business sphere, transboundary relationships have a long history. Some things have always been better, cheaper, or more readily available abroad than at home. Sports cars, stereo equipment, wine, cheese, watches, carpets, shoes, high fashions, and, until recently, abortions are typical examples. In addition, in some countries essential raw materials are either completely lacking or not available in sufficient quantities; in the United States, tropical fruits, natural rubber, bauxite, chromium, and petroleum lead a long list of materials in this category. To pay for imports, a country must export; to be able to make full use of its own resources and industrial capacities, a country needs access to foreign markets.

Although the international business activities that come to mind most readily are exports and imports, foreign trade in merchandise or tangible goods is only a fraction of total international business today. Just as goods are traded across national boundaries, so are services, stocks and bonds, industrial technology, and managerial expertise. Just as foreign goods are attractive to domestic consumers, so foreign factories, department stores, and banks are attractive to domestic investors.

A country's dependence on international business activity tends to vary inversely with its size; larger countries have more diverse resources and markets and thus can be more self-sufficient than smaller countries. For example, per capita exports in 1979 were $1,650 for Belgium/Luxembourg, $500 for France, and only $240 for the United States. But larger countries also have larger needs and capabilities, especially if they are highly industrialized. Therefore, their international activities have a significant effect on the rest of the world.

Large or small, industrialized or not, all countries can benefit from international business. The basic question has never really been whether or not a nation should have international business relations, but rather, what kind of and how much international involvement it should have. With constantly increasing interdependence, the scope and composition of international business are an increasingly important priority in both governmental and business policy.

International business is a composite of four subareas: trade and payments, investments, and multinational enterprises. Thus, it encompasses not only international transactions but also institutions and organizations that cross national boundaries. These four subsystems are interrelated in many ways, as we shall learn in later chapters.

International Trade and Payments

The oldest type of transboundary business activity is international trade. It consists of *exports*—sales of home country goods to foreign buyers—and *imports*—purchases of goods from abroad. Exports and imports are called *autonomous* or *primary transactions*, because they are presumed to have been undertaken for their own sake; that is, the trader expected a profit or some other benefit from the transaction.

International trade gives rise to *international payments*. Every export transaction causes an *inbound payment* or *international receipt*, and every import transaction causes an *outbound payment* or *international remittance*. Since the payments are a consequence of the export and import activities they are known as *induced* or *secondary transactions*.

The Balance of Trade   Another way to describe foreign trade is to say that it embraces buying and selling between residents of different countries. For the seller's country the cross-boundary transactions are exports; for the buyer's country they are imports. Since every export transaction of every country must simultaneously be some other country's import transaction, worldwide total exports always equal total imports. From the global perspective, then, international trade is always balanced.

However, this equality need not hold for an individual country. Although a country may be both an exporter and an importer, it is not necessarily always able to balance exports and imports. Some countries find their products in great demand abroad while their domestic demand for foreign-made goods is low; the result in this case is called an *export surplus* or a *positive balance of trade*. Other countries may have an imbalance of trade in the opposite direction; their consumers are eager purchasers of imported goods, while their exporters have difficulty selling abroad. Here the excess of imports over exports creates an *export deficit* (*import surplus*) or a *negative balance of trade*. Such imbalances in the foreign trade of a country, unless they are offset by other kinds of inflows and outflows, may have serious repercussions on international monetary relations and on the economic policies of the country and its trading partners.

Effects of Trade Balance on Individual Firms   The trade balance is significant for national governments, but an individual business firm is affected only indirectly by its country's balance of trade, unless the country is running a serious and persistent deficit or surplus. A serious, persistent trade deficit may induce the government to impose import restrictions such as *quotas*, which hurt importing firms directly by limiting the quantity of goods that can be imported, or *foreign exchange controls*, which indirectly limit the quantity of goods that can be imported by denying the importer's access to the foreign exchange necessary to pay for the imports. The government might also introduce export expansion programs; it might send trade missions to other countries, organize international trade fairs, provide tax relief for exporters, or even directly subsidize export activities in order to enable private traders to sell at competitive prices abroad. Obviously, all the measures would be helpful for the exporting firms. An excessive trade surplus, on the other hand, may lead to governmental restrictions on exports or import incentives, which would again affect the opportunities of companies engaged in international trade.

Except for these governmental interventions during balance of trade disturbances, an individual firm's international trading activities are generally independent; trade is a function of the firm's knowledge and managerial capabilities, which enable it to identify and cultivate profitable export and import opportunities. Some firms not only specialize in international trade, but further specialize by product line or geographical area. Thus, both the purposes and perspective of a trading company are different from those of a government. This difference must be recognized if we are to avoid the rather common misconception that trading policies of businesses will or should coincide with the international commercial policies of a government. Only under a centrally planned system, in which the business function is carried out by the state, would the government's and the firm's objectives become more or less the same. In free enterprise countries it is the business managers' independence and initiative, rather than governmental direction, that are the primary determinants of international trade.

International Investment

Although international trade is the oldest and most familiar kind of international business, foreign investment—the transboundary purchase of financial assets—is a much more important and dynamic international business activity today. Foreign investment falls into two broad categories, portfolio investment and direct investment. The essential differences between these two categories involve managerial control and the allocation of the investment funds.

Portfolio Investment International portfolio investment, or indirect investment, is the purchase of foreign securities (stocks, bonds, and commercial paper) in order to earn a return in the form of interest, dividends, or capital gains. When an investor buys foreign securities he acquires an indirect claim to the assets of some foreign enterprise, but he does not acquire the specific, tangible assets that comprise the earning power of the enterprise whose securities he has purchased. Nor does he have a direct say in where the enterprise's products are to be sold or at what price. In other words, the purchase of an indirect claim to ownership of a foreign enterprise does not confer managerial control on the owner of the securities, regardless of how large or diversified his investment portfolio may be.

A United States investor might decide, for example, that because of the company's superior marketing and production abilities in consumer electronics, the stock of Matsushita Electric Industrial Company of Osaka, Japan, is a sound investment. If the United States investor purchases Matsushita stock (he will actually acquire American Depository Receipts, ADRs, which represent shares owned in the United States but held on deposit physically in Japan), he will be engaging in international portfolio investment. Likewise, if a Swiss citizen purchases shares of IBM through one of the more than 250 foreign branches of United States securities firms, he will be engaging in international portfolio investment.

The international portfolio investor is primarily a creditor whose main concern is the placement of his capital among the existing enterprises of different countries. The investor does not actively participate in the management of the enterprises involved. Although entitled to a vote in proportion to the share of stock held, the investor normally plays a negligible role in the managerial affairs of the enterprise. Only in the exceptional case, where they provide the means for acquiring the ownership interest necessary for ultimate managerial control, do portfolio investments play a role. This happens only when the investor attempts a takeover.

Portfolio investments tend to fluctuate with stock prices and interest rates. When securities can be purchased more cheaply on La Bourse in Paris than on the New York Stock Exchange, outbound portfolio investments or security imports soar; when the reverse is true, foreigners enter the American market, causing inbound portfolio investments or securities exports. The responsiveness of securities purchases to stock market prices and interest rates means that there is always a considerable amount of cross-trading of international portfolio investments. For example, Europeans might purchase $5 million of equity shares in United States industry in a period in which United States investors purchase $4 million of bonds and other interest-bearing obligations of European enterprises. The total volume of indirect investment between the United States and Europe in this period would be $9 million, but the net impact of indirect investments on the U.S. balance of payment would be an inflow of $1 million.

Portfolio investments may have a life of only a few days, weeks, or months, as such securities are bought and sold in response to the different investors' needs and assessments of future changes in securities prices.

Direct Investment   Direct foreign investment involves acquisitions by domestic companies of foreign-based operating facilities, such as factories, warehouses, packaging plants, hotels, banks, or insurance companies. The investor buys specific tangible assets that possess the capacity to produce either goods or services outside the investor's home country. Direct private foreign investment represents a commitment that is not only long term but that also implies managerial control over the assets or enterprises acquired.

Direct investments are the vehicles for the birth and growth of multinational enterprises, but the two can never be considered synonymous. The central concerns of the multinational enterprise are production, distribution, and other operational activities that generate outputs and profits. Investments play only a supporting role in this complex of activities. Furthermore, the typical multinational company minimizes its international capital transfers by drawing upon indigenous resources for both equity and loanable funds where feasible and by plowing profits back into the affiliates in different countries. Regrettably, these important distinctions are not yet assimilated into many text books.

In the past it was assumed that trade and investment, taken together, measured the total scope of international business activity. This traditional concept was not too far from the actual reality so long as foreign investments were primarily portfolio investments and a trader's national identity was the same as that of the country in which the company operated. Under those conditions international business activity consisted exclusively of *transboundary transactions*—sales and purchases of either goods or securities across national borders, plus the international payments caused by such sales or purchases. No other kind of business relationship was recognized between different national economies.

This traditional concept is no longer adequate. Although occasional direct investments date back to the last century, it is only since the 1950s that direct investments have grown to challenge trade and portfolio investments in importance. The rapid rise of direct investments in the recent past has caused much conceptual confusion and heated controversy. The rise to dominance of multinational companies (MNCs) has added a new mode of operation across national borders that extends the scope of international business far beyond the limits of trade, investment, and payments transactions (see Figure 1.1).

Multinational Companies

Acquisition of foreign operating facilities—generally called *affiliates*—causes a company to transfer not only investment capital but also technology, material inputs (machines and equipment, component parts and supplies), and management expertise, in order to make the affiliate as efficient and profitable as possible. The affiliates in turn generate outputs and income that may never leave the host economy, may flow back to the headquarters company, or move from one affiliate's host country to another affiliate's host country, or be divided among the three alternatives. The result is a network of intracompany international relationships and activities that integrates all the different entities of the firm into a multinational whole.

Key Characteristics   The most important characteristic of the MNC is its simultaneous possession of operating capacity (factories, warehouses, branch offices) in several national economies. The capacity to produce and market products, whether tangible or intangible, in a number of countries may be acquired through ownership (*direct investments*), through cooperation with firms of the host nation (*joint ventures* and *licensing*), or through long-term contracts to manage enterprises that are owned by nationals of foreign countries (for a discussion of these points, see Chapter 9).

From this multicountry capacity derive multilateral transboundary relationships. Take, for example, a car manufacturer who has acquired an engine factory in England, a transmission factory in Germany, an electric components plant in Switzerland, body plants in Italy and the United States, and assembly plants in these and some other countries. From the British affiliate engines are shipped to all the assembly plants; similarly, from Germany, transmissions are dispatched, from Switzerland the electric components, and from the United States and Italy bodies. Each affiliate not only produces its respective product but also generates sales revenues and incomes.

A. *FOREIGN TRADE* (transboundary sales of goods and services)

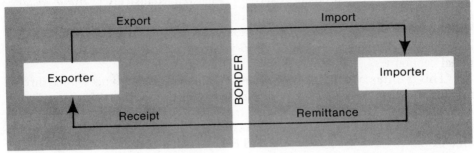

Exports cause receipts from abroad.   Imports cause remittances abroad.

B. *PORTFOLIO INVESTMENT* (transboundary trade in securities)

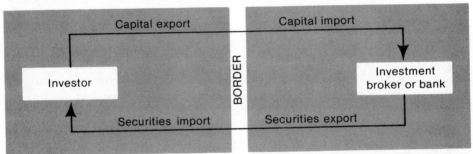

Purchase of foreign stocks or bonds
causes capital export and securities
import.

Sale of domestic stocks or bonds to
foreigners causes capital import and
securities export.

C. *DIRECT FOREIGN INVESTMENT* (acquisition of operating assets abroad)

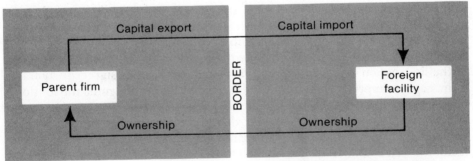

Establishing or acquiring assets
abroad causes capital export and
ownership import.

Establishing or acquiring assets
from abroad causes capital import
and ownership export.

Figure 1.1   Component Concepts of International Business

D. *MULTINATIONAL COMPANY* (managerial control over a group of affiliated enterprises in several countries)

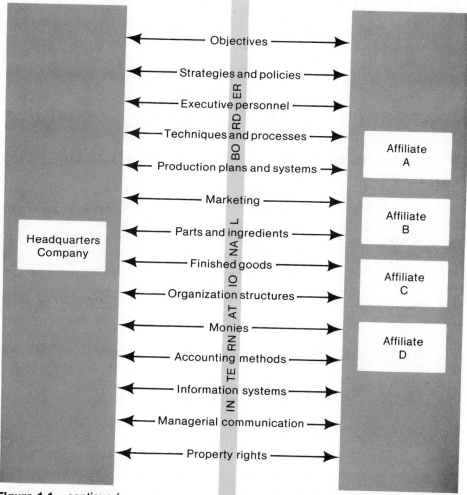

Figure 1.1   *continued*

Management must organize and coordinate the operations of all the affiliates so as to achieve a synchronized system of the multinational company as a whole. Since the possession of operating affiliates by a firm is normally a permanent or at least a long-range condition, the MNC cannot be conceived as a collection of international transactions; it is an ongoing process of both creation and allocation of assets in a multinational context. In addition to export, import and investment transactions, MNCs generate permanent, non-transactional cross-boundary business relationships. These range from the ownership of real estate to possessing managerial authority and from integrating production systems to pooling cash flows. MNCs have also greatly extended the list of transboundary transactions, as we shall learn in later chapters.

Heterogeneous Environment   The possession of operating capacities in many countries is the defining characteristic of the multinational company, but this fact has wide ramifications. Each affiliate must comply with its particular host country's laws and regulations; each is part of a different national economy with its own resource base and local markets; each must adapt to the social and cultural norms of its host society to be an acceptable corporate citizen; and each is staffed by employees from a different nationality who often speak a different language. Each of these facts creates managerial complications for the MNC. In brief, multinationalization changes both the external and internal environments of the headquarters company.

The more countries a company enters, the greater are the changes in that company's environment. Every country imposes something new and makes the overall environmental framework more heterogeneous. The increasing heterogeneity requires organizational and managerial changes that pervade the whole company. Directly affected are such important functions as financing, marketing, purchasing, tax liabilities, ownership policies, educational requirements for executives, and even the philosophical outlook of corporate planners and policy makers. Indirectly, the increasing heterogeneity of the multinational business environment causes most management systems and processes to take on new dimensions and to become more complex and sophisticated, as we will see in Chapter 2.

INTERNATIONAL INFLUENCES ON DOMESTIC BUSINESS

Direct and Indirect Influences

Many international influences on domestic business are so subtle and roundabout that they are confused with domestic developments. For example, a U.S. Food and Drug Administration clearance permitting the sale of a given pharmaceutical may not be related in the public's mind with the Swiss patent by which it is manufactured, nor would a drug store and its clientele be aware of the international investments, production and marketing organizations, and competitive shifts in the drug market that the Swiss-invented product may have caused. Other international influences may be more direct: a Japanese quota on American beef or a price rise of OPEC crude oil will be more widely understood. But whether direct or indirect, the international influence is real. Often the total impact of the indirect influences is even greater due to the fact that indirect influences are less likely to elicit an informed counteraction by the affected domestic businesses.

The international influences on domestic business originate in three basic sources as shown in Figure 1.2. These three sources are interlocked in numerous ways. Although sovereign in theory, the U.S. government does not act in disregard of other nations or its own business community; rather, it acts in the context of both the domestic and international forces at play. The same is true of businesses. Though a firm may be privately owned, it does not enjoy

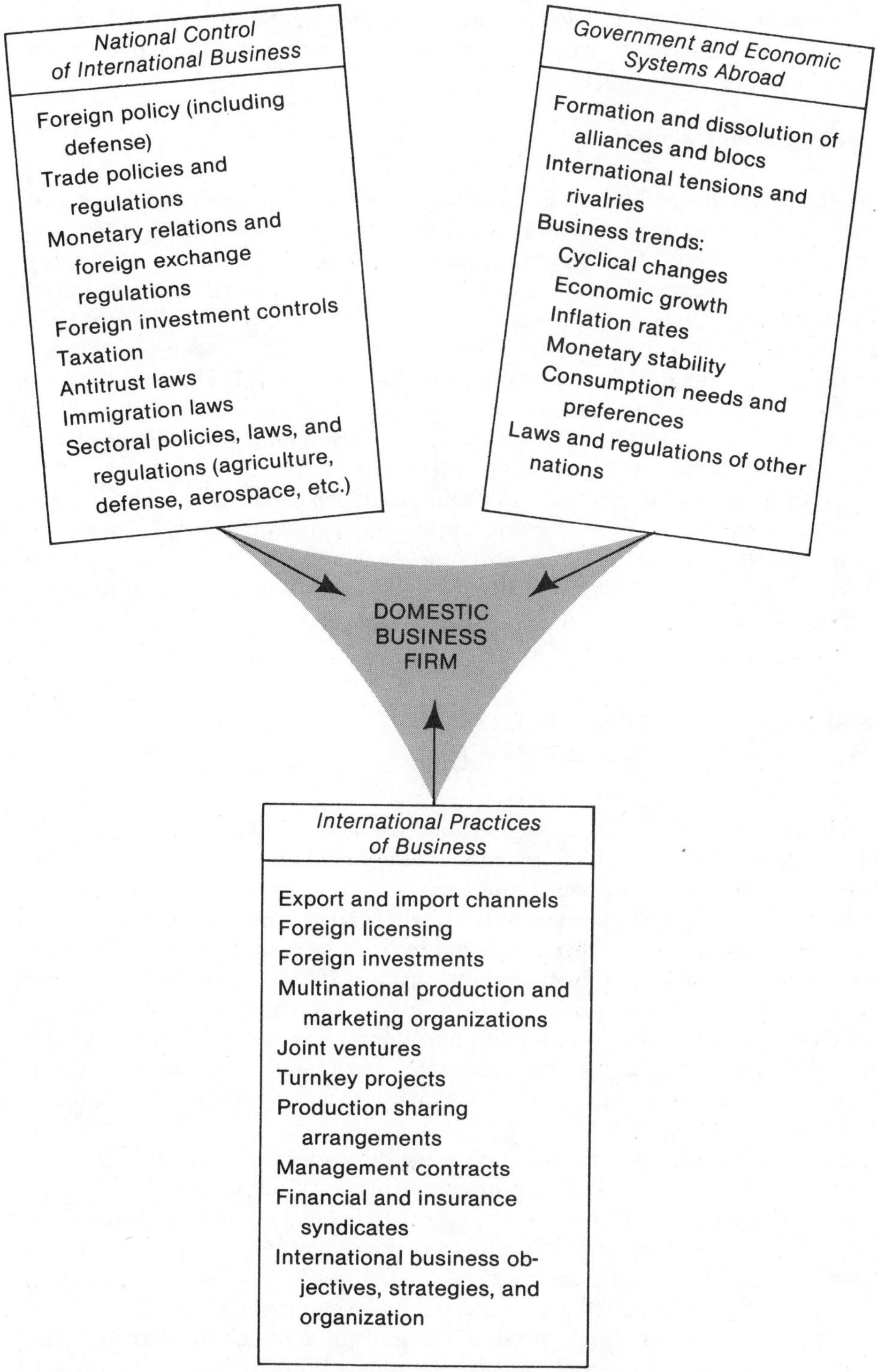

National Control of International Business	Government and Economic Systems Abroad
Foreign policy (including defense)	Formation and dissolution of alliances and blocs
Trade policies and regulations	International tensions and rivalries
Monetary relations and foreign exchange regulations	Business trends:
	Cyclical changes
	Economic growth
Foreign investment controls	Inflation rates
Taxation	Monetary stability
Antitrust laws	Consumption needs and preferences
Immigration laws	Laws and regulations of other nations
Sectoral policies, laws, and regulations (agriculture, defense, aerospace, etc.)	

DOMESTIC
BUSINESS
FIRM

International Practices of Business

Export and import channels
Foreign licensing
Foreign investments
Multinational production and
 marketing organizations
Joint ventures
Turnkey projects
Production sharing
 arrangements
Management contracts
Financial and insurance
 syndicates
International business ob-
 jectives, strategies, and
 organization

Figure 1.2 Overview of How the International Environment Affects Domestic Firms

unlimited freedom, for the actions of both government and other businesses, particularly competitors, usually compel it to follow a relatively narrow path.

Profiting from Change

Due to the adaptive and interactive tendencies among the main sources of change, any specific international influence on domestic business may be shaped by all three. The trigger mechanism for any influence on business is change. To be successful, a firm, through its management, must be able to anticipate what changes it will face, make timely preparations for adapting to the changes, and learn to profit from the changes. The essence of business management is the management of change. In politics and diplomacy the same necessity is expressed in the slogan "the art of the possible." In substance this, too, refers to the adaptation to and benefiting from change. Without change no art is necessary; the status quo maintains itself.

Management's effectiveness in dealing with change is a function of both knowledge and time. Grasping the causes and consequences of change and being able to anticipate it allows an optimal response to it; conversely, either the inability to understand the change or insufficient time to respond to it may spell disaster.

ASSESSING THE IMPORTANCE OF INTERNATIONAL BUSINESS

Growing interdependence among nations has accelerated the increase of international influences on U.S. business. The same is true for other countries. Since the traditional business education has been almost entirely inward-looking, U.S. managers are generally intellectually unprepared to cope with the new business realities that are rooted in the international sphere. Statistics such as the percentage of gross national product (GNP) generated by foreign trade or the number of jobs created by export activities are useful only for some purposes. Despite their limited usefulness, they are still propounded to prove how self-sufficient the U.S. economy is. Such statistics, however cleverly devised, are false representations of the total impact of international affairs on U.S. business.

To illustrate the point, take such apparently simple factors as imports. A common fallacy equates the importance of imports with their dollar value. This says nothing about the effects imports may have on other industries and on consumer welfare. Imported finished goods enrich consumers' choices; though such enrichment is unmeasurable statistically, it is absurd to deny it any value. For imports of raw materials and semimanufactured goods, the fallacy is even greater. Such imports are used in combination with domestic materials, technology, capital, and labor to make finished goods. Hence, the imports serve as the basis for jobs, payrolls, and an ultimate output of goods and services whose aggregate value is normally several times the value of the imports themselves.

Consider for a moment one basic material, aluminum. This strong but lightweight metal, so important to so many industries—including transportation (imagine a Boeing 757 without aluminum), building and construction, electronics, consumer durables, and packaging—is made from bauxite ore. The United States must import about 85 percent of the bauxite it consumes as aluminum. In a typical year the value of the imported bauxite is about 0.005 percent of our GNP. But if the imports of bauxite were suddenly unavailable, would the United States GNP shrink only 0.005 percent? What would be the impact on quality and availability of inputs to other industries and of consumer goods?

Obviously, imports provide the basis for a far greater share of the GNP than the value recorded in the import statistics. Although the total value of imports is approximately only 6 to 9 percent of the United States GNP in recent years, it would be fallacious to say that the elimination of imports would reduce GNP only by 6 to 9 percent. In most import-dependent industries the decline would be much greater. In the absence of key imported ingredients, the domestic productive facilities of certain industries might well become idle, or production would be curtailed because of higher cost or lower quality of substitutes for the imports. The cutbacks in the import-dependent industries, would, in turn, tend to have secondary effects in the other sectors of the economy.

How other international factors may have similar multiplier effects in the domestic economy will become clearer in later chapters. Our purpose here is to emphasize that the study of international business is necessary not only for people who are involved in some international organization—business or non-business—but also for people aiming for a managerial career in domestic business. It is for this reason that the Association of the Collegiate Schools of Business in 1976 established international business as part of the required core curriculums.

PROBLEM AREAS

A general outline of the main areas with which international business must cope is shown in Figure 1.3. In the center lie the objectives of the enterprise (usually either profit maximization or the fulfillment of norms prescribed in a national plan). To achieve the objectives, management must formulate and implement appropriate strategies, programs, and policies. From a functional standpoint, the managerial responsibilities fall into four main categories: finance, production, marketing, and the organizational and institutional structure within which the enterprise is to function. Each of the four contains subareas, of which three main ones are shown. An explanation of how these, in turn, proliferate into clusters of component fields will occupy much of this book. These are all part of the internal environment of an enterprise.

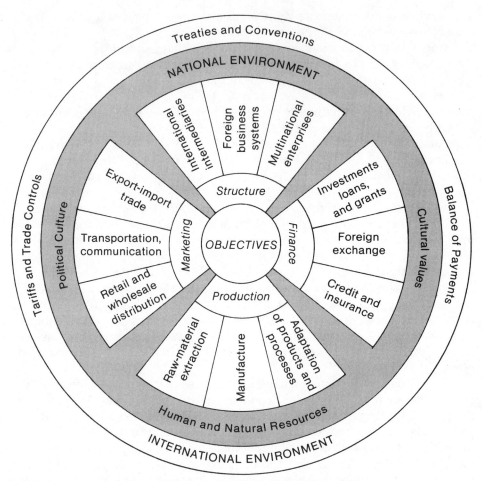

Figure 1.3   The Scope and Composition of International Business

From the outside, the company encounters both positive and negative elements that must be identified and understood before rational choices can be made among the alternatives available in different parts of the world. The environmental effects on business enterprise are among the most subtle and complex influences in an international context. As an enterprise moves beyond a single country and extends successively to more countries, the environmental diversity grows progressively. From such diversity arise new opportunities, uncertainties, incentives, impediments, and necessities for the enterprise and its management. Multinational diversity may also transmute the previous norms, managerial conduct, executive action, and corporate behavior as a whole. The multinational environmental framework, within which international enterprise must function and in reference to which its administrative decisions must be made, is, therefore, of paramount importance to the understanding of international business.

Some have argued that the need for study of international business as a field could be obviated if the traditional subject areas of business administration would broaden their coverage to include the international aspects. The experience of multinational companies has strongly discredited this view, but the point may still be worth making that no amount of "internationalization" of the specialized subfields of business administration can take the place of studying international business per se. Technical and functional disciplines such as finance, marketing, and production are often helpful and sometimes vital for the study of international business. But, since none of them deals with the multinational framework as a whole, they can neither singly nor collectively cope with the basic problems of international business administration. Not only is the sum of the parts smaller than the whole, but also many of the parts, including the most important ones, would never be included if the environmental framework of international business were not subjected to thorough analysis and study. It goes without saying that the problems peculiar to foreign societies lie far beyond the purview of the traditional subfields of business administration as we know them today and as they are taught by colleges in this country.

The growth of multinational business operations and the increasing interdependence of world economies create the need for people who are competent to handle international problems and situations. As a result, schools have come under pressure to offer educational programs that go beyond the U.S. experience in both business and other fields. U.S. schools have not been able to respond adequately to the accelerating demand for international expertise. The lack of international competence has not only troubled the management profession but has also been implicated in numerous political and cultural fiascoes, such as the Iranian hostage crisis and the Cuban sea lift.

The failure of the schools to keep abreast of the increasing needs for international expertise led to the appointment of a presidential commission to study how to remedy the situation. Since the commission was headed by James A. Perkins, distinguished former president of Cornell University, it is generally referred to as the Perkins Commission. Completing its work in 1980, the commission found that the inadequacies of U.S. citizens to handle international problems stem from long-held biases in the country's educational system. Because of the nation's physical distance from other cultures, education in the United States has had a distinct insularity. Neither the schools nor the public have until now recognized the necessity of studying other peoples. Now that the need has suddenly arisen, educators are ill-prepared to do anything about it. Most instructors, from high school teachers to university deans, have had only minimal exposure to international studies themselves. To remedy the situation the commission recommended:

1. Expansion of international programs at all universities
2. Requirement of at least two to three courses of international subject matter to all university graduates (in addition to languages)
3. Reinstatement of foreign language requirements in high schools and colleges
4. Inclusion of an international educational requirement in the certification of all teachers, including university professors

As noted earlier, business schools are in the forefront of internationalizing academic programs by requiring that all graduates have at least some international study. The basic pedagogical task of international business is to broaden the executive's perspective by giving him or her a wider and a structurally more flexible frame of reference and a more diversified conceptual grasp than he or she otherwise would possess. This knowledge will increase the manager's powers to perceive, compare, and adapt. International work done in the base subjects such as finance, marketing, and production is a direct benefit to international business since it contributes to the total store of relevant knowledge and enables more sophisticated, higher-level treatment in the integrative and behavioral analyses that international business must pursue. Conversely, a solid international business program benefits all other fields of business administration by providing the frame of reference in which they can more effectively pursue international objectives of their own.

SUMMARY

Multinational business includes all economic activities and relationships that extend across national boundaries. Its main components are trade (exports and imports), international payments, foreign investments, and the organization and behavior of multinational companies (MNCs). Thus, multinational business includes not only international transactions, but also much more. Multinational companies and their influences, both business and nonbusiness, have become particularly important, if not predominant, aspects of the field. They incorporate not only international activities but also all concurring types of business operations which take place in host countries but never or rarely cross the national borders of the headquarters country. Since the MNC organizes ties with many countries, its behavior is a particularly complex and comprehensive subject.

Familiarity with sociocultural systems in different host nations is necessary to managers of MNCs. Multinational business studies, therefore, must draw on anthropology, geography, world politics, psychology, and sociology, in addition to other branches of business administration, such as finance, marketing, personnel, and systems management. Even art, linguistics, and literature as expressions of the social values and cultural characters of different countries, are significantly linked to multinational business realities.

Because of such intermingling with many academic disciplines, the boundaries for multinational business as a field of study defy exact delineation. Its peripheral subtopics are seldom discrete parts but more often continuous extensions that bridge multinational business with some other field. There is no clearcut way to separate the two. Therefore, it is best to conceive the borders of multinational business studies not as a fixed line but as a flexible zone of subjects that may or may not be included, depending upon their relevance to any particular problem. Our main concern in this book is not definitional detail, but the topics that form the main body of multinational business. It is not the periphery, but the central core, where the most useful learning and rewarding preparation for multinational managerial careers can be found.

The central objective of international business as an academic field is to study the problems that arise when business operations and organizations cross national boundaries and become multinational in structure and scope. In recent years, international expansion has become commonplace in U.S. businesses, making international problems an organic aspect of management. As a result, there is an increasing need to understand foreign environments, business methods, and the techniques of adapting management processes and organizational behavior to new and different conditions.

FOR REVIEW AND DISCUSSION

1. How would you differentiate between domestic and international business?

2. Do you agree that the basic purpose of international business is making profits? Explain.

3. What is meant by exports and imports of securities?

4. Why is it erroneous to regard MNCs as synonymous with international investments?

5. Identify the parts of Figure 1.3 that you rate as the most important elements of international business.

6. Do official statistics of exports, imports, and foreign investments overstate or understate the true significance of international business? Explain fully.

7. Domestic firms are unaffected by international business. Substantiate or refute.

8. Cite examples of how foreign events have influenced business in your city or state.

9. If all subfields of business administration, such as accounting, finance, and marketing, would cover the international aspects of their subjects, there would be no need for any course in international business. Comment.

10. It has been argued that international studies are more difficult for U.S. students than for students in European countries because of the geographical isolation of the United States. Is this a valid argument? What other factors might motivate students to become interested in international studies?

2

The Environmental Context of International Business

The primary distinction between international business and national (domestic) business lies in the differences in their environments. The environmental differences lead to behavioral and managerial differences. Although the objectives of a company may remain the same, its organization, strategies, policies, and operating practices undergo a multitude of adjustments or even complete revisions when the firm expands its operations beyond its home country. International expansion confronts management with new problems as well as new possibilities in each host economy. Thus, international expansion requires managers to cope with increasing environmental complexities. To do so, they need information and insights that for purely domestic managers may be quite inconsequential.

In this chapter we will survey the main factors in business environments that change significantly at international boundaries. The purpose of the chapter is twofold: to provide an overview of the international business environment by placing in perspective the more detailed subjects of subsequent chapters, and to give concrete meaning to international environmental contrasts.

CROSS-NATIONAL ENVIRONMENTAL CONTRASTS

A systematic overview of the environmental discontinuities represented by international boundaries will help make more explicit the differences between international and national business environments. To prevent the details from concealing the underlying structures, it is useful to focus on categories of related factors instead of specifics. Since most readers of this book are U.S. citizens, it is appropriate to use the United States as an illustration. A reader from another nation may wish to construct a similar scheme for his or her home country. Such a study will help to identify a number of environmental commonalities that apply to all businesses in a given country. They serve as common ground rules for all firms throughout that national economy. At the

23

national boundary, these ground rules come to an end and some other nation's system begins.

The Government System

The United States Constitution is the supreme law of the nation. It sets forth the principles to which all other laws and regulations must conform. It is the law of laws; no human or organizational conduct, no economic or social relationship is beyond its scope. Although many specific areas of human conduct are not expressly mentioned in the Constitution, by implication they are all covered. Because it is the ultimate law, nothing unconstitutional can be legitimately practiced by any citizen or business firm of this country.

The Constitution establishes the basic framework of government institutions. First, it requires tripartite division of powers among the legislative, executive, and judicial branches; second, it delineates matters of jurisdiction reserved for the federal authorities and those left for the individual states and localities; and third, it provides for separation of religion from law (church from state).

Thus, the Constitution creates the basic structure of public institutions and provides principles that must be followed by nonpublic institutions such as businesses and nonprofit organizations.

The federal format is followed by individual states as they exercise the powers reserved for them. For this purpose, states have designed their own constitutions, agencies, and laws, extending and adapting the federal system to their different needs and preferences. The state systems add variety and specificity but can never supercede the federal system. Together, the federal and state systems have created an elaborate set of principles, laws, institutions, regulations, and public policies that apply to all businesses of a given industry in the United States and that form a common framework for business activity.

This elaborate system comes to an abrupt end at the national boundaries. Neither the U.S. Constitution nor the legal and institutional structures created under it have any validity whatsoever in any other country. If it were not for the fact that nations borrow ideas and models from one another there would be no resemblances among different national environments in this respect. In reality, nations do borrow and imitate, just as individuals do, but this is purely coincidental. Thus, when a business crosses the national border it enters an entirely different ball park, with different rules, different referees, and different ways of keeping score.

The Enterprise System

Under the United States Constitution, the business of producing the goods and services for the nation are left to private enterprise. However, the ground rules for business activities are set forth in great detail in a large and constantly growing body of laws, regulations, precedent-setting court rulings, and public policies.

All of these apply to businesses in the United States only. Other countries have their own rules for business. As a result, the entry into any new country confronts a U.S. firm with a number of different requirements. The types of company charters; the responsibility for the forms and enforcement of contracts; the methods of calculating costs, incomes, and profits; the responsibilities to consumers; the rights of employer and labor unions; the methods of financing; and the tax liabilities are but a few of the major subjects in this intricate framework which is relatively uniform in the domestic context but highly variegated internationally.

The most fundamental feature of the U.S. economic system is its reliance on market competition. Monopolies, cartels, and collusion among potential business competitors are outlawed and the methods of pricing, promotion, and distribution subjected to elaborate surveillance by both federal and state agencies. Thus, the U.S. free enterprise system is far from free. It is structured, regulated, and constrained in countless ways.

Though certain similarities to many of the elements characteristic of the U.S. competitive system are found in other nations' economies, no economy duplicates it. From an international perspective, therefore, the U.S. system represents a separate set, a vast rule book for business in the United States. In each other country, a new text is required. Each has its own enterprise system, with a different mix of actors, roles, and rules.

The Monetary System

Another commonality of the U.S. business environment is its monetary system. Its centerpiece is the dollar, the national currency. All financial transactions are measured and settled in dollars. The institutional and operational machinery of the monetary system is an extension of the free enterprise system. It consists of three main segments: the federal reserve system—the banker's bank, the national banks, and the various state banks and credit associations. All money market dealings of U.S. businesses take place within this framework. There is no other way. Thus, the kinds of deposits and loans, interest rates, credit instruments, and banking practices are to a high degree standardized throughout the national economy. Since nearly all normal business transactions involve money in some way, the importance of the national monetary system as a unifying force in the U.S. business environment can hardly be overstressed. At the border, however, this system ends and another country's currency and money market institutions start. There is an abrupt break and, behind it, a new monetary environment.

The Capital Market

Though part of the monetary system in the general sense, the capital market deserves separate mention because of its strategic role in financing private enterprise. Here, too, U.S. business has its own environmental framework. The types of securities (stocks and bonds), the rules and regulations of floating them, the brokerage houses, the two central markets (the New York Stock Exchange and the American Stock Exchange), as well as the guardian federal agency (the Securities and Exchange Commission), are all unique.

But like the U.S. money market, the U.S. capital market ends abruptly at the national border. To be sure, there are linkages between the different nations' capital markets, but in the main each is quite distinct.

The Demographic Environment

The people of the United States are perhaps the most important aspect of the business environment. The absolute size, age and sex distributions, growth rates, geographic distribution, ethnic subdivisions, and household units of the nation's population represent quantitative indicators of markets for goods and services as well as the availabilities of human resources for business pursuits. But that is only the beginning. The demographic environment of business in the United States gains greater depth when we add information on education, occupational characteristics, work habits, income classes, consumption requirements, leisure and recreational preferences, and other qualitative characteristics of the population. The United States demographic environment turns out not only to be unique to this economy but also to be increasingly more differentiated from its counterparts in other countries as we delve deeper in studying it.

The Labor Market

International borders represent also a discontinuity of wage rates, fringe benefits, and working conditions. These discontinuities are particularly sharp when the living standards in the two countries involved are far apart, as between the United States and Mexico or West Germany and Czechoslovakia.

Labor unions, too, change at the border. In each country business must deal with new unions, which are subject to different labor laws, and redesign its personnel policies accordingly.

The Physical Environment

From a physical standpoint, too, each nation is unlike all others. Its territorial size, geographic location, natural resources, climate, topography, lakes, rivers;

all are unique. So are the formations of real capital through investments in infrastructure—roads, bridges, canals, harbors, sewers, water and power systems, public buildings, and residential dwellings. As a composite they form the physical framework for business.

THE SOCIOCULTURAL ENVIRONMENT

The influences of social and cultural forces on international business are more subtle and often more indirect than the influences of economic variables, yet none are more pervasive. Because of the subtlety of these influences, they are often ignored or misjudged. Many failures in international management, therefore, can be attributed to managers' weaknesses in bridging cross-cultural differences and adapting business behavior to the norms of other lands.

Culture-Conditioned Behavior

Each nation is a unique and complex system of values, norms, and relationships. Because of their common heritage, joint experience, and shared learning (schools, games, sports, and social activities), individuals in any particular country tend to identify with similar values and priorities.

Deep down, on the strictly biological level, all human behavior derives from genetically inherited drives and impulses that demand gratification—hunger, shelter, sex, social interaction, recreation, rest. How these needs are satisfied is determined by the culture within which the individual is *socialized* or *encultured;* that is, taught how to live and provide for the needs of life. Through learning from others, the individual adopts and internalizes the values and behaviors of the particular culture (see Figure 2.1 on the next page).

Much of what is learned sinks beneath rational consciousness and is fused with the genetically inherited drives. Thus, the learned behaviors form the structures and methods by which our biological requirements are met. In addition, the learned behaviors greatly expand the spectra of human needs as they define what is right or wrong, humorous or grotesque, exhilarating or tragic; that is, they form complex sets of psychological needs that are distinguishable from the purely biological ones only by the aid of psychiatry.

Cross-Cultural Differences

For the ordinary individual the biological and psychological needs are one and the same. For example, we eat not just to get calories and nutrients; we also eat to gratify our needs for flavor, aroma, appearance, and all those aspects of what the anthropologist would call the food culture of our particular national society. In the United States the individual thinks in terms of sirloin, onion dip, turkey, apple pie, hamburger, hot dogs, and a number of other socially

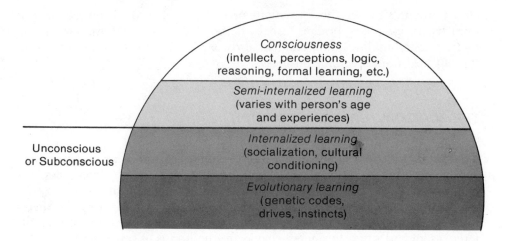

Consciousness
(intellect, perceptions, logic,
reasoning, formal learning, etc.)

Semi-internalized learning
(varies with person's age
and experiences)

Internalized learning
(socialization, cultural
conditioning)

Unconscious
or Subconscious

Evolutionary learning
(genetic codes,
drives, instincts)

Figure 2.1   The Human Psyche

defined combinations of nutrients; the German consumer conceives food culture in terms of bratwurst, dumplings, sauerbraten, wiener schnitzel, and beer. In Japan it is an entirely different story; in Nigeria again a new one; and so in every country. The biological need for food has been cast into culturally defined recipes and menus and has acquired significant psychological dimensions that vary from country to country. As a consequence, the products and business processes by which this need is met are different in each culture.

Similar cross-boundary contrasts can be shown in many other aspects of life. Clothing, housing, furniture, games, mannerisms, even the use of facial expressions and hands and eyes in everyday communication carry distinct investments of national culture. So do ways of thinking, conceptions of the world and man's relations to it, and the relationship of these ways of thinking to various phenomena of life. Therefore, what people consider important or unimportant becomes an international variorum.

Cross-cultural differences are easily confused with subcultural (based on regional or minority group status) or interpersonal differences within a culture. As shown in Figure 2.2, behavioral variations arise on each of three levels. No individual can internalize the entirety of his or her culture, either regional or national. It is essential for managers of international business to develop the skills to distinguish the cross-cultural differences from the subcultural and interpersonal variations.

Cultural Borrowing

Modern communications technology has greatly increased exposure to foreign cultures, resulting in more borrowing and interaction among national cultures. But much of this is rather superficial (pop music, blue jeans, and Coca-Cola) and limited mainly to the upper classes. The general populations have remained relatively unaffected.

Cross-Cultural Differences	Intracultural Differences	Interpersonal Differences
National culture system (different attitudes, beliefs, values, behaviors)	*Subculture* (differential identification with social class, ethnic group, or region)	*Personality* (differential internalization of cultural norms)

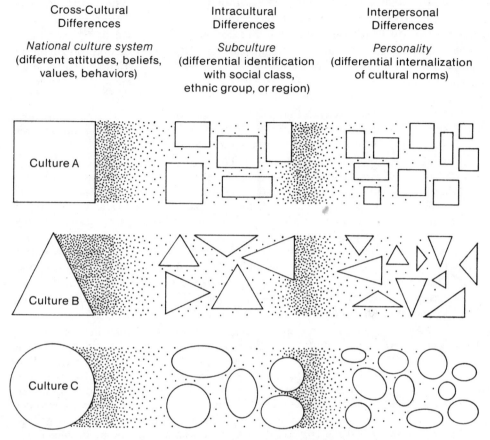

Figure 2.2   Sources and Levels of Cross-Cultural Differences

Predictions of a rapid cultural homogenization are ill founded. All cultures are inherently conservative, resisting change and fostering continuity. People need a frame of reference against which to plot their experiences, and culture provides that frame of reference. If everything were in a flux it would be necessary to map the environment afresh every moment. No people could cope for long with such a situation. It is precisely for this reason that all societies at all times have established habits and traditions, the main building blocks of culture.

The Effect on Business Behavior

Most of the psychological aspects of a national culture have a bearing upon business behavior and managerial activity. Business is an integral part of its host society. Whatever it does, the activity always has emotional or psychological dimensions in addition to the purely economic or technical dimensions. Thus, products of business must conform with the psychological requirements of the particular country, but there is much more to it. The manager must behave as expected by the indigenous society. Deviations from the local social norms quickly isolate an executive and seriously jeopardize his power base. The following psychological variables, all of which tend to take on different scope and connotations from country to country, are particularly important for managers:

1. *Social class structure.* What is the class stratification of the society? What constitutes higher classes and lower classes? What interactions are accepted as normal between the classes? What impedes or restricts interclass mobility?

2. *Status of managers.* Where in the social class structure do business executives and managers of various business activities belong? In some countries, promotion from managerial rank to higher corporate office tends to elevate the person to a higher social class. In the United States, for example, a senior executive of a major company becomes almost automatically a member of upper class society. In other countries, managerial rank bears little if any relation to social standing. This is particularly the case in cultures in which traditional forms of social stratification have long been the accepted norm, such as in Great Britain, India, and Sri Lanka.

3. *Leadership style.* What is generally expected from a business leader? How is leadership supposed to be exercised—by example, by command, by direct action, by indirect indication, or by some other model?

4. *Problem solving.* How do people approach business problems, such as choosing occupations, dealing with competitors, or filling executive positions? Who is consulted? Who is informed? Who is excluded? Who actively participates? What information is gathered? What processes are followed? Who occupies the culturally recognized position of proper authority for a particular kind of problem? How problems and solutions are viewed also varies. Some cultures are strongly dominated by tradition; solutions to problems are sought by sifting through past procedures to find the correct, that is, the traditional, solution. Problems that require new solutions present great difficulty in such societies. Solutions to them come slowly and are often wrought with controversy. In other cultures, logic and scientific method have been internalized as the means of solving new problems and solutions are perceived as progress or improvement. This may lead to problem solving for the sake of problem solving, without any real improvement in the situation.

5. *Decision-making styles.* How and by whom are decisions supposed to be made? Although this is in many respects related to problem solving, it is by no means synonymous with it. Solutions to problems express intellectual outputs; decisions transmit power, that is, carry commands and about how the organizational membership is to proceed, and what its responsibilities, duties, and rewards will be. Successful decision makers use the proper and culturally accepted methods of problem solving to reach their decisions, but they must also follow the proper institutional and procedural implementation of the decision itself.

Attitudes toward risk, toward authority, toward individual responsibility, toward participation in group activity, and toward social responsibility form another important group of variables in the psychological sphere of the multinational business environment. Most people do not usually realize that the culture to which they belong has shaped these attitudes, as it has shaped most

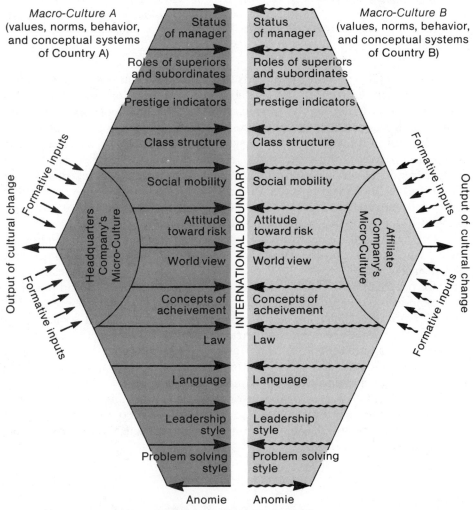

Figure 2.3 International Culture Conflicts in a Binational Business Organization

of their values and behavioral patterns. It is hard to be conscious of the eyes through which one looks. The inability to see how one is shaped by one's own culture makes cross-cultural conflicts difficult to predict. Special awareness and culture sensitivity are required of managers of international business—an awareness that only careful training and much experience can yield.

Ethnocentrism

It is perfectly right and legitimate that we should consider as "good" the manners which our parents have taught us, that we should hold sacred social norms and rites handed down to us by tradition and culture. What we must guard against, with all the power of rational responsibility, is our natural inclination to regard the social rites and norms of other cultures as inferior.[1]

A widespread fallacy in the West holds that all nations' cultural growth follows a unilinear path. Citizens of the United States, England, or France are apt to place their own nation at the pinnacle of this path and look upon all other peoples' cultures as backward and inferior. In these technologically advanced countries, cultural maturity is rationalized to be a function of technology and economic progress. Similarly, in the less developed countries ethnocentrism finds a frequent manifestation in the belief that the relative lack of material wealth and technological considerations is evidence of cultural superiority over industrially advanced nations who, due to their material successes, are condemned to moral decay and spiritual degeneration.

This is dubious logic. Cultural forms have meaning only in relation to their particular historical context. Societies are relative to one another, not higher or lower on some absolute scale. Primitive cultures have values that are valid for people in high industrialized countries, and all the norms and practices of the modern industrial societies are by no means beneficial. There are elements of primitive behavior in the most modern technological society; it is only that the taboos are more sophisticated, the votive offerings and sacrifices ritualized on a different level. The industrialized countries have translated tribal idiom into modern behavioral terms, but they have not removed the cultural and psychological bases for human action.

Each society, however primitive or advanced, must always retain a self-generating system of values, institutions, and social structures. Cross-cultural differences will be, therefore, inherent in any intersociety comparisons, including international business.

POLITICAL CULTURE

Principles and Applications

Since nationhood is first of all a political concept resting on sovereignty—a society's independence in regulating human activities and relationships—the political culture of a country represents an especially vital part of its national culture. How political elites make decisions, their priorities and attitudes, as well as the norms and beliefs of ordinary citizens and their relations to government and to their fellow countrymen, are all cultural components.

Such factors as suffrage, the legislature, participant policy, political freedom, and national loyalty vary from country to country, but are always pres-

---

1. Konrad Lorenz, *On Aggression* (New York: Bantam Books, 1970), pp. 79–80.

ent. They are just as much a part of the totalitarian patterns of countries, in a formal if not functional sense, as they are of the democratic and autocratic ones. The political typologies themselves—democratic, autocratic, dictatorial, totalitarian—are but skeletons that take on different tissues and forms, even in semiautonomous satellite countries such as those in eastern Europe.

Understanding the political dimensions of national culture requires much more than understanding the formal institutions of governments, just as understanding the economic dimensions requires much more than knowing that the country's economic organization is feudalistic, socialistic, communistic, or capitalistic.

Powers of Constituencies

The distribution of power, government policy making, and electoral processes are all country-specific phenomena. So are the dynamics that change the political environment for business: the changes in the relative powers of different constituencies, official attitudes toward private enterprise and foreign firms, the access of business to societal resources, and public expectations on disclosure of information by business, as well as national priorities in such complex intangibles as the quality of life, distribution of wealth, and social progress.

Even if we limit discussion to the broadest constituent groups—business, labor, consumer, and government—sharp contrasts exist in the international scene. In the United States, the emphasis has been on the stockholder and corporate needs; although the consumer has been receiving increasing attention and power, there has been no doubt who runs the business. In Europe the most powerful constituency is labor. As a consequence, government policies in Europe are motivated by labor union interests to a far greater extent than they are in the United States. In Great Britain, the unions form the central cadre for the Labor party and supply the funding for most of the party's activities. In West Germany and Sweden, unions have the legal right to appoint members to corporate boards of directors. They also play influential parts in other aspects of national affairs, especially those involving economic and social policies. The so-called codecision and works council laws in effect in many European countries require public disclosure of corporate information and the inputs of labor and the general public in major business decisions. Because of such differences in the political power structure, business in Europe must rely on a cooperative rather than a confrontational model in its relations with labor or government.

Government involvement in industrial planning, regional development, and risk sharing is another variable in the political environment. The majority of nations have adopted the principle of governmental control and direction of business activity, but what concrete form that control takes, how extensive it is, and how it alters the potential opportunities and risks of businesses vary. For example, the European Community, under its regional policy, restricts new business growth in major industrial districts such as the Ruhr, Milan, and Paris while subsidizing new businesses in less developed regions such as southern Italy, eastern France, and parts of Great Britain.

Many of the factors in the sociopolitical environment are basically similar in several countries. But how the factors are assigned priorities and how they generate specific constraints or incentives for business are very dissimilar in different countries.

Reciprocal Effects of Political and Business Values

The ordinary citizen's political values, including his propensities either to participate in or to abstain from social action decisions (involvement in causes) are not just a matter of governmental system; they relate also to folkways, to demographic conditions such as population sparcity, to archaic transportation systems, or to generally backward technology, all of which may make frequent communication impossible between much of the citizenry and the government.

Recent research in international politics has emphasized the relationship between the political activities and workplace experiences of people in different countries. The results suggest that the two have a reciprocal effect: where people are oriented to participate as decision makers in one area, they will tend to seek similar roles in the other. But the reciprocity is rarely complete. In some countries, political involvement coexists with relative docility in the workplace; in other countries, a low level of political involvement does not prevent a participatory work culture with considerable self-reliance and group-oriented decision making.

The research further shows that the structure of authority at the workplace can be a most persistent source of influence on the political practices of a nation, due to the repetitiveness of daily contact and the tangible rewards attendant to it. Also, job group membership always coexists with any political involvement for the ordinary citizen, by economic necessity, while political involvement is not a necessary condition for having a job.

Studies of some developing countries indicate that more basic than either governmental or job experience is educational attainment, which produces basic changes in citizens' intellectual capabilities, values, and aspirations. However, whether this also holds true in the developed countries, where the educational frontier is above elementary and secondary levels, remains obscure.

The most important characteristic of the political culture in any country is its mixed quality. It encompasses not only the official governmental system but to varying degrees all the other social systems and relationships of the citizenry. There is political activity in parochial, functional, vocational, recreational, and business sectors. In its full meaning, *political* is a pervasive idea; all involvement and commitment, factional cleavage, loyalties, and orientations combine to make up the political reality of a country.

THE TECHNOLOGICAL ENVIRONMENT

Technology is another basic variable in the multinational business environment. Since technology determines the methods and organizations of productive activities it is an integral part of any country's business system. But its effects are not limited to business. Dictating how things are to be done, which machines and tools are to be used, which skills and educational preparations are best for which productive activity, and in which sequence various business operations should be arranged, technology tends to intermesh with social organization and traditional humanistic ideas regarding the organization of relationships and occupational values. Technology thus performs a dual function: it serves the need of productive efficiency in business as well as in other economic sectors of the country, and it injects its own logic and requirements into the social life of the country.

The interaction between technology and the outside social system is not without friction. On the contrary, the two often clash. The basic reason for the clash derives from the fact that technology is science-based, derived from objective rationality and scientific method, and as such, is insensitive to human values and relationships. The whole fabric of social and cultural norms that rest upon emotional considerations, traditional beliefs, and other nonscientific value systems is, therefore, potentially hostile to technology.

How great a role technology plays in a country depends upon the level of industrialization, education, and the national policies and regulations. In a highly developed country such as West Germany or the United States, technology-based procedures and modern machine systems are commonplace. In Nepal or Ethiopia they are rare. Hence, organizational values and managerial philosophies differ accordingly.

The conflict between technological values and traditional values also varies with the stage of industrialization. In the less developed countries, major confrontations between the two are now in progress. This is so because the introduction of modern technology into a traditional subindustrial society creates a social shock wave of tremendous magnitude. In a primitive society, relationships are built upon a hierarchy of traditionally determined power distribution, which rests mostly on seniority and hereditary privileges. Modern industrial technology and business organizations undermine and threaten to destroy the traditional structure. It therefore incites political terror and moral conceit, especially in minds that have not been educated to understand either science or technology. To put it another way, infusion of industrial technology and modern business organizations into a preindustrial society generates a process in the economy that tends to restructure not only the business sector of the country but also the society at large. It causes change, confusion, and conflict.

Although the most far-reaching restructuring of the society and its value system takes place in the early stages of a country's industrialization, the process is never fully complete. Even in the most industrialized countries, technological requirements and humanistic requirements clash frequently.

Scientists and humanists disagree on whether technology is destructive or constructive of human values and whether technological imperatives could or should be allowed to displace the traditional cultural values. The clashes continue because technology is never static; as science advances, new technology enters the productive system. New technology requires changes in business organizations and corresponding adjustments in the society at large.

ORGANIZATIONAL CULTURE

Micro-Macro Relationship

Any organization is a creature of culture. The structural and behavioral characteristics of every productive enterprise derive from the attitudes, values, and beliefs of the society in which it exists. A multinational business enterprise must by definition also be multicultural. Each corporate entity in an MNC's structure is subject to a ceaseless intrusion from its host country's culture. Though reciprocating with its own inputs to the national culture, the business entity remains but a local constituent. The corporate culture is but a microcosm in the national macrosystem. Thus, the different functional variables of the national culture are reflected in the functional aspects of the corporation's internal culture. Although the transfer from the national macroculture to the corporate microsystem is never complete, it is irresistible. The two systems can seldom sustain irreconcilable contradictions. Their differences are either temporary or limited to the acceptable deviation from national norms.

Deviations from National Norms

The deviations of company values from the national norms stem primarily from one of four sources.

1. The company is often not only the recipient of national culture, but a contributor to it by originating and introducing new cultural dimensions, which the national culture can absorb only after a period of maturation and dissemination. The reverse situation, one in which the company lags rather than leads in cultural progress, produces deviations in the opoposite direction.

2. To the extent to which information flow between the corporate and national cultures is impeded, there can unintentionally arise in the company organization norms different from the society's norms. If laws require corporate disclosure of information, only small deviation from social norms is allowed; in the absence of such laws, the corporation can, over time, establish its own norms.

3. Motivational indifference between management and the society as a whole may allow divergences to occur between the corporate and national cultural concepts that underlie organizational design and behavior. It is simply a case of nobody being affected or concerned about the divergent values. Motivational indifference and impeded information flows are in reality closely linked and can be unscrambled only after considerable study of any particular case.

4. National culture is always much broader in scope and more pluralistic in composition than the corporate culture, as long as the company remains uninational in scope. National culture can wholly absorb not only a single company's culture in its entirety, but all domestic company cultures in the nation's domain. The reverse—corporate culture absorbing the complete national culture—is an apparent impossibility. Consequently, the corporate culture can receive inputs from its national environment only on a selective basis, accepting what is necessary or irresistible and screening out the rest.

In this screening and selecting the management's philosophy and personal biases significantly affect the outcome. Managerial attitudes affect also the tempo and timing of organizational adaptation to environmental changes. On the lag end of the adaptive process are companies whose internal power structure responds only after the changes in external culture have become manifest in overt new norms with clearly perceived costs associated with deviant behavior. On the lead end are companies practicing anticipatory adaptation. They constantly scan the horizons to detect the sources of new or pending environmental change. This involves risk. The scanning requires a definite allocation of resources that can promise only plausible yields; its cost-benefit ratio is statistically indeterminate and, as such, a matter of managerial judgment.

Any company's culture consists of a combination of norms that in certain ways is unique. The probabilities are infinitesimal that two companies would make identical acquisitions from the national culture and have precisely the same sensitivities and abilities to internalize the various environmental impacts.

Thus, each organization develops its own microculture, or personality. But this differentiation is confined to the national culture unless the company is operating in a transnational space. Suggestions that cross-cultural research need not go beyond interorganizational studies within the same country fail to recognize this fundamental fact. There may be, and certainly are, some similarities between interorganizational culture conflict in uninational settings and international culture conflict, but to equate one with the other would be absurd.

ORGANIZATIONAL CULTURE IN MNCs

Adaptation to Heterogeneous External Cultures

If we widen our perspective from a single country setting to the heterogeneous cultural bases of a multinational firm, the problem of company culture takes on new dimensions. No longer is the organization receiving inputs from a cohesive national culture. Instead, it finds itself not only able to choose from all the national cultures harboring its affiliates, but, even more importantly, also compeled to reconcile the idiosyncracies among its various affiliates for which culture contrasts are responsible. Thus, adaptation of company culture to all national cultures in the company orbit becomes imperative and the expansion of company culture to incorporate certain elements from each national culture axiomatic.

That kind of cultural bridge-building can succeed only if both the structural materials and traffic patterns avoid incompatibility with the national cultures concerned. No direct one-to-one correlation between the transnational corporate culture and its various host country cultures is conceivable. Rather than equating cultural compatibility with cultural identification, experience has shown it to be more realistic to limit the goal to the avoidance of cultural incompatibility, to aim toward a neutrality status for the corporate culture vis-à-vis its multinational environmental cultures, rather than to seek intimate identification with them. The neutrality criterion offers the only viable basis for harmonious relations between a multinational company and its heterogeneous cultural environments. International conflicts make impartiality, that is, equalization of involvement in all its host countries, impossible for the company. However, commitment to the cultural system of one or a few from among its many host environments will sooner or later expose the firm in a countercultural or even counterinternational light in the others. This would unstabilize and undermine the company's continued existence in those countries whose cultures are deemphasized.

Constructive Neutrality

What is neutrality? It is easier to say what it is not. First, true neutralism is never synonymous with negativism, although prejudiced partisans, especially in the political field, have attacked neutrality as being negative. Second, neutralism is not hypocritical; its central strategy is not to play both ends against the middle or to shield partisan machinations. Such negative connotations accrued to the term during the cold war, when a number of governments raised the neutralist banner to qualify for maximum foreign aid from both the West and the East or to create a false facade for their own aggressive designs. Since the cold war such pseudo neutrality has lost much of its strategic luster and is now a much lesser factor.

For the purpose of the multinational corporate culture, *neutrality* can be defined as a positive system of principles and norms to guide the decision-making processes of all its entities and affiliates so as to avoid or to minimize clashes with its various national environments and to facilitate optimal involvement and participation of the company in the productive systems of all its host countries.

Cultural Change and Managerial Modernization

Under colonialism, optimization of business operations was attempted through economic and political exploitation and social and cultural subjugation, that is, coercion. Due partially to ethnocentrism and partially to cultural unawareness, some MNCs still continue the colonial practice; they try to impose upon all their foreign affiliates the value system of the headquarters country. This is a self-destructive strategy.

Culture is conservative. It rejects external change as a threat to the psychological infrastructure upon which it rests. To maintain the integrity of a culture, it is necessary to introduce change through the culture's own system; by enlarging its scope, modernizing its processes, and opening up areas for innovation. En bloc infusions of alien culture, such as is the case when corporate foreign-based affiliates are imbued with U.S. corporate values and norms under headquarters pressure, is often counterproductive. Mutilation of the indigenous ways tends to unstabilize the social climate, increase anomie, and induce hostility toward the MNC, its methods and conduct, and toward the home nations' culture, which is viewed as the ultimate source of the evil. For the Iranian revolutionaries, the United States was the great Satan because of its values and conduct.

Though cultures are intricate and basically conservative, they are never inherently rigid. Each has built-in laws of dynamics. Change comes slowly or, more precisely, at the speed the internal dynamics can accommodate. Any effort to change the cultural patterns has a domino effect; breaking one pattern leads to dislocations in others. There exists, thus, what might be called the *change-absorptive capacity* of a culture: a culture can accommodate only a given amount of change at any particular time if it is to remain structurally stable and operationally balanced.

It is not only a matter of the methods by which cross-cultural transfers are made, but also the magnitudes of change that the transfer precipitates in the recipient culture. If the absorptive capacity is exceeded, by either too extensive or too sudden external infusion, as was the case in Iran under the Shah, a dual system of mutually inimical norms results. The conflict between the native and imported values may embroil the perceived source of the alien values, as the agent of anomie and decay in the cultural ecosystem of the host nation, in social and political turmoil, ranging from labor stoppages to terrorism.

Too often, the notion still prevails that a U.S. national abroad is first of all a *change agent* with a mission to Americanize the host country. Such ethnocentrism elicits only animosity and ill will from local nationals.

To achieve empathetic integration between the corporate culture and its multicultural environment—a condition necessary for mutually supportive growth—no unilateral transfers, especially from a financial or political power base, will do. The resistance to such imposition may not be immediate or even overt but in time it never fails to materialize, often through covert expressions. Management cannot approach this problem with only thinking of the balance sheet or organization chart. Cultural empathy can be achieved only through sensitivity toward the living realities of the national societies concerned. Appreciation of all the cultures involved and attitudes sympathetic to their cardinal values are required from those responsible for shaping the company's cultural milieu.

The complexity of the problem depends upon the number of countries involved. As the corporation's territorial scope expands the probabilities of cultural conflict multiply, as each new country adds new complications to the mix. Conversely, the opportunities for culturally indifferent corporate values shrink, leaving fewer and fewer alternatives and neutral possibilities. The pressure for knowledge of how to handle the situation intensifies geometrically.

The Cosmopolitan Management Culture

Cooperation Among MNCs   In a common peril—the pressures for alignment with host societies as evidenced by rising public criticism, official attitudes, and nationalizations of affiliates—multinational firms have sought aid through cooperation and mutual assistance. Formal and informal exchanges of experience with one another, trade association activities, conventions and seminars for executive groups and functional specialists, and various other ways of disseminating information about successful experiences have created the means for collective corporate learning about cross-cultural conflict resolution. There is developing among international executives a brotherhood of intense necessity that has fostered close fraternal relations regardless of the individual's own nationality or the domicile of his or her parent company.

Standardization of decision modes and policy provisions have become quite commonplace among MNCs. Intercompany differences, while always present, have shown a tendency to decline, especially in the problem areas that are of general, and therefore common, concern to the majority of MNCs. From the shared experiences is emerging a new international code of managerial values and behavioral norms, a *cosmopolitan management culture*, which may be visualized as a functionally oriented superstructure bridging the national cultures of different countries.

In an idealized concept, this emergent superstructure rests on the different host countries' cultural systems, maintaining neutrality toward each. In practice, pure neutrality has been neither achievable nor sufficient for corporate needs. In many respects the cosmopolitan standards in multinational business have, in fact, progressed beyond the neutrality objective; in others, they are only in a formative stage. Because of its pragmatic base, the development has been far from uniform and lacks internal consistency.

Diffusion of Enmity   Despite its theoretical vagueness, the emergent cosmopolitan management culture introduces something very original into the relations between the multinational firm and its heterogeneous cultural environment. It takes the focus off any particular firm and its national origin and creates a broad-based corporate culture that has greater influence and stability than any individual company culture could. In a sense, it takes the firm out of isolation in its external cultural relations and places it in the context of this transnational normative system, which maintains relative constancy throughout the world. If clashes between this corporate culture and any particular national culture occur, they do not expose the company as a deviant culprit but as a member of a cosmopolitan elite against whose standards the indigenous

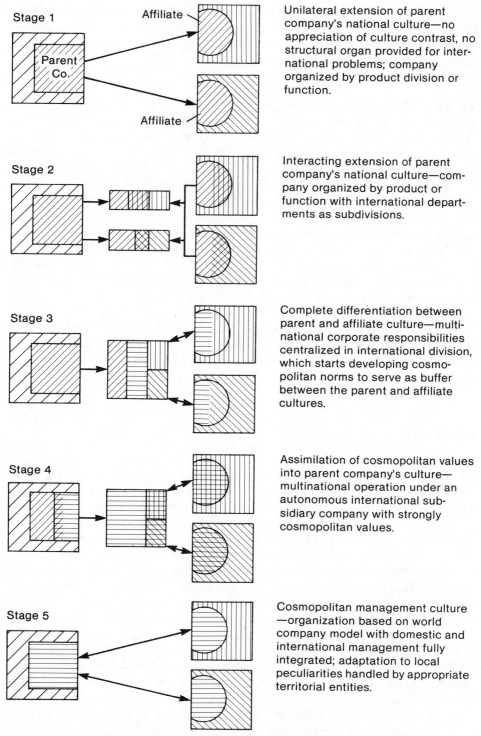

Figure 2.4 Evolutionary Stages of Cosmopolitan Management Culture

norms do not enjoy the popular presumption of moral superiority. This cosmopolitan management culture thus provides a real basis for a social discourse, an intercultural dialogue, that opens rational approaches for eliminating the conflicts.

Vanguard of Indigenous Change   The MNC that is identified with the cosmopolitan management elite can greatly contribute to the adaptation and development of indigenous value systems in favor of free initiative and enterprise. This would help reorient indigenous values toward economic achievement and productive activity, thus making them socially desirable values.

In this context of the cosmopolitan management elite, the company, rather than being an intruder, can become identified with the vanguard of modernity, deserving of glamour and bestowed with institutional charisma to lead. It can, in brief, become a prime mover of indigenous change in its host countries' normative systems. Such leadership, unlike direct cultural imports, will not mutilate and disrupt the intricate social systems of the different host cultures but will, instead, engender growth and development through the indigenous culture toward the values essential for the efficient utilization of the host country's natural and human resources.

That the process of consolidating cultural differences is a difficult and slow one has already been emphasized. Only over time can the internal cultural system be fully synchronized with its multinational environment and converted to the cosmopolitan management culture.

SUMMARY

Differences in environmental settings are the source of behavioral and organizational differences between domestic and international businesses. As a firm expands internationally, its environment takes on new dimensions, each country adding a new set of laws, economic and political institutions, markets, and sociocultural systems. The greater the geographic scope of a firm's activities, the more varigated and complex is the environment in which it operates.

Cross-national differences involving laws, engineering, and accounting can present serious problems to managers, yet these differences lend themselves to factual study and concrete definitions, by means of which competent analysts can usually resolve the problems. The same cannot be said of sociocultural differences, which are often subtle and elusive. The difficulty for managers is compounded by their lack of expertise in cross-cultural studies. Development of this skill has not been part of traditional business school curricula. International business and managerial behaviors are most affected by social stratification, leadership style, modes of problem solving and decision making, attitudes toward various elements of business activity, ethnocentrism, and the role of technology in the economy.

When firms become multinational, their internal values must be adjusted to the cultural systems of their different host nations. This presents complex problems, which require many compromises and innovative approaches. Of particular significance to the firm's welfare is neutrality, the avoidance of partiality, both political and cultural. If the existing culture of a host country represents a hurdle for modernization and business efficiency, the right course of action is to introduce change by utilizing the change-producing mechanisms of the indigenous culture rather than attempting to inject the change directly. Since cross-cultural differences pose problems that are common to most international businesses, a process of formulating cosmopolitan corporate values has started to gain momentum. Known as cosmopolitan management culture, these values can ultimately eliminate managerial dilemmas arising from cross-cultural conflicts.

FOR REVIEW AND DISCUSSION

1. The international boundary may be regarded by business as the line of discontinuities and break-off points of environmental variables. Discuss.

2. If the United States had been formed as a loose confederation of autonomous states rather than as the federal union it is, how would business relations among states be different?

3. Do differences in consumer preferences in different countries derive mainly from learned tastes or physical needs? Elaborate.

4. The notion of "right time" is a cultural variable; the time to start work, the time for lunch, the time to go home, the time to eat dinner, the time to take a vacation, the time to celebrate, all vary from country to country. So also do the notions of being on time, being late, or being early for various kinds of functions and business appointments. If you were assigned to manage a U.S. company's subsidiary in a country in which the notions and attitudes toward time were very different from those in the United States, what problems would this create for you?

5. If you were asked to take a managerial position in a country characterized by a dictatorial government and by authoritarian attitudes in business and social organizations, how would you prepare yourself for this assignment? Would you have to modify your own attitudes and behaviors? Could you rely on U.S. ways of relating to your subordinates, superiors, and clients?

6. A large Japanese company conducted a thorough factual study of the feasibility of establishing a subsidiary in Brazil. The study showed a great profit potential for the intended venture. However, after the factory had been built and operations begun, the optimistic results of the study failed to materialize. The Japanese executives learned, to their dismay, that the Brazilian workers shared neither the attitudes toward work nor the loyalty to the company of their Japanese counterparts. Why could a technically impeccable economic study fail to reveal potential problems regarding the attitudes toward work, achievement, and one's employer?

7. What causes ethnocentrism? Can a person overcome it? Would this be desirable?

8. Would you agree with the assertion that "What is bribery in one country is a human right in another"? Consider tips to bank clerks, truck drivers, customs inspectors, and a host of other lower level functionaries, which is a traditional practice in many countries. Consider also lobbying activities, political contributions, and the so-called white collar crime prevalent in the United States and other industrial countries.

9. Describe company culture. Try to identify the main factors that tend to vary from firm to firm.

10. How essential do you think it is that MNCs be successful in developing a cosmopolitan corporate culture? Try to explain how this would relate to or affect the indigenous cultures of each affiliate.

SUGGESTED READINGS FOR PART ONE

Brock, Jan O., and Webb, John W. *A Geography of Mankind*. New York: McGraw-Hill, 1973.

Brown, S. *New Forces in World Politics*. Washington, D.C.: Brookings Institute, 1974.

Case, Pierre. *Training for the Cross-Cultural Mind*. Washington, D.C.: The Society for International Education Training and Research, 1980.

Daniels, John; Ogram, William; and Radebaugh, Lee. *International Business: Environments and Operations*. Reading, Mass.: Addison-Wesley, 1976.

England, George. "Managers and Their Value Systems: A Five Country Comparative Study." *The Columbian Journal of World Business*. 13:35–44, 1978.

Farmer, Richard, and Richman, Barry. *International Business: An Operational Theory*. Homewood, Ill.: Irwin, 1970.

Haire, Mason, et al. *Managerial Thinking: An International Study*. New York: Wiley, 1966.

Kolde, E. J. "Culture Context of Multinational Organizations. In E. J. Kolde, *The Multinational Company—Behavioral and Managerial Analysis*. Lexington, Mass.: Heath, 1974.

New Directions in International Education. The Annals of The American Academy of Political Social Science 449 (special issue):1980.

Nordyke, James. *Comparative Business Environment*. Cincinnati: Southwestern, 1977.

Robock, S., et al. *International Business and Multinational Enterprise*. 2nd ed., Homewood, Ill.: Irwin, 1977.

Toyne, Brian. *Host Country Managers of Multinational Firms: An Evaluation of Variables Affecting Their Managerial Thinking Patterns*. New York: Arno Press, 1980.

Terpstra, Vern. *Cultural Environment of International Business*. Cincinnati: Southwestern, 1978.

Vernon, Raymond, and Wells, Louis. *Economic Environment of International Business*. Englewood Cliffs, N.J.: Prentice-Hall, 1976.

Part Two

INTERNATIONAL TRADE

Of all the problems we call "economic," few have so baffled the expert and the nonexpert alike as those that involve the relations between nation-states. Indeed, one might even go so far as to say that economics, as a "science," got its start from efforts to explain how gold and goods traveled from nation to nation, working their various effects on the countries they left and those they entered.

—Robert L. Heilbroner

In Chapter 3 we will examine the basic concepts of trade theory and evaluate its strengths and limitations. Chapter 4 explains how nation-states control their international trade relations and how the various government controls affect business activities. Chapter 5 identifies the U.S. government's objectives and policies in concluding trade agreements with other nations.

3

Economics of International Trade

Why do businesses cross international boundaries? For private profits? Yes, but not exclusively. Government agencies also participate in transboundary activities; in the United States the diplomatic service, cultural exchanges, foreign aid, the Federal Reserve System, the armed forces, the General Services Administration, the Bonneville Power Administration (in charge of hydroelectric projects on the Columbia River system), and a great multitude of other public agencies at all levels conduct sizeable volumes of international business. The same is true of many nonprofit organizations, from religious missions to the National Audubon Society. In addition to profits for private enterprise, multinational business investments must yield a social good—a gain to the nation as a whole—or all the nonprofit transboundary businesses would be senseless wastes.

Even those countries whose laws prohibit private enterprise and preclude business profits are active participants in international business, and both their interests and involvements seem to receive increasing emphasis. Clearly, they must have reasons other than profits.

What, then, are the reasons for multinational business? How are private profits and public purposes involved? How can managers use the theoretical tools to unravel complex relationships in multinational business? These are the main questions to be addressed in the next two chapters.

THE THEORY OF INTERNATIONAL TRADE

In economics, multinational business is assumed to be limited to foreign trade and payments. This assumption no longer corresponds to reality. However, trade still makes up a large share of multinational business, and the economics of trade continue to be important, especially for economic planners, politicians, and regulatory authorities. It is, therefore, necessary to start our explanations of the reasons for multinational business with the theory of trade. We shall

articulate the essence of the theory without resorting to mathematical formulations or pursuing technical points.

In economic theory international trade is explained by the principle of
national advantage; that is, a nation trades because it derives an economic gain
from the trade. In the absence of a gain international trade will cease. But how
can we tell which trade relations will be advantageous to a nation? And how
can a nation avoid disadvantageous trade? What should a country export and
what should it import? According to the theory of trade, a nation's gain from
international trade may be derived from either an absolute advantage or a
comparative advantage.

Absolute Advantage

Suppose we select at random two nations, Q and R, and discover the following
facts:

	Labor input required	
Output	*Q*	*R*
20 tons of food	1 day	2 days
10 tons of fiber	2 days	1 day

In the absence of trade, Q can produce 20 tons of food and 10 tons of
fiber, and R can produce 10 tons of food and 20 tons of fiber. The aggregate
physical product for each country would be 30 tons per three days of labor
input, or 60 tons of physical product output per six days of labor input for
both countries combined.

From the input figures we can see that the costs of production (labor input)
are not the same in the two countries. Q is the low-cost producer of food, and
R is the low-cost producer of fiber. If Q specialized in food production and R
in fiber production, both would stand to gain, as follows. In three days of
labor Q can produce 60 tons of food and R can produce 30 tons of fiber. Their
combined output would be 90 tons. Hence, the gain from international specialization would be 20 tons of food and 10 tons of fiber, or a total physical
product of 30 tons. But to be able to specialize, the two countries must trade;
otherwise, Q would have no fiber and R no food. To realize this gain of 30
tons of output, the two countries must strike a bargain on how to divide the
gain between them; that is, they must determine what the ratio of exchange
between food and fiber should be.

The condition for *absolute advantage* is met whenever one country can
supply a given product at a lower absolute cost than its trading partner, while
for another product its own cost is higher than that of the trading partner.
Such is the case, for example, with trade in tropical agricultural products
(bananas, coffee, cocoa) and temperate agricultural commodities (wheat, corn,
rye), as well as with trade in Russian caviar and U.S. cowboy music.

Comparative Advantage

What happens if one country can produce both products at lower absolute costs than its neighbor? Does this mean that the country would be better off by not trading with its neighbor? Could the neighbor export anything at all? Common sense would argue for no trade under those conditions, but the theory of international trade disagrees. It postulates that trade can be beneficial to both countries, regardless of the level of absolute costs. What matters is the relative cost, or *comparative cost*. To fully understand this, we should back off a bit and start from the very beginning.

Role of Resource Endowments   The theory of trade regards each country as an autonomous economy resting on its own resource base. The resource endowments vary: some countries are richer in agricultural land than in forests or fisheries; others may have abundant mineral deposits but very small food resources. Each country has its own unique mix of resources, having relatively more of one resource than of some other. There also may be absolute gaps, in that some resource, such as oil or iron ore, is not found at all in a given country.

Human factors, too, vary internationally. Differences in natural aptitudes, education, and skills are translated into cost differentials in actual production processes. Often the human aptitudes and skills are correlated with the natural resource endowments through experience and tend to compound the natural resource advantage. Where a particular activity has been a mainstay of economic life for many generations, such as watch making in Switzerland, high fashion in France, silk weaving in Japan, or cheese making in Denmark and Holland, the art of production has not only been raised to the highest attainable level but also perpetuated as part of the national heritage. To a greater or lesser degree this socioeconomic training is applicable to most types of production activities. Thus, differences in human efficiency combined with differences in resource bases encourage international specialization, each country capitalizing on the aptitudes and skills in which its people excel.

Opportunity Costs   The endowments of natural and human resources determine two factors in a national economy: the production possibilities and the opportunity costs. *Production possibilities* are best for goods requiring the resources that are most abundant in a country, and they are worst for goods demanding the least available resources. Denmark has good arable land but poor forests; it can produce food products much more readily than wood products. Finland is relatively much better endowed with forests than with agricultural resources; correspondingly, its production possibilities are skewed toward wood products.

But resource endowments play an even larger role in shaping a nation's economy. They also determine the opportunity costs of producing any particular product. *Opportunity cost* is the value of the opportunity foregone to produce a product, that is, the value of what was given up or sacrificed. Take, for example, a given plot of land, which can grow grain, meat, or fruit. If the plot is sown with wheat, the opportunities for raising animals or growing fruit are foregone; if it is used for meat production, the opportunities for crops will automatically be sacrificed. Suppose the expected values of the three outputs are grain, $900; meat, $700; and fruit, $950. The opportunity cost of producing any given commodity is the value of the best alternative that must be sacrificed. Thus, the opportunity cost for grain is $950, for meat $950, and for fruit $900. Since the opportunity cost for the first two commodities exceeds the value of the commodities themselves, they are obviously uneconomic alternatives for this plot of land.[1]

Optimal Use of Resources   The concept of opportunity cost, the value of goods given up to produce a particular product, is fundamental for the modern theory of trade. Economic rationality requires that all resources be employed in their *optimal use*, that is, for making goods whose opportunity costs are less than (or at most equal to) the value of the goods themselves. For any single country this objective is unobtainable. The reason is lack of symmetry between resource potentialities and consumption requirements. What people need comes first. Resource utilization must be adjusted so as to best meet the needs of the society. A self-sufficient economy is thus forced to use resources for suboptimal purposes. For example, suppose that the production possibilities of all suitable land resources in country *X* as shown in Figure 3.1.

The country could produce 40 tons of meat if it used all land for this purpose, but would then have no fruit at all. At the other extreme, it could produce 160 tons of fruit if it could get by without any meat. Since normally

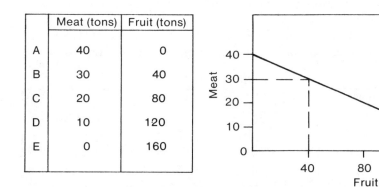

	Meat (tons)	Fruit (tons)
A	40	0
B	30	40
C	20	80
D	10	120
E	0	160

Figure 3.1   Production Possibilities in Country *X*

1. The opportunity cost should not be confused with business or accounting cost. Suppose that in the illustration actual production costs would be $670 regardless of which product is chosen. Hence, the owner could make a business profit of $30 by raising meat animals while suffering an economic loss of $250.

consumers would want both, the land resources would have to be divided between meat and fruit production, as indicated, say, by point B in the chart.

Gains from Trade

Two-Country Trade   It becomes a matter of trade-offs between the two products; the more meat, the less fruit, and vice versa. The trade-off ratio is 40:160 or 1:4. Every ton of meat output requires the same amount of land as 4 tons of fruit output. Consequently, each ton of meat will exchange for 4 tons of fruit and each ton of fruit for 0.25 ton of meat. These would be relative prices in Country X as long as it has no international trade.

Add to the picture country Y. Its production possibilities are shown in Figure 3.2.

For Country Y, the opportunity cost or trade-off ratio between the two products is 100:200 or 1:2, each ton of meat is worth 2 tons of fruit and each ton of fruit exchanges for 0.5 ton of meat in the domestic market. Compared to Country X, a ton of meat buys only half as much fruit here (2 tons versus 4 tons) while a ton of fruit buys double the amount of meat (0.5 ton vs. 0.25 ton).

Consequently, both countries can benefit from international trade with the other. If the pretrade position of Country X was combination B (30 tons of meat and 40 tons of fruit), it can now shift to combination E and increase its fruit output by 120 tons (from 40 to 160). Exporting this surplus fruit to Country Y, it can exchange it for 60 tons of meat, which will not only make up for the 30 tons that had to be sacrificed for the increased fruit production but yield another 30 tons of meat as a net gain to the country's economy. If that is more meat than the people in Country X need, some of it can be traded for some third commodity such as wine or textiles. Either way, the country has derived a real gain from trade.

Country Y will also benefit from the trade. By satisfying its needs for fruit more economically through imports from X (paying for each ton only 0.25 ton

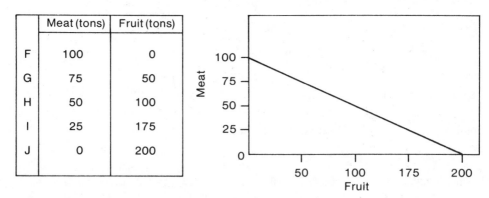

Figure 3.2   Production Possibilities in Country *Y*

of meat as against 0.5 ton of domestic meat), it can now shift its domestic resources to meat production, for which they are better suited.

Three-Country Trade   Would all countries enjoy similar gains from international trade? Is a gain from trade automatic? No. Add a third country, Z, with the production possibilities shown in Figure 3.3. If this country produced 60 tons of meat the opportunity cost would be 240 tons of fruit; conversely, if it wished to put all the land in fruit the opportunity cost would be 60 tons of meat. Therefore, meat could be traded for fruit at the ratio of 60 to 240 or 1:4 in Country Z. This trade-off ratio happens to come out exactly the same as in Country X. Now, try to initiate international trade between countries Z and X! There is no way either country can make a profit trading with the other. Obviously, benefits from international trade are not automatic. Consider now trade possibilities between countries Z and Y. There profitable trade is clearly possible. Z can export fruit and get more meat for it than at home, and Y can export meat and get more fruit for it than at home. Hence, the gains from trade are mutual.

Why? Why can countries Z and Y or countries X and Y trade while countries X and Z cannot? What determines the possibilities for gainful international trade? It is the opportunity cost expressed on a per unit basis, which we call the *domestic trade-off ratio*. When the ratios are different (1:2 vs. 1:3) the basis for gainful trade exists between the two countries; if the ratios are identical (1:4 vs. 1:4), gainful international trade is impossible.

To illustrate how traders profit from comparative advantage, examine the following example, in which M stands for meat and F for fruit.

Transaction	Country X	Country Y
1	a. Exporter buys 100 F at cost of 25 M and exports it.	
		b. Exporter trades 100 F for 50 M.

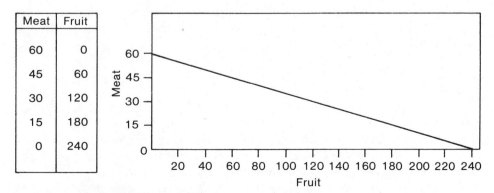

Meat	Fruit
60	0
45	60
30	120
15	180
0	240

Figure 3.3   Production Possibilities in Country Z

Transaction	Country X	Country Y
1	c. Result: Exporter brings in 50 M. Subtracting original cost of 25 M yields net profit of 25 M (minus transport costs).	
2		a. Exporter buys 100 M at cost of 200 F and exports it.
	b. Exporter trades 100 M for 400 F.	
		c. Result: Exporter brings in 400 F. Subtracting original cost of 200 F yields net profit of 200 F (minus transport costs).
3	a. Exporter buys 100 M at cost of 400 F and exports it.	
		b. Exporter trades 100 M for 200 F.
	c. Result: Exporter brings in 200 F. Subtracting original cost of 400 F yields net loss of 200 F (plus transport costs).	
4	Work out the fourth possibility yourself.	

The domestic opportunity costs indicate which commodity to export and which to import. If Country X were to export meat and import fruit, as in the third transaction, it would lose on both transactions; by doing the reverse, it can profit. Similarly, Country Y would lose if it tried to export fruit and import meat, but gains by exporting meat and importing fruit. Why is that? The source of gain from trade is the difference in relative domestic prices (how much meat equals a unit of fruit) between the two countries. Each country will export the product the relative price of which is lower at home than abroad and import the product the relative price of which is lower abroad than at home. The country has a comparative advantage only in the exportable product; in the importable product it has a comparative disadvantage. Comparative here refers, of course, to comparison of the relative prices of the two countries involved; and relative price refers to the domestic trade-off ratio or per unit opportunity cost.

Terms of Trade

The price equalization process will go through two phases. First, when trade begins merchants start arbitrage transactions: buying fruit in Country X and buying meat in Country Y for export to the other country. Since a ton of fruit in X costs only 0.25 ton of meat and will sell for 0.50 ton of meat in Y, the gain from arbitrage is 100 percent, less transportation and other costs associated with the transaction. Similarly, since a ton of meat in Y costs only 2 tons of fruit but sells in X for 4 tons of fruit, the arbitrage there is equally lucrative.

However, this profit pump is self-destructive. First, as the demand for fruit increases in Country X, so does its price; the same happens to meat in Country Y. This will go on until the *terms of trade*, the ratio at which the two commodities are exported and imported, have stabilized. If both nations have equal bargaining power, that is, have equal potential to help or hurt the other, the terms of trade will settle halfway between the domestic cost ratios of 1:2 and 1:4, that is, at 1 ton of meat for 3 tons of fruit. If, however, one nation is economically more powerful, the terms of trade may settle anyplace between the two domestic cost ratios. Beyond these limits (the domestic cost ratios), no trade between countries X and Y can take place. If the terms go from 1:2 to, say, 3:4, both countries would profit by exporting fruit and importing meat; if they go from 1:4 to, say, 1:5, both countries would become exporters of meat and importers of fruit.[2]

The second mechanism stopping these terms of trade, according to trade theory, is that as the trade continues, factor costs will rise in Country X for producing fruit and in Country Y for producing meat. This will reduce the comparative cost differential and may ultimately lead to absolute price equality.

Trade Under Money Prices

To this point the discussion has been in terms of real as distinguished from money prices as a way of focusing the analysis on the theory. This section demonstrates the validity of the principle if money prices are used. Start by assuming that domestic prices are as follows:

	Meat	*Fruit*	*Ratio*
Country X	40 pesos	10 pesos	4:1
Country Y	100 rupees	50 rupees	2:1

Assume further that there has been no trade between the two countries to this point, so no peso-rupee exchange rate exists. When trade starts, the following situation develops:

Transaction	*Country X*	*Country Y*
5	a. Exporter buys 10 F at cost of 100 pesos and exports it.	
		b. Exporter sells 10 F for 500 rupees and with those rupees buys 5 M.
	c. Result: Exporter brings in 5 M and sells for 200 pesos. Subtracting original cost of 100 pesos yields net profit of 100 pesos (minus transport costs).	

2. If you wish to have further proof of the impossibility of trade when terms go beyond the domestic cost ratio, use terms of 3M to 4F in the example in Figure 3.1.

Transaction	Country X	Country Y
6		a. Exporter buys 10 M at cost of 1,000 rupees and exports it.
	b. Exporter sells 10 M for 400 pesos and with those pesos buys 40 F.	
		c. Result: Exporter brings in 40 F and sells for 2,000 rupees. Subtracting original cost of 1,000 rupees yields net profit of 1,000 rupees (minus transport costs).

The result is that international trade under money prices produced the same advantages as it did in the barter situation.

To move another step closer to reality, assume that there is a pre-existing exchange rate of 1 peso equaling 3 rupees. How would the comparative advantage in the previous examples be affected?

Transaction	Country X	Country Y
7	a. Exporter buys 10 F at cost of 100 pesos and exports it.	
		b. Exporter sells 10 F for 500 rupees and exchanges proceeds into 167 pesos at rate of 3:1.
	c. Result: Exporter brings in 167 pesos. Subtracting original cost of 100 pesos yields net profit of 67 pesos.	
8		a. Exporter buys 10 M at a cost of 1,000 rupees and exports it.
	b. Exporter sells 10 M for 400 pesos and exchanges proceeds into 1,200 rupees at rate of 3:1.	
		c. Result: Exporter brings in 1,200 rupees. Subtracting original cost of 1,000 rupees yields net profit of 200 rupees.

As these transactions show, the advantage still exists. But when the exchange rate changes, the per-unit export advantages have to change also. Take, for instance, an exchange rate of 1 peso equaling 6 rupees: no trade would take place with this exchange rate because X can sell neither product without suffering a loss and Y can profit on both.

Transaction	Country X	Country Y
9	a. Exporter buys 10 F at cost of 100 pesos and exports it.	
		b. Exporter sells 10 F for 500 rupees and exchanges them for 83 pesos (6:1).
	c. Result: Exporter brings in 83 pesos. Subtracting original cost of 100 pesos yields net loss of 17 pesos.	
10	a. Exporter buys 10 M at cost of 400 pesos and exports it.	
		b. Exporter sells 10 M for 100 rupees and exchanges them for 167 pesos (6:1).
	c. Result: Exporter brings in 167 pesos. Subtracting original cost of 400 pesos yields a net loss of 233 pesos.	
11		a. Exporter buys 10 M at a cost of 1,000 rupees and exports it.
	b. Exporter sells 10 M for 400 pesos and exchanges them for 2,400 rupees (6:1).	
		c. Result: Exporter brings in 2,400 rupees. Subtracting original cost of 1,000 rupees yields net profit of 1,400 rupees.
12		a. Exporter buys 10 F at cost of 500 rupees and exports it.
	b. Exporter sells 10 F for 100 pesos and exchanges them for 600 rupees (6:1).	
		c. Result: Exporter brings in 600 rupees. Subtracting original cost of 500 rupees yields net profit of 100 rupees.

The shift of the exchange rate from 3:1 to 6:1 destroyed all comparative advantages that X previously had and simultaneously conferred on Y an absolute advantage in both products. Consequently, the relative values of the two currencies, expressed in their exchange rate, can either create or negate the prerequisites for profitable international trade. But to what extent? The answer can be found by establishing the international price ratios for both products. Meat costs 40 pesos in X and 100 rupees in Y, hence the ratio is 1:2.5; fruit costs 10 pesos in X and 50 rupees in Y, giving a ratio of 1:5. These ratios set the upper and lower limits for the exchange rate. As the exchange rate fluctuates, it shifts the advantages more toward the country whose currency depreciates and away from the country whose currency appreciates. On the limits, one of the countries will break even and the other will derive all the advantage from the trade. Beyond the limit, as shown above, the comparative advantages disappear, and trade must stop, since one of the countries cannot export and thus cannot earn the other's currency to pay for any imports.

LIMITATIONS OF TRADE THEORY

The theoretical prediction of uniform prices and qualities has seldom been fulfilled. The real world has always been characterized by sharply differentiated prices, qualities, and even types of products from country to country. Part of the differentiation can be blamed on artificial trade barriers such as tariffs, import quotas, and other restrictions imposed by governments upon export and import businesses (we shall explore these governmental controls in Chapter 4); however, most of the differences have persisted in an arrogant contradiction to the theory of comparative advantage.

The Theoreticians' Dilemma

The contradictions between theoretical predictions and actual conditions stem from the fact that the model of comparative advantage is too simplistic: it can cope fully only with a two-country and two-commodity world, that is, with the very minimum condition for any international trade. If it is applied to multicountry and multiproduct trade, the model becomes vague. A real country exports and imports from thousands to millions of different products, depending upon how developed and diversified its economy is. No one has yet come up with a method of applying the comparative advantage theory to each specific item or even to each main classification of goods. Instead, economists have resorted to devices that attempt to simplify the real-life complexity enough to reduce it to the same level as the theory. The simplifying devices are of two kinds. First, assumptions are substituted for certain factual information. The main assumptions are as follows:

1. All countries use a free enterprise system with perfect competition (no oligopoly, monopoly, price fixing, or public enterprise).
2. Each country and each firm possesses the same technological and managerial capacities to produce any good; that is, technology and management know-how are public goods equally accessible to all firms.
3. There is perfect factor mobility within each country (but not internationally); thus, firms can change from one production mix to another at no cost or risk.
4. Import and export trade represent the only transboundary business activity. There are no multinational companies that operate in many countries simultaneously.

The second simplifying device is to lump all goods into two broad categories: *labor intensive* (those that require more labor than capital) and *capital intensive* (those that require more capital than labor). For example, if it costs $3 to produce a bushel of corn and wages account for $2 (67 percent of the cost), corn is a labor intensive product. Similarly, if it costs $50 to make a tape recorder and $30 is spent on capital goods (machines, factory buildings, raw materials), the recorder is a capital intensive good. By lumping all goods into these two categories, the vast numbers of products traded in actuality can be reduced to two, which would then theoretically be perfectly manageable under the comparative advantage theory.

Leontief's Paradox

The attempt to link comparative advantages to a nation's relative endowments with capital and labor suffered a catastrophic setback when Professor Wassily Leontief at Harvard undertook to analyze U.S. exports and imports in terms of their actual labor and capital contents. Because the United States is the most capital-rich country in the world, Leontief predicted that the United States would export only capital intensive goods and import only labor intensive ones. When his calculations had been completed, the results showed not only that the country was exporting and importing both kinds of goods but, even more surprisingly, that, taken as a whole, U.S. exports were actually less capital intensive or more labor intensive than import-competing goods. These factual findings, contradicting what at the time (1953) was accepted as immutable truth, became known as *Leontief's paradox*. Although much theoretical labor has been spent since on endeavors to explain it, the paradox not only remains but also keeps reappearing in factual studies of other countries' export-import data.

Technology Content

A more recent method of predicting comparative advantage is to classify all exports and imports into high technology and low technology goods. The technology content is measured by the cost of research, engineering, and other high skill inputs that a product requires.

According to this classification, the United States has had a trade surplus (exports minus imports) in high technology goods and a deficit in the low technology goods. This is certainly much closer to what the theory of comparative advantage predicts than was the case with the capital intensive and labor intensive classification. However, the reference here is to the aggregate balances. A study of the complete data reveals that a number of products of both categories flow in the direction opposite to what the theory predicts: many technology intensive goods are imported and many low-technology goods are exported by the United States.

Hence, even in its latest formulation, the theory of comparative advantage yields at best rough approximations in a macroeconomic context. For any specific product and for any individual company, the predictive powers of the theory remain limited. Business firms, therefore, must supplement economic theoretical analysis with market research in order to pinpoint specific opportunities.

SUMMARY

The theory of international trade is succinctly summed up by one authority as follows:

> Trade takes place when relative prices differ between countries and continues until these relative differences—aside from transportation costs—have been eliminated. In a more roundabout way, trade tends to bring about the equalization of factor prices. The export of products of the abundant factor (or resources) increases the demand for its services and makes them relatively less abundant. The import of products embodying large amounts of scarce factors (resources) makes those factors less scarce in the domestic market.[3]

Paraphrased, the theory of international trade postulates that countries will specialize according to comparative advantage, each producing the goods for which its resource endowments are relatively best suited and importing other goods. The international specialization and trade will tend to iron out price differences among national markets except those that are due to transportation costs, and will lead to rather uniform prices and qualities of products throughout the world.

Factual verification of the theory has been less than conclusive. Leontief's paradox has never been satisfactorily resolved. Even more serious contradictions to the theory seem to be presented by the rise of multinational enterprises and international technology transfers.

FOR REVIEW AND DISCUSSION

1. Explain the meaning of natural resources and their relationship to international trade.

2. If two countries had identical endowments of natural resources, could they trade at all?

3. Is it conceivable that the skills of its labor force could influence a nation's ability to trade?

4. Explain the principle of absolute advantage. Give examples.

---

3. Charles P. Kindelberger, *International Economics* (Homewood, Ill.: Richard D. Irwin, 1973), p. 30.

5. Suppose two countries, X and Y, are capable of producing annual quantities of oil and soybeans in the combinations given below.

Country X		Country Y	
Oil (lbs)	Soybeans (tons)	Oil (lbs)	Soybeans (tons)
0	200	0	300
20	180	80	240
60	140	160	180
100	100	240	120
120	80	320	60
200	0	400	0

What would the domestic real prices of each commodity be in each country?

6. Using the data in the previous question, determine (a) if either country enjoys any comparative advantage; (b) which product each country should export; and (c) what would be the gain from trade for each country.

7. Which of the assumptions underlying the theory of trade do you find most objectionable? Why?

8. Two requirements for any good theory are that it be a true reflection of basic reality and that it enable us to predict the outcome of future events. Assess the theory of trade in terms of these two criteria.

9. Leontief's paradox is still a controversial issue among economists; some accept it and others do not. Can you think of reasons why the matter has not been laid to rest long ago?

10. What do the terms of trade show? Could it make any difference if we computed the terms of trade by using the prices of goods traded or the prices of the factors of production?

4

National Control
of International Trade

Nations are sovereign entities. Each shapes its own economic and social affairs. Each also forms its own *foreign policy*, the ways in which it interacts with the outside world. Foreign policy covers national security and defense, cultural exchanges, and foreign economic policy. Each of these subareas of foreign policy, in turn, consists of a number of component fields, each with its own specific subsets of policies.

The purpose of the international economic policy of a nation is to define the goals that guide its business relations with other countries and to identify the ways and means by which those goals are to be achieved. As such, international economic policy embraces all international economic or business matters of a nation. Trade, payments, investments, the activities of multinational companies, foreign aid, patent and trademark controls, standardization of weights and measures, postal service, international transportation and communication, and a number of other specific areas fall within the scope of this policy.

FOREIGN TRADE POLICY

A most important part of foreign economic policy is foreign trade policy, also called *commercial policy*. Foreign trade policies are designed to cause export and import flows to conform to national goals. What the goals are is up to government authorities to decide. However, no government is free to follow any goals. The choices are limited.

In theory, the choices of trade policy available to a nation range from complete self-sufficiency (independence) to absolute free trade (interdependence) as shown in Figure 4.1.

Any shift toward one extreme will always exact a cost in terms of the other. A nation cannot simultaneously enjoy self-sufficiency and free trade. All it can do is search for the point on the continuum that best serves the total national interest as perceived by the nation itself. There is no objective measure of what the total national interest is or ought to be; it is determined by the

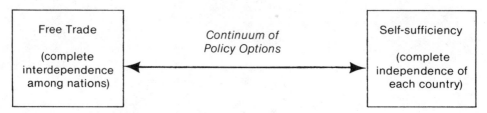

Figure 4.1   The Range of Trade Policy Choices

political process. Because of ideological priorities and economic necessities, different nations assign different values to independence and interdependence. Therefore, the policy continuum is not a straight line with objectively measurable trade-off costs, but an infinite variety of curved paths. Each country moves in its own particular path.

In reality, the limits of trade policy available to a nation are set by its economy's capacity to compete in the world market, its capacity to produce exportable surpluses, and its dependence on imports. A government's power to influence and to bargain with other governments is also limited. No government is normally in a position to dictate unilaterally to other countries what the terms of their economic interactions should be; no government can impose its own policies on others. There is always give and take. Even a large country, though usually more influential than a small one, must adjust its international trade policies to those of other countries. To benefit a country, trade policies must be effective; that is, they must lead to commercial interactions that serve the national interest. Trade policies and regulations that disregard the policies of other countries may fail to produce the desired effects because international trade is a multilateral process with each country's actions eliciting reactions and counteractions from others. Unilateral initiatives can, therefore, succeed only if accepted and supported by other countries.

Our aim in this chapter is to examine the instruments and rationalizations that governments use in regulating transboundary business activities and to show how business operations and managerial decisions are affected by them. How the United States has used these instruments to forge its trade policies vis-à-vis different parts of the world will be discussed in Chapter 5.

TARIFFS

Types of Duties

The oldest and most widely used trade control device is a tax levied on transboundary movements of goods, commonly called a *tariff* or *duty*. If levied by the country of origin on outgoing cargo, the tariff is known as an *export duty*; if levied by the country of destination on incoming cargo, it is called an *import duty*; and if levied by a country through which the cargo must travel en route from its origin to its destination, the tariff is known as a *transit duty*. A particular shipment may be subject to all three kinds of duties. In the United States, export tariffs are unconstitutional and transit tariffs have not been enacted; only import duties are used.

Duty Rates

Duty rates are based on either the physical unit or the monetary value of the imported article. If the duty is levied as a fixed amount per physical unit, such as $91.50 per ton or $6.25 per dozen, it is referred to as a *specific duty*. The amount of specific duty on any cargo is unaffected by its price or other costs; the total assessment depends entirely upon the physical quantity imported. If the duty is levied as a percentage of the value of the imported product, it is known as an *ad valorem duty*. In this case the total duty obligation varies with the price and quality of the imported cargo and bears no relation to the physical quantity imported. Quite frequently the two duties are combined by super-imposing an ad valorem rate on a specific duty; for example, $3 a pair plus 10 percent ad valorem. Such duties are called *compound duties*.

Since the number of articles that move in international commerce is very large and constantly changing, no tariff schedule can list all products individually; instead, they are classified into a hierarchy of groups and subgroups for which different duty rates are established. Through the differentiation of rates the government can influence the international trade of each category. Products that a government does not wish to be imported in large quantities will be assigned high tariffs, and products that it considers more desirable will be subjected to relatively low or even zero rates of duty.

Theoretical Relationships

The theoretical effects of a tariff are best shown by graphic analysis. For simplicity, it is assumed here that transportation costs are negligible and that there are no government controls or any other artificial restrictions to prevent the quantities that are exported and imported to respond to prices and costs. It is further assumed that only two countries and a single commodity are involved. Such a situation is presented in Figure 4.2.

In the absence of tariffs, the exporting country will sell to the importing country a quantity that equalizes prices in both countries (p_1). At this price the total demand and supply in the exporting country are equalized at the volume q_1; the demand is determined from d_1 (domestic consumption) and e_1 (export sales), and the output is determined by the supply schedule S. In the importing country, the demand and supply are equated at v_1; the supply is made up of S_1 (domestic output) and i_1 (imports), and the demand is determined by schedule D. Hence $d_1 + e_1 = q_1$; $s_1 + i_1 = v_1$; and $e_1 = i_1$. If an import tariff t is now imposed on the movement of the commodity, the price in the importing country rises, as the importers are trying to pass the tariff on to the

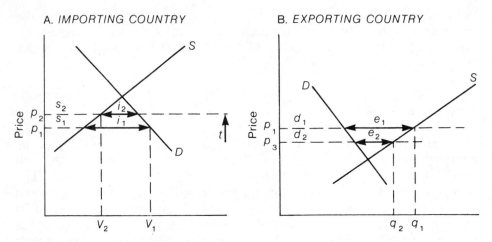

Figure 4.2   Effects of Tariffs

consumer. Since all consumers are not willing to pay a price higher than p_1, the demand for the commodity shrinks and only a smaller volume, v_2, can now be sold. The shrinkage of demand in the importing country leaves a surplus in the exporting country and intensifies competition among suppliers. As a result, the price declines to p_3, the point where the quantity offered equals the quantity demanded; that is, where $d_2 + e_2$ equals the supply (changed from q_1 to q_2). Under these supply and demand conditions, the effects of tariff t will be to raise the price in the importing country from p_1 to p_2 and to lower the price in the exporting country from p_1 to p_3; the difference between the new prices will be equal to the tariff t. At the new prices the quantity of exports will have declined from e_1 to e_2, and the volume of imports will have declined correspondingly from i_1 to i_2; $e_2 = i_2$ and $p_2 = p_3 + t$.

How the tariff effect will be distributed between two countries depends upon the relative slopes of their supply and demand schedules. If, for instance, the demand curve of the importing country were flatter in the above illustration, a price lower than p_2 would be necessary to balance supply and demand; this change would mean that a greater part of the price effect would be borne by the exporting country and p_3, too, would be lower than now shown. The reverse would hold if the supply curve in the exporting country were steeper. The reader who wishes to carry this reasoning to its ultimate numerical conclusions is advised to use the formulas of elasticity, which can be found in any good text on price theory.

The essence of the relationship can be summarized in two conclusions:

1. The imposition of a tariff by one country affects both countries of a trading relationship by creating a price spread equal to the amount of the tariff between them.
2. The burden of the price spread falls primarily on the country that has the steepest supply and demand curves for the commodity involved.

The Effects of Tariffs from a Unilateral Perspective

In practice, trade relations are usually multilateral, and the two-country assumption seldom holds. In a multilateral context, the total effect of a tariff becomes diffused and difficult to ascertain. Although this effect does not change the nature of the relationships, it distributes the results among a greater number of countries and makes them difficult to trace. Therefore, the arguments and reasoning employed in actual tariff policy formulation are normally centered on the effects in the importing country itself rather than on those in the international trading community as a whole.

Viewed from such an unilateral perspective, the effect of an import tariff can be (a) negligible, (b) a price rise lower than the tariff, (c) a price rise equal to the tariff, or (d) a price rise greater than the tariff. A price rise lower than the tariff is the typical case.

The no-effect situation exists whenever the exporting country is willing to lower its export prices by an amount equal to the tariff and thus neutralize the effect of the tariff upon the importing country's demand. This is usually the case when the exporting country has idle production capacity, has surplus stocks on hand, or is afraid to lose the import country's market to a competitor. Another no-effect situation exists when the duty is imposed on a product that the country is both importing and exporting. To illustrate, suppose the United States imposed an import tariff of $0.50 per bushel on wheat in the hope of raising the domestic price. What would the effect be? Since large quantities of U.S. wheat are exported, any price rise that might initially follow the tariff would quickly be drowned by exporters, who would divert their entire supplies to the domestic market as soon as the U.S. price rose above the world price. Thus, any price rise that did occur would be short-lived. However, the tariff would still affect the quantities traded, and both imports and exports of the United States would decline.

A price rise equal to the tariff is theoretically possible only when the pretariff price differential between the two countries is either larger than or equal to the duty, or when prices are set in ignorance of the true supply and demand relationships. Both these situations do occur.

A price rise greater than the duty may occur when the imported article moves through a chain of middlemen after being cleared through the customs. Each middleman adds his markup based on the landed cost. The figures below illustrate such a situation:

	No Tariff	25% Ad Valorem Tariff
Importer's cost, insurance, and freight price	$5.00	$ 5.00
Duty		1.25
Landed cost	5.00	6.25
Importer's markup (40%)	2.00	2.50

The result is the cost to the retailer shown on the next page.

	No Tariff	25% Ad Valorem Tariff
Total cost to retailer	7.00	8.75
Retailer's markup (40%)	2.80	3.50
Price to consumer	9.80	12.25

Hence a tariff of $1.25 has led to a price rise of $2.45.

Nominal Versus Effective Tariff Rates

How much protection against import competition a tariff provides is not readily reflected by the actual rates charged on a product by the customs; it depends also upon the relationship of this rate to the duty rates of the product's ingredients. Consider, for example, a finished product that is subject to an ad valorem rate of 15 percent. Suppose that the product is a Scandinavian desk and that its value has been derived 40 percent from raw material—Asian teakwood—and 60 percent from manufacturing. If the United States assessed a 15 percent duty on raw teakwood, the effective protection of the U.S. furniture industry would be, in fact, the same as the numerical or nominal rate, that is, 15 percent. If the United States imposed no duty whatsoever on teakwood, the entire weight of duty on the finished desk would fall on the manufacturing share of its value, giving an effective rate of protection to U.S. furniture manufacturers not 15 percent but $0.15 \div 0.6$, or 25 percent. Consequently, domestic manufacturers' costs of converting teakwood into Scandinavian desks can exceed 25 percent of that of its foreign competitors before any real import competition can occur. The effective protection is 10 percent greater than the nominal protection by official numerical rates.

Since most countries' tariff rates rise with the degree of finality of a product—raw materials have the lowest rates, semimanufactured goods medium, and finished goods the highest—the effective protection provided to the domestic manufacturers tends to exceed the level of the nominal rates of duty. The difference between the two depends on the relationship that the rates on raw materials and other inputs bear to the rates on finished goods. This can be concretely illustrated by broadening our example of the teak desk to four countries, all of which depend on imported teak. Start with these costs:

Cost of teakwood at world market price	$ 400
Value added in manufacturing	600
Value of desk (free of duty)	$1,000

Assume the following ad valorem import duty rates:

Country	Teak Lumber	Desks
A	0	20
B	10	20
C	20	20
D	30	20

The result is the following effective protection:

Country	Dollar Equivalent	Effective Rate
A	200	$\frac{200}{600} = 33.3\%$
B	$200 - 40 = 160$	$\frac{160}{600} = 26.7\%$
C	$200 - 80 = 120$	$\frac{120}{600} = 20.0\%$
D	$200 - 120 = 80$	$\frac{80}{600} = 13.3\%$

Although all four countries have the same ad valorem rates of duty on finished desks, the protection provided to domestic furniture manufacturers varies from 13.3 percent to 33.3 percent, due to differences in raw material duties. We must, therefore, conclude that the actual protectiveness of a country's import tariffs to any particular industry or economic sector is not accurately reflected in the nominal duty but is affected also by any differences in the structure of the rates between the industry's input and output goods. Differences in the effective rates will, in the long run, affect business decisions as to the location of manufacturing plants, that is, the importation of materials for further processing versus the importation of finished goods.

ISSUES OF TARIFF POLICY

Since tariffs affect different segments of society in different ways, tariff policy is always a controversial subject. The main interest groups are government, business, consumers, and labor. Each of these has an input, though not an equal one, to a nation's tariff policy. Familiarity with their attitudes toward tariffs are, therefore, fundamental to understanding the policy formulation processes.

Government

Governments use tariffs for three main purposes: (a) to control the direction of foreign trade; (b) to provide public revenue; and (c) to bolster national security.

In poorer countries, the tariff as a source of revenue ranks first, as the tax base in such countries is usually too limited to support the government budgets. In addition to import tariffs, developing nations frequently resort also to export and transit tariffs.

In the industrially advanced countries, including the United States, the use of tariffs is limited to the control of import trade. This, however, does not render the issue noncontroversial. The use of import tariffs involves discrimination against those whose consumption requirements are better met by foreign than domestic goods. They also discriminate against the foreign producers and marketers as compared to their domestic counterparts; tariffs shield domestic business from foreign competition. The use of import tariffs implies that foreign competition is not only different from domestic competition but also inadmissible in the national interest.

The last point is particularly relevant to industries that are considered important for national defense. In order to maximize endogenous capacity to provide strategic goods, the economic considerations are subordinated to the security needs as perceived by the government. If the militarily strategic industries cannot meet import competition, they may be built and maintained in the shelter of protective tariffs. The national security argument defies any conclusive economic analysis. In the United States, it has been used with consistent success by watch manufacturers, the maritime industries, and a number of producers of military supplies. For small countries, whose capacity to subsidize defense contractors is limited, a tariff policy based on this argument could be suicidal in today's world of weapons systems, atomic bombs, and supersonic aircraft, all of which demand mammoth investments in plant and equipment.

Business

In business, attitudes toward tariffs vary according to their effect upon the particular industry. For industries that depend upon foreign materials or finished goods, import tariffs mean higher costs of doing business. Under competitive conditions the tariff cost cuts directly into the industry's profit margin; under monopolistic conditions it forces higher prices and a consequent reduction in the volume of sales. Import-dependent industries, therefore, are strongly opposed to tariffs and support trade liberalization policies.

On the opposite side are industries whose products must compete against imports. For them import tariffs are a protective wall that reduces competition and raises the profit margin. The higher the tariffs, the smaller the foreign competition. Import-competing industries, therefore, are the strongest advocates of high tariffs. They engage in intensive lobbying in support of protectionist measures and policies. From their aggressive behavior comes the erroneous public belief that the business community as a whole seeks high, protectionist tariffs.

Industries that are neither import dependent nor import competing have no direct stake in tariffs. They constitute, so to speak, an *indifference zone* between the other two groups. However, they may be indirectly influenced by either side. For example, a company whose customers compete with imports will tend to take a protectionist stand; conversely, another whose customers depend on imports will lean toward free trade as a matter of solidarity. The attitudes of business toward tariffs is depicted schematically in Figure 4.3, which is shown on page 73.

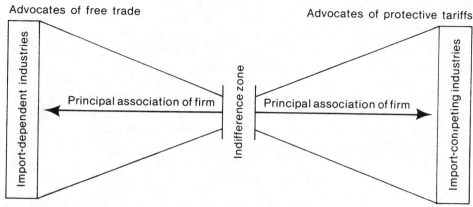

Figure 4.3   Business Attitudes Toward Tariffs

Consumer

For the consumer, tariffs mean higher prices. In spite of this, the consumer's influence on tariff policy is small. Public attitudes toward tariffs are usually vague and seldom motivated by the economic self-interest of the individual. This is true partly because foreign trade is a complex matter, much of which the consuming public does not comprehend, and partly because those who do comprehend have professional or business interests that are more influential in determining their attitudes than their consumer interests. A business manager whose profits depend on tariff protection is likely to oppose tariff cuts although his personal consumption expenditures might be reduced by a cut. The consumer interest, though universal, is frequently secondary to professional interest and, therefore, motivates very few to act. In addition, consumers are too diffused and unorganized to have much influence on a country's tariff.

Labor

From the perspective of labor, tariff policy should aim toward increasing employment and safeguarding domestic wage standards. Since raw materials, technology, and capital are essential for jobs, labor organizations lobby for low import restrictions on such imports. However, they are even more vehement on preventing the export of these job creating factors.

Protection of Jobs   On manufactured goods, labor's stand is rather universally protectionist, as such imports are seen as substitutes for actual or potential domestic jobs. The central thesis here is that all imports have a certain labor content that displaces domestic labor and contributes to unemployment in the importing country; therefore, the objective of tariff policy should be to minimize imports of all products that could be produced by domestic workers. This means high tariffs for the great majority of industries.

In certain instances this argument may be valid, but only to a point. Domestic employment can benefit only if the demand for the protected article is highly inelastic; that is, if the rise in price the tariff will cause will not destroy its effective demand. Otherwise, there will be little, if any, gain in employment and a loss to the consumers who are deprived of the product by the higher, after-tariff price. In addition, if a country's imports are curtailed, its exports, too, tend to decline, as other countries' abilities to buy from it are reduced by an amount equivalent to the value of the imports that are eliminated by the tariff or as other countries often retaliate with high tariffs of their own. Whichever the case, the resultant restriction in exports creates unemployment in the export industries.

Thus, the real question is, which of the two opposing effects of an import tariff is greater, the gain of employment in import-competing industries or the loss of employment in export industries? If the two are equal, the tariff will not contribute to total employment but will merely redistribute it between the two types of industries. As workers may not readily shift from the stagnating export industries to the newly protected industries, a structural dislocation in the labor force may result, with unemployment in one and overemployment in the other. If the loss of exports is greater than the reduction of imports, the whole argument collapses completely. However, since tariff advocates are normally concerned with their own particular labor union, community, or industry rather than with the nation as a whole, they often see in this argument an instrument for pursuing their own purpose.

Protection of Wage Standards   Labor unions in the industrial, high-income countries contend that their high wages must be protected by high tariffs against imports from low-wage countries. They claim that a free trade policy pauperizes domestic workers by destroying their standard of living.

The argument can be either true or false. More often it is false, because it rests on the assumption that differences in wage rates represent identical differences in the costs of production. This is the case only if the productivity of labor is identical in both countries. But if productivity differs, the wage rates alone reveal nothing, for the cost of labor is not equivalent to the hourly or weekly wage rate but to the total wage bill that a product must bear. This bill is determined by the hourly wage rate times the number of hours of work required to produce a product.

Suppose that a U.S. worker is paid $12 per hour and that 10 hours of work are required to make a particular article; the cost of the labor then is $120. Suppose further that the wage rate in Algeria is $3 per hour and that it takes 50 labor hours to produce the same product. The Algerian cost of labor is thus $150, or 25 percent higher than the U.S. cost, despite the fact that the wage rates are four times lower.

This is not an exaggerated illustration. Many U.S., European, and Japanese industries have, in fact, vastly higher productivity per labor hour than producers in less developed countries. The principal reasons for the superior productivity are greater capital investment in plant and equipment, superior technology, and better preparation of the worker, the investment in education and training. Any one or all three of these factors may affect productivity significantly. Since the conditions vary from industry to industry, the vulnerability to foreign low-wage competition varies accordingly. As a rule, the older industries with relatively stagnant technology, such as textiles, shipbuilding, and glass, are least able to compensate for relatively higher wage rates by correspondingly higher productivity. In the more dynamic fields the wage rate has no direct significance for tariff policy.

The Infant Industry Argument

Since 1791, when Alexander Hamilton wrote his *Report on Manufactures,* the thesis that new industries require protection against foreign competition in their early years has been widely accepted as a justification for high tariffs. According to this thesis, certain industries in a country cannot develop because of competition from already established producers in other countries even though, once developed, they will have a comparative advantage.

The argument rests on a reasonably sound theoretical base. With a small demand and limited capital resources, an infant industry is bound to have higher per-unit costs than an already established competitor operating at or near the optimum on the cost curve (see Figure 4.4). If it is not protected, the infant industry has no chance to reach optimum capacity, since the foreign industry can undersell it, and the only customers it will have are those willing, for patriotic or other noneconomic motives, to pay a higher price. Also, the

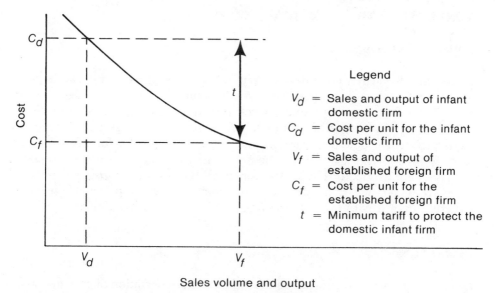

Legend

V_d = Sales and output of infant domestic firm

C_d = Cost per unit for the infant domestic firm

V_f = Sales and output of established foreign firm

C_f = Cost per unit for the established foreign firm

t = Minimum tariff to protect the domestic infant firm

Sales volume and output

Figure 4.4   Per-Unit Cost for Infant and Established Firms

established foreign industry can perpetuate the advantage by continued improvement of techniques, product quality, and marketing methods. As a result, the country's resources remain idle and its industrialization is retarded. Given tariff protection, the new industry is encouraged and, as it grows in size and strength, the tariff barriers can be reduced and at its maturity completely removed.

For obvious reasons the infant industry theory appeals strongly to industrially underdeveloped countries. Like the United States in the eighteenth and nineteenth centuries, the developing nations of Asia, Africa, and Latin America in the present time are avid supporters of it. In the developed countries, its backers are primarily small businesses.

If one could predict with certainty which industries, if started and given tariff protection, would ultimately reach an efficiency comparable to or greater than that of their foreign competitors, the infant industry thesis would provide a sound basis for tariff policy. However, policy makers can only hope and guess. They have no sure way of forecasting the relative successes of different industries. Hence, they run the risk of protecting the wrong industry, one that never will reach competitive maturity and that will always remain dependent on tariff protection. Such misallocation of resources not only defeats the purpose of the tariff but also retards the development of other industries that might put the resources to more efficient use.

Another problem of applying the infant industry theory is the practical difficulty of removing the tariffs as the industry matures. Once enacted they tend to be forgotten and stay on the books like any other tariff. Nevertheless, the infant industry theory is the most widely used justification for high import tariffs throughout the Third World.

NONTARIFF METHODS OF TRADE CONTROL

Surtaxes and Special Levies

In addition to tariffs, government may impose special *surtaxes* or *border levies* on international cargo. These are usually temporary measures designed to correct a short-term disturbance or self-liquating maladjustment in trade relations. A typical cause of import levies or surtaxes is a serious balance of payments deficit. The levies are imposed to restrain imports for a few months or so to save foreign exchange; when the critical deficit has been eliminated, the levies are dropped. The reason for using the surtax is legislative convenience. It is a much more cumbersome process to revamp the whole tariff structure than it is to impose temporary levies as corrective devices.

Export Subsidies

Export subsidies or *bounties* are used to stimulate the exportation of certain goods. The subsidy enables the exporter to sell in foreign markets at prices lower than nonsubsidized competitors.

Export subsidies may be direct or indirect. Direct subsidies are cash payments by the government to the exporting firms based on the quantity exported. For example, the Spanish government may pay $20 a ton to olive exporters. If the unsubsidized price of the olives were $200 a ton, the subsidy enables the trader to sell the olives at $180 a ton and cover the deficit of $20 by the subsidy. This gives the Spanish olive exporter a competitive advantage in world markets. It is, however, an artificial advantage, not one based on the actual cost.

Indirect subsidies may take the form of low freight rates, reduced domestic taxation, government guaranteed low-interest loans, government help for research and development, or other assistance that leads to a lower than normal cost for the exported commodity. The indirect subsidies are used much more widely than is generally recognized. Because of their disguised nature, indirect subsidies are difficult to discern, not to mention measure.

From the trade control standpoint, a subsidy is merely an extension of the tariff effect into the positive side of the zero-line; the tariff restricts, the subsidy augments a nation's trade. Governments view their own subsidies simply as export stimulants, but this view is not shared by the governments whose countries are the target markets of the subsidized exports. For them the subsidies represent trade distortions. The subsidized price may nullify the restrictive effects of their own import tariffs and may even undercut the domestic prices if the foreign subsidies are actually greater than the domestic import tariffs, thus leading to unfair competition.

Corrective Duties

Countervailing Duties To prevent trade distortion by means of export subsidization, many countries impose extra duties on subsidized goods when they are imported. In the United States these charges are called *countervailing duties*. They are normally set at the same amount as the foreign subsidy, restoring the amount of tariff protection that regular import tariffs are intended to provide. In case of direct subsidies the application of countervailing duties is relatively simple; in the case of indirect subsidies their use is often greatly complicated by the lack of available evidence. We shall return to subsidies and various other nontariff trade distortions in Chapter 5, in which concrete issues of trade policy are discussed.

Anti-Dumping Duties *Anti-dumping duties* are imposed on goods imported at a price lower than they command in their country of origin. The main motivation for dumping—exporting at a lower price than selling the same goods in the producer's home market—is the profit that results from the economies of scale. If a producer is operating below full capacity level, an increase of output will reduce costs per unit.

For example, a plant's cost of making product X may be $5.00 a unit if it produced 6,000 units, which is all the domestic market can absorb. But at 8,000 units, the cost would drop to $4.00 per unit. To increase the output to

8,000 units the firm must export 2,000 units. Suppose competition will permit it to enter an export market only if it sells at $4.20 a unit. If its shipping and export marketing costs are more than $0.20 a unit, as they normally should be, the $4.20 will not suffice to cover the full cost of the exported goods. Taken separately, then, the exports result in a loss to the firm. But this is out of context. The reduction of production cost from $5.00 to $4.00 applies not only to exports but to the entire output. On the 6,000 units sold in the producing country the manufacturer now nets an extra $6,000—$1.00 per unit—since the price is still the same as before. Thus, despite the fact that it exports at slightly below the break-even point, the company's total profit picture has been improved by dumping on export markets.

As a general rule, economies of scale induce dumping when most fixed costs can be charged to domestic sales and export prices are based on variable costs only. Another incentive for dumping may be sporadic accumulations of distress goods, such as excess inventories or defective items, which are dumped on foreign markets to avoid disturbing the domestic price structure. Sometimes dumping is used to weaken competition. Known then as *predatory dumping*, the practice aims at gaining monopolistic control of the particular export market and thereafter profiting from substantially higher prices, which could go unchallenged.

Like subsidized shipments, dumped exports can cause chaos and disturbances in the target markets. To protect their market against dumping, many countries, including the United States, use anti-dumping duties. Their main purpose is to nullify the price differential between the dumped and the normally priced products.

Penalty duties include a variety of levies and charges that customs authorities are authorized to assess in cases of faulty documentation of cargo, noncompliance with customs procedures, attempted smuggling, or some other infraction of the import regulations. Depending on the infraction, the penalty rates range from an increase of a few percent over the regular rate to several times the regular rate, and they may include confiscation.

Quantitative Trade Restrictions

Tariffs and surcharges restrict trade by making the goods more expensive, but they do not set any absolute limits. Trade goes on as long as there are buyers willing to bear the higher cost. To set absolute limits to trade, governments use quotas and licenses. A *quota* specifies the quantity of a given good that can be imported or exported; for example 10,000 sports cars or 800 gross of diamond rings. Quotas can also be stated in terms of value: $50,000 worth of sports cars or $144 thousand worth of diamond rings.

The quota is parceled out to traders by issuing licenses on fractions of the quota. Usually some set of criteria is followed in allocating the quotas to traders. Sometimes the criterion is simply first come, first serve; other times the criterion is political. When the limit of the quota is reached no more licenses are issued, and no further trade can take place in this particular commodity.

Since the quotas set absolute limits they can cause more drastic restraints on trade than tariffs. High tariffs can be absorbed by consumers who have a high enough propensity for the imported product coupled with the ability to pay for it. In other words, people and businesses with an elastic demand will tend to drop out of the market when high tariffs are imposed; consumers with an inelastic demand will still continue buying imported goods even though they may be subject to high tariffs. As a result, tariffs do not completely shut out imports or exports. Quotas do. It matters not what the elasticity of demand or supply is or what the consumer's preferences are—the quota ends it all. Therefore, quotas are generally regarded as the potentially most restrictive of government trade controls.

In recent years, there has been a tendency to negotiate so-called *voluntary quotas* for certain products. Most prominent among the voluntary quota imports to the United States have been textiles, automobiles, electronics, and stereo equipment. The purpose of the voluntary quotas is to head off protectionist congressional action that might seriously threaten trade in a particular sector. The foreign government and industry involved have been persuaded to limit their exports (imports to the United States) voluntarily, that is, to self-impose quantitative limitations on their exports. Japan has agreed to more voluntary quotas than any other country.

Monetary or Exchange Controls

An indirect but equally efficient way to restrict trade is to cut off foreign exchange, without which payments for foreign purchases are impossible. Foreign exchange controls are used either as a substitute for tariffs and merchandise quotas or, as is more common, as a new dimension of the control apparatus. The monetary controls can help to impose the government's influence, to place under its value judgments such matters as which goods are to be regarded as necessities and which as luxuries, which trade transactions are to be rated more important and which less important, and which countries should be favored and which disfavored as either sources of imports or markets for exports. In sum, the monetary controls enable a government to fine-tune foreign trade activity not only to fit an officially desired commodity mix but also to reflect government priorities in terms of product qualities and foreign trading partners.

The currency controls usually take the form of exchange quotas and licenses that are operated not too differently from the merchandising quota systems. Limited sums of foreign exchange are allocated for trading in specific commodities. The quotas are parceled out among trading companies by means of issuing exchange licenses without which foreign exchange cannot be obtained. Additional features of the monetary controls may include *multiple exchange rates* both for buyers of exchange and sellers of exchange. Under such a system a particular foreign currency will have several prices in terms of domestic currency depending upon the purpose for which it is used by an operating firm. If it is bought for the purpose of importing something considered essential by the government, the currency can be acquired at a low rate of exchange; but if it is to import something considered unnecessary or a luxury, the rate of exchange is considerably higher. Such rates make it artificially cheap to import the favored goods and artificially costly to import the disfavored goods. For exports the reverse system of preferences can be applied.

Multiple exchange rates thus give premiums to certain businesses and impose penalties on others, depending upon what commodity they are trading in and which country they are trading with. They are an instrument for commercial discrimination employed by some governments.

EFFECT OF TARIFF RATES ON BUSINESS COSTS

The duty rate is of more than statistical interest to traders. A *specific duty* applies equally to low-priced and high-priced goods. Suppose the duty on sunglasses is $2 a pair. For very high quality sunglasses valued at $25 a pair that rate is the equivalent of 8 percent, but for sunglasses at the lower end of the quality spectrum, which may wholesale for $1 a pair, the rate is 200 percent. It is highly unlikely that the low-priced sunglasses could be imported at all under such conditions since the duty would require that the price be at least tripled. The high-priced glasses could absorb the same duty with relative ease. Consequently, specific duties are more restrictive for low-priced goods than for high-priced goods.

Another important consideration with specific rates is prices. Since prices in the world market often fluctuate, the effect of the specific rate of duty fluctuates accordingly. When prices rise while the rate remains unchanged, the effect of the duty declines; when prices decline the effect of the rate increases. Since in recent years inflationary pressures have caused rapid price increases, the effect of specific rates on trade has been constantly declining.

Ad valorem rates keep the duty obligation proportional to the value of the dutiable cargo. If we applied an ad valorem duty of 8 percent to the sunglass example above, both the high-priced and the low-priced sunglasses would be assessed an equal proportion of their actual value; the low-priced glasses would be assessed $0.08 per pair and the high-priced glasses $2.00 a pair. From the standpoint of customs clearance the specific duties are preferred. They require no valuation of the cargo and are thus easier to process, whereas ad valorem duties require very accurate valuation and classification of imported goods. This leads to frequent disputes between traders and customs authorities. It is an inherently confrontational situation. The custom officials are in essence tax collectors. Their job is to see that the tariff laws are properly applied and all duties collected. If they err, they would rather overcollect than undercollect; for them it is better to be in the position of making refunds than having to chase down traders who were underassessed.

Thus, even under the best of circumstances, international traders run the risk of being overassessed by customs. To minimize this risk most trading firms utilize the services of *custom house brokers;* qualified specialists who are licensed by the government of the importing country (in the United States, through the Treasury Department). U.S. law permits only an importer in person or a certified custom house broker to clear goods through customs. Nobody else can do it.

POSTPONING DUTY OBLIGATION

The Need to Postpone Duties

For some business firms, import duties may have some unintended side effects. For example, they may prevent a company from importing in large enough quantities to enjoy a most advantageous purchase price or to ship the cargo at the lowest freight rate (shipload or carload lots). Some other companies could benefit from importing in unpackaged bulk if they still could keep the integrity of the packaged product intact, that is, prove to the consumer that the bulk imported product is in no way different from the one packaged in the country of origin. For example, if the label reads,"Imported and bottled by X & Sons, San Francisco," the consumer has no absolute certainty that he or she is getting the real thing. The company says so, but that makes it neither true nor convincing. If the product is Scotch whiskey, for example, the consumer has no safeguard that no domestic whiskey was blended with the imported product before it was bottled.

It is not the point here to argue how many people do or do not believe the importers. The factual credibility depends on the product, the importing company, and the particular consumer's sophistication. Rather, the point is that bulk importing introduces the possibility of tampering with the product during the packaging process. The existence of this possibility reduces the consumer's confidence in the authenticity of the product.

Import duties must be paid or a bond posted to guarantee their payment before the cargo is released by customs. For any large quantity of dutiable imports the duty obligation represents a formidable financial burden. For example, take a manufacturer who uses imported raw materials or parts. By buying its annual supply at one time and shipping it in shipload lots the firm could significantly reduce the cost of these imports. However, to pay the import duty on a full year's supply at one time may be more than the firm's cash flow can finance.

To alleviate such undesirable and uneconomic side effects of tariffs, U.S. laws provide for two major institutions that enable importers to postpone and prorate over time their duty obligation, and to process, package, label, and to perform even some manufacturing operations before clearing the imports through customs.

Bonded Warehouses

Under U.S. tariff law, storage facilities that are operated under the lock and key of customs authorities can be organized. These are known as *bonded ware-*

houses. The bonded facilities may be owned either by private firms specializing in selling warehousing services or by companies who use large amounts of imports. In either case, the owner must be bonded to guarantee that he will observe and fulfill all customs regulations.

The main function of the bonded warehouse is to enable incoming cargo to be put in storage without payment of duty. As long as the goods are kept in the bonded warehouse the duty obligation is postponed. The goods must remain in the bonded facility under custom's lock and seal and can be moved only in a bonded carrier from one bonded warehouse to another or to a port for re-exportation. The bonded carrier may be a railroad car, truck, cargo plane, barge, or coastal vessel carrying the bonded goods in an enclosure under custom's seal. In order to place the goods on the open market, the importer must first clear them through customs and pay the assessed duty. The advantage of the warehouses is that the law permits the importer to withdraw the goods in small lots and to pay duty only on the lot withdrawn. Thus, the total duty obligation on a large import shipment can be distributed over many months.

Bonded warehouse facilities can also be used for processing and limited manufacturing activities. For example, Scotch whiskey or French perfume imported in bulk can be bottled *in bond*, which guarantees the integrity of the product to the ultimate consumer. Woolens can be cut to the patterns of jackets, trousers, or whatever is to be made of the material and the cuttings discarded; since the import duty on woolens is based on weight this operation reduces the burden of duty for an apparel manufacturer. Many other processing, labeling, and even assembly operations are carried out in bonded facilities.

Bonded warehouses may also be used for re-exportation. In that case, imported goods will be stored in the bonded warehouses until a satisfactory market for them is found abroad. If these goods are not placed in a bonded warehouse, the importer pays duty on them at the time of entry and later claims a refund of the duties paid, known technically as a *drawback*, after they have been re-exported. The drawback is limited to 99 percent of the duties paid. Use of the bonded warehouse eliminates all the work, delay, and costs connected with customs clearance and drawback application connected with re-export.

Free Trade Zones

Storage in bonded warehouses is usually more expensive than in ordinary storage facilities. The additional cost is due to the expenses of customs inspection and surveillance. To provide a less costly alternative, Congress created *free trade zones* (FTZ), limited areas adjacent to major commercial centers that have been excluded from the U.S. jurisdiction for all customs purposes. Foreign goods may enter and exist in these zones without any customs formalities so long as their destination is a foreign market.

Goods can be processed, packaged, and further manufactured in the zone area. After that they may be cleared through customs and entered as any other imports for consumption or they may be reshipped to third country markets without customs formalities. For example, in a newly established FTZ at Kansas City, pool tables and related equipment are assembled using slate from Italy, frames from the United States, rubber from Japan, balls from Belgium, and cue sticks from Portugal and Taiwan. If the finished product is sold in the United States, the company will pay duty only on the imported components; if the equipment is exported, no U.S. duty obligation is incurred. In one of the oldest FTZs, in Seattle, complex optical equipment is assembled combining prisms from Germany and lenses from Japan, precision mechanisms from Switzerland, plastic castings from England, and control instruments from France.

SUMMARY

Foreign trade is subject to a multitude of government restrictions as well as stimuli. Since trade affects various constituencies (business, labor, consumers, and the military) differently, public pressure on government is often contradictory. In formulating foreign trade policy, a government attempts to consolidate the diverse pressures so as to best serve the nation as a whole.

Tariffs, quotas, subsidies, and monetary exchange restrictions are the most widely used instruments for trade control. Each provides a wide range of options by which both the direction and the composition of a nation's trade can be changed. In combination, they lead to a complex system, the operations and effects of which are not readily understood.

FOR REVIEW AND DISCUSSION

1. Compare the uses and relative effectiveness of tariffs, quotas, and foreign exchange restrictions. Would you expect business firms to prefer one over the others if given a choice? Why?

2. Should importers prefer specific or ad valorem tariffs? Would all importers agree? How would a government trade official view the two tariff categories?

3. Explain the meaning of effective tariffs. Should business pay more attention to the official tariff rates set by government or try to determine the effective rates? Elaborate.

4. Which segments of U.S. society would benefit if import tariffs were sharply increased? Which segments would suffer? How would such an increase affect the common good?

5. To increase exports of product *X* by $100 million, U.S. firms must spend $5 million on advertising abroad. If the U.S. government subsidized the exporters by $4 million they would be able to achieve the $100 million expansion of exports by lowering their prices instead of incurring the advertising cost. Would you support an export subsidy to this industry?

6. What are the pitfalls of the infant industry tariff?

7. Would dumping be possible by a firm that operates under near perfect competition at home? Explain fully.

8. In Europe, free ports and free trade cities evolved during medieval times; in the United States the free trade zones have been established only since World War II. What factors might explain this lag?

9. What, if any, are the connections between wage rates, living standards, and cost of labor, viewed from an international perspective?

10. Self-sufficiency is a political luxury that burdens the society with unbearable economic costs. Comment.

5

United States Trade Policy

Trade policy is the composite of official attitudes and formal actions, including laws and regulations, which form the objectives and rules for a nation's international trade relations. As such, trade policy is a complex subject. It is not something that any one official, any one government, or even any one country alone can make. The formulation of trade policy is an ongoing process. Many divergent interests within the country itself as well as in other countries with which it interacts participate in this process. The policy is never complete nor fully articulated. Its formation, elucidation, and interpretation require an historic perspective to be understood.

POLICY CHANGES IN THE 1930s

Under the U.S. Constitution only Congress can make tariffs; the president has no such powers.[1] Congress used to exercise this power directly by passing new tariff laws and repealing old ones. The last such law was the Tariff Act of 1930, which is still the basic tariff law of the land. However, congressional tariff making was a slow and cumbersome process. As the pace and importance of international business grew, a more flexible system was needed. In 1934 the Reciprocal Trade Agreements Act was passed. This act introduced a system that allows the executive branch of the government to take over the leadership function in tariff matters and to induce other countries to reduce their tariffs by offering concessions.

Under this act Congress delegates to the president the authority to negotiate reciprocal tariff reductions with other nations. It provides maximum limits of the tariff cuts (such as 50 percent of existing rates) and the time period (such as three or five years) within which the negotiations must be completed.

---

1. Also, Congress can only create import tariffs. Export tariffs are prohibited, and transit tariffs have never been needed because of the country's location.

After that, all the tariff making power reverts back to Congress until it passes a new trade act. The reciprocal trade law has been renewed twelve times since 1934.

The reciprocal trade agreements themselves make no changes in U.S. tariffs or trade; they only enable the president to negotiate with and make commitments to other nations. If the negotiations are unsuccessful or are not completed before the act expires there is no change whatsoever; if the negotiations are successful and trade agreements reducing tariffs are concluded, the reductions take effect as amendments to the Tariff Act of 1930, which remains the country's basic trade law.

From Bilateralism to Multilateralism

When the reciprocal trade agreements were introduced, the world was in the grip of the great depression. Panic-stricken governments had resorted to ultraprotectionist devices in the naive hope of stimulating domestic business through supression of international trade. The United States itself had fallen victim to the depression hysteria by enacting the 1930 Tariff Act, which holds the notoriety of having been more protectionist than any other piece of U.S. legislation.

The fast shrinking world trade was based on the bilateralist system. As its name implies, this was a system in which each country negotiated with only one other country at a time and entered into a separate bilateral arrangement—trade and payments agreement or commercial treaty—with each foreign nation. Being a product of separate negotiation, each bilateral arrangement was in some or most respects different from all others. That this must have resulted in a bewildering number of different rules and regulations of trade is an algebraic inevitability. A nation trading with, say, one hundred other countries would have one hundred sets of trading rules; the same would hold for each of the other one hundred countries.

Under bilateralism, due to the bureaucratic complexity of transboundary transactions, management of international trade became a technical profession. Ordinary marketing personnel were usually not able to cope with the legal and technical aspects of international transactions. Special training and considerable practical apprenticeship were required before one could acquire the necessary experience to handle competently foreign trade transactions.

Why, then, did bilateralism gain dominance in the interwar period, and why does it continue to be advocated by policy makers of certain countries? It is inherently a system of *international commercial discrimination* and as such holds the lure of enabling an anxious government to take shortcuts in improving the relative trading fortunes of its own country at the expense of the rest of the world.

The overall character of the bilateralist system may be summed up by saying that it was a disruptive and corruptive system that bred international commercial discrimination, undermined fair and open negotiations and agreements, and greatly complicated foreign trade practices. It is this system that the reciprocal trade agreements program had to change if its objective of general trade liberalization was to be achieved.

General Agreement on Tariffs and Trade

To remove the bilateralist obstacles the General Agreement on Tariffs and Trade (GATT) was negotiated soon after World War II, an epoch-making event. GATT is a multilateral agreement signed by some 90 trading nations, with the objective of making multilateralism the cardinal principle of international trade relations. It provides an open forum for simultaneous trade negotiations to all member countries (this is where the name *GATT round* originates). All member countries participate on an equal basis in negotiations and have access to any deliberations of other members. Thus it provides an open forum that can be used not only for negotiation of tariff matters but also to air any grievances that any member country might have against any other, such as mistreatment of its goods or carriers, commercial discrimination, unfair competition, or any other international misbehavior.

The second key provision of the GATT is to outlaw international commercial discrimination. Any member country is required to treat *all* other members as equals and is entitled to the same consideration. All forms of favoritism or disfavoritism are violations of the GATT principle. Thus, any particular product should be treated the same by the importing country regardless of its origin if the producing country is also a member of GATT.

The practical vehicle for implementing the nondiscriminatory provision is the *most favored nation* principle, which is a universal requirement for all tariff adjustments within the GATT framework. The most favored nation (MFN) principle provides that a country will not impose higher restrictions on imports from the other country than those it imposes on imports coming from any third country. The MFN clause does not eliminate discrimination against imported goods as compared to domestic goods, but it does prohibit discrimination among imported goods coming from different countries of origin. For example, if Country X levies 10 percent ad valorem duty on shoes from Italy and 18 percent on shoes from Japan it must grant the 10 percent rate to any other shoe exporting nation with whom it enters into an agreement that contains the MFN clause. (The tariff on shoes from Japan will remain at 18 percent as long as it doesn't have MFN status.) Over time, the country granting MFN treatment will thus tend to treat all imports alike. This says nothing about the absolute level of tariffs or quotas. All imports may be treated very badly or very well compared to domestic goods. But in the long run the use of the MFN clause leads toward a general liberalization of trade. GATT requires that negotiations between any pair of member countries on any specific product or rate of duty will be shared automatically with all others, making it generalized. Since the MFN principle has been applied also to invisible tariffs, such as import licenses, quotas, and various legal restrictions and bureaucratic procedures, as well as to actual tariffs, it has played a very decisive role in reducing trade barriers.

The MFN principle may be applied not only to goods but also to investments, vessels, entrepreneurs, or any aspect of business relations. The MFN principle is not to be confused with the *national treatment principle*, which requires that foreign goods, vessels, and so forth be accorded the same treatment as their domestic counterparts; no tariffs or import quotas can be imposed at all under this principle. The use of the national treatment principle has so far been limited to internationally integrated economic systems such as the European Common Market, which are discussed in Part Eight.

THE EVOLUTION OF U.S. TRADE POLICY

Trade policy is a multifaceted phenomenon. It is composed of multiple decisions, both legislative and administrative, which must somehow balance the conflicting goals of all the different interest groups in the economy. While some decisions are more significant than others, none can singly determine what the policy is. To understand the policy we must review its evolution. The main body of the policy is a carryover from the past. The new policy measures focus on additions to and deletions from this main body.

The evaluation of U.S. trade policy is best achieved by reviewing the trade agreements that have been negotiated on the basis of the reciprocal trade legislation within the GATT framework. The *reciprocal trade agreements acts* (RTAAs) were based on two principles:

1. Reciprocity in trade liberalization, especially in tariff reduction. That is, if one country removed some trade barriers, it was entitled to similar concessions from the country or countries benefiting from this action. It was hoped that the reciprocity requirement would set in motion the process of general trade liberalization among all trading nations.
2. Prevention of injury to domestic industry, known as the *noninjury principle*. This meant that tariff cuts should not be made when they would lead to an increase in imports that would be harmful to the import-competing domestic industry.

The Peril Point and Escape Clause Mechanisms

The noninjury principle was harnessed for the dual tasks of defining what tariff concessions would be contemplated by the United States and of adjudicating claims for protection against existing import competition. For the implementation of these dual aims, the *peril point* and *escape clause* mechanisms were invented.

Peril Point   Under the peril point provision of the RTAAs of the 1950s, the president was required to have the Tariff Commission ascertain what size tariff concessions could be offered to other countries without threatening injury to U.S. business. The commission was directed to review for each product item that was to be negotiated and to make precise determinations of the point below which the tariff could not be cut without injury to domestic producers. These studies were costly and time-consuming. The commission, never having enough money to determine the peril points for all goods, had to rely mainly on industry claims. Since the most active participants in the commission's hearings were the industries lobbying for the greatest possible protection, the peril points were, as a rule, set so high that little room was left for effective tariff reduction.

In the 1962 Trade Act, the precise peril point was eliminated, although a weakened remnant of the concept was retained, mainly to appease the protectionist hard core in Congress than for any presidential application. The replacement of the peril point with other criteria removed the rigidity that had immobilized U.S. tariff negotiations in the past.

Escape Clause   Under the escape clause provisions any business that felt it had suffered serious setbacks because of increased competition from imports occasioned by tariff cuts could appeal to the government for tariff relief. If the Tariff Commission found that injury had been caused or threatened, it was required to make specific recommendations to the president regarding necessary tariff or quota relief to remedy the damage.

For the purpose of illustration, let us suppose that because of an official trade agreement an industry in Country X could project a substantial volume of exports to the United States and that to meet that demand it must make large investments in new production capacity. A year or two later, when the new factories have been completed and their output starts flowing to the U.S. market, the affected U.S. industry claims injury and demands a new peril point investigation. Let us suppose further that the concessions granted to Country X two years earlier do indeed violate the peril point criterion. The Tariff Commission would then recommend that the president invoke the escape clause of the trade agreement with X and nullify the concessions. Country X would thus loose the market for the new factories and be left with investments sunk in idle capacity. The mere possibility of this happening placed U.S. intentions in doubt abroad and tended to serve as an invisible tariff against imports.

Policy Crisis

The peril point and escape clause not only symbolized the schizophrenic dilemma of the U.S. position, but also blocked the achievement of tariff reduction in an increasing number of commodity classifications, the peril point setting an absolute floor, and the escape clause creating an uncertainty that kept both negotiators and traders guessing as to what was or was not permissible. Under those circumstances, the principle of reciprocity could have only limited application.

A new impetus came from the creation of the European Economic Community (EEC) in 1958. While the GATT program had been losing momentum, six European nations concluded a customs union and embarked upon a program of complete economic and social integration of their countries. This provided the prospect of a mass market and ultimately a mammoth economy comparable to that of the United States.

The new union provided two kinds of incentives to the outside world for trade liberalization. First, there was immediate danger of trade diversion from nonmember countries to the member countries, since the internal import duties were to disappear while a uniform external tariff was to be imposed. Second, there was a longer range prospect of mass marketing and mass production that had never existed outside the United States. Thus, the business community in the United States as well as in other nonmember countries began to demand concrete steps for obtaining an easy access to the European market. From the EEC side a prerequisite for starting negotiations was the elimination by the United States of the peril point and escape clause system. In the Trade Expansion Act of 1962, which was the twelfth extension of the RTAA program, the noninjury principle was relegated to a hollow rhetoric. The central core of the act was the legitimizing of import competition under the so-called *trade adjustment program*.

In his 1962 message to Congress, President Kennedy stated:

> Once given a fair and equal opportunity to compete in overseas markets and once subject to healthy competition from overseas manufacturers for our own markets, American management and labor will have additional reason to maintain competitive costs and prices, modernize their plants, and increase their productivity. The discipline of the world marketplace is an excellent measure of efficiency and a force for stability. To try to shield American industry from the discipline of foreign competition would isolate our domestic price level from world prices, encourage domestic inflation, reduce our exports still further, and invite less desirable governmental solutions.

THE KENNEDY ROUND

Worldwide recognition of the new initiative symbolized in the trade adjustment program was expressed by the GATT's membership naming the negotiations following the 1962 trade legislation the Kennedy Round. These marathon negotiations lasted for five years and resulted in significant tariff reductions for some five thousand product groups. These could not have been achieved without the trade adjustment program. But equally important were previously overlooked dimensions of U.S. trade relations which the Kennedy Round deliberations brought to light. These were *tariff structures* and *nontariff barriers*.

Tariff Structure

Under the earlier trade acts, the U.S. delegation had been required to negotiate tariff cuts product by product. Such tedious procedures made it necessary to negotiate on a very selective basis and to focus the attention on tariff rates of specific imports rather than on the overall structure. The 1962 act authorized across-the-board cuts, which could apply either to all manufactured goods or to broad sectors of them.

When the U.S. delegation proposed an across-the-board cut of 50 percent of the then-existing tariff rates other nations objected. The main advocate for the opposition was the European Common Market. The issue arose because the U.S. tariffs varied across a wide range, some products having zero rates, others extremely high rates. The European rates were much more even, mostly in the 10 to 20 percent range. What would happen if the 50 percent across-the-board cut was applied to such different structures is shown in Figure 5.1.

If 50 percent is cut off the top of the Common Market structure, there is a new tariff level that will clearly allow a greater inflow of imports in all categories; there is liberalization throughout the whole structure. However, if 50 percent is cut off the top of the U.S. tariff structure, some new rates are still prohibitively high (cut from 80 percent to 40 percent, for example). In those product classifications, the cut will have no effect on imports because the remaining tariff is still high enough to keep all imports out. Such tariff cuts are a statistical fiction, quite irrelevant to actual trade.

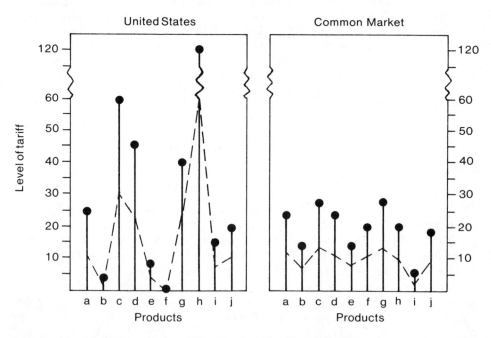

Figure 5.1   Tariff Structures at the Start of the Kennedy Round

The Common Market, therefore, demanded an alignment of tariff structures, that is, a cutting down of the high peaks, before any across-the-board reduction was attempted. The United States strongly resisted this demand and the negotiations remained deadlocked for several months. It was finally agreed that where large disparities existed the reductions by the other nations could be smaller than those of the United States.

Nontariff Barriers

Previous trade agreements had been narrowly limited to tariff problems; they were in reality only tariff agreements. Although the 1962 act was equally barren in this respect, the issue of nontariff barriers to trade surfaced during the Kennedy Round as an important new aspect of international trade relations. Once the issue had been raised, it quickly led to accusations and countercharges from all directions. The constructive contribution of these accusatory proceedings was not any reduction of the nontariff barriers—the Kennedy Round was not prepared to cope with them—but the proof that import quotas, export subsidies, trade taxes, restrictive customs and administrative procedures, labeling and marking requirements, health and safety regulations, dumping and antidumping practices, buy-national laws, and other forms of regulatory restraints on international trade were widely used.

The inescapable implication was that the actual trade liberalization achieved under the reciprocal trade agreements was considerably smaller than it had been perceived to be. Earlier tariff reductions had been followed by imposition of new nontariff barriers. Figure 5.2 illustrates what had happened in the United States as an example. The neglect of nontariff barriers had led to a distorted view of trade liberalization. While one barrier, the tariff, had been reduced, many others had taken its place. Obviously, the main problem was no longer tariffs but the various forms of nontariffs. This problem was addressed at the next GATT negotiations.

THE TOKYO ROUND

In 1973 foreign ministers of 90 nations met in Tokyo to plan for the next multilateral trade negotiations. They agreed upon an agenda that was made public in the Tokyo Declaration; from this came the name *Tokyo Round*, which in many publications is referred to simply as MTN, or *multilateral trade negotiations*. (The ensuing negotiations were actually conducted in Geneva, Switzerland.) In addition to emphasizing tariff reductions, the Tokyo Declaration emphasized the need for reduction of nontariffs, coordination of trade liberalization by economic sectors, liberalization of agricultural trade, special treatment of tropical products, and the establishment of the so-called *multilateral safeguard system*—how to handle a fast rise in imports or collapsing exports.

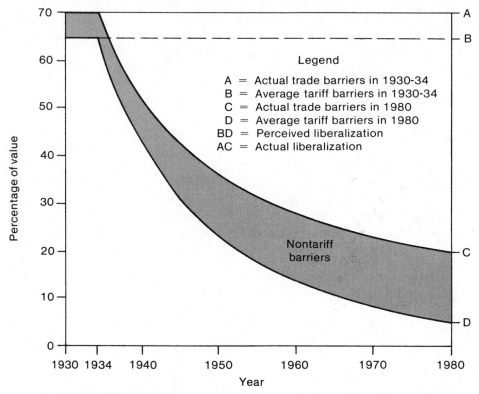

**Figure 5.2   Perceived and Actual Reductions of Trade Barriers
by the United States**

Special attention was to be given to trade problems peculiar to developing countries.

The Tokyo Round represents the first comprehensive approach to trade liberalization. Its results are far-reaching. Since the agreements concluded in 1979 will be implemented step by step over an eight-year period, their impact on world trade will grow annually until 1987. The agreements will affect all types of international businesses as they will form the framework for international trade relations in the 1980s and possibly beyond. The contents of the Tokyo Round agreements are of utmost significance not only to traders and multinational companies but also to domestic firms.

The objectives that the United States sought to achieve at the Tokyo Round were set forth in the Trade Reform Act of 1974, the latest in the series of reciprocal trade agreements acts. The law authorized the president to negotiate with other nations to:

1. Reduce duties above 5 percent by a maximum of 60 percent and to eliminate existing duties of 5 percent or less
2. Enter into agreements for the reduction, elimination, or harmonization of nontariff barriers, providing that implementing legislation is approved by Congress

3. Seek agreements to ensure fair and equitable access, at reasonable prices, to supplies important to the U.S. economy
4. Improve certain aspects of the GATT's rules
5. Impose controls to relieve injury to domestic producers caused by imports
6. Adopt a generalized system of tariff preferences for the benefit of developing countries

To facilitate the adjustment of domestic business to the possible increase of import competition, the 1974 law extended and refined the adjustment assistance concept first introduced in the 1962 act. The refined adjustment assistance consists of three separate programs: assistance to workers, assistance to firms, and assistance to communities. As detailed in Table 5.1, the eligibility

Table 5.1   Revised Trade Adjustment Assistance Programs

ASSISTANCE TO WORKERS

Eligibility for assistance no longer requires that increased imports be the primary cause of loss of jobs; a finding that the imports contributed importantly to unemployment is sufficient.

The range of benefits offered includes readjustment allowances of up to 70 percent of the displaced employee's wages, payments for retraining and related services (counseling, testing, job search).

Maximum benefit period is 52 weeks for workers under 60 years of age and 78 weeks for older people.

ASSISTANCE TO BUSINESS FIRMS

Eligibility criteria: (a) that substantial numbers of workers are laid off or threatened to be laid off, (b) that sales or production have declined, and (c) that increased imports contributed importantly to the actual or threatened unemployment of workers and the decline of sales or production.

An eligible firm qualifies for government assistance for (a) direct loans or loan guarantees for the purpose of expansion or modernization of production facilities or for working capital; (b) technical assistance allowances to upgrade engineering, product design, production, marketing, or other aspects of management.

ADJUSTMENT OF COMMUNITIES (A COMPLETELY NEW PROGRAM)

Eligibility criteria: (a) community has been or is threatened by significant unemployment, (b) sales or production of firms in the area have declined, and (c) increased imports or the transfer of businesses to foreign locations have contributed importantly to the existing or feared unemployment.

An eligible community is required to form a *Trade Impacted Area Council* with representation from business, labor, government and general public; the Council's task is to prepare a plan of how adjustment assistance could be used to rejuvenate the community's economy.

If the U.S. Department of Commerce certifies the plan as feasible, the community becomes entitled to adjustment assistance to fund the implementation of the plan.

criteria for adjustment assistance have been considerably relaxed and the benefits greatly increased compared to the Kennedy adjustment law.

Canada and the United States are the only industrial nations who have specific trade adjustment assistance programs. All other industrial countries have adopted policies aimed at facilitating structural adjustments of any kind in their economies. Trade adjustment is but one factor in such comprehensive approaches to structural change. In the past, the United States has resisted government participation in, not to mention planning and programming for, structural changes in the economy. However, since both industrial and developing nations (see Chapter 19) have been seeking international linkages between such programs, it is likely that the extended trade adjustments assistance system may take on even wider dimensions in the future.

THE NEW WORLDWIDE TRADING SYSTEM

The Tokyo Round negotiations produced a series of multilateral agreements on detailed rules for a new international trading system. As these new rules are adopted during the 1980s, both government trade contracts and international business policies will undergo significant changes.

Tariffs

Table 5.2 shows the average tariff levels of major industrial trading partners at the start of the Tokyo Round (see page 96).

The agreed-upon reductions are shown in Table 5.3 by major sector. They come out to a 33 percent overall reduction on imports to the United States,

Table 5.2   Comparative Tariffs Before Tokyo Round

AREA	DUTIABLE GOODS		ALL GOODS	
Manufactures	*Weighted Average*[a]	*Simple Average*[b]	*Weighted Average*[a]	*Simple Average*[b]
United States	8.8%	12.1%	6.8%	11.1%
European Community	8.1	7.5	4.5	6.9
Japan	11.6	11.2	6.3	10.1
All industrial nations	9.8	10.7	5.9	9.0
Agricultural Products				
United States	8.5%	16.8%	4.8%	15.1%
European Community	13.9	17.9	8.4	16.5
Japan	39.7	44.2	27.4	40.6

[a]Weighted by actual imports
[b]Arithmetic average of rates in official schedule

Table 5.3 Reductions of Tariffs on Dutiable Imports at Tokyo Round

COUNTRY	ALL DUTIABLE GOODS	DUTIABLE AGRICULTURAL GOODS	DUTIABLE MANUFACTURES	DUTIABLE MINERALS[a]
United States	29.6%	17.2%	30.9%	51.2%
European Community	29.3	30.0	29.0	31.4
Japan	10.7	3.6	11.8	5.9

[a]Includes oil.

Source: United States Tariff Commission

a 40 percent reduction on imports to Japan, and a 30 percent reduction on imports to the European Community.

Once these reductions have been implemented tariffs will cease to be a major trade barrier. The industrial nations have come very close to the 5 percent level below which tariffs are generally regarded to be dysfunctional—they are more of a nuisance than a protection. The next move could well be a complete abolition of tariffs, though one major hurdle to such a move remains. There are still some very high rates in the U.S. tariff structure. The industries behind these rates are shielded against import competition. They will not give up the shield without a major political battle.

With these few exceptions, the problem of trade liberalization in the industrial world has clearly shifted to nontariff issues, which are discussed later in this chapter. This cannot be said about the less developed countries. Their basic objective is to use tariff protection for their infant industries and to insist on free access to the markets of industrial countries.

Less Developed Countries' Preferences

In the past, GATT provisions required that international trade concessions be based on the principle of reciprocity, mutually equal treatment. This basic rule was changed by the Tokyo Round. The new system assures less developed countries (LDCs) the right to nonreciprocal priviledges. They do not have to grant full reciprocity to participate in GATT agreements, especially in areas in which reciprocity would be inconsistent with their developmental needs. Their exports are to receive special preferences in regards to entry into the industrial countries and they are entitled to restrict foreign competition in their domestic markets. In the longer run they are to phase down their import barriers and move toward reciprocity.

The preferential treatment of LDCs by the United States was made possible by the 1974 Trade Act, which includes the provision for a *generalized system of preferences* (GSP). Other developed countries have enacted similar legislation. The GSP gives the president the power to exempt from duty eligible imports from any developing country except communist nations and members of the Organization of Petroleum Exporting Countries (OPEC). To be eligible the law requires that at least 35 percent of the invoice value of the product originate in the exporting LDC, either in the form of material inputs or value added in processing. The only LDC products ineligible for GSP treatment are those directly competitive with *import sensitive* domestic products. The act defines import sensitivity in terms of national security and economic significance. It specifically lists textiles, apparel, watches, and certain footwear as import sensitive and excludes electronics, steel, or glass from consideration, but for most imports the GSP leaves the decision to the president. (Other trade issues relating to developing nations will be covered in Chapters 19 and 20.)

Nontariff Codes

Subsidies and Dumping   Government subsidies can hurt another country by creating unfair competition. The United States has in the past unilaterally applied countervailing duties to nullify foreign subsidies. This has been a controversial issue. The Tokyo Round established rules under which all countries may impose countervailing duties against subsidized imports only if they cause serious injury to the importing economy.

As we learned in Chapter 4, dumping occurs when a firm sells its products abroad at a price lower than at home or below the cost of production. The rules about how and when anti-dumping duties may be applied were also standardized internationally by the negotiations.

Product Standards   It is not always clear when technical or health requirements are used for bona fide purposes and when they are imposed as import restrictions in disguise. The European Community has excluded U.S. electrical goods as unsafe; the Japanese have excluded U.S. pesticides as hazardous to health, and the United States has kept Mexican tomatoes out by requiring that they be packed in cartons into which they do not fit. Thousands of similar tricks have been invented to manipulate product standards.

Because such abuses are difficult to detect and to correct, the new agreement requires that governments use open procedures, and it prohibits regulatory standards that create unnecessary obstacles to international trade. The agreement has also created an international committee to handle complaints and suggest corrective actions.

Customs Valuation   The U.S. system of customs valuation has long been criticized by importers as an invisible tariff because of its multitude of alternatives and the unpredictability of applicable rules. Foreign countries have been particularly critical of the use of U.S. selling price as the basis for assessing ad valorem duties on certain chemicals, footwear, and shellfish. For example, if tennis shoes made in Korea were priced at $10 but U.S.-made tennis shoes sold for $30, the import duty was computed by using the U.S. price as the base, which resulted in a duty three times higher; if the rate was 12 percent, the duty was $3.60 instead of $1.20.

Two technical agreements resulting from the Tokyo Round lay these disputes finally to rest. All countries agreed to switch to actual transaction value (invoice value at the port of export) for import valuation. If the transaction value should be unknown, the agreement provides for three other standards, to be applied uniformly in all countries.

Safeguards   The Tokyo Round legitimized emergency protection against disruptive imports (those causing serious payments problems, say, or massive unemployment), but such action must be preceded by international consultations and it must apply to all supplier countries. Discrimination entitles the affected country either to retaliate or to accept negotiated compensation. On this point compromise was difficult because the Scandinavian countries were insistent on their right to selective protection; and since in the past selective measures have been used in Europe mainly against Japanese imports, Japan was relentlessly opposed to their international legitimation. An international surveillance committee was set up to oversee the use of the safeguard rules.

Other Tokyo Round agreements establish new rules for government purchasing and for sectoral trade such as aircraft and agriculture. These agreements go into great detail, which can best be appreciated by a thorough study of the actual agreements.

Challenges for the New System

International Forces   Conversion to the new trading system is certain to be challenged on several fronts. In the raw materials trade there has been a shift from the free market toward government cartels. This poses a wide range of problems that are far beyond the scope of the GATT trading rules. We will explore this topic at length in Chapter 19.

A second trend is the rise of state-owned enterprises as major actors on the world market. All trade of communist nations goes through state trading monopolies (see chapters 22 and 23). In the less developed countries, state-owned enterprises show significant growth, and even in Europe and Japan significant sectors are run by public enterprises. The new trading rules provide that state traders should follow commercial trading principles. It remains to be seen to what extent they will and what, if any, disciplinary action can be taken against them if they violate those rules.

A third change involves mergers of national markets through international integration. As is explained in Chapters 24 and 25, this tends to weaken the competitive position of those nations who are not parties to any such integration scheme. For the United States the main challenge in this regard has come from the European Community (Common Market). It has been proposed that the United States, Canada, and Mexico join their markets to counterbalance the integrated markets elsewhere.

Domestic Pressure Groups   Finally, there are domestic political pressures, which all democratic governments must heed. If some important industries fail the test of adjusting to a greater openness of the national economy to international economic forces, governments will come to the rescue. The recent bailouts of the Lockheed and Chrysler corporations in the United States are cases in point. Steel and textiles are other obvious problem industries. Even when Congress was debating the 1979 Trade Agreements Act, which made the agreements and codes of the Tokyo Round part of U.S. law, federal authorities were using so-called voluntary quotas, diplomatic pressures, and a bag of other devices to restrict imports of textiles and footwear from a score of less developed countries and Japan; cane sugar from the tropical nations; television sets from Korea, Taiwan, and Japan; stainless steel from Europe; and beef from Argentina and Australia.

Government Inconsistencies   U.S. trade policy has also suffered from diffusion and cross-purposes. Seven different departments of the federal government participate in making and carrying out trade and other international business policies. As a result, trade policies are not only fragmented but frequently tangled up with unrelated pursuits: promotion of human rights, protection of the environment, preventing payoffs and other fraudulent behavior, fighting the Arab oil boycott, or aiding Jews to emigrate from the U.S.S.R. Such disparate applications of trade policies have severely reduced U.S. trade and other international business activities and robbed the economy of countless jobs.

To combat this problem, many experts believe, a separate department of trade or, preferably, of international business should be established by the federal government. Many other nations have long since recognized this necessity. By having a cabinet ministry exclusively for this purpose, international business receives not only top level attention but will also enter into the process of government policy making as a comprehensive whole rather than as scattered bits and pieces that have often been overhauled by domestic issues.

SUMMARY

The fundamental structure of trade policy in the United States is determined by federal legislation and international trade agreements based on multilateral negotiations. Presidential actions may either strengthen or weaken the trade policy, depending upon changes in international tensions, involving national security, or domestic problems such as unemployment, economic recession, or monetary instability.

Before the Kennedy Round, U.S. trade policy was based on the principles of multilateralism and prevention of injury to domestic industries. The MFN theory was used to combat international commercial discrimination, which had become rampant during the interwar period, and the peril point and escape clause mechanisms concessions were used to prevent import prices from dropping below those of domestic producers.

The Kennedy Trade Expansion Act added a new dimension, the trade adjustments program. It was designed to open the U.S. market for foreign competition by allowing tariff concessions to reduce import prices below the peril point. The domestic industry injured by such concessions became eligible for federal assistance aimed at lowering its costs sufficiently to meet the import competition.

The Tokyo Round of multilateral trade negotiations shifted the focus of trade policy from tariffs to nontariff distortions of trade. A series of nontariff codes was adopted. The codes do not completely eliminate differences in nontariff practices, but they set forth a consistent set of ground rules that go a long way toward uniformity and reciprocity in nontariff matters.

FOR REVIEW AND DISCUSSION

1. If a trade war broke out, which nations would suffer the most, the nations with trade surpluses or those with trade deficits? Explain.

2. Bilateralism provides each nation with more choices than multilateralism. It also allows a nation to synchronize trade and political relations closely. Would it not be wiser, then, for a nation to follow a bilateralist rather than a multilateralist trade policy? Are factors other than trade relevant to such a decision?

3. Suppose Congress passed a law substituting the use of the MFN principle with the national treatment principle in all trade agreements. What difference would this make to different businesses, to labor, to consumers, to defense, or to other segments of society?

4. How many different ways can the average tariff of a nation be computed? Explain. Are any of them satisfactory for international comparisons?

5. Which factors do you believe were responsible for the fact that each round of tariff reductions under the reciprocal trade agreements program between 1934 and 1979 were followed by new nontariff barriers?

6. If the United States government would not be ideologically opposed to central planning of the economy, the trade adjustments program might not be needed at all. Comment.

7. Will the objectives of trade liberalization more likely be achieved under the system of reciprocity or nonreciprocity of concessions? Why? In light of your reasoning assess the long-range outlook for the GPS.

8. Do anti-dumping duties impose an unfair restraint on price competition? Explain.

9. Which of the nontariff codes is the most important? Why?

10. The United States does not have a foreign trade ministry. Many other nations do. What do we gain or lose by not having one?

SUGGESTED READINGS FOR PART TWO

Balassa, B. *Changing Patterns in Foreign Trade and Payments.* New York: Norton, 1978.

Bergsten, C. F., and Krause, L. *World Politics and International Economics.* Washington, D.C.: Brookings Institution, 1975.

Caves, R., and Jones, R. *World Trade and Payments.* Boston: Little, Brown, 1977.

Destler, I. M. *Making Foreign Economic Policy.* Washington, D.C.: The Brookings Institution, 1980.

Ingram, J. *International Economic Problems.* New York: Wiley-Hamilton Publications, 1978.

Kindleberger, C., and Lindert, P. *International Economics.* 6th ed. Homewood, Ill.: Irwin, 1978.

Mason, H. *The Economics of International Business.* New York: Wiley, 1975.

Patrick, H., and Rosowsky, H., Eds. *Asia's New Giant.* Washington, D.C.: Brookings Institution, 1976.

"Reconciliation of Conflicting Goals in the Export Administration Act of 1979—A Delicate Balance." *Law and Policy in International Business* 12:415–460, 1980.

Root, F. *International Trade and Investment.* Cincinnati: Southwestern, 1978.

Rosenblatt, S. M. "Trade Adjustment Assistance Program: Crossroads or Dead End." *Law and Policy in International Business* 9:4, 1065–1100, 1977.

Snider, D. *International Economics.* Homewood, Ill.: Irwin, 1979.

Symposium on the Multilateral Trade Agreements. Law and Policy in International Business 11:1263–1526, 1979; 12:1–333, 1980.

Walter, I. *International Economics: Theory and Policy.* New York: Ronald Press, 1976.

Part Three

FINANCIAL ENVIRONMENT OF INTERNATIONAL BUSINESS

We often buy money very much too dear.

—W. M. Thackeray

The use of money is intrinsic to all business activities. Since each country has its own national currency, banking system, and government controls, international business activities are complicated by the cross-national differences and incongruencies in the financial environment.

Three categories of problems are basic to international finance. One relates to international payments transactions—how they are carried out, what risks they entail, and how the exchange rates are established. These topics are covered in Chapter 6. The other problem complex involves the effects of international payments on a nation's economy and its international financial position. These topics are discussed in Chapter 7. A third source of the international financial complications derives from trends that are not directly traceable to the existence of separate national financial systems but tend to function on a transnational plane. These are treated in Chapter 8.

6

International Payments

*E*very nation has its own monetary unit, which serves as the common measure of value and the legal medium of exchange in its territory. All economic relationships, business transactions, and accounts of assets and liabilities are based on this unit. The issuance of currency is a government monopoly. Only a government can mint the bills and coins that are recognized as official money, that can be tendered and that must be accepted as the normal means for settlement of financial claims.

MONEY IN INTERNATIONAL BUSINESS

The Need for Currency Conversion

In the international realm no legal tender exists. Values must be measured, accounts kept, and payments made by conversion of one currency into another. For example, assume a U.S. exporter wishes to sell to a Swiss importer a cargo worth $2,000. The Swiss importer assesses the value of the cargo in Swiss francs. If this business transaction is to be carried out, the number of francs that are equivalent to $2,000 must be calculated and the francs somehow converted into dollars.

The conversion is handled by the banking systems of the two countries. Basically it is accomplished by some U.S. banks holding franc deposits in Swiss banks, and some Swiss banks holding dollar deposits in U.S. banks. When the U.S. exporter sells to the Swiss buyer who pays francs, the U.S. bank will acquire the francs for its franc deposits and pay the U.S. exporter from its dollar assets; when a Swiss exporter sells to a U.S. importer the bank will acquire dollars and pay out (or sell) francs. Banks specializing in international banking make hundreds of such conversions daily. In recent years some banks have multinationalized.

106

The Rate of Exchange

The other aspect of the payments process, namely, determining the dollar equivalence in francs or the franc equivalence in dollars, is more complicated. How many francs will the bank have to get to be able to pay out $2,000? In theory, currencies are exchanged on the basis of their *purchasing power parity;* that is, a dollar should be worth the sum of francs that buys exactly the same amount of real goods as one dollar, and one franc should be worth the sum of dollars or cents that buy exactly the same amount of real goods as does one franc.

In practice, this principle defies direct application. A dollar may buy more beef and less perfume than a franc and both may have equal value in purchases of steel. Since relative costs and prices differ between the United States and Switzerland for the vast majority of goods and services, there is no way of computing an exact purchasing power parity. The job is left to the invisible hand of the marketplace. Currencies are sold and bought on the foreign exchange market. Here currencies become commodities that are traded and, as anything else that is traded, each currency acquires a price, called the *rate of exchange*. If the dollar in New York is worth 1.50 francs, the rate of exchange is $0.667; conversely, if the franc in Geneva is worth $0.667, the rate of exchange is 1.50 francs. The rate of exchange is expressed in the number of units of the domestic currency per unit of foreign currency, except in England, where the reverse practice is followed (number of foreign units per pound sterling).

The rate of exchange is subject to supply and demand. It has a tendency to fluctuate in response to the amounts of the currency offered for sale and demanded by traders, investors, speculators, and others who participate in international transactions. However, the determination of exchange rates has never been left entirely to market forces. Governments jealously guard their monetary systems and introduce constraints into the foreign exchange process. Some countries regulate official rates of exchange from which no deviations are allowed; others allow a greater play to supply and demand but intervene actively in the market as buyers or sellers to keep the rates in targeted intervals. The role of a government in the exchange market depends in part on the prevailing international monetary system and in part on the country's own requirements as perceived by its government.

ANALYTICAL MODELS

In pure theory, international monetary relations are limited to three alternatives: (1) an international or universal currency, (2) a complete exchange monopoly, and (3) an absolutely free exchange market.

The Gold Standard

Although other international media of exchange are conceivable, the only one that has in fact been used is the *gold standard*. In its pure form the gold standard links all national currencies to gold. Although the unit denominations, the numerical scales, and the actual circulation media differ from country to country, each currency has its official gold cover, called either the *gold par* or *mint parity*. Thus, all currencies are convertible into gold at their respective mint parities. Gold thus serves as the common denominator of all national currencies or, more correctly, as the universal money upon which the values of national currencies rest. This system is shown schematically in Figure 6.1.

If paper notes or nongold coinage are circulated by a nation, as was typical under the gold standard, the relationship between such circulation media and

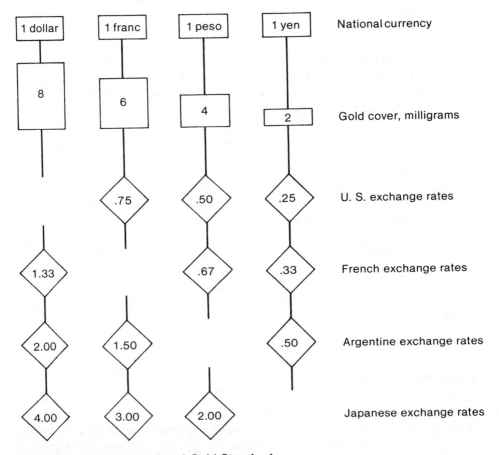

Figure 6.1   The International Gold Standard

gold is maintained through the freedom of any bearer or holder of the nongold media to demand redemption in gold at the official mint parity. This right of redemption compels the monetary authorities of the nation to keep the money supply in the parity prescribed relationship to its gold reserves at all times. Any change in the gold reserve will cause a corresponding change in the money supply. It will thus tend to adjust the country's price level either up or down, depending upon whether the gold is flowing in and augmenting the money supply or flowing out and contracting it. Consequently, the gold standard serves as the basis not only for national monetary systems but also for the international monetary system.

Despite the establishment of gold as the foundation of currencies, day-to-day exchange transactions are executed in legal tender rather than in gold for two reasons: the instruments of exchange must be made out in a particular legal tender; and importers, exporters, and other parties to international transactions need sooner or later to convert their proceeds into their own domestic money. Therefore, the short-run exchange rate is subject to the current supply and demand relationship on the exchange market and may even shift away from the mint parity rate at which gold standard currencies should theoretically exchange. But such shifts cannot exceed the cost of redeeming a currency in gold, for at that point gold will be demanded by the party against whose interests the rate is shifting. The redemption cost consists mostly of transportation, insurance, and handling costs for the gold shipments plus, possibly, some loss of interest.

The extent and the limits of exchange rate fluctuations are illustrated graphically in Figure 6.2. In part A, if the demand for Norwegian krone in New York exceeds the mint parity rate of $0.20, as shown by lines S_1 and D_1, the exchange rate will move about the mint parity to R_1 (about $0.204 per krone); if, on the other hand, the supply outstrips the demand, as shown by lines S_2 and D_2, the rate will drop below the mint parity (in this instance, to about $0.191 per krone).

If the demand for the krone (supply of the dollar) still exceeds the supply of the krone (demand for the dollar) when the exchange rate reaches the gold export point, dollars will be converted into gold to satisfy the excess demand, as illustrated by the line R_3 to D_3 in part B. Such a situation may arise because of a sudden increase in Norwegian imports to the United States or a decrease in U.S. exports to Norway. In this case, only q_1 krone are earned through U.S. exports, and the q_1 to q_2 amount is paid from the gold reserve. Conversely, if the demand for the krone (supply of the dollar) is insufficient to absorb the supply of the krone (demand for the dollar), as under D_4 and S_4 condition, the exchange rate will drop to the gold import point; and, since there are still not enough buyers of the krone in the New York market to enable all holders of krone assets to settle their dollar obligations, that is, there are not enough dollars to clear the krone supply, gold will be imported to make up the difference. Despite the fluctuations in the supply and demand, the exchange rate remains fixed to the narrow interval between the gold export point and the gold import point.

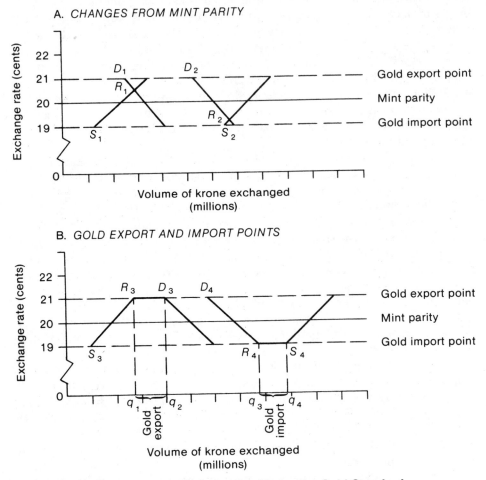

Figure 6.2   Exchange Rate Determination Under the Gold Standard

National Exchange Monopoly

The establishment of a government monopoly over foreign exchange allows the government to direct all receipts of exchange into a national pool in order to subject it to rigorous inspection and control. More specifically, the exchange-control authority fixes the exchange rate by an official decree, requires all recipients to surrender their foreign exchange assets to the central bank or to some other agency at the official buying rate, and rations the exchange through quotas, licenses, and exchange permits.

The country's exchange rate is rigidified. Supply and demand in the exchange market can affect neither money supply nor prices. The domestic economy is entirely shielded against foreign influences, and the government experiences no international restraint or compulsion regarding domestic monetary affairs.

All governments exercise their monopoly power in the exchange market to some degree, but only the communist nations, including both China and the U.S.S.R., rely exclusively on this model. That none of the communist currencies is convertible on a free market at its official exchange rate is a poor testimonial to the claimed values of exchange monopolies.

Free Exchange Market

The *free exchange model* postulates that the exchange market is perfectly competitive; completely free from monopolistic imperfections and government interventions. Currencies are readily convertible and parties to any transactions are free to execute payments in any currency, in any amount, at any time, for any purpose, at any place, without interference from any source. The exchange rates are determined by the unhampered interplay of supply and demand, very much as commodity prices are determined; and, like commodity prices, the rates respond to variations in the supply and demand relationship—hence they are called *freely floating exchange rates*. The amplitude of the rate fluctuations depends entirely upon economic forces, mainly traders' and investors' needs, which determine how much of a given currency is sought and how much of it is offered at any particular time. If the underlying forces remain relatively stable, so will the exchange rate; if they swing wildly, so also will the exchange rate. Figure 6.3 illustrates how exchange rates respond to different changes in the supply and demand of exchange.

According to *purchasing power parity theory*, exchange on a free market will seek the level at which the internal purchasing powers of the two currencies are equal. Disturbances in the exchange market may cause the short-run rate to deviate from the purchasing power parity, just as disturbances cause similar deviations from the mint parity under the gold standard, but such deviations are postulated to be short-lived and the market to have the tendency to correct itself and to restore the equilibrium or parity rate. In other words, the short-term market rates revolve around the parity rate, which in the long run equalizes the real values of the domestic and foreign currencies in terms of their real purchasing powers. Should inflationary or deflationary tendencies change the real purchasing power relationship of two currencies, the exchange rates move accordingly. For example, suppose the parity or equilibrium rate for U.S. dollars and Swiss francs in the base year was $0.40 per franc. If, in a subsequent period, the price index in the United States climbed from 100 to 120 while in Switzerland it declined from 100 to 80, the new parity rate would be:

$$\$0.40 \times \frac{120}{80} = \$0.60$$

Attempts to put the theory into practice by working out precise mathematical formulas for purchasing power parities have encountered immense

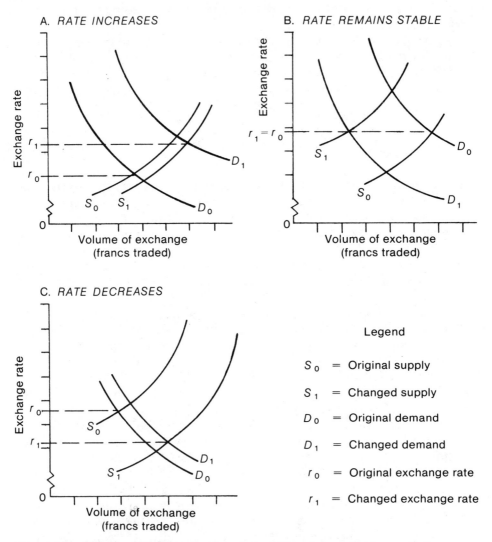

Figure 6.3   Effects of Changes in Supply and Demand on Exchange Rate

difficulties for three reasons: (a) international payments other than those for exports and imports also affect the supply and demand of exchange; (b) the product mix of one country is never identical to that of another—certain goods are unique to certain countries and others vary in grade and quality; and (c) price indexes are misleading in that they conceal the actual price structures, that is, the relative value of one product in terms of another, and create numerical comparisons that are fictitious. For example, a typewriter in Country A may be equal in price to ten pairs of shoes or two woolen suits or two pounds of liverwurst; in Country B the same typewriter may be worth fifteen pairs of shoes or one woolen suit or eight pounds of liverwurst.

In order for the price levels of two countries to be equated, the product mixes of the countries must contain the same products in the same proportions and their price structures must be identical. Consequently, though it is undisputable on grounds of logic, the free exchange market theory refuses direct verification. Its ultimate proof can come only through actual testing—the creation of a free exchange market—which the world has yet to do.

THE INTERNATIONAL MONETARY FUND

From World War II to 1971 international monetary relations were structured rather rigidly, according to the rules established by the *Bretton Woods Agreement* of 1944. A product of the experts of 44 nations, the agreement created two institutional entities, both supranational in character: the International Monetary Fund (IMF) and the International Bank for Reconstruction and Development, usually called the World Bank.

The IMF Fixed Rate Regime

The World Bank has relevance to foreign exchange only to the extent that it serves as a source of assistance credit for financially weak nations and thereby adds to their foreign exchange supply. The IMF, however, was designed to regulate and coordinate international financial relations. Its main objectives were as follows:

1. Promotion of exchange rate stability
2. Maintenance of orderly exchange arrangements
3. Avoidance of competitive currency depreciation
4. Establishment of a multilateral system of payments and the elimination of exchange restrictions
5. Creation of a standby source or exchange reserves available to individual countries in case of maladjustments in international payments

The emphasis on stability, orderliness, and multilateralism reflected the fears that the financial disorder, instability, and discriminatory bilateral payments arrangements that followed World War I and persisted throughout the great depression would occur again at the end of World War II. To prevent this unhappy history from repeating itself, the exchange rates used by different countries were to be standardized and subjected to a continuous surveillance by the IMF. The exchange rate standard adopted was a composite of the best features of the three theoretical models: the gold standard, the exchange monopoly, and the free exchange market. At the time of admission to the IMF, a country's currency was assigned a par value based on its rate of exchange in U.S. dollars at that time. The dollar par was in turn converted into a gold par on the ratio of $35 per ounce of pure gold (then the only legal price of gold in the United States). Thus, regardless of whether a currency had any legal gold cover internally, it was given a gold parity by the IMF. The purpose of the gold par was to give the system a double foundation. If a member nation felt that the key currency was overvalued, it could demand gold instead. This right was limited to national monetary authorities only; private parties could not demand gold.

Like the gold standard, the IMF exchange standard was predicated upon exchange rate stability. In place of the gold points, the rules of the agreement prescribed that governments keep exchange rate fluctuations between 1 percent above or below the official parity. The parity requirement applied also to gold; all official purchases and sales of gold by members had to be made at parity rates. And the membership was prohibited from engaging in any exchange practices that might jeopardize the rate structure without prior approval from the IMF.

The IMF rules permitted greater than the 1 percent adjustments of rates by setting new parities for a currency if its relationship to the key currency (the U.S. dollar) had substantially changed in terms of purchasing power. But setting of new parities was used only in acute financial crises. Most of the exchange rates of IMF members remained fixed for extended periods. In the end, it was the excessive rigidity, rather than the excessive instability it had been designed to avoid, that caused the collapse of the IMF fixed rate regime.

Whether it had been a wrong diagnosis or an overdose of medicine that killed the patient remains open for debate. As domestic price trends followed divergent paths in each country the fixed exchange rates veered constantly farther from purchasing power parties. And when inflation in the United States started to accelerate, the key currency itself depreciated more rapidly than a number of other currencies.

Directly after World War II other nations had been content to hold dollars as exchange reserves. This universal acceptability of the dollar derived from the fact that the holdings were convertible into gold at any time at $35 an ounce and that at the same time the dollars could be invested in interest-earning instruments such as U.S. government bonds. Since gold itself bears no interest, under the initial IMF system dollars were better than gold for foreign monetary authorities. But this situation lasted only so long as the dollar remained stable in terms of purchasing power.

When inflation started to erode the dollar, the situation changed. Now the sinking dollar induced foreign monetary authorities to start redeeming their dollars in gold. Since the foreign holdings of the dollar had swelled to exceed the value of U.S. gold reserves by nearly five times, there was no conceivable way for the dual parity system of the IMF to continue to function; nor was the United States willing to allow its monetary gold reserves to be completely depleted. In August 1971 the U.S. government terminated dollar convertibility into gold. This was the end of the IMF fixed-rate regime.

Table 6.1   The IMF in the World of Floating Exchange Rates

The International Monetary Fund is an organization of countries that seeks to promote international monetary cooperation and to facilitate the expansion of trade.

To achieve its purposes the Fund has a code of economic behavior for its members, makes financing available to members in balance of payments difficulties, and provides them with technical assistance to improve their economic management.

The Fund maintains a large pool of financial resources that it makes available to member countries—temporarily and subject to conditions—to enable them to carry out programs to remedy their payments deficits without resorting to restrictive measures that would adversely affect national or international prosperity. Members make repayments to the Fund so that its resources are used on a revolving basis.

The Fund helps members to coordinate their national economic policies internationally. In effect, it provides a permanent international monetary forum.

To enable the Fund to carry out its policies, member countries continuously supply it with a broad range of economic information.

Membership in the Fund is a prerequisite to membership in the World Bank (International Bank for Reconstruction and Development), and close working relationships exist between the two organizations, as well as between the Fund and the General Agreement on Tariffs and Trade and the Bank for International Settlements. The Fund is a specialized agency within the United Nations system, cooperating with the UN on matters of mutual interest.

Source: International Monetary Fund.

Managed Float

The *managed float* has evolved as the successor of the IMF fixed-rate system. While the IMF mechanism was basically patterned after that of the gold standard, the managed float utilizes the free market model. Rates are allowed to respond to market conditions, but only within limits set by governments. As shown in Figure 6.4, rates are allowed to float within a targeted band, between r_l and r_b. If the rate drops to r_l, the monetary authority enters the market and buys the quantity g_1, thereby pushing the demand from D_0 to D_{il}; if the rate rises to r_b, the government starts selling quantity g_2, causing the demand to move from D_1 to D_{ib}.

These interventions are justified by the belief that governments are morally obliged to prevent their currencies from suffering violent exchange rate fluctuations and to shield the domestic economies against speculative forays from abroad. Apart from references to petroleum exporting countries, the identities of the feared speculators have remained obscure.

The management of the float is internationally orchestrated. Officials of central banks stay in almost continuous contact, with frequent conferences held under the coordinating auspices of the Bank of International Settlements

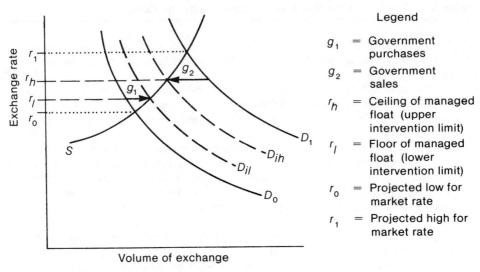

Legend

g_1	=	Government purchases
g_2	=	Government sales
r_h	=	Ceiling of managed float (upper intervention limit)
r_l	=	Floor of managed float (lower intervention limit)
r_0	=	Projected low for market rate
r_1	=	Projected high for market rate

Figure 6.4   Managed Float Under Shifting Demand

in Basel, Switzerland. Though the consultations lack the force of a formal agreement, countries tend to abide by the international consensus and deviate from it only in severe crises. The ad hoc format allows the conferees the flexibility to change the rules of the exchange market without lengthy political formalities. This system and the other exchange systems are summarized in Table 6.2.

EXCHANGE RISK

The fact that the rate of exchange fluctuates is of great significance in international business. First, fluctuations cause the value of domestic money to change relative to foreign money. When the exchange rate goes down, domestic money appreciates in value; it buys more foreign money. When the exchange rate goes up, domestic money depreciates in value; more dollars have to be paid for a unit of foreign currency.

Changes in exchange rate due to appreciation and depreciation create *exchange risk*, a possibility of gain or loss. These gains and losses are caused by changes in the international monetary environment, more specifically, in changes in the exchange market. Like other market factors, exchange rate fluctuations are beyond the control of individual firms and managers. Take, for example, an importer transacting to buy 600,000 Swiss francs (SF) worth of mountaineering equipment from Zurich. The exchange rate is $0.5000 (per franc) on the date of purchase, giving a total of $300,000. The terms call for cash on arrival of goods, estimated 90 days hence. Should the exchange rate rise in the meantime from $0.5000 to $0.5120, the importer would suffer a loss of ($0.5120 − $0.5000) × 600,000, or $7,200; if the rate dropped during the tenor of the transaction, the importer would stand to make a windfall.

Table 6.2 Summary of Exchange Rate Regimes

FIXED RATES

1. *Complete government exchange monopoly* — Rates officially fixed by national authorities for indefinite periods, sometimes for several years. Adjustments made by substantial devaluation or revaluation, causing windfall profits and losses to holders. All legitimate payments based on official rates; currency normally overvalued; black market and smuggling inevitable corollaries. Used in pure form in communist economies and in modified versions in less developed countries.

2. *Gold standard* — Monetary unit linked to gold by fixed par (gold content); parity rates determined by relative gold contents. Deviation from parity limited to costs of gold exports and imports. Exchange risk minimal.

3. *IMF treaty rates* — All currencies linked to key currency (U.S. dollar) through par values set by IMF; key currency linked to gold by official price. Governments committed to restricting rate fluctuations to ± one percent of dollar parity; greater adjustments under IMF supervision. System dominated international monetary relations from World War II to 1971.

FLOATING RATES

4. *Free exchange market* — Rates fluctuate with supply and demand conditions in exchange market; no government intervention at all. Crises and speculation may cause wild rate swings and financial chaos. Theoretical model only, never used anywhere in pure form.

5. *Managed float* — Rates determined by governmentally managed supply and demand; government monitors rate movements and intervenes as buyer or seller to keep rates in targeted range. Intergovernment consultations avoid offsetting foreign measures. Evolved since 1971 in the developed market economies.

Similar risks accompany all transactions involving a future remittance or receipt in a foreign currency. They introduce a speculative element that both businesses and private persons often wish to avoid. This is accomplished by converting all transactions to a domestic currency basis when they are first made, thus avoiding any open exposure to exchange risk.

Hedges Against Exchange Risk

The Spot Exchange The import firm in our illustration could buy the SF 600,000 right away on the spot market, hold them for 90 days, and then pay off the Swiss supplier. The firm's cost would be $0.5000 × 600,000, or $300,000 plus loss of interest for 90 days on $300,000, which at 1 percent a month will bring the total maximum cost of the franc's to $309,000. If the firm is able to deposit the francs in an interest earning account in a Swiss bank, interest loss would be hedged unless the interest rate in Switzerland is significantly lower than in the United States. However, unless the importer is a multinational company with a subsidiary in Switzerland, either depositing or borrowing there could prove difficult or involve high transaction costs. Therefore, it is often impractical for nonmultinationals to cover their foreign exchange exposures through foreign bank accounts or other money market transactions abroad.

The Forward Exchange   A better method of hedging against the exchange risk is the *forward exchange*—buying or selling a given currency for future delivery. In our example, the U.S. importer would buy SF 600,000 90 days forward, thus fixing the dollar amount required to pay for the mountaineering equipment. The forward rate, determined by market forces, may be either higher (*forward premium*) or lower (*forward discount*) than the spot rate. If the 90 days forward rate for the Swiss franc is $0.5085, the importer will pay $0.5085 × 600,000, or $305,100, and will be assured of receiving SF 600,000 90 days hence to pay off its Zurich supplier. Recipients of foreign currency would act in the opposite way.

Foreign Borrowing and Lending   Where access to a foreign money market is not restricted, foreign exchange risks can be covered by borrowing instead of by forward exchange. Suppose a U.S. engineering firm is promised payment of 500,000 pesos by its Mexican client six months hence. The firm will borrow 500,000 pesos from a Mexican bank and convert them into dollars at the spot rate. It can now deposit the dollars in a U.S. bank or put them to some more profitable use. On the date of maturity, the firm will collect the 500,000 pesos from its client and pay off its debt to the Mexican bank. Whatever happened to the peso exchange rate in the meantime is of no consequence to the firm.

The same method can be used between third and fourth country firms. Suppose a Japanese firm acquires a claim on a British company of £1 million due six months from now. To avoid exchange risk exposure the firm will immediately enter the exchange market and sell £1 million six months forward. The receipts will become part of its current cash flow, like its domestic revenues. Six months later the firm will collect its receivable from the British company and pay off the forward contract; that is, it will deliver the £1 million it has sold forward. Since in many countries banking laws and foreign exchange controls restrict access to the money market by foreigners, opportunities to use this alternative are not always available.

Short and Long Positions   Exposure to foreign exchange risk exists whenever someone (a firm or an individual) has differing amounts of assets and liabilities in a given foreign currency; the difference is called the *net position* in that currency. If the liabilities, including future cost streams, are greater, the net position is short; if the assets, including future income streams, are greater, the net position is long. Any change in the exchange rate of the currency causes a corresponding change in the holder's net position; either a gain or a loss will result from the change in the exchange rate. Thus, holding a net position (either short or long) over time constitutes *speculation* in exchange rate fluctuations.[1]

Most participants in the exchange market engage in some form of hedging to avoid an open position. This is particularly true when a firm's perception of the future behavior of the spot rate will yield an exchange loss. If, however, the projections tilt toward a speculative windfall, there is a tendency to stand pat with net positions and to accept the eventual speculative results.

The Determination of Forward Rates

In traditional theory, the forward rate for one currency in terms of another is determined by the differential between the prevailing interest rates of the two countries concerned. If the interest rate is higher in Italy than in Japan, lira exchange at a discount from the lira-yen spot rate because funds held in lira yield a higher return over the forward period than those in yen; and yen exchange at a corresponding premium over the yen-lira spot rate since funds kept in yen yield relatively less in interest than those in lira. For example, if the interest rate for a six-month deposit was 9 percent in Italy and 6 percent in Japan, funds held in lira would produce 3 percent more interest income than funds held in yen. Therefore, investors in search of a higher yield will engage in *covered interest arbitrage*, that is, in converting their holdings from yen into lira. To hedge their conversions, to make sure they can convert the lira back into yen, they will sell lira six months forward. As a consequence, the Tokyo exchange market will experience an increase of demand for spot lira, pushing the spot rate up, and a simultaneous increase in the supply of forward lira, forcing the forward rate down. This process will continue until the forward discount equals the interest rate differential, in our illustration 3 percent. At this point the covered interest arbitrage will cease, since the forward discount cancels the profit from the higher interest earnings in Italy. For the Milan exchange market, the relationship is reversed; the forward rate for yen will rise until it commands a 3 percent premium over the spot rate.

In general, the forward market will value the currency of the higher interest nation at a discount and the currency of the lower interest nation at a premium from their spot rates. The size of the discount or premium will be determined by the interest rate differential and the length of the forward period, as follows:

$$(r_I - r_J) \times t = \text{forward rate}$$

1. Speculation is defined as profiting from price changes over time.

where r_i denotes the interest rate per month in Italy, r_j the interest rate per month in Japan, and t the forward period in months.

When the actual discount or premium equals the interest rate differential, the forward exchange rate between the two countries is at *interest rate parity*. Such a forward rate induces no arbitrage transactions.

Inflation has a direct effect on forward exchange rates. If, for example, the annual inflation rate is 30 percent in Brazil and 11 percent in France, the cruzeiro will be projected to drop 25 percent against the franc within the next twelve months. Given interest rate parity, the cruzeiro in Paris would fetch a discount as follows:

Months Forward	Forward Discount
12	25.00%
6	12.50
3	8.33
1	2.08

The inflation effect is particularly pronounced on longer term forward rates. If interest rates and inflation rates both differ between two currencies, their effects on forward rates will be compounded, either magnifying the deviation from spot rates or offsetting each other.

The actual forward exchange rates may deviate from the interest rate and inflation rate parities because of sudden changes in trade and investment flows, regulatory interferences, political uncertainties, or speculation by major actors in the exchange markets.

ORGANIZATIONAL STRUCTURE OF THE EXCHANGE MARKET

The foreign exchange market has no formalized structure comparable to that of the stock and commodity exchanges. It embraces the entire banking industry that participates in the financing of commercial enterprises, plus exchange brokers and dealers who specialize in certain aspects of the exchange process. The institutional structure of the market is determined by three basic functional relationships: dealings with the buying and selling public, dealings among banking institutions, and dealings among domestic and foreign exchange institutions. These may be called the retail, wholesale, and foreign sectors of the exchange market.

Retail Sector

Commercial banks serve the exchange needs of their local communities and provide the auxiliary banking services necessary for efficient handling of international payments. For this purpose the banks maintain foreign exchange departments, which may be independent or may be a subsection in the international banking operations division, a new development in bank organization.

In the United States, the major metropolitan banks and many inland banks maintain their own working balances in the form of deposits in their own foreign-based branch banks or in correspondent banks abroad. These overseas balances are replenished by the purchases of exchange assets from business firms and individuals and from sales of domestic currency to foreign exchange institutions. Inland banks that do not have their own exchange deposits abroad maintain correspondent relationships with large metropolitan banks in New York City or San Francisco, under which they can utilize the latter's exchange resources either in this country or abroad. Normally, the inland correspondent is authorized to draw drafts directly against the foreign balances of the metropolitan bank and to accept deposits of drafts at specified rates and in predetermined amounts.

Along with banks, foreign exchange dealers are active in some areas in buying and selling exchange to the general public. In the United States, the exchange dealers tend to operate in the marginal, high-risk markets, and their importance varies with the international financial climate. Since the dealers are not subjected by law to the same government supervision as banks, they can engage in more venturesome, higher-risk operations and thus can undertake transactions beyond the legitimate capabilities of a bank.

Wholesale Sector

In the course of its retail trading activity, each bank can use purchases to offset sales and thus can finance much of the local demand from the local supply. In large cities with diversified international activity, the opportunities for such internal clearinghouse operations are good. In less diversified centers, imbalances between demand and supply may cause large surpluses or deficits in a bank's foreign exchange accounts. To even out any imbalances banks must turn to the interbank or wholesale exchange market.

In the United States the interbank exchange market has no uniform pattern. Some banks seek to clear their daily balances first on the local and regional basis; others deal directly with the New York market, which is the principal foreign exchange center in this country. Most of the larger banks refrain from direct trading with one another but depend upon the foreign exchange brokers for their interbank transactions. The brokerage firm's main function is to bring together the buying and selling banks and to arrange the necessary supply or placement of exchange that a particular bank may need. Like other brokerage houses, it does this through continual contact with the market and an intimate knowledge of the supply and demand conditions at any particular moment.

SUMMARY

Money is a creature of national law. Payments across international borders require conversion from one currency to another, and the pricing of foreign currencies in terms of domestic money, that is, establishing rates. How the rates are arrived at depends not only on the market forces but also on government policies and monetary regulations. The existence of exchange rates translates into dual pricing of international business transactions: the price of the product or service traded, and the price of the foreign currency involved. The second price, the exchange rate, introduces possibilities for both losses and profits that are not present in domestic transactions. International managers must understand how exchange rates are made, which factors and processes affect them, and which methods minimize the risks.

FOR REVIEW AND DISCUSSION

1. Is it true that under a complete gold standard system, mint parities would become synonymous with purchasing power parities among different nations' currencies? Explain.

2. What are the main causes of exchange rate fluctuations?

3. Why does the exchange rate fluctuate at all under the gold standard?

4. Why do governments intervene in the foreign exchange market?

5. Evaluate each of the five exchange rate regimes in terms of their advantages and disadvantages. Why do some countries prefer certain rate regimes?

6. What are the main sources of exchange risk? How can business protect itself against such risk?

7. Can forward exchange rates be predicted on the basis of spot rates? Why or why not?

8. Do banks like to hold open positions in foreign currencies? Explain.

9. Is it true that the U.S. dollar became an inconvertible currency after 1971? Explain.

10. Could the U.S.S.R. make the ruble convertible to noncommunist currencies? If so, what steps would it have to take?

7

The Balance of Payments

*T*he balance of payments is a system of accounts designed to show how a nation finances its international activities. Unlike domestic activities, international activities require external purchasing power; that is, the ability to finance transactions in foreign exchange. The external purchasing power is obtained through sales of goods and services to foreign residents or by borrowing abroad; it is used for imports and for lending to foreigners.

INTERNATIONAL ACCOUNTING

To keep track of the sources and uses of external purchasing power, nations use *balance of payments accounting*. This is a system of government accounting based on the same double-entry principle as business accounting. Technically speaking, balance of payments is a misnomer; the system covers not only payments but all transboundary transactions, whether in money or in kind, that move in or out of a country and possess any monetary value. Business transactions, private transactions, government transactions, gifts, lottery wins, inheritances, royalties, penalty payments, and even a Nobel prize are subjects for balance of payments entries.

The balance of payments registers the changes in the nation's financial claims and obligations vis-à-vis the rest of the world. It is a tabulation comparable more to a firm's profit-and-loss statement, which shows what has happened during a year, than to a balance sheet, which presents the total assets and liabilities at a particular point in time. The balance of payments does not measure the total foreign assets or liabilities that a country's citizens may possess at any particular moment. Rather, it shows what changes are taking place in them and how these changes affect the external liquidity and other financial relations of the nation. It also shows what forces are causing the changes and how business is affected by them.

Residents

Since only transactions between residents of different nations are included in the balance of payments, we need a definition of resident. The term *resident* is defined as all persons and institutions identified with the country concerned. Resident institutions include all business enterprises, government agencies, and nonprofit organizations. International agencies are regarded as special cases and are not treated as resident institutions of the countries in which they are located. Government officials and members of armed forces stationed abroad are treated as residents of the country of citizenship. Foreign branches and subsidiaries of business firms are treated as residents of their host countries. Individuals with dual or multiple residency, such as international executives, temporary residents, and transboundary commuters, are classified by the *center of interest* rule, which assigns them to the country of their principal interest. In general, residency refers to normal location rather than to nationality.

Credits and Debits

The tabulation of international transactions in the balance of payments is based on double-entry accounting. Every entry must have a counterentry; for every debit there must be a corresponding credit and for every credit a counterbalancing debit. If a transaction causes a payment or indebtedness to foreigners, it is a debit. If it results in a receipt from or a claim on a foreigner, it is a credit. The appropriate debits and credits for typical transactions are shown in Table 7.1

As a general rule, all credit entries in balance of payments accounting indicate additions to the nation's international liquidity (external purchasing power) and all debit entries indicate deductions from it. The credits, reflecting the nation's sources of foreign exchange, originate in three broad categories of transactions: exports of goods or services; liquidation of existing foreign assets, such as investments; and increase in foreign liabilities, that is, foreign loans or credit.

The debits show the nation's uses of the exchange. They, too, fall into three broad categories of transactions: imports of goods and services; acquisitions of assets abroad, mainly investments; and reductions of foreign liabilities, such as payment of debts to foreign banks or other creditors.

Two-Country Perspective

To this point we have viewed the balance of payments from one nation's perspective. Since entries always involve another nation, however, we must expand our perspective to include both nations. Each business transaction, except unilateral transfers (gifts and donations), gives rise to a claim of resources by one country and a counterclaim for payment by the other. Thus, an export

Table 7.1 Typical Entries in Balance of Payments Accounting

TRANSACTION	DEBIT	CREDIT
Export of goods	Short-term capital account, because the payment adds to bank balances abroad or reduces the other nation's U.S. bank balances.	Merchandise account, because it creates a claim of payment against a foreigner. It also reduces the merchandise assets.
Import of goods	Merchandise account.	Short-term capital account, because the payment decreases bank balances abroad or increases the other nation's U.S. bank balances.
Foreign travel	Foreign travel account, because the transportation, food, and entertainment the traveler consumes abroad creates a claim against the United States. It also adds to the domestic assets by not consuming them.	Short-term capital account, because U.S. bank balances abroad are decreased or liabilities to foreign banks are increased.
Dividends from foreign stocks	Short-term capital account, because when the affiliate distributes the dividends, U.S. bank balances are increased or foreign bank balances in the United States are decreased.	Investment income account, because the declaration of dividends by the foreign firm creates a U.S. claim on the other country's assets.
Aid to a developing nation	Unrequited transfer account, because the United States incurs an external liability.	Short-term or long-term capital account, because the aid payment reduces U.S. external assets by increasing recipient country's bank balances in the United States.

of goods creates a claim for payment in the country of origin and a counterclaim for receipt of the goods in the country of destination; a purchase of French securities by a Canadian capitalist creates a claim for ownership by the Canadian and a claim for payment by the French concern. There is a mutuality or a mirror effect in all international transactions. Therefore, opposite double entries are made in the balance of payments accounts of the two countries involved, in the same way that they are made in the books of interacting business firms. What is a credit for one is a debit for the other.

Information Sources

For the purposes of data collection, international transactions recorded in the balance of payments are grouped initially by the specific activity, such as exports, imports, air cargo charges, port fees, or book royalties. On subsequent levels the specific item accounts are combined by the degree of homogeneity into aggregates. How the specific accounts are set up varies from country to country, because of national tradition and the system of data collection used. Unlike business accountants, balance of payments accountants do not have direct access to many of the original records upon which their entries are based. Much has to be entered by approximation or sheer estimation. It is particularly difficult to get data on tourist purchases, gifts, loans, and acquisitions transacted directly among residents of different countries without going through any bank or government agency keeping records for balance of payments purposes.

Official practice in the United States is to use customs records for export and import entries and bank records for the corresponding payment entries. Both are entered as aggregates. Since the merchandise entries come from a different source from the financial entries, they seldom match exactly. The inaccuracies stem mainly from the bank records since banks are the conduits of a bewildering variety of financial transactions; it is often difficult for them to separate accurately trade related payments or, for that matter, any other specific type of international financial transfer.

The use of both customs and bank records purportedly maximizes the coverage and completeness of the balance of payments statement, but it does not strictly comply with the principle of simultaneous offsetting entries required by double-entry accounting. Both the magnitude and the timing of the debit and credit entries may differ greatly in practice. As a result, *internal disbalances* may arise, due to the differences in the data on which any particular pair of debit and credit entries are based. This weakness, it is argued, can be tolerated and the internal disbalance is not an unreasonable price to pay for scrutiny of all sources of data.

The French system requires that balance of payments debits and credits be taken from the same, or very closely related, source. The nerve center for this so-called *symmetrical system* is the foreign exchange control administered by the central bank. If all international transfers are subject to exchange control, the system works well; if most transactions are free, the control authority becomes dependent for information on commercial bank records. In such a case, the difference between the U.S. and French systems is not that great.

Regardless of system, no government has come up with data accurate enough to make debits exactly equal to credits for any particular category of international transactions. The discrepancies are recorded in the *Errors and Omissions* account, which is universal in all nations' balances of payments. In the true sense, it is not an account at all, for no actual transactions are ever recorded in it. It serves merely as a receptacle for the corrective entries that are necessary to make the substantive accounts balance.

THE SYSTEM OF ACCOUNTS

Logical interpretation of accounting results is possible only if the system of accounts is consistent with informational needs. In balance of payments accounting the needs are not limited only to measuring the foreign exchange, but also to generating data for understanding the causes and consequences of international transactions. Since transactions differ in respect to their causes and consequences, they must be recorded in separate accounts. Although in practice balance of payments accounting has scores of specific accounts for sundry peripheral reasons, its conceptual structure consists of four main accounts: the current account, the unrequited transfers account, the capital account, and the official or government reserve account. Each of these is subdivided into narrower accounts.

Current Account

Merchandise Trade   For most countries, exports and imports of merchandise are the largest single component of total international payments, often accounting for two-thirds or more of the overall international transactions. As we have already observed, exports of goods from a country give it a claim upon foreigners for payment, and the value of the goods is therefore listed as a credit entry. On the other hand, imports represent a payment obligation and are therefore entered as debit entries in the account. The net result of the merchandise account is *balance of trade*, a concept often confused by the layman with the balance of payments itself. Merchandise transactions are referred to as *visible trade*, as distinguished from *invisible trade*, or trade in services.

International Service   Trade in services can be broken down into four areas: foreign travel, investment income, private services, and government services.

1. *Foreign Travel.* Foreign travel includes all tourist expenditures—fares, lodging, food, entertainment, and articles purchased abroad. Such expenditures are comparable to imports. Conversely, foreign visitors' consumption and purchases in the host country are similar to exports. For many countries, such as Switzerland, Denmark, Italy, and Spain, receipts from foreign tourists constitute a major source of foreign exchange. For the United States it has been a debit item, as more is spent by U.S. citizens abroad than by people of other nations in the United States, although the depreciation of the dollar is starting to entice more foreign visitors to the United States.

2. *Investment Income.* Investment income comprises transfers of dividends, interests, and repatriated profits of foreign branches and subsidiaries of transnational firms. Dividends are entered when officially declared, interests when credited or paid by the bank, and profits when paid or due. Income from portfolio investments is treated the same way as dividends from direct investments. All these data are entered at their book value.

3. *Private Services.* Under the heading of private services come payments to various private parties—royalties; rents; consulting and engineering fees; reinsurance commissions; charges for international cable, radio, and telephone operations; motion-picture rentals; and all other international charges for services rendered and received by nongovernment institutions and personnel. Since the available data for some of the service subaccounts are quite incomplete—such as those for purely personal services, copyrights, and travelers' expenditures—this account

represents the least accurate component of the balance of payments and contributes greatly to the errors and omissions account.

4. *Government Services.* The principal transactions recorded in the government services account are the regular international transactions of a country's government—diplomatic and military representation, administrative and operating expenses, salaries and wages to foreign employees of embassies and consultates, purchases of foreign products, payments for land and buildings; membership fees in international organizations, and similar expenditures. In the case of the United States, the transactions of government-operated business enterprises such as the postal service and the Panama Canal are also recorded in this account. Goods shipped and services rendered under U.S. military aid programs are not in this account, for they do not affect external liquidity.

Unrequited Transfers Account

Included as unrequited transfers are both private and government noncommercial transactions.[1] Personal gifts of all kinds, philanthropic activities, such as Ford Foundation grants, and relief-organization shipments (CARE packages, Red Cross aid, and so forth) are the main categories. Although such transactions flow in both directions, the U.S. net has been heavily outward for many years.

Due to foreign aid, the government's portion of this account is particularly important. It consists of transfers by government agencies of money, goods, and services as aid to other nations, including grants made under economic aid and defense support programs but excludes direct military aid. This account has been a large and controversial debit in the U.S. balance of payments ever since World War II. For countries receiving aid, it is a significant credit.

Where the foreign aid grant takes the form of goods and services, the debit entry is offset by crediting either the exports of the services account, and there is no immediate effect on the country's liquidity; where the aid is given in the form of cash transfers, it represents a corresponding reduction of the country's liquid reserves. It is this latter type of aid that causes serious deficit problems unless it is neutralized by surpluses from other accounts.

Capital Account

Long-Term Capital The long-term capital account shows the inflow and outflow of capital commitments that have a maturity longer than one year. The account is divided into subsections for private and for public or government capital transactions. Private long-term capital items range from the extension of commercial credit to direct investments in physical properties such as mines, mills, and factories. Stocks, bonds, new issues of securities, redemptions, long-

---

1. Most nations have, in the last few years, substituted the terms of *unrequited transfers* for *unilateral transfers* or *donations* in their balance of payments accounting. This has been purely a change in terminology with no effect in the content of the account.

term bank claims, and miscellaneous other interests in property constitute the majority of the entries.

Government long-term capital loans to and from other governments; financial support of economic development projects abroad; and, particularly significant for the United States, loans by the Export-Import Bank, subscriptions to the Inter-American Development Bank, and participation in the financing of other foreign projects either directly or through international institutions, are all included in this account.

Short-Term Capital   Short-term capital movements are generally confined to commitments with a duration of less than one year. Frequently the maturity date is only 30, 60, or 90 days. Movements in short-term foreign capital accounts commonly include additions to or subtractions from foreign bank balances; purchases or sales of marketable foreign government bonds of relatively short maturity; and acquisitions of bank deposits, other foreign currency holdings, foreign exchange instruments (commercial paper), and other liquid or near liquid assets. These are normally used to finance international trade, to pay for international services, and to settle other accounts. The short-term capital account is also divided into private and government subaccounts. The basis for the division is the same as that for long-term capital accounts. For the balance of payments analysis, particularly for forecasting financial conditions, this division is a significant one, since the two groups react quite differently to certain changes in the economy.

Official Reserve Account

The phrase *monetary-gold movements*, although in general use, is misleading. A large number of international transactions in gold involve no physical movement but are handled through earmarking operations, by which the title to the gold is transferred from one nation to another while the bullion remains in Fort Knox, Berne, Paris, or London. Such passing of ownership is a sufficient basis for the appropriate balance of payments entry. Exports and imports of nonmonetary gold are treated as merchandise transactions.

Convertible Currencies   Official holdings of other currencies that are freely convertible on the international money market are kept by monetary authorities for the purpose of settling any deficits that may occur in the nation's balance of payments. Only purchases and sales by official monetary authorities, such as the U.S. Treasury and Federal Reserve Board, the Bank of England, or the Swedish Riskbanken, are entered in this account.

Drawing Rights   The International Monetary Fund provides credits in the form of regular and special drawing rights (SDRs) and loans, which have become increasingly important reserve assets to its member countries. Each

Table 7.2 Special Drawing Rights

The special drawing right (SDR) is an international reserve asset created by the Fund to supplement existing reserve assets. All 141 member countries of the Fund are participants in the Special Drawing Rights Department of the Fund. They may use SDRs in transactions and operations with other member countries and other holders.

The SDR is the Fund's unit of account. Increasingly, commercial transactions and private financial obligations are being denominated in SDRs. Its valuation and interest rate are determined on the basis of a basket of five currencies—the U.S. dollar, deutsche mark, French franc, yen, and pound sterling. The value of the SDR is calculated daily.

Following is the SDR valuation on January 16, 1981.

CURRENCY	CURRENCY AMOUNT[a]	EXCHANGE RATE ON JANUARY 16, 1981[b]	U.S. DOLLAR EQUIVALENT[c]
U.S. dollar	0.5400	1.00000	0.540000
Deutsche mark	0.4600	2.01720	0.228039
French franc	0.7400	4.65970	0.158809
Japanese yen	34.0000	202.67000	0.167760
Pound sterling	0.0710	2.39950	0.170365
Total	—	—	1.264973
		SDR value of U.S. $1 =	0.790531
		U.S. dollar value of SDR =	1.26497

[a]The currency components of the basket.

[b]Exchange rates in terms of currency units per U.S. dollar, except for the pound sterling, which is expressed as U.S. dollars per pound sterling. All rates are at noon in the London foreign exchange market.

[c]The U.S. dollar equivalents of the currency amounts in Column 1 at the exchange rates in Column 2—that is, Column 1 divided by Column 2 except for the pound sterling, for which the amounts in the two columns are multiplied.

Source: International Monetary Fund.

member nation is allocated a quota of the drawing rights. In case of a deficit it can receive convertible currency or IMF credit to be able to pay its international debt.

Comparability of Balance of Payments Figures

To facilitate the analyses of different countries' payments data, the International Monetary Fund has established a standard format. All IMF members are required to supply their data broken down as shown in Table 7.3 on pages 134–35. The results are published by IMF for worldwide distribution. This classification has become by far the most important source of international payments data.

BALANCE OF PAYMENTS DISEQUILIBRIUMS

Balance of payments data have great significance to the entire national economy—business, government, and consumers. Their significance derives from disbalances, which vary with the changes in international activities. The greater the disbalances in the balance of payments, the greater are their effects on the economy. Understanding and interpreting balance of payments data requires an understanding of why international payments disbalances occur and how they are linked with domestic activities.

As an accounting proposition, the balance of payments is always in balance; every credit entry is matched by a debit entry. But this does not mean that a nation's financial position vis-à-vis the rest of the world stays in a balance. Its external liquidity—holdings of cash and other assets that are usable as means of payment abroad—may either deteriorate or improve while the total entries in the balance of payments balance by definition. To say that the balance of payments importance is reflected in its disbalances may sound like a play on words. It is not. Only the word *balance* is used in a double sense. This semantic paradox is avoided if we substitute *equilibriums* and *disequilibriums* for *balances* and *disbalances* in the balance of payments accounts.

The Concept of Equilibrium

Equilibrium refers to the relationship between a nation's international receipts and remittances during a given period. If the aggregate value of receipt-producing transactions coincides with the aggregate value of remittance-producing transactions, the two flows neutralize each other and the nation's financial position vis-à-vis other nations remains unchanged. This is the equilibrium position. All foreign purchases (goods, services, and securities) can be financed from the proceeds of foreign sales, and no excess of international receipts or remittances is created. Since the only mechanism necessary for carrying out international payments is an efficient implementation of the clearinghouse principle, there will be no delays or other constraints retarding the receipt-remittance neutralization process.

In theory, then, a country that is able to maintain a continuous equilibrium experiences no balance of payments effects at all. Its payments are both self-generating and self-liquidating.

In practice, such zero effect equilibrium cannot be maintained. First, the receipt-remittance neutralization is not instantaneous, primarily because both flows comprise countless autonomous transactions, which follow their individual and independent paths. Second, the international clearinghouse process takes time to work itself out, as the banking channels through which it flows are not entirely free from rigidities and restraints. Thus, short-term (less than one year) disequilibriums between receipts and remittances are inevitable and universal. In light of this fact, the practical definition of equilibrium allows for temporary disequilibriums during the period under consideration. If the duration of the disequilibriums does not exceed one year, which is the normal accounting period, that is, if the cumulative receipts and remittances equal each other by the end of the year, the nation is in reality considered to have its balance of payments in equilibrium. However, unlike the purely theoretical nation with the continuous equilibrium, a real nation with a cumulative equilibrium experiences inescapable economic effects of its temporary disequilibrium.

The most obvious effect is a need for foreign exchange reserves to bridge the leads and lags in its receipt and remittance patterns during the year. What the nation earns as excess external purchasing power during some months must be reserved for other months when current exchange earnings are less than obligations. The *equilibrium reserves* may be thought of as a country's minimum requirements for external working capital. The numerical relationship of the equilibrium reserves to the total volume of international business depends on the oscillations characteristic of that business. The more subtle effects of the excess receipts and payments are better explained in connection with more enduring disequilibriums.

Disequilibriums

When the aggregate value of receipt-producing transactions differs from the aggregate value of remittance-producing transactions, the balance of payments is in *disequilibrium*. If the receipts (credits) are greater, the disequilibrium is a *surplus;* if the remittances (debits) are greater, the disequilibrium is a *deficit*. In either case, the nation's international equilibrium has been disturbed. A surplus signifies an increase in external liquidity, and a deficit a decrease in liquidity. Even with that distinction, balance of payments accountants find it difficult to measure disequilibriums. We shall review the various methods used, pointing out the problems involved in each.

The surplus is reflected first in the nation's foreign bank balances and holdings of liquid assets abroad, which will increase, or, alternatively, in foreign balances in its own banks, which will decrease, and later in the inflow of IMF drawing rights, convertible currencies, or gold. Conversely, the deficit is first manifested in the decline of the nation's bank balances and liquid assets abroad or in the rise of foreign deposits in its own banks, which may ultimately lead to an outflow of convertible currencies, IMF drawing rights, or gold.

The sum of the drawing rights, convertible currencies, and gold equals the nation's international monetary reserves, a figure watched carefully by governments and international financial agencies, as well as by business firms.

Measurement of Disequilibriums

To compute the deficit or surplus in the balance of payments, *autonomous transactions*—those that take place for reasons of their own, such as exports,

Table 7.3   IMF Standard Balance-of-Payments Schedule

Reporting country _____ Period covered _____

Currency _____ Unit _____ Exchange rate: US$ _____ per _____

ITEM	CREDIT (RECEIPTS)	DEBIT (PAYMENTS)	NET CREDIT (+) OR NET DEBIT (−)
A. CURRENT TRANSACTIONS			
1. *Merchandise* (1.1 plus 1.2)			
1.1 Exports and imports (both f.o.b.)			
1.2 International services			
2. *Nonmonetary gold movement* (*net*)			
3. *Foreign travel*			
4. *Transportation* (4.1 plus 4.2)			
4.1 Gross freight			
4.2 Other			
5. *Insurance*			
6. *Investment income* (6.1 through 6.3)			
6.1 Direct investment			
6.2 Other interest			
6.3 Other equity			
7. *Government, not included elsewhere* (7.1 plus 7.2)			
7.1 Military expenditures and surplus property			
7.2 Other			
8. *Miscellaneous*			
Total goods and services (1 through 8)			
9. *Unrequited transfers* (9.1 through 9.4)			
9.1 Personal and institutional remittances			
9.2 Other private transfers			
9.3 Reparations			
9.4 Official grants			
10. *Total current transactions* (1 through 9)			
Errors and omissions (16 minus 10)			

ITEM	NET MOVEMENT INCREASING (+) OR DECREASING (−)		
	Assets	Liabilities	Net Assets
B. MOVEMENT OF CAPITAL AND MONETARY GOLD			
11. *Long-term capital* (11.1 through 11.6)			
11.1 Direct investment			
11.2 Portfolio securities: bonds			
11.3 Portfolio securities: shares			
11.4 Amortization			
11.5 Other contractual repayments			
11.6 Other			
12. *Short-term capital* (12.1 plus 12.2)			
12.1 Currency, deposits, government obligations			
12.2 Other			

Table 7.3 *continued*

		NET MOVEMENT INCREASING (+) OR DECREASING (−)		
	ITEM	Assets	Liabilities	Net Assets
C.	OFFICIAL AND BANKING INSTITUTIONS			
13.	Long-term capital (13.1 through 13.6)			
	13.1 Official loans			
	13.2 Bank loans			
	13.3 Portfolio securities			
	13.4 Amortization			
	13.5 Other contractual repayments			
	13.6 Other			
14.	Short-term capital (14.1 through 14.4)			
	14.1 Payments and clearing agreements			
	14.2 Liabilities to IMF and IBRD			
	14.3 Other liabilities to official and banking institutions			
	14.4 Other			
15.	Monetary gold			
16.	Total movement of capital and monetary gold (11 through 15)			

imports, investments, travel expenditures—must be distinguished from *compensatory* or *settlement items*—those that are carried out by the government for the purpose of correcting disequilibriums or coping with the country's international financial position. The settlement transactions consist mostly of sales and purchases of reserve assets (gold, foreign exchange, drawing rights, and so on).[2]

Basic Balance In theory, then, the disequilibriums are measured by the difference between autonomous receipts and autonomous payments. The amount by which autonomous payments exceed autonomous receipts shows the size of the deficit, and the excess of autonomous receipts over autonomous payments shows the surplus. In practice, the problem is not that simple. Neither the power nor the will always exists for a complete and correct separation of autonomous transactions from settlement items. While there is little difficulty with such things as merchandise exports and imports, transfers of capital often defy any easy classification since the balance of payments authorities have no way of telling what their purposes were. Consequently, their classification cannot be based on factual record but must be left to accepted accounting practices and professional judgment.

Therefore, there is no absolutely correct or precise measure of a deficit

2. When autonomous transactions cancel out over a month or a quarter, there is no need for settlement items; that means the balance of payments is in equilibrium.

or surplus. The reported figure is always affected to some degree by the judgment used in classifying capital transfers. Since such judgment is required, the monetary authorities can deliberately increase or decrease the reported figure by juggling the questionable capital transfers to suit their political purposes. However, their latitude to do so is limited.

For the United States the problem is further complicated by the fact that many foreign countries keep a certain amount of their monetary reserves in the dollar. When they make settlements these reserve dollars are shifted in and out of the country, showing up as international capital transfers on the U.S. balance of payment. Were they autonomous or settlement items? Neither, so far as the United States is concerned.

Liquidity Balance   Traditionally U.S. balance of payment accountants have used a method called the *liquidity balance*. A deficit computed by this method includes a loss of official gold and foreign exchange reserves plus any rise of foreign holdings of short-term claims—bank deposits, treasury bills, market-

Table 7.4   Summary of U.S. Balance of Payments in Selected Years from 1960 to 1980 (billions of dollars)

	1960	1965	1970	1975	1976	1977	1978	1979	1980[a]
Exports	19.5	26.3	42.5	107.0	114.7	120.8	142.1	182.0	222.5
Imports	−14.7	−21.5	−39.9	−98.0	−124.0	−151.6	−175.8	−211.5	−242.7
Trade balance	4.8	4.8	2.6	9.0	−9.3	−30.8	−33.7	−29.5	−20.2
Net investment income	3.4	5.4	3.5	12.8	16.0	18.0	20.1	32.5	31.3
Net military	−2.6	−1.9	−3.4	−0.7	0.6	1.6	0.9	−1.3	−3.0
Net travel and transportation	−1.0	−1.5	−2.0	−2.8	−2.6	−3.3	−3.2	−2.7	−1.2
Other services, net	0.6	1.4	2.2	4.6	4.7	5.1	6.0	5.8	6.3
Balance on goods and services	5.2	8.2	5.8	22.9	9.4	−9.5	−9.2	4.9	13.2
Unrequited transfers	−2.4	−2.9	−3.2	−4.6	−5.0	−4.6	−5.1	−5.7	−5.8
Balance on current account[b]	2.8	5.3	−0.3	18.3	4.4	−14.1	−14.3	−0.8	7.4
Net change in U.S. assets abroad	−7.3	−6.5	−6.0	−39.7	−51.3	−35.8	−61.2	−61.8	−27.0
Allocations of SDRs	—	—	0.9	—	—	—	—	1.1	1.2
Errors and omissions	−1.0	−0.4	−0.2	5.7	10.4	−0.9	11.4	23.8	5.9
Capital account balance[b]	−2.8	−5.3	0.3	−18.3	−4.4	14.1	14.3	0.8	−7.4

[a]1980 figures based on the first three quarters of 1980 plus an estimate of the fourth quarter based on a trend analysis.

[b]Balance on current account equals capital account balance except the signs are reversed.

Source: U.S. Department of Commerce, *Survey of Current Business,* various years.

able or convertible U.S. government obligations (even long-term bonds because of their ready marketability), bank acceptances, and similar short-term exchange instruments. All long-term capital transactions are excluded from the computation and viewed as settlement transactions. A surplus is measured by reversing the signs in the above formula.

A peculiar feature of the liquidity method is the treatment of short-term private capital transactions asymmetrically. Changes in U.S. liquid liabilities to private holders abroad are counted as part of the imbalance, while changes in private U.S. claims on foreigners are counted as reserve account transactions or settlement items. If, for example, a U.S. company acquires 1 million Swiss francs in a Zurich bank and an indebtedness equal to 1 million francs to a Paris bank, the first transaction is treated as an autonomous capital outflow (a claim on the Swiss bank) increasing our deficit, but the second transaction is counted as an indirect or settlement transfer (an added liability to the Paris bank) and is not included in the computation.

Because of its asymmetry, the liquidity method results in overstatements of the reported U.S. deficit and understatement of its surpluses. When exchange rates were fixed under the IMF regime the United States regarded this overly cautious technique as the best indicator of its ability to defend the system's key currency—the U.S. dollar—against any pressures for exchange rate fluctuations. Conversion to a floating rate system has made the liquidity balance a dubious concept.

Official Reserve Balance   Differing from the liquidity balance method, the *official reserve balance* method treats private foreign claims, either long-term or short-term, as autonomous transactions, changes in which are included in the computations, and regards all transactions of monetary authorities as reserve account or adjustment entries. By treating U.S. and foreign short-term capital alike it eliminates the asymmetry of the liquidity method and avoids its distorting effects.

It should be noted, however, that to make the distinction between official and private holdings of dollar instruments is not always easy. Central banks can and do influence the foreign exchange methods and holdings of private banks and business firms in such a way that the official balance can be affected. The official reserve balance has gained wide acceptance during the years of floating exchange rates.

Money Supply Balance   Monetarist economists regard changes in *money supply* as the prime cause of other changes in the economy. In their view, the most important purpose of balance of payments accounting should be to show how international payments affect a nation's money supply. They have, therefore, advocated the addition of a money supply or money account balance.

This balance would include only the international items that affect the money supply, but how these could be determined remains obscure. Many international transactions of central banks and national treasuries have no effect on money supply; others do. For example, if the Bank of England obtains dollars from the Federal Reserve Board and invests the dollars in England, the U.S. money supply is affected; if the Bank of England uses the dollars to buy U.S. treasury bonds on the open market, there is no effect whatsoever on American money supply. Many international transactions have a similarly unpredictable relationship to the domestic money supply because when a foreign institution buys dollars, there is no certain information on how the funds will be employed. Thus, the money account balance remains too vague for practical application. However, should monetarism emerge victorious over other economic theories, the rules and regulations of international payments transactions could conceivably be changed so as to make the money supply balance a usable measure.

Causes of Deficits and Surpluses

Deficits and surpluses are more likely to persist when exchange rates are officially fixed or managed than when they are free to move. A disequilibrium in the balance of payments means there is a corresponding disequilibrium in the foreign exchange market; that is, that the supply and demand of foreign exchange are unequal. If the exchange rates are unregulated, the disequilibrium will cause the exchange rate to move until the supply and demand equality is restored and the market cleared.

Disequilibriums may be caused by several reasons. Developing nations tend to be the most vulnerable because their international business is heavily concentrated on a few products. If the world demand for these products declines, their international receipts tend to plummet, partly because prices go down but sometimes even more because the export demand drops more than the consumer demand. The reason for this accelerated decline is inventory drawdown. Merchants and manufacturers in the importing country cut back their inventories when consumer demand drops. For a while they supply their customers from the drawdown of excess inventories, buying very little if any at all from the exporting nation.

This *accelerator principle* applies not only to raw materials but also to manufactured producer goods such as machine tools, construction equipment, and various intermediary or semimanufactured products. Since these manufactured goods originate mainly in the industrial economies with a highly diversified export base, however, the impact of a decline in demand on the balance of payments is normally much less violent than that of primary product.

Structural shifts in export markets are another major cause of balance of payments disequilibriums. Structural shifts include such things as rapid changes in consumer preference and in competition and market shares. Import markets undergo analogous shifts. The normal remedy for structural disequilibriums is a reallocation of productive resources; developing new or improved products, employing different technology, adopting a new marketing system, or switching to an entirely different line of activity. Since all these take a long time and are often associated with high risk of failure, structural disbalances are more prone to become chronic than other disbalances.

A third source of disequilibriums are *cyclical movements* in business conditions. People's spending patterns change with the business cycle. First to fall when a recession starts are luxuries and recreational expenditures. This decline is transferred to the capital goods industries that supply the recessionary consumer sectors. In other sectors equipment relacements are postponed and materials inventories reduced. These purchases from both domestic and foreign sources are curtailed. Thus, exporters of such goods will find their markets dwindling. During the recovery phase the processes are reversed.

A fourth reason for payments disequilibriums is in older literature often labeled *speculation*. Speculation is a situation in which someone holds an amount of asset in a given currency that is greater than the amount of liabilities held in that currency; that is, any holding of a long or short position in a foreign currency is regarded as speculation. The purpose of speculation is taken to be profiting from exchange rate fluctuations. By this definition the exchange speculator is but a short step removed from an outright gambler. The luck of the draw, the clairvoyance of assessing future rate movements, and the subjective urge for quick profits are the speculator's traits. To be sure, there are people of means so endowed, but nowhere near enough to make a dent in the world exchange markets.

The great bulk of what are called speculative holdings of foreign currency and speculative capital movements are in reality both rational and completely impersonal. They are undertaken not by the mythical semigamblers, but by multinational enterprises—banks, industrial corporations, and service firms with operating entities in several countries. MNCs would rather hedge their foreign exchange positions than speculate, but such firms do move large sums of money from country to country, sometimes for only a few days. However, these movements derive from interest rate differentials or other factual conditions increasing (or maximizing) the return on the liquid reserves that must be held to meet budgetary needs. Although the MNCs have become the largest single group of actors for any category of international transactions, save foreign aid, the balance of payments terminology has yet to accommodate this fact without serious distortions.

The final two sources of disequilibriums are unilateral transfers (foreign aid, foundation grants, gifts and bequests), for which there is no payment, and foreign direct investments, which may take a long time before they start generating any return flows. In its initial years, a direct investment often causes a deficit, although in later years it may become a source of surplus through profit repatriation.

EFFECTS OF PAYMENTS DISEQUILIBRIUMS ON BUSINESS

Deficits and surpluses in the current account affect a nation's economy in a number of ways. National income, money supply, prices, employment, interest rates, and foreign exchange reserves rank among the most important factors affected by the disequilibriums. Changes in these may induce changes in other aspects of the economy. Thus, balance of payments effects are not limited to firms in international business but extend to domestic business as well. Indeed, a payments deficit or surplus, especially a sizable one, leaves nothing untouched as it sends shock waves throughout the economy.

How domestic and international activities interact is perhaps the most complex part of economics. A great deal of it remains both unclear and controversial, not because there is any lack of theoretical models. The problem is scarcity of factual verification of the operational validity of the models. In this book, we are exploring knowledge that is applicable to managerial and government purposes; we will, therefore, emphasize the principles and relationships most tested by experience. From this perspective, the linkages between payments and domestic activities fall in two separate yet interrelated categories: income effects and price effects.

Effects on National Income

National income is calculated by aggregating the market value of all goods and services produced in a year, done by adding all expenditures on goods and services in a country's domestic market and adjusting the total for depreciation in its capital stock. Since exports represent expenditures by foreigners in the domestic market, they are included as part of the national income. Imports are excluded from national income since they require expenditures by domestic buyers outside the country. The monies spent on imports are part of other nations' incomes. The share of national income spent on purchases abroad is called the *propensity to import*. This ratio varies from country to country: it may be only 2 percent to 3 percent in a relatively closed economy such as Albania, China, or the U.S.S.R. and reach to 50 percent or more in some ministates with wide-open borders such as Luxembourg, Monaco, or Liechtenstein. In any given country, the average propensity to import is a relatively stable statistic. It rarely shows any abrupt change, though it responds gradually to major changes in the economy.

A slightly different measure of the linkage between imports and national income is the *income elasticity of demand for imports*. It is computed by dividing the percent change in imports by the percent change in income. For example, if the demand for imports increases 8 percent and national income increases 12 percent, the income elasticity of imports is 8:12, or 0.667. This means that any change in national income will cause imports to change but only at a rate equal to 67 percent of the income change.

Foreign Trade Multiplier

To analyze the causal linkages between payments disequilibriums and national income, it is useful to start with a mythical country whose international business consists solely of exports and imports. Once we understand the effects on domestic business of surpluses and deficits in trade balances, we can apply the insights to other transboundary transactions.

Effects of Surpluses Suppose our mythical country has enjoyed a perfect equilibrium between exports and imports. All monies spent abroad on imports have been earned at home by export sales to foreigners. There is no residue of international payments to affect the country's national income. The *income leakage* to imports has been completely offset by the *income injection* from exports. Though this perfectly balanced trade has enriched consumer choice and allowed economic specialization for greater efficiency, it has had no payments effect on the economy.

What if the export-import equilibrium is disturbed? Assume the country finds itself with an excess of exports over imports of $1 million. Since there are no nontrade transactions, the export surplus is synonymous with balance of payments surplus. Will this surplus have any effect on the country's economy? Yes, indeed.

Since exports are part of national income, the immediate effect of the surplus is to increase the country's national income by its whole amount. But this is only the beginning.

The recipients of this new income, the exporters, will spend it, just as they would spend any other income, on wages, raw materials, and other inputs. The exporters' expenditures are income to the employers, raw materials producers, and suppliers of the other inputs. They, in turn, will proceed to spend the new income on whatever best suits their needs. A chain of successive rounds of spending is set in motion. If all the recipients spend their payments surplus, all their new income, national income would grow by $1 million (the size of the total surplus) during each round, and the income growth would continue forever. In reality, this can never happen. Some of the new income is spent on imports, which is income to foreigners, and some of it is saved or hoarded, that is, left unspent. Therefore, each spending round generates less new business in the domestic market than the preceding one. The increments of national income keep shrinking.

If the propensity to import were 0.24 and the propensity to save 0.16, there would be a total leakage of 40 percent during each round. What the effects of the payments surplus would be in such a case is shown in Table 7.5.

Although the increments dwindle from round to round, their cumulative total is 2.5 times the size of the payments surplus from which they are derived. Had the leakages to imports and hoarding been different, the cumulative addition to domestic business also would have been different. The smaller the leakages the greater the growth effect of the surplus, and the greater the leakage the smaller the growth.

The numerical coefficient showing how great a contribution to national income, that is to say, to domestic business activity, a given payments surplus creates is called the *foreign trade multiplier*. In the above illustration the multiplier is 2.5. The multiplier may be computed arithmetically, as in Table 7.3, or by the algebraic formula for an infinite geometric progression:

Table 7.5 Multiplier Effects of $1 Million Export Surplus

SPENDING ROUND	INCREASE OF NATIONAL INCOME	INCREASE OF SAVINGS	INCREASE OF IMPORTS	INCREASE OF DOMESTIC SPENDING
Initial injection	$1,000,000	$160,000	$240,000	$ 600,000
Second round	600,000	96,000	144,000	360,000
Third round	360,000	57,600	89,400	216,000
Fourth round	216,000	34,560	51,840	129,600
.	.	.	.	.
.	.	.	.	.
.	.	.	.	.
Total Increase	$2,500,000	$400,000	$600,000	$1,500,000

$$1 + r + r^2 + r^3 + \ldots + r^n = \frac{1}{1 - r}$$

Applying the formula to our mythical nation, the foreign trade multiplier would be:

$$\frac{1}{1 - 0.6} = \frac{1}{0.4} = 2.5$$

Had the import and savings leakages totaled 0.25, the foreign trade multiplier in our mythical country would have been:

$$\frac{1}{1 - 0.75} = 4$$

and the cumulative growth of national income would have been $4 million.

Effects of Deficits The foreign trade multiplier is activated by both surpluses and deficits. In the case of a deficit the multiplier becomes negative, setting in motion a chain of decreases in domestic income. Suppose, for example, that another mythical nation experienced a $1 million deficit instead of the surplus. The deficit would represent an income ejection (negative injection) from the economy. The ensuing process is easiest to describe if we assume further that the cause of the deficit was a decline in exports that is expected to be permanent.

The decline of exports causes an equivalent drop in sales for the domestic firms who supply the exports. These export firms cut back their production, causing reductions in the incomes of employees and suppliers. The latter groups must now curtail their expenditures, which are incomes to a third group of firms and individuals. So the process of income shrinkage spreads throughout the economy. Although in each spending round the cutbacks decline due to imports and savings, the cumulative total of the income decreases in the domestic economy will always exceed the size of the original payments deficits. If the propensities to import and save totaled 0.4, as in our earlier example, the multiplier would be -2.5 and the cumulative income contraction $2 million.

The cumulative multiplier effects, though true in theory, tend to overstate the actual consequences of payments disequilibriums. This is so because the composition and growth of national income are subject to a great many other variables. Also, because the national economy is so large, the national income may remain relatively irresponsive to payments disequilibriums for extended periods. Normally the multiplier effects are most noticeable in the early spending rounds, perhaps for a year or a year and a half. As the effects dwindle in the later rounds they are wiped out by other autonomous changes in the economy unless a given payments disequilibrium persists.

Effects on Prices

Among the intervening factors we must first consider the level of employment. If an economy is operating at full capacity, there is no room for a real increase of national income to take place. Injection of new money income through a trade surplus will add only to the nation's money supply but cannot bring forth a corresponding increase in output of goods and services. The result will be price inflation.

In principle, payments surpluses tend to fuel price inflation whenever the economy is unable to expand real production at the same rate as the new income is spent. The lag may be due to an insufficiency of resources or it may be due to the fact that spending expands at a rate faster than production.

Conversely, a deficit causes deflationary tendencies. As funds are drained out of the economy to finance the deficit, the money supply shrinks. Lacking clairvoyance, businesses may attempt to keep production at the same level as before in the hope of better times. Inventories pile up and sooner or later prices have to be cut to clear the stock. The price deflation (or a reduction of the general inflation rate relative to that of other countries) will make the country's goods more competitive abroad and foreign goods less competitive at home. Exports will increase and imports decrease. A country with payments surplus will have the opposite experience. As price inflation at home is accelerated, exports suffer and imports pick up. The size of the price effects on trade depends on price elasticities of the export and import sectors. Though individual commodities may be price inelastic, a nation's overall foreign trade mix is normally price elastic.

As prices rise in the surplus country and decline in the deficit country, terms of trade between them will shift in favor of the surplus country—an average unit of its exports will buy more imports—and against the deficit country—an average unit of its exports will buy fewer imports than before. Thus, in real terms, the surplus country would seem to gain at the expense of the deficit nation. This is not necessarily true.

When a deficit in payments occurs, more goods and services are imported than are exported, the difference being equal to the deficit. The excess of imports makes a net addition to the country's supply of goods and services but it does not increase the country's national income. Consequently, a deficit in payments means that the economy is absorbing more goods and services than it is producing. In other words, the country's absorption of goods and services is greater than its national income. Clearly the nation is not paying its way. A likely cause of the deficit is too high prices, which impede exports. Therefore, the shift in the terms of trade may well be the necessary adjustment of relative prices between the two countries to bring the prices in both countries into closer alignment with real (as distinguished from monetary) values.

Payments disequilibriums affect not only prices of goods but also the factor costs. By changing the money supply they induce changes in interest rates, the cost of capital, investments, and employment. No prices are left untouched.

SUMMARY

Balance of payments disequilibriums are of interest to government, business, and labor alike, but any intervention with the economic and business processes that are set in motion by deficits or surpluses in the balance of payments can come only through government action. Governments may countervene the deflationary effects of a deficit by increasing the supply of money, by printing more currency, or by reducing the reserve requirements for banks; governments can counter the inflationary effects of a surplus by removing some currency from circulation or raising the reserve requirements for banks. More directly, governments can manipulate exchange rates, introduce trade and payments restrictions, or intervene in the market in many other ways. Since any government must grapple simultaneously with all variables, both economic and political, its treatment of payments disequilibriums is rarely consistent and predictable. As a result, each deficit or surplus represents a new opera and must be analyzed in its own context of realities.

FOR REVIEW AND DISCUSSION

1. Explain the basic rationale of balance of payments accounting.

2. Why are the balances of the merchandise account and the current account the figures of balance of payments data most often cited by the business press?

3. Assess the appropriateness of the system of accounts now in use. Would the information needs of business be better served by changing the system somehow? Explain.

4. What is meant by official reserve assets? Explain their sources and uses.

5. Is it realistic to assume that the conflicting theories about methods of measuring

the balance of payments disequilibriums will ultimately be resolved and a single method adopted? Why or why not?

6. Of the different causes for disequilibriums, which would you expect to be the most persistent in the future?

7. To what uses can business firms put the concept of propensity to import? Would they encounter any practical complications?

8. Explain the relationship between the balance of payments and the foreign trade multiplier.

9. Can we tell from balance of payments data if a nation is producing more goods and services than it consumes or consuming more than it produces? Explain.

10. Prices affect the balance of payments and the balance of payments affects prices. Comment.

Transnational Dimensions of International Financial Environments

*I*nflation and Eurocurrencies have come to play significant roles in international finance since the 1960s. Though each has its own origin and effects, these two factors are similar in that neither lends itself to national regulation in the normal sense, and each may influence exchange rates, capital and credit flows, and balance of payments adjustments in all parts of the world.

Neither inflation nor Eurocurrencies derive from any one nation's business activities; instead, their causes must be sought in the context of a multitude of economies and business relationships among them. Yet, these factors leave no nation's business activities untouched; they influence not only foreign trade and investment flows but also dominate markets and business conditions in general. Because of such scope, inflation and Eurocurrencies are better described as *transnational* or *supranational* than as international phenomena.

For business firms the two factors have brought both opportunities and complications. Since they are causally unrelated we shall discuss each separately.

THE EUROCURRENCY MARKET

Eurocurrency denotes banking operations specializing in loans and deposits of currencies outside their countries of legal tender. These activities originated in the 1950s, when a few banks in Paris and London started the practice of accepting dollar-denominated deposits and making dollar-denominated loans, providing a non-U.S. alternative to owners of dollars for banking their holdings and enabling borrowers of dollars to satisfy their requirements through European sources. The practice of using Eurocurrency has spread to other financial centers and is now worldwide in scope.

The Rise of Eurocurrency

The initial reasons for its emergence were (a) the desire of the communist-bloc banks to have their dollar working balances in Europe rather than in the United States during the cold war, and (b) the need of countries whose own currencies were inconvertible—and nearly all were in the 1950s—to use dollars as the unit of account and means of payment in international transactions. Widespread convertibility after 1960 did not destroy the Eurodollar but accelerated its use. The main reason for its continued growth has been a far greater freedom for banks to operate in the Eurodollar market than in national markets because such transactions are not subject to domestic banking regulations. In periods of tight monetary restriction at home, businesses and even governments have, therefore, sought rescue through the Euromarket.

Much of the original supply of Eurodollars came from the U.S. balance of payments deficits, which left many foreign banks with large holdings of dollar claims, most in the form of deposits in U.S. banks. However, with its present volume in hundreds of billions, the Eurocurrency market has far outgrown this initial source. Now, the Eurodollar supply, just like the domestic money supply, derives in most part from *fractional reserve banking*. Eurodollar deposits, like domestic dollar deposits, can exceed multifold a bank's actual dollar reserves on hand. In any period, because a bank not only pays but also receives dollars, it can redeem most of its cash obligations from day to day as a matter of course. The same principle applies to Eurodollar deposits in U.S. and other banks. Like currency, deposits need be only a small fraction of assets since the bank is in a continuous process of remitting to and receiving from other banks, and this process to a very large degree balances the bank's positions. Reserves are needed only to provide for temporary discrepancies between remittances and receipts.

The Eurocurrency banks, including the foreign branches of U.S. banks, are not subject to U.S. reserve regulations. Each country has its own banking laws. In many countries they are more liberal than in the United States. A typical Eurodollar bank, therefore, can cascade its reserves in dollar currency plus its initial dollar holdings in other banks into a volume of loans and deposits that is several times greater.

Some analysts have tried to explain the Eurocurrency movement in terms of traditional foreign exchange transactions. They claim, for example, that the amount of Eurodollar business done at any time is limited to the volume of dollar transfers from U.S. banks. This is erroneous. Evidence shows that once a foreign bank has launched its Eurodollar operations, its initial dollar holdings have little further significance. From that point on, the only limitations on the bank's ability to expand its Eurodollar business are its total assets; the need to have a certain, though yet undeterminate, share of the bank's business in the local currency; and the banking regulations regarding reserve requirements of the particular nation.

The bulk of Eurodollar business volume is neither in dollars nor in Europe. It consists mainly of dollar-denominated credit instruments from short-term drafts to multiyear term certificates and Eurobonds, which the banks abroad create, carry, and trade. Their holdings at U.S. banks are helpful but not essential to this business.

When the dollar started to fade in value, the Eurodollar system of accepting nonresident-denominated deposits was expanded to include a number of other currencies, Swiss franc, West German deutsche mark, Dutch florin, French franc, Japanese yen, and some others. This turned the Eurodollar market into the *Eurocurrency market*. The widening of its base has rendered the Eurobanking system a highly competitive market. Entry into the business is unrestricted; banks of any nation can participate. Due to the competition, Eurobanks have at times accepted higher risks (both in terms of borrowers and longer maturities) and lower margins than have national banks.

The Eurocurrency market draws funds from depositors in countries with excess liquidity, low interest rates, and high devaluation risks, and channels the money to borrowers in countries with high credit, high interest rates, and appreciating currencies. Eurocurrency interest rates vary with supply and demand; they are neither fixed nor uniform. Though arbitrage prevents persistent differences among financial centers such as London, Tokyo, Frankfurt, Paris, Zurich, Singapore, and Hong Kong, temporary deviations are a constant occurrence.

The Eurocurrency market caters to large customers, the typical transaction falling between $10 million to $20 million; many transactions are in hundreds of millions of dollars. As a means of spreading the risk inherent in such large scale loans, Eurobanks rely on *syndicating;* that is, many banks participate in a transaction with one bank managing the loan. The syndicating technique enables small and medium banks to participate in Eurocurrency transactions. It also makes it possible for the market to undertake extremely large lending programs. In some cases as many as one hundred banks of a dozen different countries have cooperated in a Eurocurrency syndicate. Comparable transactions would be inconceivable in traditional international finance except as government transfers.

The Eurocurrency market is closely geared to inflationary trends. Medium and longer term loans are made as rollover credits with a so-called floating interest rate, which is fixed anew every three or four months. The interest rate is usually geared to current rates charged by Eurocurrency banks on their interbank transactions. Another safeguard is a multicurrency clause, which has become standard for most Eurocurrency loan agreements. By providing the flexibility to fulfill the obligation with one of several currencies, this clause helps to reduce the risk for both lenders and borrowers in a turbulent world economy.

Eurobonds

Once the Eurocurrency market had become established its basic principles were adapted to financing long-term capital needs by the introduction of *Eurobonds;* for instance, bonds issued in Belgium but denominated in duetsche mark or bonds issued in Singapore but denominated in Japanese yen. Initially all Eurobonds were denominated in U.S. dollars, but, as with the Eurocurrency market, the Eurobond market has diversified into a number of other currencies.

Compared to regular corporate bonds, Eurobonds offer several new options. Since they are issued in a foreign currency and sold to foreigners, Eurobonds create no export of capital; therefore, they are not normally subject to the foreign exchange restrictions of the country of issue. If they are marketed in third countries, that is, in countries other than that whose currency is involved (Eurobonds issued in England, denominated in U.S. dollars, and sold in Australia), they are subject to minimal, if any, import restrictions, as most governments welcome the inflow of long-term foreign capital. The holders of Eurobonds are free from any withholding of taxes on interest earned that may apply to domestic holders of bonds denominated in the same currency. The borrowers may benefit from being able to fund long-term capital requirements in a given country despite regulatory restrictions on traditional capital movements. No government is in a position to regulate the Eurobond market; it transcends all domestic capital markets. As a result, it increases the freedom and international mobility of capital.

The Eurobond market has been growing in volume, diversity, and geographic scope. Such bonds are now available in many parts of the world. Beside bonds with fixed interest rates and fixed terms, there are Eurobonds with floating interest rates and Eurobonds convertible into common stock at their holder's option—these latter came into being in the recession-ridden 1970s, when low stock prices made it difficult to raise equity capital. The newest variety is multicurrency Eurobonds, which are issued in a designated currency, such as the U.S. dollar, but which buyers can redeem in some other currency of their choice or in a combination of currencies, such as *European currency units* (ECU). The value of the ECU is determined by a composite index of the national currencies of European Economic Community member nations. (The organization and function of the European Economic Community are discussed in Chapter 24.)

Many Eurobond issues are considerably larger than domestic bond issues. To facilitate such large financing and to spread the risk, investment banks from a number of countries join into underwriting syndicates to float the issues.

The Eurobond market has been generally limited to borrowers from the private sector, but more recently public agencies requiring sizable amounts have patronized this market in increasing numbers from all parts of the world.

INFLATION

Inflation represents the most insidious factor in international finance. Its effects are pervasive and continue to confound both national economies and individual firms.

The pressure for prices to rise has been universal in recent times. No country has been completely successful in suppressing it, and all currencies, therefore, have declined in real value. In earlier times, inflation was primarily a domestic rather than a world phenomenon. The countries whose currencies inflated more rapidly experienced increasing payments deficits as their exports suffered and imports soared. Sooner or later these countries ran out of reserve assets and were forced to devalue their currencies. Under the fixed exchange rate regime of the International Monetary Fund the exchange market itself was usually less than adequate to bring about exchange rate adjustments that would have been adequate to keep currencies at their purchasing power parities.

The United States escaped the adjustment pressures despite its payments deficits because the dollar was the official reserve asset for other IMF members. Foreign central banks used the U.S. Treasury's and major U.S. banks' debt instruments as international reserve assets, thereby helping to finance the U.S. payments deficits. By 1970, however, other countries' central banks possessed more dollar reserves than they needed or could afford, and they started to trade their dollars for gold. This demand led to the rapid erosion of U.S. gold reserves and the consequent closing of the gold window in 1971. With this, the so-called gold-exchange standard of the IMF came to an end. Until 1971, dollar assets of foreign central banks were convertible to gold; after 1971, they were not.

U.S. Inflation

Since under the IMF system the values of all other currencies were measured in dollar parities, the decline of the dollar due to domestic inflation before 1971 was synonymous with the de-escalation of the entire international monetary structure. Within this structure, each national currency had its own history of rates and patterns of purchasing power declining, and, as a consequence, the real, as distinguished from the official, values of currencies shifted in countless ways. But the onus of adjustment was on other currencies.

Domestic Effects Though not unrelated, the domestic and international effects of U.S. inflation were quite different. In the domestic economy, the decline in the purchasing power of the dollar affected primarily those whose incomes were fixed by pre-existing contracts, especially pensioners and holders of long-term bonds. In the rest of the domestic economy, the value of the dollar was not as important as were the offsetting flows of incomes and costs, both of which showed nominal increases more or less paralleling the rate of inflation. This meant that individual dollars bought less but there were more of them streaming in and out, so the real purchasing power of the individual or firm was not decreased. In other words, it was not the value of the dollar but the relationship between the revenue stream and the cost stream that determined real purchasing power.

If there were leads and lags in a firm's revenue and cost streams, there were corresponding gains or losses caused by inflation. The point here is not that inflation was inconsequential, but that in the domestic context the inflationary process created, and still does create, its own counterbalance, to a substantial degree, by inflating both the incomes and expenditures of employees and businesses.

International Effects   In the international context this is not so. When the dollar is held as a reserve asset by a foreign central bank there is no revenue-cost relationship. The foreign government acquires the dollar for its own currency and thereafter depends upon the value of these dollars, just as the pensioner or other fixed contract holder in the United States. To a very slight extent the loss in the dollar's value may be reduced by increases in interest yields of U.S. Treasury bonds or other government debt instruments. If the foreign country involved experienced a slower rate of inflation than the United States, the value of its dollar-denominated reserve assets deteriorated not only in real terms but also relative to the country's own currency. That exposed the other country to a risk of loss. To realign its own currency with the constantly depreciating dollar, it had to revalue its currency periodically.

Experience shows revaluation to be politically a more difficult move for a government to make than its opposite, devaluation. The reasons for this are not entirely clear, although one major reason can be identified: the fear that the country's international trade position as well as its balance of payments will suffer. Apparently, governments would rather accept distorted currency values than accept the public and business reactions associated with revaluation. Since no country was willing to undertake periodic revaluations to neutralize the effect of the inflation upon international monetary relations, the problems of purchasing power disparity and key currency instability emerge as critical dysfunctions of the IMF system.

Distortion of Parity Rates   Under the key currency system with fixed dollar parities, rapid inflation in the United States was tantamount to a de facto devaluation of other nations' currencies whenever their own inflation rates were lower. Their exports were stimulated and their imports impeded by the process. To the United States itself, the inflation put a brake on exports and accelerated imports. That pushed more dollars into foreign coffers.

As a consequence of this process, a number of other currencies kept gaining in strength compared to the dollar. As their IMF parities were not adjusted to offset the gain (except minor revaluations of the German mark and Dutch gulden), their purchasing power parities suffered serious distortions. Thus, besides the general undervaluation of gold, the dollar became overvalued vis-à-vis many other currencies, though in different degrees. The IMF system's lack of flexibility to harmonize purchasing power and exchange rate parities became painfully evident as prolonged international currency maladjustment endured.

Collapse of the Fixed Rate Regime   When the dollar was made inconvertible to gold, the IMF's fixed exchange rate regime became untenable. Despite desperate efforts to save it by widening the band for allowable rate fluctuations, the crisis continued until rates were set afloat, in 1973. With this, the shield against international inflation was removed and a new chapter in international monetary relations started. Let us hasten to add that it was not the official closing of the gold window that caused the demise of the IMF system; it merely administered the coup de grace. The system died of incurable natural causes. Accelerating rates of inflation world over eroded the premises on which the IMF system had been built.

Causes of Inflation

Inflation is a basic, yet poorly understood phenomenon of the contemporary world. Traditional theory explains inflation by demand-pull, cost-push, and structural changes; more recently other explanations have been offered.

The *demand-pull theory* postulates that inflation is caused by increases in aggregate demand in the economy that are not neutralized by matching increases in the aggregate supply of goods and services. The demand may go up either because the stock of money in the economy expands or because production shrinks.

Keynesian modifications of inflation theory emphasize income and expenditure flows, which are determined by the *liquidity preferences*—preferences for money rather than for real assets—of different segments of the society. A sudden drop in the liquidity preference would release cash for purchases of goods and services, thereby increasing the velocity of circulation. Thus, inflation can occur even in the absence of any expansion in the money supply. An increase in the liquidity preferences slows down the velocity and leads to price deflation. Liquidity preferences vary widely from country to country.

The *cost-push theory* explains inflation by wage increases that outstrip productivity and thus raise the cost of production. The higher cost results in higher prices of goods.

The wage demands may stem either from increasing profits, which on the one hand encourage labor leaders to demand wage increases and on the other hand enable employers to yield to those demands, or from labor shortages, which induce employers to lure workers from other industries by higher wages. Regardless of their cause, wage increases cannot normally be absorbed by business unless productivity can be increased simultaneously at the same rate. If productivity remains constant, management has to raise prices or reduce employment to keep its total cost at its previous level.

The *structural theory* of inflation holds that, even though the aggregate demand is not excessive, the demand in specific industries may be excessive while in others it may be insufficient. In the industries with the excess demand, prices will rise. This rise will not be balanced by corresponding price declines in industries with insufficient demand because both prices and wages in the contemporary world are flexible upward, but rigid downward. Therefore, the excess demand will raise the price and wage standards of the entire economy.

Structural inflation may arise initially from the rapid growth of a particular industry, a concentration of population in a particular region, a social policy, or any other change that causes excess demand in some sector. It leads to a general inflation because wages and prices tend to be cost determined and their flexibility, for institutional and social reasons, is relatively immune to downward pressures but sensitive to upward trends. Thus, neither the upward push of costs nor the aggregate demand can fully explain inflation.

The *monetary theory* assigns the cause of inflation to an excessive quantity of money in the economy. It differs from the demand-pull theory in that the monetarist views inflation as a purely monetary phenomenon, not created by either demand or supply factors, but by government. When the government allows the quantity of money to increase more rapidly than the quantity of goods and services available for purchase (output), prices will go up. Other factors can cause temporary fluctuations in the rate of inflation, but they do not produce any lasting effect unless they induce further expansion of the money supply. Since deficit spending on public services tends to add to the money supply, the monetarists, as well as demand-push theorists, consider government budget deficits as tantamount to printing currency.

The *growing scarcities theory* disagrees with the monetarist diagnosis. Studying long-term production and consumption trends in the world, these analysts conclude that the root cause of the inflation that now engulfs the world is not permissive monetary policies of governments but increasing scarcities of real resources. These research studies were originally sponsored by the Club of Rome, an international group of leading individuals from industry and academia. What they achieved is perhaps better referred to as a synthesis than a theory. These analysts point to a bent-up curve of long-term production that has dwarfed the combined discoveries of new natural resources and their synthetic substitutes. As a result, per capita ratios of all essential resources have declined. The ratios in the industrial world are now further depressed by the ex-colonial nations' drive to develop their own resources, which leaves few resources available for export.

In recent decades the scarcity crunch has been compounded by skyrocketing military expenditures. Since these expenditures divert massive amounts of materials from the fulfillment of human needs to the building of weapons unavailable for human consumption, they are wholly inflationary. The total quantities of resources diverted to military purposes in the world just about equals the aggregate GNP of the less developed nations, in which nearly one-half of the world population lives. The U.S.S.R. and the United States are responsible for most of the military expenditures. The growing scarcities of resources may be overcome only at higher costs and prices than in the past.

In a given context, each of the theories can be useful. As a full explanation of inflation none is equal to the task. The phenomenon has proven itself too complex to be explained by any single theory.

EFFECTS OF INFLATION

Social Effects of Inflation

Inflation affects the entire society. It is most damaging to people living on fixed incomes, especially for passive income claimants such as the aged and pensioners who lack the means and opportunities to hedge against rising prices. It benefits those groups whose earnings rise at a rate equal to or higher than the prices. In some Latin American countries, for example, industrial wages have kept pace with inflation while the earnings of the rural population have not, resulting in a redistribution of purchasing power. Such redistribution affects nearly all segments of the society.

The resultant income disparities cause social stress and political instability. This is particularly pronounced in underdeveloped countries, where the redistribution of income has been primarily in favor of the very few highly developed industries and secondarily in favor of industrial labor as such. As a consequence, there has been an influx of population to urban centers; this population increase in turn puts unbearable strains on the cities' abilities to provide housing, sewerage, water, and other public services. Vast suburban slums then form around these industrial cities of the developing world, accentuating their unemployment problems and creating social conditions laden with political explosives.

Inflation also weakens the general confidence in money. By reducing purchasing power, inflation makes currency as well as other monetary assets unsuitable for protecting real income. People therefore attempt to convert these assets into price-flexible and quick-yielding tangible properties. Thus, inflation discourages investment in price-rigid infrastructural sectors, which are a prerequisite for industrial development and economic growth. Also, when confidence in monetary assets is undermined, the public's will to save is weakened, thrift is discouraged, and spending habits are changed in favor of consumption expenditures. The savings that do accumulate often escape the country and seek safety in a hard currency abroad. In most developing countries the problem is further aggravated by the nonexistence of a security market through which savings could be channeled into productive investments.

Accounting for Inflation

The Problem of Cost Accounting   For the decision maker the redistribution of costs, prices, and purchasing power poses serious complications. How inflation affects a firm depends upon which sector of the market is undergoing the fastest rise. The firm will reap a windfall if its selling prices lead the increases in its factor prices; conversely, the firm will suffer if its selling prices lag behind the increases in the prices of inputs such as raw materials, semi-manufactures, and wages. The most immediately sensitive cost elements are those that are part of the firm's variable cost inputs. Investments in plant and equipment respond only within a longer time frame.

In a multinational company (MNC) the problem is complicated not only by each country's rate of inflation but also the difference in leads and lags among the relevant prices in each economy. For example, wages may be rising by 12 percent in Germany, 15 percent in Australia, and 20 percent in Brazil; but at the same time selling prices may be rising by 6 percent in Germany, 20 percent in Australia, and 35 percent in Brazil. If we attempted to expand such comparison to all the thousands of cost elements of an MNC we quickly realize the labyrinthine complications that world inflation produces for international managers.

Looking at it in a different way, inflation causes the real values of host and home country currencies to change. This renders accounting records based on historical costs fallacious unless exchange rates move in a perfect harmony with inflation. Since changes in the exchange rates may be influenced by other factors, such as the composition of the export and import mix, investment flows, foreign aid transfers, and government intervention, the rate of inflation and the rate of exchange at times differ considerably.

Replacement Cost Accounting   This problem can be solved, at least to some extent, by the use of *replacement cost accounting*, which attempts to adjust the financial statements to take the effects of inflation into account. In doing so, it pushes aside the traditional accounting assumption that fluctuations in the purchasing power of local currency may be ignored in preparing financial statements. Instead, historical cost figures of transactions and ending balances are converted to the current value of money, as measured by a wholesale or retail price index or by a specially constructed index.

To illustrate the conversion procedure assume the following index numbers:

1978	100
1979	120
1980	168
1981	180

If the analysis concerns the year 1981, all assets, current liabilities, and capital stock items, except inventory and plant assets, are in terms of that year's currency; so no adjustment is made, except for the two items; inventory and plant assets. To adjust the preceding year's statement it is necessary to divide the 1981 index number, 180, by the 1980 index number, 168. Each item in the financial statement for 1980 is then multiplied by the resulting quotient, which converts the statement to 1981 dollars. The same procedure is followed for 1979: divide 180 by 120 and multiply each item in the 1979 statement by the new quotient.

Inventory, plant assets, and accumulated depreciation are composed of both current dollars and past years' dollars, depending upon the date of acquisition. For the 1981 statement, a portion of these three items is in current dollars. However, that portion representing 1980 acquisitions is adjusted by that year's index, as described above, and so are the portions acquired in 1979 and in each of the previous years. When all the items are adjusted, the three annual statements conform with current purchasing power and are directly comparable with one another. Each noncash item on the financial statements is expressed in a common denominator, the purchasing power of the currency at the balance sheet date.

Constant Cost Accounting   This is a somewhat less satisfactory method than price level accounting, yet much more acceptable than using the traditional historical cost. The *constant cost* technique uses a base year value of a currency as the accounting standard for a period of years. All currency transactions in subsequent years are converted to that base. For example, assume that changes in exchange rates reflected accurately the changes in purchasing power (which is not always true) and that the exchange rates were as follows:

Currency	Base Year	Current Year
Franc	$0.40	$0.50
Peso	0.15	0.10

The MNC using the constant cost method would multiply all accounting data of its French affiliate by 50/40, or $1.25, and all accounting data of its Argentina affiliate by 10/15, or $0.67, to convert them to base year equivalents.

This means that the company records and current transactions are in different purchasing power figures. If the changes in the purchasing power of the currency are accurately measured, the substantive results are compatible with those of price level accounting. The advantage of the price level technique is the continuous updating of records and the alignment of the firm's financial data with the prevailing price level. This facilitates decision making because decisions involve the present and future rather than the past.

Potentially, the greatest sources of accounting error for MNCs under current worldwide inflation are three: inventory valuation, depreciation of plant and equipment, and dividend distribution.

Corporate accounting practice has been slow to adjust to the realities of inflation. The results can be catastrophic. For instance, the crises of the Chrysler Corporation could have been detected far earlier using replacement cost accounting than they did on the historical cost accounts. In the meantime, the firm was paying taxes and distributing dividends on nonexistent profits.

Effects of Inflation on Inventory Policy

Rapid inflation requires a company to have a careful inventory re-evaluation procedure to avoid fictitious profits. For example, consider this illustration. The cost of goods is $2.00 per unit and the price is $3.00; the firm sells 10,000 units and realizes $30,000. Disregarding operating expense, the profit is $10,000, which conceivably can be distributed as dividends to the owners. But if during the sales period the price of inventory purchases rises to $2.50 per unit, the company will be able to replace only 8,000 units with the remaining $20,000. To put it another way, the company will be short $5,000 to maintain the inventory requirements.

The *last-in, first-out method* (LIFO) of inventory pricing is suggested for firms involved in inflation. This method assumes that the merchandise that is purchased last is the first to be used up or sold. The time interval between the purchase and sales dates is thus substantially reduced and the inventory is valued at close to the current costs of acquisition.

If this is not close enough, due to a slow inventory turnover or very rapid inflation, the company must adopt the *current cost method*. Under this system, the current market price of each item in the inventory is determined and the composite of these values is calculated. The resulting value replaces the traditional inventory value figure on the balance sheet, and the retained earnings figure is correspondingly adjusted to make the sheet balance. The income statement, of course, will show a greater cost of goods sold and a correspondingly smaller profit.

Effects of Inflation on Depreciation Policy

Inflation requires accelerated depreciation methods to assure that enough is saved to replace the capital assets of the firm. Under straight-line depreciation the historical cost of an asset is written off at a fixed, unchanging amount each year, depending on the estimated life of the equipment. If an asset costing $20,000 has an estimated useful life of ten years, one-tenth of $20,000, or $2,000, is depreciated for each of the ten years. If at the end of that time a replacement asset can be bought for $20,000, the depreciation charge, which allows cash to accumulate to that extent since no money is spent for depreciation, theoretically provides the funds for replacement.

However, if the price of the asset increases during its life from $20,000 to $40,000—as occurs under inflation—the depreciation accumulation is clearly insufficient to pay for its replacement. Hence, an accelerated depreciation must be substituted for the traditional straight-line method to prevent erosion of company assets under inflation. From the legal standpoint, however, the matter is subject to specific restrictions, which vary widely from country to country. Most foreign countries have more liberal depreciation laws than the United States. Therefore, MNCs should decentralize their depreciation policies to take full advantage of the local laws.

Effects of Inflation on Dividend Policy

A firm may have dividend problems not only because of exchange controls but also because of inflation. If old costs are matched with current revenues, the resulting net profit is higher than if current costs are matched with revenues. For instance, with an apparent large profit, management may plan to pay out 60 percent of the reported income in the form of dividends. However, if the profit and loss statement is adjusted for uniform dollars, the apparent profit may be reduced more than 60 percent, indicating that the profit contained a large element of inflated prices and a small portion of real income. In this case the payment of a dividend may take all the real profit, in terms of purchasing power, and may even take part of the equity. Such a policy, if pursued for some time, will eventually drain the company of its cash, causing slow payment of trade debts or making it impossible to replace inventory or plant as needed.

Effects of Inflation on Liquidity

In a period of rising prices firms suffer losses in the purchasing power of their cash and in the value of assets that are claims against cash, such as accounts receivable. In a multinational setting, a firm keeps cash at the minimum in countries with the highest inflation rates. Any surplus cash is invested in assets that tend to increase in price along with the inflationary trend. Such assets may include securities, gold, hard currencies, rights to natural resources, and real estate. MNCs often adjust their intracompany transfer prices so that the excess cash will be shifted through intracompany trade to some country with stable currency (see Chapters 14 and 15). Investment in larger inventories is perhaps the most common device employed by business under rapid inflation. Direct foreign investments in the form of plant and equipment are also common.

As far as trade credit is concerned, inflation requires both a strict and a restrictive policy. To keep the accounts receivable from deteriorating in real value during the credit period, it has become customary in many countries to mark up the current selling price by an amount equal to estimated depreciation of the currency during the credit period. Since inflation may drain a company's cash resources, it is imperative that tight control be exercised over collections and receivables in general.

Effects of Inflation on International Business Relations

The decline in savings and the tendency of capital to flee the country dry up the supply of capital available for business purposes. At the same time, the demand on the capital market increases because of the failure of business firms to raise their depreciation charges to offset the price escalation. If the inflated profits are distributed as dividends, business will be consuming its capital stock and sapping its internal strength for growth even further.

Since inflation discourages saving at the expense of consumption, its general effect is to stimulate the demand for goods and services. But the degree of the stimulus varies across a broad range. On the positive extreme are the countries whose incomes in real terms are increasing the most; on the negative end are those whose purchasing power is decreasing the most. Since the consumption patterns of the gainers and the losers are likely to differ and to become even more different as inflation progresses, the international redistribution of income is followed by an international redistribution of market demand among different goods and services. Suppliers of the inflation-benefited segments of the world market gain, while the suppliers of the other market segments lose. If the world demand of the two segments is composed of different product mixes, as is normally the case, the redistribution of the demand will be reflected not only in changing market shares of different nations but also in the relative profitabilities of different industries and companies. Thus, the redistributive effects of inflation are transposed from the consumer level down to the production level in each economy. Windfall profits attract new investment to the inflation-benefited countries, while the other countries stagnate.

These effects of inflation shift the demands for exports and imports. For trading nations this is crucial. Inflated costs weaken the competitive position of the country's industries in export markets, and simultaneously the inflated prices stimulate imports. This in turn puts pressure on the exchange rate and undermines the country's balance of payments position, both potential sources of restrictive government action and curtailment of business opportunity.

SUMMARY

Inflation and the Eurocurrency market are both related to the growth of interconnectedness among national economies. Eurocurrency is a direct outgrowth of an ever-increasing international business. Its market now embraces all major financial centers of the world and is used heavily by both business firms and many governments.

Inflation is not new, but what is new is the rapidity and apparent ease with which inflation in the contemporary world spreads from one country to the next. In earlier periods, inflation was more a national phenomenon, with national borders containing its spread. This is no longer true. The growing interdependencies of national economics has created a multitude of transboundary linkages through which inflation can spread from country to country. It is unclear if the increased number of cross-boundary conduits for inflationary flows only facilitates its spreading or if they also have become a factor contributing to the rate of inflation.

Inflation requires businesses to adjust many aspects of management to adapt their operations to inflationary changes. Most problems arise with accounting, financing, and pricing practices.

FOR REVIEW AND DISCUSSION

1. Are there any advantages to business firms in using the Eurocurrency market instead of the traditional foreign exchange market? Can all businesses benefit?

2. Why have governments become increasingly involved in the Eurocurrency market?

3. If Eurobonds were sold in small denominations by security firms, would you buy them for your personal investment portfolio? Why or why not?

4. In old days inflation stayed home, today it travels. Comment.

5. What are the cause and effect relationships between inflation and exchange rates?

6. In which respects does inflation affect domestic and international business in the same way? In which respects are its effects different?

7. Is the growing scarcities theory of inflation more convincing than the older theories? Explain.

8. If businesses used the replacement cost method all the distorting effects of inflation on financial statements would be eliminated regardless of whether the firm was operating only domestically or in a number of countries. Analyze.

9. Can international business ignore the social effects of inflation? Explain.

10. Is the balance of payments affected by inflation? How?

SUGGESTED READINGS FOR PART THREE

Brown, B. *Money, Hard and Soft on International Currency Markets.* New York: Wiley, 1978.

Bryant, R. *Money and Monitary Policy in Interdependent Nations.* Washington, D.C.: Brookings Institution, 1980.

Crockett, A. *International Money.* New York: Academic Press, 1977.

Dufey, G., and Giddy, I. *The International Money Market.* Englewood Cliffs, N.J.: Prentice-Hall, 1978.

Einzig, P., and Quinn, B. S. *The Eurodollar System.* New York: St. Martins Press, 1977.

Eliteman, D., and Stonehill, A. *Multinational Business Finance.* Reading, Mass.: Addison-Wesley, 1979.

International Monetary Fund, *Annual Report.* 1979.

Jacque, L. *Management of Foreign Exchange Rates.* Lexington, Mass.: Lexington Books, 1978.

Kolde, E. J. *International Business Enterprise.* 2nd ed. Englewood Cliffs, N.J.: Prentice-Hall, 1973.

Robock, S., et al. *International Business and Multinational Enterprises.* Homewood, Ill.: Irwin, 1977.

Root, F. *International Trade and Investment.* Cincinnati: Southwestern, 1978.

Snider, D. *Introduction to International Economics.* Homewood, Ill.: Irwin, 1979.

Stein, H. "Mystery of the Declining Dollar." *AEI Economist* September, 1978.

Stern, R. *The Balance of Payments.* Chicago, Ill.: Aldine, 1973.

Vernon, R., and Wells, L. *Manager in the International Economy.* Englewood Cliffs, N.J.: Prentice-Hall, 1976.

Willett, T. *Floating Exchange Rates and International Monetary Reform.* Plaino, Texas: American Enterprise Publications, 1977.

Part Four

THE GROWTH AND STRUCTURE OF MULTINATIONAL COMPANIES

*T*he multinational company has become a global phenomenon in both scope and significance. Despite some superficial similarities to certain forerunners, it is essentially a new and still evolving mode of economic enterprise. Transcending national economies and the analytic frameworks of existing theories, it has posed baffling problems and great new expectations to the contemporary world.

The rise to dominance of the multinational company has been swift and startling. While businessmen, politicians, labor leaders, and many other leaders of society have focused on its nature and potential, the multinational firms themselves have forged a global network of production and marketing that integrates the economies of different nations. In the process, they have demonstrated great dynamism and flexibility.

Because this new mode of enterprise pervades all spheres of modern life, understanding the multinational company is imperative for any educated person. The most difficult barriers to understanding the multinational company derive from its scope and complexity. It is simply too large and multifaceted to fit the conceptual framework or analytic techniques of any one discipline. Therefore, it cannot be adequately researched in the context of ordinary business or economic studies. Though this fact seems to be widely accepted, publications on the multinational company remain narrowly based. Direct investments, the product-life-cycle and strategy-leads-structure hypotheses, and the traditional functional fields define the foci and problem formulations for most of these publications. By starting with the assumption that the multinational company is but a geographic extension of the domestic firm, many of these studies are stillborn. The motives and inner logic that are unique to the multinational company and, thus, its most important aspects, receive little notice.

This book has adopted an interdisciplinary approach in order to avoid the pitfalls of specialism and to rid the scene of sacred cows. Theories, analytic techniques, and facts from all social sciences, including law, have been used along with those from business administration itself. The result is a more realistic synthesis of the contemporary multinational company than is possible by any unidisciplinary method.

The five chapters in Part Four systematically review the evolution and organization of multinational companies. Chapter 9 provides background information. Chapters 10 and 11 explain, both conceptually and factually, why multinationals have spread and prospered. Chapters 12 and 13 discuss the organizational ideas and models by which we can differentiate different types of multinational companies.

9

Concepts and Growth
of Multinational Companies

The *multinational company (MNC)* is a company involved in producing and marketing its outputs in several countries. The outputs may be goods, services, or various combinations of both. To develop the capacity to produce and market multinationally a firm must acquire managerial control over operating entities in a number of countries; in other words, it must establish subsidiary companies in all host economies and endow each with the necessary operating assets, such as factories, mines, department stores, hotels, banks, or whatever is required in the particular company's field of activity. The MNC may bring such assets under its managerial control either through ownership or through some contractual arrangements with foreign owners.

The capacity to act simultaneously in numbers of countries sets the MNC clearly apart from the *domestic* or *uninational company (UNC)*. The UNC has all its operating assets and organizational subunits (departments, divisions, subsidiaries) in its home country. It may on occasion engage in exporting or importing by transacting with foreign firms, but its own capacity to function is limited to the domestic market.

The demarcation between the MNC and UNC is a band covering companies who are active in two or three countries. That they are not UNCs is obvious; but it is not obvious if they are MNCs. The problem here is akin to the question, how many birds does it take to make a flock? Will it be two, three, or five? Nor does this lack of a sharp line present any great problem. The two- and three-country firms are usually in the first stage of multinationalization and will soon add subsidiaries in other countries. The few firms that do not add more subsidiaries may best be treated as exceptions to the rule.

In the popular view all MNCs are alike. This is a misconception. All MNCs are no more cut from the same cloth than are domestic firms. Every MNC has its own look and its own personality. To come to grips with this rapidly expanding sector of the world economy, we must differentiate between types of MNCs. Some of the types are more numerous than others. Some are growing more rapidly. Some are even stagnant or decaying.

Some MNCs are motivated by profits, some by raw materials, some by markets, some by growth, some by diversification, some by the stability that diversification of markets and operating environments may offer. Many pursue several or all of these objectives. Furthermore, the objectives vary with time, with place, and with circumstances. From the market perspective, some MNCs cater to individual consumers, some to government procurement, some to the industrial sector, and some to the military. Some MNCs operate in a competitive marketing atmosphere, others in oligopolistic rivalry, and some in monopolistic autonomy.

Neither in structure nor in behavior are all the MNCs alike. Rather, they are very highly differentiated and varigated economic entities, each ranking as a complex organization and each possessing characteristics of its own. Therefore, logic demands that MNCs be analyzed not as a homogeneous mass, but rather in terms of typologies, the various models and the various categories of firms who share the commonality of operating simultaneously in many economies, but differing from one another in other important respects.

TYPES OF MNCs

Equity-Based MNCs

Many older MNCs obtained their multinational capacities through direct foreign investments. They have either built from ground up or bought the equity of the desired capital assets, such as assembly plants, pharmaceutical laboratories, department stores, banks, flour mills, or whatever operating facilities they use. Either way, they have become owners of these operating entities.

Equity ownership provides the basis for managerial control over the foreign-based entities and opens the way for their affiliation or integration with one another internationally by the headquarters firm. The fact that all the older MNCs and many new ones have followed the equity ownership route has created the impression that direct foreign investment is the only way for a firm to multinationalize. This is not true. Direct foreign investments are synonymous with MNCs but MNCs are no longer synonymous with direct investments.

The MNCs in which the managerial control derives from equity ownership of affiliated enterprises in different host economies fall into four main types:

1. *Resource-based companies.* The main mission of these companies is to produce raw materials, such as metallic ores, oil, rubber, and tropical plantation crops (bananas, coffee, dates). Many of these are among the very oldest MNCs, with roots in the colonial era. Although most of them have been thoroughly reformed and reorganized, they continue to be a source of sociopolitical conflict, as many host societies are striving for complete control of their natural resources (see Chapters 19 and 20).

2. *Public utility companies.* These companies, which include military arsenals, differ from other economic sectors in that they are either natural monopolies or they serve a monopsonistic (single buyer) market such as the national airline of the host nation. A relationship between a monopolistic producer and a monopsonistic

buyer is often typical for these MNCs, the MNC being the single or near single supplier and the national airline, the defense ministry, or the municipality the single buyer. Such monopolistic-monopsonistic relationships harbor both the opportunities and incentives for bribery and corruption.

3. *Manufacturing companies.* These were the largest growth sector of multinational business from the 1950s to the 1970s. In many instances the host countries were instrumental in attracting the manufacturing MNCs. Foreign investment incentive programs have been the common device for luring inbound industrial investments. Intricate schemes of tax privilege, protection against import competition, relaxation of foreign exchange restrictions, and government loan guarantees are parts of such arrangements. Compared to the extractive industries, public utility, and military suppliers, the multinational manufacturing sector has been conspicuously absent from the political scene. The few troubles that have arisen in this sector have been caused more by faulty organizational structures and managerial inexperience in international affairs than by the phenomenon of the MNC as such.

4. *Service industry MNCs.* The largest components of this category are banks, carriers, retail stores (Woolworth, Sears, Takashimaya), and some hotel chains. Consulting, accounting, and advertising firms and firms that sell similar management services have followed the multinationalization of industrial companies.

Technology-Based MNCs

A new generation of MNCs has started to emerge in which the source of multinational managerial control is technology, including management expertise, instead of ownership of operating assets. These are known as nonequity MNCs. The hotel, mining, and construction industries have pioneered this new generation of MNCs. They offer an increasingly viable alternative to the older, equity-based model.

Management Contracts   The main vehicles of the nonequity MNC are long-term contracts with owners of suitable operating facilities, such as hotels or mining properties. Often the contracts are either formally or informally sanctioned by the host government. Under such a contract the owners will let the MNC take over the possession and management of the business and the MNC will obligate itself to share profits with the owners by some agreed-upon formula.

Many international hotel companies, for example, own none or very few hotels in their global chain. The buildings and grounds are mostly owned by a variety of local national companies or other financial interests, all quite distinct from the MNC that runs the hotels. These separately owned properties are bound into a multinational system by a set of long-term contracts that not only transfer the management of the hotels to the company but also provide for profit sharing to assure a strong incentive for efficiency. A number of the international equity-based hotel chains have adopted this model for their new expansion, thus creating mixed MNCs in which some affiliates have ownership ties and others nonequity contractual ties.

The management contract model of the hotel industry has become the basis for a number of variations that are rapidly gaining status not only in other service industries but also in the manufacturing and high-technology sectors, where they have the potential for even greater importance.

Production Sharing Arrangements In mining, crude oil production, and other resource-based businesses, the profit sharing may be replaced by output sharing. These arrangements provide that the MNC not only may produce in an extractive sector (iron ore, coal, petroleum), but also must meet specific obligations for the development of indigenous supplier industries, for training engineers and managers, and for keeping pace with developments in the industry concerned. This formula rests on an agreed sharing of the output of the venture. For instance, if the contract provides for a 40:60 output sharing of a mining property, the MNC will retain 40 percent of the tonnage and turn over to the owners or, what is more typical, market on the owners' behalf the remaining 60 percent.

With rampant inflation and fluctuating raw materials prices, the product sharing is generally preferred by host countries in resource-based industries. Public attitudes in many countries have become negative toward foreign ownership of natural resources. The production sharing arrangement alleviates these objections while permitting the employment of the superior techniques and know-how that a MNC can often provide; at the same time, the MNC gains access to the natural resources it needs.

In a broader sense, the emerging production sharing agreements are contracts in kind where long-term economic growth considerations, such as raw material or energy needs of the developed partner, or the industrialization objectives of the developing partner, displace the traditional short-term profit considerations. As such, these contracts promise to become by mutual necessity long-term international linkages that offer greater stability and more cross-boundary cooperation than the equity-based MNCs.

Industrial Lease Agreements These are contracts under which an owner, sometimes a government corporation, leases a complete industrial facility, such as a factory or chemical laboratory, to a MNC. The rent consists normally of a fixed annual sum plus a scale of payments based on the output of the plant. Such lease arrangements are as yet limited to manufacturing activities in which there have been rapid technological advances or in which complex specialized facilites are required.

Technology Transfer Agreements In the high technology industries (electronics, aircraft, computers, biochemicals) where the host government lays the highest priority on indigenous production capability, the new mode is a joint venture between the MNC, whose responsibility it is to provide the technology, and one or several indigenous companies, which are responsible for financing, often with government assistance.

The communist countries (U.S.S.R., Poland, Romania, and others) have spearheaded negotiations to obtain from Western firms technologies for high-volume, low-cost products that are internationally competitive in quality. The agreements completed so far cover not only the transfer of hard technology (patent and trademark rights) but also efficient adaptation of a product to suit the strategic objectives of the host enterprise, effective development of actual production capacity by long-term enterprise-to-enterprise cooperation after the plant starts production, and marketing of the output outside the host country.

Though still modest in total business volume compared to equity-based MNCs, the industrial leases and technology transfer agreements signify the entrance of the technology-based MNC into the manufacturing sector, which the equity-based model has held as an exclusive domain in the past.

THE STRUCTURE OF MNCs

Regardless of which of these alternatives the contract provides, the organizational effect is the same. It transfers the management of the operation to the MNC and motivates the latter to maximize its productivity. This calls for the application of the most efficient alternatives in technology and management know-how available to the MNC.

Objections to foreign ownership of major business firms have risen in many countries. Simultaneously, the national goals and economic development plans of host countries are placing greater priority on technology imports and modernization of management practices. These trends are favoring the new nonequity model at the expense of the old ownership model for multinational growth. It is no surprise, then, that equity-based MNCs are showing signs of branching out into nonequity operations.

But this point should not be overstated. The equity-based MNC is still by far the most dominant type. The political resistance that it has met is gradually being eroded. More and more host countries are becoming also headquarters countries, through the establishment of their own equity-based MNCs. As a rule, political aversion to MNCs is inversely correlated with a nation's own holdings of foreign investments. Acquisition of MNCs makes the condemnation of other countries' MNCs hypocritical and self-destructive.

The equity-based and technology-based models do not present an either-or proposition. The two basic alternatives can be used separately or in combination with each other. In either case, the final outcome is the same: a cluster of production and marketing entities distributed multinationally but subject to managerial control and coordination by the headquarters company. Figure 9.1 presents two such clusters. The four-country complex consists of a headquarters company and three foreign-based affiliates, each located in a different country. The four units of the structure function together. From the headquarters company (and country) flow direction and control, and from the affiliates come products, revenues, and information. Among all the entities (affiliates as well as the headquarters company) there are operational interties for cooperation in planning, technical services, and intracompany trade. The

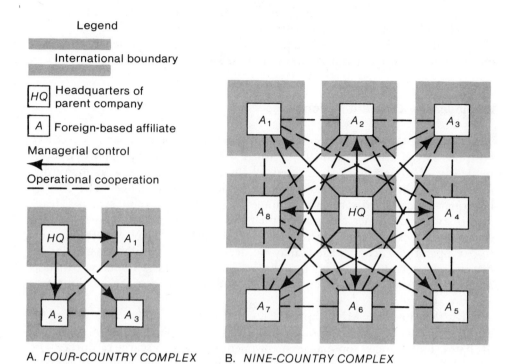

A. *FOUR-COUNTRY COMPLEX*   B. *NINE-COUNTRY COMPLEX*

Figure 9.1   Spatial Models of Multinational Enterprises

nine-country complex is analogous but has a much more intricate network of interties among its national entities. Both these models are *monocentric*, in that all affiliates have a direct relationship to the headquarters company, and *equiponderant* in that the affiliates are assumed to be comparable in size, character, and managerial autonomy. Neither of these simplifying assumptions needs to be present in any particular MNC.

CHARACTERISTIC DIFFERENCES OF MNCs AND UNCs

The acquisition of operating entities outside the headquarters country induces other changes that further differentiate the MNC from the UNC.

Global Perspective

Top management planning and strategies can no longer be confined to the opportunities present in the domestic economy but are extended to include the opportunities offered by other nations' economies. The range of management choice is thus greatly expanded, and management decisions become correspondingly complicated. To equal the task, managers must expand their own horizons and develop international sophistication. Domestic data sources no longer suffice, nor do domestic education and business experience. Foreign, international, and comparative know-how become imperative.

Employees of Different Nationalities

The executive corps itself becomes multinational. Sooner or later, executive positions in the affiliates tend to be filled with host country nationals. Consequently, the operating management of the MNC will include as many different nationalities as there are host countries to its affiliates. The MNCs headquarters can hardly remain immune to the differing value systems, leadership styles, and other cultural peculiarities each nationality contributes. In the early phases, the growing pluralism on the affiliate level, where the day-to-day operations are managed, may be dealt with by employing experts on different host countries. The function of such experts is to serve either as advisors to headquarters executives or as liaisons between the headquarters and the affiliates.

By the time the MNC approaches maturity, the more able among its affiliate managers will have outgrown the top positions at their particular affiliates. Experienced top management talent is always a scarce resource. The MNC's best interests dictate that these promising affiliate managers be promoted to more responsible positions with the MNC structure. That means transfer either to another host country where the company has larger operations or to headquarters.

It is an inherent tendency, therefore, for the MNCs to add host country nationals to its managerial cadres both at middle and top management levels. To be sure, nationalistic and cultural prejudices retard the process, but over time superior performance erodes the barriers.

That the work force of an MNC must include all the different host country nationalities is axiomatic. How else can affiliates of a factory, store, or bank function in different countries? Here again the MNC differs from a UNC in both the resource base—the size and variety of labor supply—and the knowledge and experience required of managers to recruit, motivate, and compensate the work force.

Internationally Adapted Products

The MNCs have tended to adapt their products to differences in consumption requirements of different countries. The adaptation may be rather simple, such as putting prepared foods into metric size packages and using local languages for labeling, or very extensive, such as bringing out an entirely different model of a piece of machinery, a car, or a refrigerator. Technically the UNCs could do the same, but economically it seldom pays. Since the UNC's access to any foreign market can be only through exporting, the UNC is exposed to the risk that higher tariffs or other trade restrictions may cut off its access to the particular market. The UNC is, therefore, reluctant to invest heavily in product adjustment, not to mention the production of competely different models, for foreign markets. The MNC, on the other hand, is not similarily constrained. Through its affiliates it is a permanent resident of the host countries' economies. Its access to those markets is assured.

EVOLUTION OF MNCs

Colonial Companies

The MNC has often been confused with the companies expanding nations set up during the colonial era to exploit their overseas colonies. These were giant companies. The mother countries granted them charters to establish trading and production monopolies in particular colonies and endowed them with political powers of the state to enforce compliance with their policies by native people. Among the best-known commercial companies of that era were the British East Indian Company, the Levant Company, the Dutch East India Company, and the Hudson's Bay Company.

The following quotation reflects the nature and scope of their activities:

> The merchants of [the British East India Company] received the entire rights over all of India that they could bring under their sway. . . . As its director, Sir Josiah Child, once boasted, the India Company was "a sovereign state in itself." It declared war on the Mogul Empire, it had a fleet, an army, and fortified settlements, it could coin money and make laws. Businessmen administered India in their own fashion, and a very lively fashion it was for a long time.[1]

Objectives and Behavior of Colonial Companies These companies exploited the colonies to supply the mother country with raw materials that could be converted into manufactures for export or substituted for imports. Colonies were considered an appendix to the mother country's economy. Trade of the colonies was regulated by strict laws aimed at centralizing all exports and imports of each colony upon the home country. Diversion of trade to other areas was minimized by discriminatory tariffs.

Economic development in the colonies was limited to products wanted in the home country for consumption or re-export; duplication of home country industries and development of competing products were suppressed. There was very little transfer of technology or management know-how from the colonial company to the indigenous society. The colonial company existed in isolated enclaves. The investment multiplier was rendered inoperative by the enclave strategy combined with the exploitative goals of the firm.

---

1. P. T. Ellsworth, *The International Economy* (New York: The Macmillan Company, 1964), p. 33.

The colonial company was endowed by the crown with political powers, often reinforced by military force. It had power over the indigenous society. The company did not have to adapt itself to the society; it was the colony that had to make the adaptation. The company's privileged status and political powers enabled it to impose its own objectives and motives upon the native population.

To confuse the contemporary MNC with the colonial company is a serious error. The vast majority of MNCs have come into being in postcolonial days. They have no political or legal, not to mention military, power over the host government. They must apply for permission to enter and to qualify for a charter from the host government before any organization can be set up. They remain under the sovereign jurisdiction of their host nation.

Any MNC misguided enough to endeavor to emulate the colonial company's behavior would find itself promptly facing expropriation proceedings and would consider itself lucky if permitted to leave the host country without the loss of its investments. Most such corporate efforts are stillborn in the contemporary world. An expatriate enterprise that fails to justify itself and to make a genuine contribution to the host country's best interest as conceived by its government and people is disqualified before it ever comes into being. Contrary to the colonial era, the political power now lies with the host countries, not with the company. The MNCs only power is its economic power, its business muscle, which at times can be considerable. But this power can be exercised only within the legal, economic, and social structures of the host society. In Chapters 13 and 14 we shall study how the conflicts and accommodations between the MNC and the host nation are worked out.

Management Attitudes During the Colonial Era   The colonial company's privileges and power aroused envy, and its methods and attitudes were copied and imitated by business everywhere. The colonial company became a role model to overseas business operations during the colonial era. How the colonial companies acted set the norms for overseas business behavior. That these norms seem atrocious to the contemporary reader make them no less valid or dominant in the colonial setting. Historical facts, especially those involving mores and values, must be interpreted in the context of their own time.

The colonial company has been extinct since the 1960s, but its shadow lingers on, confusing both the public and the manager. A number of today's MNCs have their roots in the colonial era. Some, particularly British, Dutch, Belgian, and French headquartered firms, are direct descendants of colonial companies. Others, such as the early international ventures of some U.S., Swiss, and Swedish companies, though never legally chartered as colonial companies, often had adopted the colonial company's behavior.

To what extent the early MNCs were patterned after the colonial companies was a joint function of geography and product specialization. In Europe, due to educational and technological parities among nations, colonial exploitive practices were politically infeasible. Therefore, international business ventures were based on arm's length dealings and were not significantly different from their contemporary counterparts. In the other continents that was seldom true. There the colonial format dominated.

The companies in extractive industries (mining, petroleum, and tropical agriculture) were the most apt to adopt the colonial model, with its ethnocentric managerial attitudes and exploitive operating policies. Several expropriations and nationalizations by postcolonial governments in the extractive sector are attributable, at least in part, to this inheritance.

Manufacturing firms were generally less directly committed to the colonial company model. Since their international success was derived from their technical superiority rather than from the control of host country natural resources, a sharp contrast with the mining, oil, and tropical agriculture companies, the manufacturing companies had from the start much less in common with the colonial company.

Early International Ventures of U.S. Business

Throughout its colonial era the United States had served England as an agricultural outland, supplying the metropolitan motherland with cheap food and raw materials. The British imperial policy was to prevent industrial development in the colonies and to limit their trade to the imperium, centered on London, by severely taxing extraimperial trade through a punitive system of tariffs. Nevertheless, a considerable amount of industrial development did take place in the American colonies.

When independence came, the newborn nation had already achieved what in the late eighteenth century was a semi-industrial stage. The immenseness of the new nation and its rapidly growing home markets fully absorbed all indigenous industrial energies for the first hundred years of its existence. Export and import trade developed, but very little else. It was, therefore, only toward the end of the nineteenth century that U.S. business made its debut on the international business scene.

Markets for Inventions   Unlike the European colonial companies, the early U.S. direct investors abroad were not seeking raw materials and foodstuffs but markets and profits. The frontier was still open and untold natural treasures remained untapped; there was no shortage of natural resources. Technolgy and markets, however, were another matter. Interestingly enough, the search for technology led to the discovery of new markets for technological inventions and ultimately to foreign manufacturing operations. The U.S. companies that pioneered in multinational industrial operations in the late nineteenth century invariably received their initial impetus from some technical invention or product that, on the one hand, confronted the company with the opportunity to acquire a legal monopoly on an almost global scale through patent rights and, on the other hand, impelled it to establish foreign-based production facilities to prevent local imitators from pre-empting these markets. For example, Singer obtained a patent on his sewing machine in 1851; fifteen years later his company broke ground with its first overseas factory in England. As the patent came under heavy competitive pressure in the continent, Singer affiliates in other European countries followed in a rapid succession. In those days the main markets lay almost wholly in Europe.

Thus we find among the first U.S. direct foreign investors manufacturers of sewing machines, telephones, electric lamps, airbrakes, and cameras, all of which had sprung from U.S. inventions or innovations. Western Union, Bell Telephone, Edison, and National Cash Register had almost identical early histories to Singer, though in their later development each moved along a different path. Each was based on an invention, acquired patents, and proceeded to establish its corporate presence in Europe to prevent competition from cashing in on the invention.

Not too different were the histories of Westinghouse and Kodak. George Westinghouse was first to perfect the airbrake, which revolutionized railroad transportation in his day. Since the airbrake was developed after railroad networks had been introduced or were significantly expanded in all industrialized countries, it had an immense ready-made market. In a few years the company's operations spanned the European continent from London to St. Petersburg. Kodak had built the first successful U.S. camera. When he linked up with Eastman's photographic plate firm of England in the 1890s, a marriage was consummated from which the present worldwide Eastman Kodak company has evolved.

Among other late nineteenth century U.S. manufacturers who entered into international business were International Harvester (agricultural machinery), Otis Brothers (elevators), Babcock and Wilcox (boilers), Remington (typewriters), Burroughs (calculators), Yale (cylinder locks), and Colt (guns). Again, they all were motivated by the particular technical advantages that derived from patentable inventions.

Oil Companies   Oil companies were catapulted into a global orbit by the invention of the internal combustion engine, which completely revolutionized transportation. Both the motive for and the method of international expansion in this industry were quite different from what we have seen to this point. The initial push for oil companies to globalize was the search for oil. To the present time the oil companies have remained, essentially, seekers and exploiters of petroleum resources in their international ventures. For a long time they bore a close resemblance to the colonial companies, whose shadow has never ceased to haunt them.

Legal Impetus   A new impetus to internationalize was provided by the Sherman Antitrust Act of 1890. This law prohibited collusion among business firms in restraint of trade. The rapid industrialization of the U.S. economy in the second half of the last century had inflicted upon society clandestine monopolistic schemes to bleed the consumer that threatened the economic as well as the social health of the nation.

In an attempt to curtail corporate malpractices, the Sherman Act prohibited cartels, trusts, and other forms of collusion in restraint of trade among business firms that were potential competitors. Business responded to the law in two ways. First, since cooperation was outlawed but mergers were not, a wave of corporate mergers swept the land, in a short time creating a number of large firms. These represented unprecedented concentrations of corporate power. Their expansionary force was soon felt abroad, when the U.S. "mammoths," as U.S. corporations are still often called abroad, embarked upon the practice of buying up foreign firms. Although temporarily interrupted during periods of political upheaval such as the two world wars, the policy of acquiring foreign-based affiliates has continued to date.

Cartellistic Advantage   In the early days, the U.S. judicial authorities interpreted the Sherman Act as being limited in its scope to domestic business activities. Collusion, including formal cartel agreements between U.S. firms or between U.S. and foreign firms, was a matter of official indifference when such actions were taken abroad and did not directly affect the domestic market. Thus, collusion, outlawed in the United States by the Sherman Act, could be practiced with impunity in foreign markets by U.S. firms. This provided a special stimulus for international expansion. It also broadened the base for such expansion.

While the direct foreign investors to this point had been primarily manufacturers of patentable products, they were now traders in nonpatentable goods and service industries in search of special marketing advantages. Their sudden appearance sharply underscores the lure that the relatively greater freedom to engage in market sharing, price fixing, and competitive retaliation seemed to have offered. Life insurance companies were the first to appear on the scene, and they rapidly enveloped all European countries during the 1880s and 1890s. Ocean shipping was not far behind. It started with J. P. Morgan's purchase of Leyland Shipping Lines in 1901 and was quickly followed by others.

Foreign Operations Atypical to Early Industry   Although a number of U.S. firms did move abroad in the early years, they were a small minority. The vast majority of firms were preoccupied with a growing domestic market. The principal exceptions were oil companies, mining companies, and some tropical agriculture plantations. At the end of 1940, U.S. direct investments amounted only to $7 billion, most of it in petroleum properties. Very few U.S. firms had invested in overseas manufacturing ventures designed to supply the local markets, and in service industries the idea of multinationalizing was yet to be invented. The immensity of the domestic market was still overwhelming, and isolationism discouraged international business involvements.

The Big Push

Systematic expansion of business operations beyond national boundaries started to spread in the 1950s. Once under way the process picked up speed

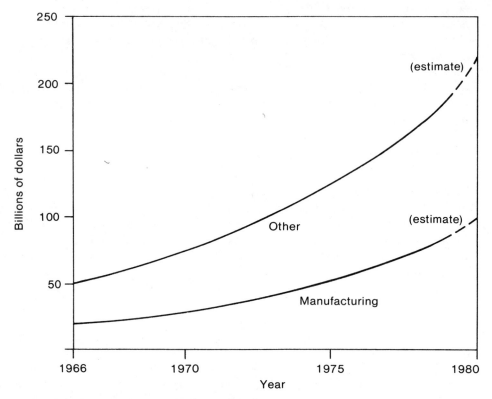

Figure 9.2   U.S. Direct Investment Abroad

Source: U.S. Department of Commerce, *Survey of Current Business,* February 1981, p. 41.

rapidly. The biggest push came in the 1960s, when the growth rate of international production was more than twice the growth rate of domestic output. But the swell of the 1960s was mainly a U.S. phenomenon. The new MNCs were headquartered in the United States.

In terms of activity, the greatest growth, more than two-fifths, was in manufacturing; the petroleum industry was second, with about one-fifth, followed by mining and smelting, construction, public utilities, and service industries.

In terms of geography, Western Europe absorbed about a third and Canada another third of the affiliates. Europe has been gaining significantly since the creation of the Common Market. Latin America, too, attracted the MNCs, but its relative importance does not show because of the exceptional growth in Europe and Canada. Japan was a latecomer to the MNC picture, but its importance has overtaken all but Europe in recent years.

Economic theory postulates that the movement of productive factors is guided by their relative scarcities, which determine their marginal productivities at different localities. Since capital is very scarce relative to labor and land in developing countries, a prediction based on the theory would show direct

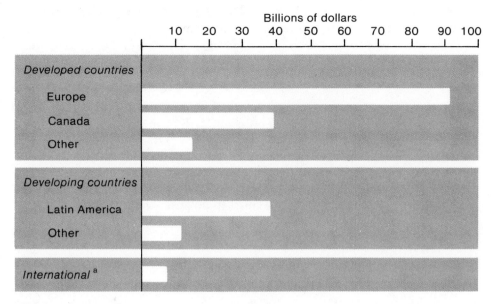

^aInvestment in enterprises under the jurisdiction of international and supranational bodies (United Nations, various common markets, etc.).

Figure 9.3   U.S. Direct Investment Abroad by Area (1979)

Source: U.S. Department of Commerce, *Survey of Current Business,* February 1981, p. 41.

investments flowing primarily from the developed to the less developed parts of the world. Actual data do not conform with the theoretical expectations. Direct investors from the United States and other industrial countries found one another more attractive than the less developed areas for corporate growth. Nearly four-fifths of U.S. direct foreign investments went to the industrial countries and only one-fifth to the developing nations, many official inducements notwithstanding. A similar preference is reflected in the foreign investment statistics of other industrial countries. The tendency of capital to avoid and often even to escape from the poor countries is an old economic paradox, to which we shall return to later chapters.

Another characteristic of the period was the shift of emphasis from primary to secondary and tertiary levels of production. Investments in mining and smelting increased in dollar volume but declined relative to aggregate direct investment. Petroleum investments, although bypassed by manufacturing investments, remained a major component. Both the mining and particularly the petroleum figures concealed the escalation effect since, in contrast to earlier periods, their foreign operations shifted more and more from serving the U.S. market with crude and semicrude products to meeting overseas requirements for finished goods both locally and on an export basis. For example, petroleum industry affiliates reduced their exports to the United States to below 1 percent of their total annual sales in the 1960s. The shift in marketing objectives was accompanied by changes in product mix and an increased emphasis on non-extractive aspects in vertically integrated companies.

The Growth of Foreign-Based MNCs

In the 1970s the patterns changed. As stagflation increased and the economy hovered between recession and depression, U.S. companies cut back their plans for foreign expansion; some even divested. Other nations' businesses chose the opposite course, namely, to accelerate their foreign investments. Their prescription for economic stagnation was international expansion, a leap forward to cut the lead of the U.S. MNCs and to capture for themselves the superior leverage that the MNCs seemed to possess. Despite much dogmatic exhortation against the MNCs, factual data consistently pointed to the greater

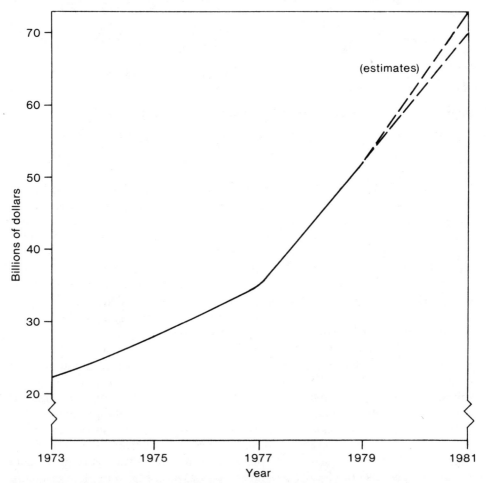

Figure 9.4   Foreign Direct Investment in the United States

Source: U.S. Department of Commerce, *Survey of Current Business,* February 1981, p. 46.

profitability of the MNCs compared to UNCs having the same technology and industry characteristics.

A large share of the non-U.S. companies' foreign investments have gravitated to the United States. In 1971 their U.S. affiliates were estimated to be worth between $14 and $15 billion; in 1980 they represented about $40 billion. Names such as Bayer, CIBA, Dunlop, Electrolux, Honda, Massey-Ferguson, Nestlé, Olivetti, Pechiney, Shell, SKF, Volkswagen, and Yamaha reflect the diversity of business activities carried out by non-U.S. companies in the United States. It is not coincidental that the acquisition of Atlantic Richfield by British Petroleum ranked as the largest international investment transaction of the world in 1969. Several other very sizable foreign acquisition prospects have made headlines in the U.S. press in recent years, including Brown Bovari of Switzerland, Mitsubishi of Japan, ICI of England, BASF of Germany, and scores of other companies from many countries.

Continuation and probable acceleration of the inflow of foreign direct investments to the United States are pointed up by the fact that more and more foreign firms are setting up sales and service subsidiaries in this country, a step frequently followed within a few years by processing, assembly, or complete production facilities.

Global Assimilation

As a result, today the MNCs are a near global phenomenon. They may be headquartered in any industrial country and in a growing number of developing

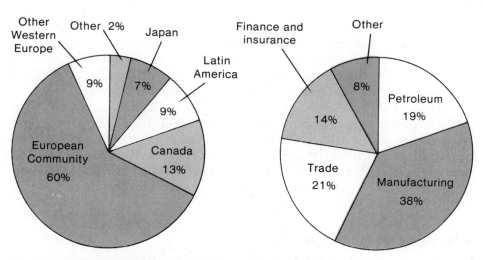

A. *BY AREA OF ORIGIN*   B. *BY INDUSTRY*

**Figure 9.5 Foreign Direct Investment in the United States
by Area and by Industry (1979)**

Source: U.S. Department of Commerce, *Survey of Current Business*, February 1981.

nations, such as Argentina, Brazil, Singapore, South Korea, India, and others. Even the communist nations are participating in this development. Whether their ideological adversion to private control of productive enterprises can be sufficiently molded to make full-fledged Marxian MNCs possible is doubtful. However, some communist facsimiles to MNCs are already in existence, as we shall see in Chapters 22 and 23.

SUMMARY

The basic definition of a multinational company is a number of affiliated business establishments located in different countries but subject to a common managerial control. The control may be based on equity ownership or on technology, including management know-how. In both categories are several subsets of MNCs, dependent upon the economic sector, level of technology, and host country characteristics.

The technology-based firms, often referred to as the new generation of MNCs, are expected to gain far greater significance in the future, mainly due to host country dislike of foreign ownership.

As a firm transcends national boundaries, it changes in form and substance. The spectrums of managerial choice and responsibilities are widened and diversified, the incentives and impediments to success multiplied, and the norms of corporate behavior varied. Its multitude of different national environments imposes unyielding demands on MNCs for adaptation of its management policies, assimilation of host country values and peculiarities, and reconciliation of conflicting forces. As a result, both the personnel and products of an MNC undergo changes that would have been unnecessary had the firm remained a UNC.

The MNC should not be confused with colonial companies. The two are very different. Since after decolonization some colonial companies were converted to MNCs, the mistaken impression was created that MNCs are the direct decendents of colonial companies. The vast majority of MNCs are of postcolonial origin and bear no resemblance to the colonial firms.

U.S. MNCs had their start at the end of the nineteenth century. The largest ventures were based on technical invention. Later, the search for oil and antitrust laws provided added impetus. The process of multinationalization remained modest until the 1950s; since then it has accelerated and spread to become a global phenomenon. The present organizational types and behavioral characteristics of MNCs have evolved mainly since 1960.

FOR REVIEW AND DISCUSSION

1. Why is managerial control more important than ownership or any other factor in defining a MNC?

2. What are the most important differences between equity-based and technology-based MNCs?

3. Why would it be fallacious to consider a firm with export markets but no foreign-based affiliate a MNC?

4. Can you think of an actual firm that uses both the equity-based and technology-based models? If not, try to construe such a hypothetical firm.

5. Both its personnel and products undergo change when a firm becomes multinational. Discuss.

6. The colonial company is dead but its ghost still haunts MNCs. Elaborate.

7. To what degree might expropriations and nationalizations of MNC affiliates have been caused by colonial practices?

8. Do U.S. MNCs still enjoy a cartel advantage over domestic firms, as they did in early years?

9. Describe the so-called big push of MNC growth.

10. Identify some foreign MNCs that have been active in the United States for some years. How are their products perceived by U.S. consumers?

10

Conceptual Perspectives on Multinational Business Expansion

*E*xpansion of operations beyond national frontiers is no longer exceptional corporate behavior. More and more firms in the United States and elsewhere are pursuing multinationalization as a general strategy. Gone is the notion that investments abroad must be unusually compelling or exceptionally attractive. Gone also is the notion that export and import trades represent the only normal conduits to foreign markets.

The new concept of normalcy denies trade even any precedence over investment for capturing foreign markets. Both are equally legitimate. Nor does the contemporary company view trade and investments as mutually exclusive. The old textbook maxim that a firm either exports or invests but not both no longer holds. In today's boardrooms trade and investments are seen as constructively interactive phenomena. Foreign trade is expected to spawn foreign investment, and foreign investment to generate more foreign trade; therefore, they can be pursued simultaneously. Multinational operating structures are not only acceptable and natural, but indicators of success.

MNCs have multiplied and continue to grow. The new managerial concepts have been translated into a new reality. In the process the MNCs have garnered both glamour and notoriety and have become highly controversial. What explains the phenomenon of the MNC? Why was it born? Why does it keep spreading? Is it beneficial or detrimental, an agent for good or for evil? Such questions have inevitably arisen as the MNC has emerged as the dominant institution in more and more types of international business activities. At stake are not only business interests. Governments, labor unions, and consumers are all affected. The answers are also important from a purely scientific point of view. They cut widely and deeply into the fabric of traditionally accepted truths about international economics and world politics.

Volumes have been devoted to the MNC in recent years. They throw much light on its origins and growth, but they have also created many contradictions. As the debate has developed, it has become increasingly clear that the MNC defies any simple explanation. It is a multifaceted phenomenon.

We shall take a systematic tour through the best theoretical and empirical explanations of the MNC up to now. In this chapter we will deal mainly with

185

theoretical and political concepts. The managerial viewpoint will be the subject of Chapter 11.

NEOCLASSICAL ECONOMIC THEORY

In economic theory MNCs are manifestations of direct foreign investments and nothing else. As such, they must be explained by the same conceptual framework that is applicable to the behavior of foreign investments. Thus, a logical point to start is with the neoclassical theory. Since it embodies the accumulated learning of the preclassical and classical eras, it obviates the need to focus on the realities of the past yet provides both a connection to as well as a contrast with the present. From the neoclassical models of economic theory we can proceed to the latest proposals to modify the theory to address more directly the question of MNCs.

The Essence of the Theory

The neoclassical theory regards international investment as a complement if not a corollary of commodity trade. It explains both trade and investment flows across international boundaries on the basis of differential resource endowments, which give rise to differential costs of production as well as to differential incomes or returns of productive factors—land, labor, entrepreneurship, and capital. These differentials provide the incentives for nations to specialize their economic activities according to their comparative advantages, exporting what they have in relative abundance and importing what they have in relative shortage.

Foreign investment flows, thus, are governed by the general principle of *differential factor income* or *factor return*. The theory assumes capital and labor to be mutually interchangeable. If wages are high more capital will be used and if wages are low more labor will be used; or, if the return on capital is high more labor is used and if the cost of capital is low more capital will be used. If a company has a comparative overabundance of capital relative to labor, for example, it will have two choices, either to import foreign workers or to export capital to a country that has excess labor but suffers from a capital shortage. Since capital is normally more mobile than labor, not to mention land and other natural resources, the relative abundance of capital leads to foreign investment.[1]

The export of capital makes it less abundant in the country of origin and increases its price there in the form of interest and profits. Conversely, the import of capital alleviates the capital deficiency in the country of destination, thereby reducing the returns on capital investments. The international flow

---

1. Bertil Orlin, *Interregional and International Trade* (Cambridge: Harvard University Press, 1935), p. 169.

of capital will continue until both the cost of capital and return on investment are equalized in both countries.[2] Given the capital-labor interchangeability, the returns on capital investment can be equalized only if wages, too, are equalized in the two countries involved. At this point international investment will stop. There is nothing further to be gained by foreign investment since the cost of capital, wages, and profits will all be identical in both countries.[3]

Consequently, according to the neoclassical theory the international investment process is a self-starting as well as a self-liquidating proposition. For developing nations, its implication is that the rich industrial countries export capital and capital intensive goods, and the subindustrial countries export labor intensive goods and labor where this is politically and sociologically possible.

The Applicability of Neoclassical Theory

Up to the 1950s neoclassical theory was generally regarded as an accurate statement of how the international economy in reality functioned. Of course, our ability to test the theory factually then was limited compared to what we can do today. The facts were simply not available. Statistical data-gathering systems of most nations were in a rudimentary state and those statistics that did exist were published years after they were gathered.

International investments were small in volume and relatively unimportant to the world economy. Portfolio investments dominated; the international investors were primarily buyers of foreign securities—stocks, bonds, and other commercial paper. The purchase of such securities gave the investor an indirect claim to the assets of the foreign business or government agency that had floated the securities involved, but the investor acquired no specific tangible property, nor did he acquire any direct voice in the management of the foreign firm or agency. Portfolio investment is an indirect investment.

Today the picture is quite different. The lion's share of international investments takes the form of direct investment; funds are used to purchase operating entities such as factories, mines, warehouses, hotels, banks, and other productive facilities. The investor acquires not only specific tangible assets in the host country but also managerial rights over these assets.

Consistency with Portfolio Investments   The portfolio investments fit well into the neoclassical theory. Outbound investments (capital exports) can be regarded as imports of securities; conversely, inbound investments (capital imports) can be regarded as exports of securities. Thus, the transactions of indirect investment parallel the transactions of commodity trade, the only difference being that the cargo consists of securities instead of commodities. Furthermore, portfolio transactions, like trade transactions, represent essen-

2. Paul A. Samuelson, "International Trade and Equalization of Factor Prices," *Economic Journal* 58:163–164, 1948.

3. Robert A. Mundell, "International Trade and Factor Mobility," *American Economic Review* 47: 321–335, 1957.

tially short-term relationships. A portfolio investment may have a life of only a few days, weeks, or months. When a particular stock or bond can be sold for a higher price on the American Stock Exchange than on the Paris Bourse, portfolio investments will flow from France to the United States. When the reverse is true, the French will become the recipients of these investments. All this is quite analogous to trade in tangible goods.

Inconsistencies with Direct Investments and MNC Assets   The same cannot be said about direct investments. There are very real difficulties in trying to fit them into the neoclassical theory. The direct investor buys specific tangible assets that possess the capacity to produce goods or services in the host country. A direct investment represents a long-term commitment of capital, which can be recouped only by the productive use of the enterprise acquired by the investment. As a practical matter, the amortization of a direct investment takes the form of depreciation charges, which are included as cost of the goods sold by the enterprise. To recoup the entire investment, the operating assets of the enterprise must be used for the period of their economic life, which normally runs into years or even decades. Hence, direct investments are not comparable to commodity trade, as are portfolio investments.

A second shortcoming of the traditional theory is that it equates foreign investment with international capital movements; it does not differentiate between capital movements and MNCs' assets. In fact, foreign direct investments by MNCs are far greater than the net capital outflows from their headquarter countries. Even the MNCs of the United States, the most capital-rich country, have never exported enough capital to equal the growth of their foreign assets. A significant share has always come from foreign sources, mainly through borrowing and reinvestment of affiliates' profits.

Furthermore, direct foreign investments are becoming more and more enmeshed with local investments. In early years direct foreign investments took the form of wholly-owned subsidiaries or branches of the parent firm; local participation was rare and insignificant in volume. Today an increasing number of MNC affiliates have some type of local participation—private shareholders, joint venture partners, or public agencies. A number of MNCs have even gone so far as to adopt the policy of deliberately limiting their ownership in any affiliate to a minority position (less than 50 percent of equity). The trend is clearly in the direction of joint ownership of foreign and domestic investments. Thus, the line between the two has started to fade.

Inconsistency with Cross-Investments   Another serious contradiction to the traditional economic theory is posed by the rise of crossinvestments: a U.S. pharmaceuticals company investing in England and a British manufacturer doing the same in the United States, or a French chemical firm investing in Switzerland while its Swiss competitor invests in France. If sectoral differentials in rates of return were the cause of international investments, such simultaneous investments in opposite directions would not take place. Clearly, two countries cannot have the highest rate in the same industry.

In the 1920s and 1930s, international cross-investments were few in number and small in consequence. Theoreticians dismissed them as exceptions that proved the rule, attributed either to lack of information or to investor eccentricities. In the recent past, particularly from 1960 onward, cross-investments have become commonplace: they now span the globe. No longer can they be shrugged off as corporate eccentricities or exceptions to the rule. They are the rule. A better explanation is needed.

The reason for the divergence between the neoclassical theory and financial reality is not that the theory is faulty in its method or logic. Rather, the culprit is the changed reality. Both the forms and motivations of international business have grown in scope, organization, and complexity far beyond the precepts and boundaries of the neoclassical theory. We shall return to this point in Chapter 11.

NEW LINKAGES AND THE NEED FOR NEW THEORY

When we look for an explanation of the MNC as an institution, neoclassical theory has nothing at all to offer. For this theory, a company is a company, the concepts of an MNC and a UNC do not exist. International economic relations are limited to transboundary transactions between independent (uninational) firms—trade, payments, and investments.

An MNC is much more than a company dealing in transboundary transactions. It involves ownership rights and management responsibilities. The foreign-based company that is established by a direct investment or a management contract is not an isolated entity but an affiliate of the parent company (the investor) as well as of sister affiliates in other host countries. The international flows and connections between the parent company and the affiliate, and also between different affiliates, that the ownership and management aspects of a direct investment create, are fundamentally different from the transboundary flows and linkages created by trade and portfolio investments (see Figures 10.1 and 10.2 on pages 190 and 191). The latter are merely buying and selling transactions; the former encompass a wide spectrum of more or less permanent linkages. Technology, management know-how, patents and trademarks, production systems, components and finished products, cash and other credit instruments, organizational design, professional personnel and services, decision making processes, and even performance standards and norms of business behavior, all are in perpetual motion in both directions across the international borders among the different affiliates of an MNC.

These transboundary linkages are organic constituents of an MNC. They are the lifelines without which no multinational enterprise can survive. Severing these conduits would be analogous to cutting a person's arteries—what is left is a corpse. Where government policies or other conditions prevent the establishment of cross-boundary channels and systems, efficient management of the international company becomes impossible and the direct investment will not be made. Thus, much depends on how open or closed a country's

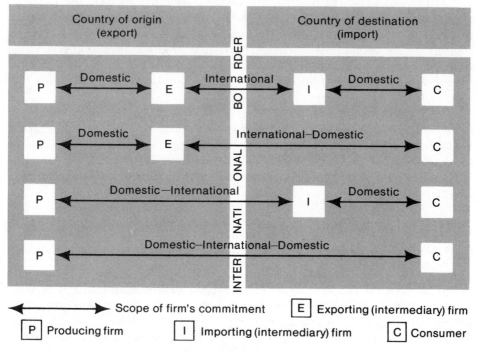

Figure 10.1   Channels of International Trade

border is and what policies are pursued with respect to the borders by the country's authorities.

This is not all. The fact that a country's borders are open for entrepreneurial purposes does not guarantee that MNCs will enter automatically. Just as an open gate guarantees no traffic, an open border and a permissive national policy in themselves cause no inbound investments. The openness of the country is a necessary precondition for but an insufficient explanation of either direct investment or MNC activity.

Investor's Advantage

The impetus for the investment process is the competitive advantage; the investor must be able to derive a perceived advantage by making the direct investment or the investment will not be made. It is a relative advantage, measured in terms of projected value of the investment relative to the value of alternative investment opportunities. In any particular instance, an MNC's primary criterion is to determine which investment opportunity promises it the greatest advantage. In this fundamental sense there is no difference between foreign investment and domestic investment; they are both competing for the available funds, which are always scarce.

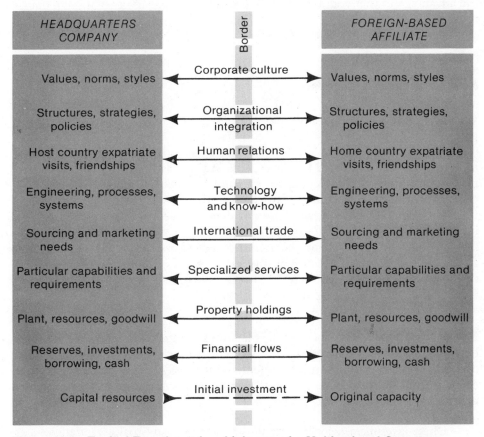

Figure 10.2 Typical Transboundary Linkages of a Multinational Company

Studies of the managerial decision-making process reveal that in practice foreign investment opportunities may be less thoroughly scrutinized than domestic ones because managers tend to be less familiar with foreign markets and more hesitant to commit substantial sums as readily as to the domestic market. They are also constrained by less confidence in their ability to foresee possible side effects of an investment, such as a reduction of exports. The perceived risk of foreign investment diminishes as the company gains experience in multinational operations and information on international opportunities becomes more readily available and reliable.[4]

Given no discrepancies in the information base, domestic and foreign investment opportunities are judged on their relative merits. For international direct investment to take place it must offer an advantage that is not available to the investor at home; for the investment to be directed to a particular country

4. Yair Aharoni, *The Foreign Investment Decision Process* (Cambridge: Harvard University Press, 1966).

the advantage in that country must be greater than that in other foreign countries. Thus, the crux of the theory of direct investment is to explain the causes and conditions that create the investor's advantage.

New Theoretical Hypotheses

Gambling Theory The traditionally oriented economists have yielded to the pressure of contradictions between economic theory and the MNC by grafting on to the neoclassical formulation a gambling theory. In this view, international investments may be caused by differences in the existing profit rates, or they may be probing ventures similar to a gambler's bets, in hope of a disproportionate return. As empirical support for this theory is cited the fact that multinational companies have used much of their overseas profits for further international growth, thus pyramiding their foreign earnings, much as a gambler leaves his winnings on the table. Needless to say, this overstretched analogy could be applied to any business that reinvests its earnings rather than distribute them as dividends. Most firms, uninational or multinational, have used profits as their principal source of growth.

Monopoly Theory Another new explanation of international investment has been derived from the theory of industrial organization. First propounded by Stephen Hymer, it has been subsequently embraced by some other traditional economists. Hymer's thesis asserts that the primary reason for foreign investment is monopoly power:

> Direct investment belongs more to the theory of industrial organization than that of international capital movements. The direct investor operates at a disadvantage in a foreign market, using foreign factors of production, and at a long distance from his decision-center. To overcome these disadvantages, he must have substantial advantage of some kind . . . the advantage may be in technology, management entry into the industry, and so on. If the direct investor can take over a competitor . . . he can establish a monopoly which may prove costly to the economy.[5]

Although it is undoubtedly true in some isolated cases, the general validity of this theory cannot be factually verified. First, the *domestic advantage doctrine*, the assumption that it is inherently more costly and less efficient for a company to operate foreign subsidiaries than domestic production units, is not supportable by the record. Foreign-based subsidiaries compare favorably both with headquarters and host country's firms in terms of costs, profits, and any other objective measures of performance. Second, factual evidence contradicts the proposition that foreign investors have a greater propensity to seek mo-

---

5. Stephen Hymer, "The Multinational Corporation: An Analysis of Some of the Motives for International Business Integration" (mimeographed), 1966.

nopolistic profits than do domestic investors. In fact, investors rarely think in these terms. Any firm, whether domestic or international, invests with an expectation of the best possible return, which implies some advantage over competitors. Otherwise, the investments would not be made. In this respect, there is no difference between domestic and international investment.

Portfolio Theory   A third new hypothesis is offered by the portfolio theory, which postulates that the ultimate source of direct investments is the saver, whose welfare is increased when investors in foreign countries come to compete for his funds. His gain may result from either higher yields, caused by the enlargement of the market, or from lower risk, which results from the geographic diversification a multicountry market creates. Whether or not any actual correlation exists between the postulated saver's gain from such international portfolio diversification and the actual flows of foreign investment is yet to be statistically proven. On the face of it, the theory is plausible.

This theory has two potentially significant implications for the multinational company:

1. If an MNC can experience a reduction of risk through wider international investments (expanding its operations to more countries), it can offset lower rates of return in some countries or on some specific projects that otherwise could not be undertaken. Thus, the MNC can make investments that for national firms are clearly uneconomic.
2. The shares of an MNC should be more attractive on the stock market to the saving public. This will increase the supply of capital available for the MNCs.

THE HEAD-START PHENOMENON

A number of the older MNCs owe their international expansion to the fact that they had a head start in a particular product line. Whatever may spark the initial entry of the firm is irrelevant. Once in business with a new product, the firm tends to improve the production methods, which give it a technological capability not available to any potential imitator or competitor, leading to successive shifts in the cost curve, as shown in Figure 10.3 on page 194. Assuming that C_0 represents the best possible cost option for a firm using the technology in public realm, it is obvious that the head-start firm will tend to extend its competitive (monopolistic) advantage by constantly adding to its proprietary technology. The gap will not start closing before some other firm takes the plunge and starts to catch up. The ultimate outcome of this will depend on the relative speed of each firm's technological progress.

The cost of production tells only part of the story. The head-start firm may have a proverbial "ace in the hole" by having decisively influenced the consumers' preferences for the new product. Its brand becomes the archetype

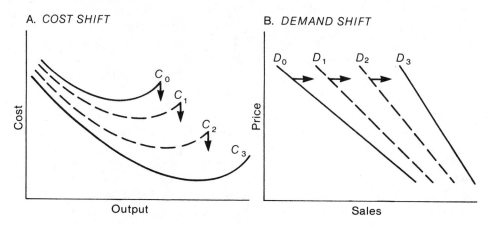

Figure 10.3   Successive Shifts of Cost and Demand Curves for Head-Start Firm

to which the consumers' loyalties and quality standards are attached. The head-start firm can, in other words, capture the new market not only as a supplier in the physical sense, but also as the architect of the value system that will govern and direct the growth of its market.

In theoretical terms, growing consumer acceptance causes the head-start firm's demand curve to shift to the right as the new product is gradually adopted by the public as the standard for the industry. It also becomes more upright as the growing prestige of the product makes the demand for it less elastic.

The more successful the firm is in building a dominant image, the more immune it becomes to competitors' efforts to challenge its position. Conversely, the more vulnerable will any prospective competitor be to the head-start firm's pre-emptive impact.

Numerous firms have been successful in building up such technological and marketing advantages, and they have maintained their leads over extended periods through constant technological improvements and vigorous marketing, including preventive promotion, which either thwarts competition in its infancy or forces it to exert massive effort and expense to make up the difference.

Dominance in the domestic market compels international expansion. To pre-empt foreign markets before indigenous competition has emerged is an almost self-evident strategy, as is the tying up of key resources or marketing channels. To prevent emerging foreign competition from becoming a menace, it must be challenged on its home ground. To fill foreign orders and to accept invitations to supply foreign requirements are natural reactions of any firm. Thus, the dominance gained during the head-start period generates its own tendency to flow across international boundaries.

PRODUCT LIFE CYCLE THEORY

A slightly different explanation of the reasons for the rise of multinational production plants is offered by the product life cycle theory. This theory hypothesizes that new products are born in high-technology, high-income countries, and that in the initial stages of their life new products are price inelastic. In the case of consumer goods, such as video recorders, the product is first bought by people for whom the novelty and prestige take precedence over price. In the case of industrial goods, such as machine tools or computers, the first buyers are similarly price insensitive. In brief, new products are bought in the high-income countries, such as the United States, which are the only countries where enough consumers can be found who have both the propensity and purchasing power to pay the high prices in the early life of a product. Since the necessary subcontractors, capital, and technical inputs are also in the developed countries, production will first remain limited to these countries.

Any sales to other countries will start as exports. As overseas demand for the product grows, the sales volume that makes local manufacturing profitable will be reached. At this point, the exporting company will become exposed to the risk that some other firm will build a plant in the importing country and take over the market. To prevent this from happening, the exporting firm is compelled to invest in its own production facilities in the importing country. The same process will be repeated in the second export market, then in the third, and so on.

The theory further assumes that, due to tariffs and transportation costs, the U.S. exporter is not able to compete with a local producer. Therefore, if it does not capitalize on the investment opportunity before some other company does, it must concede to others the earning capacity of the foreign market. At a later time the foreign competition may start its own international expansion and thus compete with the original producer of the product not only in its domestic market but also in other markets, even in its home country of the original producer. Therefore, investment in multicountry production facilities becomes mandatory both for retaining a given market abroad and also for protecting the company's position in other markets, including the headquarters country itself. The process of multinationalization creates its own opportunities and imperatives; that is, proceeds step by step from the more advanced to the less advanced countries until at an "old age" the bulk of production could originate in relatively backward economies.[6]

This theory provides a reasonably plausible rationalization of why market-oriented companies such as manufacturers of pharmaceuticals, foods, and similar goods have replaced export operations with multinational production facilities. In other words, it explains the shift from exporting to multinational

---

6. Louis T. Wells, Jr., (ed.), *The Product Life Cycle and International Trade* (Cambridge: Harvard University Press, 1972), pp. 11–15.

production. Once the multinational production system has been established by a manufacturer, any further relevance of the product life cycle becomes debatable. An established MNC may have a number of other reasons for establishing new plants.

In nonmanufacturing industries the product life cycle concept, like the head-start phenomenon from which it has been derived, is totally inapplicable. It supplies no explanation of why either the raw material producers (mining, oil, forest products, and tropical plantation agriculture) or the service industries (transportation, banking, insurance, retailing, engineering) become multinationalized.

Even for the manufacturing industries, the product life cycle theory serves better as an ex post rationalization of the initial multinationalization of some early forerunners than as an explanation of the contemporary MNC. This is true because, first, the theory is organization blind; it recognizes no differences of capabilities and behavioral rationality between UNCs and MNCs. It overlooks the greater capabilities of the MNC to integrate and rationalize worldwide production and marketing operations and to plan its strategies in terms of worldwide demand patterns and factor availabilities. The MNC's structure both presupposes and promotes a geocentric perspective that seems unattainable for the UNC.

Second, the product life cycle model denies innovative powers to all but the richest nations. This is badly at odds with empirical evidence. One must also question the relevance of export phase not only to the thousands of firms that already are multinational, but also to the unaccountable new products that are born in a multinational structure and never in their commercial life enter either the purely domestic or the export stages of the product life cycle theory.

Although helpful in some respects, such hypothetical extrapolations as the product life cycle can be misleading. A more complete and reliable explanation can be found in factual studies, to which we turn in Chapter 11.

SUMMARY

Several theories have been advanced to explain the multinationalization of business. None has fully succeeded. However, each has illuminated a different aspect of this complex process. The traditional economic theory is useful for explaining portfolio investments but not direct investments and MNCs. The greatly expanded spectrum of international linkages that the MNCs have created requires a far broader frame of reference.

Portfolio theory appears to hold some potential but its application is not yet perfected. The head-start phenomenon and the product life cycle help us to understand the conversion of manufacturing UNCs into MNCs, but beyond the initial phase of multinationalization their usefulness fails, as corporate capabilities and motivations change. A theory that provides a satisfactory explanation of nonmanufacturing MNCs is yet to be introduced.

FOR REVIEW AND DISCUSSION

1. The theory of trade deals with the causes and effects of transboundary transactions; any theory of the MNC must go way beyond this. Discuss.

2. Can portfolio investments be explained by trade theory? Explain.

3. In which respects do direct foreign investments contradict neoclassical theories?

4. Are the international linkages that MNCs create not only far more numerous but also inherently more stable and resilient than foreign trade linkages? Explain fully.

5. What factors might explain the fact that, contrary to theoretical expectations, the cost of production of foreign-based subsidiaries of an MNC is often lower than the cost of production in the headquarters country?

6. If management had as clear a picture of investment opportunities abroad as it has of those at home, much more capital would be switched from domestic to foreign investment. Comment.

7. What are some ways in which portfolio theory can be applied to studying the multinationalization of business?

8. Compare and contrast the head-start phenomenon and the product life cycle theory.

9. An established MNC may or may not follow the product life cycle theory. Discuss.

10. How would you explain cross-investments?

11

Business Stimuli for Multinational Business Expansion

When we shift our focus to the managerial analysis of international investment we must shift also the perspective from which the subject is viewed. Theoreticians and managers travel in different orbits and are subject to different constraints. Theoreticians need not be right to succeed but managers must. A theoretician's ideas never go broke; bankruptcy laws have no provision for philosophical failings. On the other hand, business firms do go broke. They face bankruptcy and extinction if their management fails to perceive the relevant realities. Theoreticians dispose of bothersome realities by making simplifying assumptions or exclusions by definition. Such conveniences are unavailable to managers. They must necessarily relate to the prevailing reality in all its complexity. Nothing can be assumed to be what it is not, or eliminated from consideration by exclusion. The managerial frame of reference, therefore, emphasizes specifics over generalizations, and it places a high priority on facts and experience.

Accordingly, research scholars who have approached the study of international investments from a managerial perspective have focused their efforts on actual policy making processes and information inputs used to establish concrete decision criteria by business managers. Since executive decisions are the ultimate determinants for all international investments, nothing can be more important than the facts and factors upon which managers rely.

The managerial information inputs come from either the external environment or the internal environment of the firm. Since the former are beyond the control of management and the latter within it, it is useful to discuss them separately.

ENVIRONMENTAL STIMULI LEADING TO MNCs

Significant changes in the world business climate in the 1950s paved the way for the surge in MNC growth. Simplification and liberalization of international transactions through the conversion to multilateralism, the addition of foreign

199

aid to traditional international economic relations, and the alliances caused by the cold war rank among the most powerful of such environmental forces. Their combined effect was to change the overall context of opportunities for foreign investment.

Multilateralism

The most inclusive among the external changes was the shift from bilateralism to multilateralism. In earlier years, business dealings among countries had been handled bilaterally. Each country negotiated separate, often exclusive, arrangements with each other foreign nation. For such things as tariffs, quotas, trading rules, formal regulations, tax and entry privileges, measurement and valuation standards, and documentary requirements, there were as many different arrangements as there were countries with which a nation maintained official economic relations. As a consequence, an incredible maze of legislative and bureaucratic technicalities surrounded international transactions in most countries. These complexities acted not only as an invisible tariff, which reduced international business by raising its cost, but also as a deterrent to all but professional specialists in any kind of international business. The mere mechanics of international transactions were often insurmountable for the typical corporate executive. There were thus compelling operational reasons for channeling international trade transactions through export and import intermediaries and for depending upon the latter's leadership in the formulation of corporate policies regarding overseas developments.

The deterring effects of bilateralism were not limited to the mechanics but went to the heart of international economic relations. Bilateralism provided a means for according different treatment to the products, investments, and enterprises of different countries. It was a vehicle for discrimination in international commerce. This discrimination manifested itself in many ways, in tariff and quota treatments, in foreign exchange regulations, in taxes and vias, and in many other aspects of international intercourse. As such, it interfered with the normal flow of goods, capital, and services, and created perverted patterns of international trade and investments. When, between the two world wars, this structure of invisible barriers was superimposed upon the highest visible trade barriers of any peacetime period, the total deterrent became a massive fortification against international trade.

Since World War II, multilateralism has greatly reduced both visible and invisible barriers. The organizational vehicle for multilateralism has been the General Agreement for Tariffs and Trade (GATT), to which nearly the entire noncommunist world now belongs. Under the GATT format, international trade matters are negotiated and settled in an open forum in Geneva, Switzerland, and any privileges granted by one country to another become automatically applicable to the entire membership. This method prevents discrimination at least in the formal schedules and rates or in whatever norms may be involved in the negotiations. Member countries have also standardized many basic practices, procedures, performance standards, and, to some degree, even customs procedures. Thus, much of the invisible superstructure of trade barriers has been eliminated, and international transactions have been greatly simplified.

The simplification of international transactions explains the relative ease with which manufacturing concerns have been able to circumvent the foreign trade middlemen and to absorb their functions in recent years. However, like bilateralism, multilateralism goes much deeper than the mechanics of international commerce. Its real meaning and value lie in minimizing the abnormalities and perversions and in enabling international business relations to develop according to price and cost patterns rather than according to arbitrary restraints. Multilateralism has opened up new areas of profitable endeavor for business and industry and has paved the way for direct contact with and among operating facilities in foreign countries. In particular, it permits the different national affiliates of a MNC to specialize in trade among themselves, thus forming an integrated international system.

Foreign Aid

Another external factor that has facilitated the movement abroad of manufacturing concerns has been the massive U.S. aid that many countries have received. Much of the aid dollar inevitably becomes a trade dollar when it is used by the recipient country. From the demands for goods and services that the aid monies have generated have sprung many foreign factories, subsidiary companies, and joint venture enterprises abroad.

Since helping other countries to industrialize has been one of the principal purposes of foreign aid, the U.S. government has often enticed, and occasionally pressured, U.S. private businesses to establish or operate production facilities in a foreign country as their contribution to the aid program. Although the government can make financial appropriations it cannot establish factories or build roads. Active participation of business is needed to make the aid program effective. Once abroad, companies have a tendency to stay, to grow, and to spread.

The Cold War

Still another external factor in the internationalization of business enterprise was the cold war, the hysterical rivalry between the capitalist and communist nations that lasted for some 25 years. The fear of communist imperialism caused the capitalist nations to tighten their military, political, and economic ties in order to find safety in collective action. Although not free from internal friction, the structure of joint defense was a formidable force not only for economic cooperation among governments but also for business participation in building the defense system. To have substance and strength, the free world military alliances and geopolitical programs had to be backed up by business capabilities to supply the goods and services necessary for the military forces.

Government Inducements

For various reasons governments at home and abroad have induced business enterprise to cooperate in public programs and to participate actively in carrying out certain government policies. Industrial development plans and programs for road building, power plants, and other projects to create a modern infrastructure require industrial know-how that developing countries usually lack. To alleviate this problem, their governments have invited MNCs to cooperate in these efforts, either as principals or as partners, often on a guaranteed-return basis.

The host country is often as actively involved in the process as the MNC itself. Direct investment not only provides the host country with necessary capital but carries with it the management know-how, technology, and industrial skills that the host country needs in order to advance industrialization and open up new avenues for economic development. Among other benefits from direct investments to the host economy are export expansion, import replacement, broader tax base, higher employment and payrolls, and a market for supplying companies.

For such reasons many countries have placed an increasing emphasis on attracting inbound investments and have aggressively pursued policies to make such investments a strategic factor in the nation's economic growth. They have initiated incentive programs to attract capital to boost their industrial growth. These programs affect corporate investment decisions in two ways. The program is nearly always given considerable publicity, built around the natural advantages and business potential in the country concerned. Even though the assessments may be quite far from accurate, the publicity does draw the attention of foreign companies, who then often institute their own studies of expected or unexpected opportunities.

This is not to say that the official incentives themselves are ineffective. As a rule they are not. A survey of investment experience made by the National Industrial Conference Board revealed that the companies of 12 industrial nations whose operations had spread to 88 countries had frequently given significant weight to the special development incentives officially offered to foreign investors by the host governments. The most effective investment incentives had been:

1. Duty waivers on imports of capital equipment
2. Duty waivers on imports of necessary parts and supplies
3. Tariff protection
4. Infant-industry benefits
5. Tax holidays
6. Tax concessions or deferrals or both
7. Liberal depreciation allowances
8. Low-cost government loans for factory construction

9. Other long-term subsidized loans
10. Government subsidies for industrial buildings
11. Preferential allocation of foreign exchange for materials and parts
12. Guarantees of profit remittance and capital repatriation
13. Subsidies for training local personnel
14. Free port or foreign trade zone
15. Government railroad subsidies
16. Favorable conditions for developing industrial sites
17. Use of government port facilities[1]

Since World War II the U.S. government has enlisted business firms in a variety of foreign economic aid programs where their technical skills and organizational capabilities have been essential. Building and repairing agricultural machinery and implements and constructing steel mills, food-processing plants, sanitation systems, and transportation facilities illustrate foreign activities that may receive their initial impetus from an economic aid assignment.

More recently, the U.S. government, confronted with a chronic balance of payments deficit, has sponsored an intensive campaign for export expansion. According to the U.S. Department of Commerce, a large number of firms have responded and have initiated programs for marketing abroad. In addition to moral suasion, the government has offered several practical aids and incentives. Among them are listings of international trade leads, trade missions to different regions of the world, and active participation in international trade fairs.

Negative Incentives

The effects of incentives have frequently been minimized by the presence of obstacles. Quite often, the principal reason for the incentive program is the existence of a generally antagonistic atmosphere for business growth, and especially international business activity. The impediments listed by managers of multinational ventures in the 88-country sample referred to above included:

1. Exchange restrictions and balance of payments deficits
2. Restrictions on foreign enterprises, investors, and executives
3. Import controls, including duties and exchanges
4. Inconsistent and unpredictable legal protection
5. Political uncertainty
6. Labor problems
7. Financial instability
8. Tax discrimination
9. Inadequate infrastructure[2]

1. National Industrial Conference Board, *Obstacles and Incentives to Private Foreign Investments* (New York: 1966), pp. 34–42.
2. *Obstacles and Incentives*, pp. 34–42.

The survey made no effort to measure the significance of the different impediments; therefore, they cannot be ranked in any systematic way.

Decision Variables

Direct investment is not only a financial proposition but also involves managerial control and transboundary operating systems. Any attempt to explain it in terms of purely financial factors would, therefore, lead to an unrealistic oversimplification. The investor's advantage arises not as an immediate response to the investment transaction but as a long-term stream of income generated by the production assets acquired. Therefore, it is the capacity to generate the income stream that creates the investor's advantge.

Studies of multinational companies show that they have not been created by a single investment decision but have evolved gradually as a process of stimulus and response over time. It is a two-way process in which the productive capabilities of the investing company and the conditions of the host economy interact. The former act as push factors and the latter as pull factors for direct investment. The investing company must seek to exploit its own factors of strength that are not available on equal terms to its competitors in the target country. Technological lead, a strong product, a famous trademark, special marketing skills, and spreading of overhead (economies of scale) are the most typical examples of such factors of strength. Any one or a combination of several may define the options open to the investor. For the host economy, there may exist particular material resources, labor force, special programs, or even location advantages that may form the basis for the investment.

Except for the initial foreign investment, a company's direct investment policy is normally an ongoing process. The relative weight given to different push factors and pull factors varies from industry to industry. Market-oriented industries (makers of perishables and light consumer goods) rely on a different calculation than do resource-oriented industries (producers of primary commodities). Similarly, high-technology industries are guided by different criteria than are the makers of low-technology products. Consequently, generalizations here can be misleading. It is the specifics that count.

Raw Materials

In general, the intensity of the search for raw materials varies with the nature of the enterprise. Resource-oriented firms have the strongest motivation to respond to international differences in the availability and cost of materials. Oil companies, steel mills, and chemical plants provide well-known illustrations of this category. As some resources near depletion and rise in cost while others are being discovered, advantages derived from foreign procurement are subject to constant change.

In complex manufacturing and refining industries, where the inputs come from a wide variety of sources, the importance of any particular raw material tends to decline, if not from a physical at least from an economic standpoint, since the price of any one input in a multi-input operation is but a fraction of the total materials cost. Accordingly, such firms are less responsive to international price differentials but tend to react vigorously if the physical availability of a critical material is in question. The search for raw materials has gained intensity in recent years, especially by Japan and Western Europe (see Table 11.1).

Markets

The search for markets had been another prime motive for international business operations. Historically, this search has been strongest among two types of companies: those facing stiff competition or market saturation at home, and those capable of economies at outputs greater than the domestic market can absorb. Mechanization and automation offer increasingly greater possibilities for lowering per-unit costs through increased output (greater utilization of capital equipment). The search for export markets is, therefore, increasingly intensified in all industries affected by them. This intensification is particularly apparent in smaller countries. It has been a major force for international economic integration in both Europe and Latin America.

It would be misleading, however, to imply that only these two types of industries have sought international markets. In recent years the search has become almost universal. Management in general has become more world oriented and has learned that, unlike domestic trade, which consists largely of the interchange of goods between businesses and consumers with similar standards, international trade can flourish on differences in production and consumption standards and, in this way, can provide alternatives and additives to the domestic market.

Table 11.1　European Industrial Strategy for Africa

The Munich Institute of Economics has been at work, in conjunction with a number of foreign research institutes and consulting firms, on a study of Africa's suitability as a location for European and in particular German industrial investment. The study was undertaken at the request of the European Commission. The immediate aim of the study is to assess the possibilities for establishing export industries in the eighteen African countries which are now associated with the European Community in accordance with the terms of the Yaoundé Agreement.

The research team has drawn up a list of no fewer than 120 industries which would be worth establishing in Africa. They are mainly labor intensive sectors involving the processing of animal, vegetable or mineral raw materials. Special attention is paid to cattle breeding and leather production, wood products harvesting, tropical fruit farming and processing, tobacco production and the electronics industry.

Source: European Commission.

Although in the past firms sought markets for their existing product mixes, more recently they have often expanded their objectives. Rising living standards and changing fashions have outmoded many products and made them economically obsolete in industrial countries, while the demand for them continues in less developed areas of the world. As the products become outmoded, so does most of the specialized machinery and equipment designed for their production. To avoid massive writeoffs and scrapping of such equipment, management has sought, often successfully, to replace the losses in domestic sales through aggressive export campaigns.

Emphasis on research and development by UNCs has created still another reason for the search for foreign markets because of the increasing number of new product possibilities such research has yielded. What to do with these possibilities has become a major unresolved problem for UNCs. More and more firms have been able to use the research results to develop different product lines primarily or exclusively for particular markets abroad.

In recent years, the main vehicle of direct investment has been the MNC. In earlier years much of the investment flow originated with companies in the process of conversion from a UNC to an MNC structure. Today the established MNCs dominate, though the conversion process continues. The MNCs are no longer a club of giants. More and more smaller companies are adopting the strategies of multinational growth.

It is from the experience of the MNCs that data can be obtained to explain the motives and reasons for international business expansion. This experience has been the subject of considerable scrutiny by a number of scholars, including the author of this book. What follows draws heavily on the conclusions drawn from the primary data that this research has produced.[3]

REASONS FOR THE INITIAL MOVE

Why domestic firms have made the initial move to start production operations abroad has long preoccupied researchers and managers alike. The first major study on the subject was published in 1931.[4] Many others have appeared since. Their main conclusions are that the initial direct investment is caused by one or more of the following factors:

1. High trade barriers, preventing exportation to the host country
2. Need to adapt the product substantially, causing loss of scale economies
3. Need to service the product (installation, repair, maintenance) in the foreign market
4. Patent laws that required the patent to be worked locally to be valid
5. High cost of transportation for bulky or fragile products

3. E. J. Kolde, *The Multinational Company: Behavioral and Managerial Analysis* (Lexington, Mass.: D. C. Heath, 1974).

4. Frank A. Southard, Jr., *American Industry in Europe* (Boston: Houghton Mifflin Company, 1931).

6. Lower cost of inputs, especially labor or raw materials
7. Inefficient indigenous marketing channels
8. Competition

Trade Barriers

Until 1968 the most frequently cited reason for establishing production operations abroad was trade restrictions. Since trade was liberalized in the Kennedy Round, other factors have been given greater weight in initial investment decisions. Among the trade barriers, three were considered by business to be the most crucial: import restrictions, especially high tariffs, quantitative controls, and licensing practices; monetary restrictions, including the lack of availability of convertible currencies for foreign imports; and artificial exchange rates. Some companies decided to get behind these trade barriers by operating from within the respective markets. Invariably these companies later extended their foreign operations from marketing to manufacturing activities.

Cost of Production

The decrease in costs obtained through employment of local labor and raw materials has ranked second only to trade barriers as an inducement for entry into foreign production. Companies that depend heavily on manual labor, such as those with intricate assembly operations, have derived significant benefits from moving to countries where wages are low.

Marketing Efficiency

A third reason for establishing marketing operations abroad has been marketing efficiency. Many foreign marketing institutions are unable to provide intensive coverage of the market and to promote the products of U.S. manufacturers aggressively. Operating within the country simplifies synchronizing domestic and foreign programs and facilitates the adoption of U.S. marketing methods. As a result, the competitive position of a company, as measured by its market share, often improves.

In certain instances, pressures have mounted for on-the-spot processing and service facilities because of changes in the foreign market and in consumption requirements. Many manufacturers have also been unsatisfied with the marketing efficiency of export-import firms. To become independent of them, they have established their own facilities abroad.

Competitive Strength

Another principal reason for the initial foreign investment has been to be able to compete more effectively. Competition in foreign markets has been increasing because of local industrial development in many countries, the growing strength of Japanese and European firms, and the increasing superiority of MNCs over exporting UNCs. More decisive than price rivalry are the nonprice aspects of competition, particularly government regulations affecting market behavior, credit terms, capacity for prompt delivery, ability to accept small orders, and customer services. All these require local personnel and facilities to avoid unwarranted risks and excessive costs of operation. Also, continuous contact with the market is important for a continuous adjustment to changing market conditions and for counteracting competitors' promotional measures before they can cause shifts in customers' patronage.

These four reasons—trade barriers, lower input costs, marketing efficiency, and competition—are closely interrelated and have a common denominator in their ultimate objective, which is increased operating efficiency.

ADVANTAGES OF MNCs

Marketing Management

Having resident affiliates in many countries provides the MNC with the ability to adjust its marketing strategies within wide ranges whenever conditions demand. Unlike the UNC, it depends neither on international trade controls nor on domestic sourcing limitations. This is not to say that the MNC is immune to changes in trade controls or in sourcing possibilities, only that it possesses means of compensating for these changes that its uninational competitor lacks. If and when conditions warrant, the MNC markets across international boundaries and consolidates several national markets; under different conditions, it can move in the opposite direction and segment its marketing operations into sharply segregated national markets, when either trade barriers or other factors make this optimal. Between these two extremes lies a wide range of possible strategies, which may be varied in reference to degrees of national market segmentation as well as to different regions of the world.

Such a broad range of options provides the MNC with a high degree of immunity against environmental adversities, whether these are internal business conditions, restrictive government policies, or disturbances in international affairs.

This flexibility is not limited to marketing of already established products but extends also to new product introductions as well as other marketing innovations. Thus, it encompasses all marketing dynamics. Take, for example, the introduction of a new product. The MNC can choose from among a wide variety of different countries the market in which to test the product. For a typical consumer product, the initial testing might be done in a small country such as Belgium, Denmark, or Finland, where regional variances in demand characteristics are small and where the pre-existence of highly refined statistical information provides an environment for completing the tests at relatively low cost. In contrast, the UNC has hardly any alternative to its own home market, regardless of how well or ill suited that may be in a given case. The lack of marketing capacity precludes any other country from serving as an operationally acceptable test market.

Its multinational structure endows the MNC with several other marketing advantages, which are summarized below:

Advantage	*Applicability*
Market access	Where host countries have high trade barriers (tariffs, quotas)
Marketing channels	Where desired marketing channels are nonexistent or underdeveloped
Promotion	Where local representatives are unable to perform the function
Supply	Where local inventories are essential for distribution efficiency
Customer service	When product requires repair and maintenance service
Brand image	When a company's trademark or brand name enjoys a strong appeal
Strategic flexibility	When changing conditions require frequent adjustments in marketing mix
Physical distribution (logistics)	When local sourcing creates savings in transportation costs over export shipments

Production Operations

Potentially, the greatest operational superiority of the MNC over its uninational rival lies in its ability to combine marketing and production arrangements throughout the world in an optimal fashion. It need not limit its product to globally standardized models, but can choose designs in which certain modules or subassemblies are standardized globally, others continentally, and still others to specific countries or even subsections of a country. This enables it to achieve any desired degree of adaptation to individual country consumption requirements without sacrificing the economies of mass production and international specialization. The MNC achieves economies of scale from mass-producing the global and continental modules at the same time as it benefits from international specialization by having each module produced in the country possessing the most advantageous conditions for it.

For complex component industries (automobiles, appliances, aircraft, computers, electronic systems) commonality is typically achievable in a significant share of components or subcomponents if production planning is focused on multinational maximization of their use.

The main production advantages derived from a multinational structure are shown on page 210.

Advantage	*Applicability*
Economies of scale	(a) Where foreign production units can utilize components produced by parent company, thereby reducing cost for both; and (b) when the scope of the foreign venture is sufficient for mass production operations at optimal cost
Raw material supply	In resource-oriented industries
Specialization	When product ingredients can be produced more advantageously in certain countries because of natural resources or sociopolitical factors
Vertical integration	When the efficiency of continuity of production operations can be enhanced by the acquisition of the suppliers of material inputs such as raw materials and semimanufactures or by the development of a system for direct marketing of the output
Labor cost (wage rate × productivity)	Under a variety of conditions that may or may not coexist: (a) in labor intensive industries; (b) in countries where wage rates are low relative to the levels of worker skill; and (c) in companies that can introduce modern machinery and production systems not possessed by host country competitors
Technological advantage	When the investor controls technologies that are not available to competition in the host country
Product design and quality	When a product must be changed to meet local consumption requirements (public taste, legal regulations, purchasing power)
Production smoothing or adaptation of production technology	In the engineering and design of plant facilities, there is a built-in tendency to stick to established systems and use the same technology, that is, to use in new branch factories what has been used in existing facilities of the company. The resistance to designing unique facilities counteracts the need for customizing products and processes to the differing requirements of different countries. The existence of a distinctly different operation environment helps to break the engineers' adversion to new designs.

Financial Advantages

Both economic and regulatory determinants of the cost of capital vary internationally. Each country has its own structure of interest rates. Even more importantly, changes within this structure may or may not be correlated with interest rate patterns elsewhere. Short-term deviations are commonplace; divergencies in long-term trends are also present. As a consequence, the cost of capital, short, medium, or long term, can vary considerably from country to country at any point in time.

In addition to interest rates, there are numerous regulatory and institutional factors that tend to widen the differences further. Many countries have programs to support or to subsidize certain types of investments. These programs may be limited to particular industries, to particular localities, to infrastructure projects, or to whatever has been deemed important by the public authorities. The support itself may take the form of guaranteed low-interest loans, direct capital contributions (usually on a participation basis) of equity capital, reduction of taxes or complete tax holidays for a number of years, accelerated depreciation and write-off privileges, special allowances for research and development, foreign exchange guarantees, and even government purchase contracts all to assure a satisfactory return on the contemplated investment.

Thus, it is not only the cost of capital acquisition but also its subsequent utilization and profitability that vary among countries. It is well to be reminded that the real measure of cost is its ratio to return. If capital from different sources can produce the same return, then the obviously rational action is to compare carefully the acquisition costs for different sources of capital and to use the lowest-cost source. This is the typical textbook prescription, which works quite well in a one-country context. In a multinational setting our calculus must go beyond the mere acquisition cost since the equal-return hypothesis no longer holds. That is to say, capital acquired in Country A may be burdened with very different utilization costs, because of different taxes, depreciation, restrictions, and so on, and be capable of earning quite different revenues, because of government subsidies, support programs, and purchase guarantees, than capital acquired in countries B or C.

In sum, capital utilization is subject to international differences on three levels: acquisition costs, utilization costs, and profitability expectations. Therefore, the financial possibilities available to the multinational firm can never be duplicated in a one-country context. The MNC consequently has a number of financial alternatives and options open to it that are unavailable to the UNC. These options must be looked upon as superior powers that a company derives from its multinational structure. They range through the whole spectrum of financial functions, from short-term borrowing to equity investments on one side and from interest earnings on liquid holdings to payback periods and amortization rates on capital investments on the other side.

In financial literature the MNC is typically viewed as a foreign investor. In point of fact, an already established MNC is neither foreign nor a new investor; rather, it holds a dual status, being both a resident enterprise and a member of an international corporate family. Its investments normally expand locally existing enterprises—its affiliates in the country—and do not cause new firms to enter the country from outside. The only exceptions are the investments that expand the territorial scope of the firm to new countries, which is the case primarily during the conversion from uninational to multinational structure. After that the push to enter additional countries weakens rather abruptly, and further outward expansion plays only a minor role in an MNC's investment expenditures.

Financial Flexibility

A UNC is wholly dependent upon its home country's constraints in any international capital transfers, whether they are short-term or long-term transactions. If there are no official restrictions, this dependence becomes academic. If, however, restrictions do exist, as has been the case in the United States and many other countries, the UNC's ability to respond to foreign opportunities or to participate in international ventures is accordingly curtailed. The tighter the regulations, the greater is this constraining effect.

The MNC, on the other hand, can develop a high degree of immunity to restrictive currency controls. It can retain its operational flexibility in spite of them. First, since it has separate juridical personalities in many countries, it has a wide range of choice as to which of these will act as the principal in any particular venture. If the U.S. exchange restrictions foreclose a particular undertaking, the Swiss or Swedish affiliate of the company may not be similarly constrained; or if no single national affiliate can fully achieve the desired objective, several of them may combine into a consortium. Second, such arrangements are reinforced by the multinational distribution of existing capital reserves as well as the potentialities to borrow. That is, the MNC may, by an appropriate distribution of its capital reserves and borrowing, participate in international investments, divestments, and transfers without violating the currency and exchange controls of any particular country. This is a much more difficult task for the UNC.

The MNC's superior flexibility is not limited to neutralizing the negative consequences of official restrictions. It applies equally in the case of government investment stimulation policies. Although varying widely in scope and continuity, government programs for stimulating growth have become an important source of corporate opportunities throughout the world. Only the companies that possess the flexibility for the transfers of the needed financial resources can capitalize upon those opportunities. Needless to add, the same is true for investment and growth opportunities unaffected by government measures.

In addition to the cost of capital and the flexibility of sourcing and use of capital, the MNCs report other financial benefits deriving from their simultaneous presence in several countries, which can be grouped under the six headings found on page 213.

Advantage	Applicability
Profit rates	To all investors whose domestic rates of return relative to risk are lower than that in a potential host country
Taxes	(a) Where substantially lower than in the headquarters country; and (b) where deferral of U.S. tax increases capital available in affiliate operations
Depreciation allowances	Where law permits greater freedom of writing off new plant and equipment than at home
Research and development allowances	In countries anxious to promote indigenous development of technology
Local capital	(a) Access to host country equity capital through local capital market or joint venture partners; and (b) ability to borrow locally
Currency convertibility	Most international enterprises

General Management

MNC managers consider the multinational structure of their firms to have created some companywide advantages that UNCs lack. These may be summarized as follows:

Advantage	Applicability
New growth options	Where growth objectives are difficult to reach in the domestic market
Stabilization of profits	When diversification of markets and production facilities is desirable
Outlet for technological slack	When company has products, processes, and/or machinery no longer needed in an industrial country and more appropriate in a less developed economy than the most advanced technology would be
Company image	To most companies, "multinational" connoting the greater corporate achievement

By becoming multinational a firm gains wider diversity of markets, resources, and other relevant factors. This increases both the number of opportunities for further international investment as well as the flexibility with which the firm can respond to its changing international environment. These new options, not available to a UNC, require that the MNC adopt significantly different international objectives.

Time Horizon

The shift from an export perspective to a multinational operations perspective takes time. In the initial stages, when a company is a newcomer to the international scene, its investment strategies tend to be narrowly based and more rigidly conceived. It looks for one or two clearcut advantages and limits its objectives accordingly. As time goes on a broader management perspective is adopted. This is basically a result of corporate learning. The initial affiliate serves as a training base for company executives in a multinational context. It also serves as a scanning device, producing better information on foreign opportunities. Each subsequent investment, each new affiliate, broadens the scanning system and increases executive expertise in foreign situations.

SUMMARY

The experiences of MNCs reveal that managerial control over operating entities in different countries offers a broad range of competitive advantages over UNCs. Initially, these advantages derive mainly from a closer adjustment of marketing activities to the specific characteristics of each host economy and from direct access to the resources—natural, human, financial, and technological—that each country possesses. As the MNC matures significant corporate learning takes place. The marketing and sourcing advantages interact to lead to a self-sustained process of examining all corporate goals and strategies from an international rather than a national perspective, and adjusting general management policies so as to capitalize on the business opportunities in a global context.

This often leads to the development of dissimilar production plants or other facilities in different host economies as each affiliate learns to draw more fully on local businesses. The result is a diversification of the firm not only in terms of markets but also in terms of products and production technologies, all of which create new frontiers of growth for the MNC.

FOR REVIEW AND DISCUSSION

1. In which ways does a bilateralist system of international business relations restrict the development of MNCs? To what extent did the shift toward multilateralism reduce or eliminate these restrictions?

.2 Some UNCs have developed into MNCs by responding to investment incentive programs of various foreign countries rather than seeking out foreign opportunities on their own initiative. Is this desirable? What risks, if any, does this practice entail (a) to the firm and (b) to the host nation?

3. Identify as many push factors and pull factors as you can. How can each of these contribute to the multinationalization of a firm?

4. Research has shown that the factors considered by management when making the initial direct investment decision, that is, when deciding to establish the first foreign-based affiliate, are some important ways different from the factors that management of an established MNC considers when adding another affiliate. What are the differences? Why do they develop?

5. In what ways does a firm gain additional flexibilities when it multinationalizes?

6. Do the added flexibilities referred to in question 5 create any new requirements for management? Explain.

7. Do the marketing and production advantages of a multinational structure accrue more or less equally to all firms or do some firms benefit more from the marketing advantages and others from the production advantages? What characteristics of a firm cause any differences in this respect?

8. How would you rate the relative importance of the different financial advantages of MNCs? Would the rating vary by industry, by home country, by host country, or by some other factors?

9. Compare several MNCs and UNCs of your choice and describe the image that each projects. Do you notice any differences? What are they?

10. Look up profit figures for an equal number of MNCs and UNCs. Does the finding that multinationalization tends to stabilize profits still hold?

12

Organization and Structure of MNCs

Any competition presumes the presence of competitors. In business, the competitors are other businesses. What the other enterprises can or cannot do has direct bearing on a company's opportunities and risks as well as its ultimate successes and failures. The competitive environment is a primary force that leaves no business untouched. To survive in the face of competition, firms must organize their resources so as to cope best with both the existing and the anticipated competition. Organization is an ongoing process that reflects how the goals and strategies of different businesses change.

The international competitive environment consists of two main groups: companies active in international business and domestic firms in each country.

In this chapter we will study international competitors. The MNCs hold a unique position among the latter. Since they transcend national boundaries in activities as well as in organization, their presence affects not only the competitive climate but also the modes and channels through which international activities are executed. How the MNCs are organized, how the different organizational models fit into host country economics, and what behavioral implications flow from each type will be discussed in this chapter.

ORGANIZATION THEORY

Formal and Informal Organization

Modern organization theory recognizes two fundamentally different aspects of business organizations—*formal organization* and *informal organization*. Formal organization is the structure for rational action: the division of work, the allocation of personnel, functions, and resources to produce the greatest efficiency. It includes the communication systems and the chain of command required for the coordination and control of the different parts as well as of the total system. The positions and relationships of functions within the organization are institutionalized; the office rather than the officer is the criterion.

Individuals are thus replaceable, and the structure is independent of variations in the personal qualities of the personnel. In its pure form, formal organization is synonymous with rational action, scientific management.

The informal organization is the social structure that develops more or less spontaneously in every company. The social positions and relationships are governed by a value system and dynamics different from those of the formal organization. The differences arise because personalities cannot be scaled to fit perfectly the particular molds that the formal structure attributes to their jobs. Instead of confining themselves to these delineated roles, individuals remain whole people whose behavior is determined by a much more intricate network of interests, hopes, and fears than that which any functional assignment in an organization encompasses. Thus, behavioristic aspects become dominant in the informal organization.

Since these two concepts constitute the bedrock of modern organization theory, it would be wise to use them in the analysis of multinational companies. Yet, they are much less useful in this study than in the study of limited structures, such as factories or stores, where the atomistic elements of the organization, the individual employee and his functional task, can be made the pivotal points. Although not unessential, the atomistic elements do not present the most complex problems or the greatest challenges in the multinational company.

De Facto or Managerial Structure

The emphasis here is primarily on the architecture and secondarily on the bricks and mortar, because the multinational company is primarily a complex of companies rather than a combination of departments or individuals. Juridically, it is a compact among autonomous units of different national jurisdictions; socially, it is a multicultural aggregation of both formal and informal structures conditioned more by the environments of their respective countries than by the environment of any particular national culture. The contrasts among its parts in economic, political, and social milieu; the differences in technology and resource bases; the obstacles to international mobility of manpower, assets, and ideas; and the divergent trends and uneven tempos of development; all combine to create organizational problems peculiar to the multinational company. These problems are in many ways of a different order and magnitude than those encountered in typical domestic situations. It is to these problems that the analysis in this chapter must be directed.

To avoid unnecessary confusion with the general literature on organization, the standard terminology of *formal* and *informal* organization is retained, but often *managerial* is substituted for *formal* and *social* for *informal*. The synonyms are used to minimize confusion from another source that to date has escaped the scrutiny of organization theorists—the legal, or juridical, form of organization is defined by a country and imposed upon a company by its official charter. Although influenced by it, the managerial organization seldom coincides with the juridical form. Usually they are significantly different from each other. Both are formal organizations; however, the juridical form can lay a greater claim to that term than the managerial form can. What is worse, international relations people, as well as the legal profession, think of the juridical form of a company as its formal organization.

Thus, perfect clarity is unattainable here. It is, therefore, better to refrain, where possible, from using *formal* organization in either sense and, as suggested above, to substitute *managerial* or *de facto* organization in the sense of organization theory, and *statutory* or *de jure* organization in the legal or official sense.

De Jure or Statutory Structure

To have legal standing, organizations must be formed in accordance with the laws of the country in which they are to function. These laws are usually more explicit the more important the potential role an organization can play. Since a business firm can involve the vital interests of the society, all countries have statutory rules for its formation and operation. Although there is some imitation and international coordination, statutes regulating business organization and activity are essentially different in each country. As such, they represent invisible internal parameters for all organizations. Furthermore, the law of any sovereign nation can be satisfied only on its own terms.

A firm must first be granted a charter and licensed for business by the government of the host country. The charter will define the form, the officers, the purposes, the ownership, and possibly the activities and methods of the organization. Since only charters consistent with the statutory provisions can be issued, any applicant is automatically restricted to the choices provided by the legislation of the particular country.

A company cannot export the juridical structure of its organization to another country in which it might wish to establish an affiliate. The affiliate must be structured in terms of the laws of the host country to qualify for its charter and license. Even if the laws of two countries happen to provide for the same form of organization, the choice of the affiliate structure must still be based upon the juridical alternatives provided in the host country law rather than the parent company's structure.

The relevant comparisons are the alternatives internal to each legal system rather than cross-system similarities. Take, for example, a U.S. firm juridically organized as a corporation planning to set up a subsidiary in West Germany. If it imitated its own domestic structure and formed the subsidiary as a German corporation (*Aktiengesellschaft*, or A/G) it would deny itself the relatively greater freedoms it could enjoy by choosing the limited liability company (*Gesellschaft mit beschränkter Haftung*, or G.m.b.H.). Many countries provide for organizational forms other than the corporation with juridical personalities separate from their owners and with the owners' financial liability limited to their equity investments. The U.S. situation, where the corporation is the only juridical form so endowed, is an exception rather than the rule internationally.

To dismiss the de jure structure as a formal shell would be to misunderstand its economic implications. Being the only officially recognized linkage of the company to the different legal systems of its host nations, it is an important organizational reality, which affects multinational corporate behavior in fundamental ways. This is particularly true in financial and legislative matters, including such strategic areas as maximizing managerial freedom of action and corporate security, minimizing taxes and exchange losses, optimizing cash flows among the various entities of the firm, and qualifying for industrial development assistance, tariff protection, or government contracts in different countries.

ORGANIZATION OF NON-MNC INTERNATIONAL TRADE MANAGEMENT

Multinational business organization has been changing rapidly. In the process new concepts have emerged that have greatly expanded the once rather standardized pattern. To capture the dynamics of this evolution it is useful to start with an analytic exposition of the non-MNC structure, namely, the international trade structure.

Institutional Zones

International trade is a process involving imports, exports, and payments, which connect the business systems of different nations. The various enterprises that carry out the trading process form the institutional structure of trade. They provide not only the channels through which world trade flows but also its content and locomotion. All trade transactions and processes are either actions of or interactions among the system's institutional components.

The organizational pattern of non-MNC foreign trade consists of institutions in three different zones of business: (a) domestic firms, including producers, distributors, and service firms in the country of origin; (b) international intermediaries, that is, exporters and importers; and (c) foreign firms that perform the distribution function in the country of consumption for exports or serve as sources of supply for imports.

The management of foreign trade is divided among three institutional zones, the firms in each zone carrying out their part of the trade process and depending on firms in the other two zones for the completion of the process. To visualize the management specialization among the institutional zones graphically, the total scope of management might be viewed as a line connecting the point of production in the country of origin with the point of consumption in the country of destination, as shown in Figure 12.1. The functions performed in each zone can then be isolated as three successive segments in the total management process. Legally and financially, the business firms in the different zones are typically independent, but in reality they are interdependent, in that the firms in one zone need those in the other two to prosper.

Requirements for executive capabilities vary from zone to zone. Managers

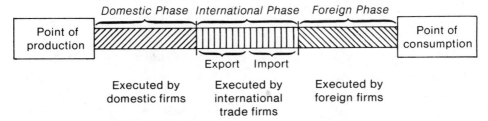

**Figure 12.1   Managerial Phases of Foreign Trade Under the
Traditional Structure**

in the domestic zone need, and typically possess, only the most rudimentary
acquaintance with any nondomestic aspect of the overall process. Since they
function entirely within the jurisdiction, both legal and cultural, of the country
of origin, they have minimal contact with the market overseas. For all practical
purposes the domestic phase of foreign trade management is not different from
domestic business itself; the same laws, costs, courts, unions, banks, interest
rates, and language apply. The transactions between the firms in the domestic
zone and those in the international zone are like transactions between two
domestic companies. The only special skills required of export management
on the manufacturing level are a thorough knowledge of the firms in the
international zone and the ability to monitor their performance. The foreign
phase in this scheme is the mirror image of the domestic phase, except that
differences in national business conditions and customary practices between
the countries distort the two in various ways.

The vitality and power in foreign trade management lie in the international
zone (see Table 12.1 on page 222). The export and import intermediaries
possess the know-how and techniques for penetrating trade barriers, reconciling
incongruities among different countries' laws and customs, and handling the
commercial and financial formalities required. The expertise required from the
managers of the intermediaries rates as specialized competence.

Analysis of the firms in the international zone is hampered by the cultural
environments that have shaped and conditioned the institutions in different
countries. However, since these environmental forces manifest themselves
particularly in the form of the organization and not so much in its substance,
a general picture of these institutions can be drawn by focusing not on organizational details that differ from country to country but on the basic patterns
of objectives, operations, and behaviors fairly common in all countries. In what
follows, then, the institutions of the international zone are described in their
prototypal form rather than in detailed terms.

The Export Subzone

The export subzone consists of four categories of participating institutions:
merchants, agents, buyers, and legal-advantage organizations. The lines be-

Table 12.1   Institutional Structure of Non-MNC International Trade

DOMESTIC ZONE—BUSINESS SYSTEM OF COUNTRY OF PRODUCTION	INTERNATIONAL ZONE—INTERMEDIARIES		FOREIGN ZONE— BUSINESS SYSTEM OF COUNTRY OF CONSUMPTION
	Export Subzone	Import Subzone	
Producers	Export merchants:	Import merchants:	Service firms
Distributors	Export houses	Import houses	custom:
	Export trading	Import trading	Custom house
Banks	companies	companies	brokers
	Pure traders		Freight
Service firms:		Import representatives:	forwarders
Freight brokers	Export agents:	Commission houses	
International	Selling agents	Residents repre-	Carriers
freight	Manufacturer's	sentatives of	
forwarders	agents	foreign exporters	Banks
Marine-insurance	Export mangement		Distributors
agencies	companies[a]	Consumer-owned	
Consultants	International brokers	import	Dealers
		establishments:	
	Export buyers:	Manufacturers	Consumers
	Commission houses	Retailers	
	(also known as	Cooperative buy-	
	indent houses or	ing groups	
	confirming houses)		
	Resident buyers		
	Producer-owned export		
	establishments:		
	(export branches		
	or subsidiaries)		
	Legal-advantage		
	organizations:		
	Webb-Pomerane		
	associates		
	LDC corporation		
	DISC (Domestic		
	international sales		
	corporations)		

[a]Called *combination export managers* in older literature.

tween these categories are sometimes blurred in practice because certain firms encompass the activities of more than one group and others specialize in borderline functions that are difficult to classify, but on the whole these distinctions apply.

Export Merchants   Export merchants include the institutions which undertake export operations at their own risk, that is, which buy products from domestic companies with the intention of reselling them abroad. The legal definition of a merchant rests on the ownership of the goods to be exported: if the export firm takes title to the goods, it is a merchant enterprise; if it does not, it is an agent. The three main types of export merchants can be described as follows:

1. *The export house.* The export house has permanent sales outlets in one or more major regions, permanent suppliers and inventories for its principle lines of goods, the capability to handle all export processes, a departmentalized organization, its own sales force, and a wide assortment of product lines.

2. *The trading company.* Trading companies include a great number and variety of export merchants who deal in one or a few related products, typically concentrating on staples or bulk commodities. Unlike the export house, which performs all marketing functions, the trading company performs only a few. Typically it is a small firm, often family operated, and has modest resources and rudimentary organization.

3. *The pure trader.* The pure trader is a business firm that specializes in a few basic commodities (often only one), carrying out arbitrage transactions in them internationally. The trader uncovers local shortages and surpluses in widely separated parts of the world and arranges offsetting purchases and sales in a short time, thus helping to stabilize international commodity markets in addition to making itself a quick profit. Pure trading firms have no operating organization besides the intelligence-gathering and buying-selling mechanisms. They handle no physical distribution and never take delivery of the goods they buy.

Export Agents   As noted before, the chief distinction between agents and merchants is that agents never take title to the goods they purchase; rather, they act on behalf of another party. Four types of agents can be identified:

1. *Selling agents.* Selling agents are large companies that distribute mostly semimanufactured or staple goods produced by small- to medium-sized manufacturers. The selling firm acts as the joint marketing agency for a number of factories or mills, pooling the sales volume of all its client producers and thus obtaining much greater competitive strength than any of the producers could manage without it.

2. *Manufacturers' agents.* Manufacturers' agents build a large volume of sales in a particular market by combining the products of several manufacturers with a minimum of competition between them. Thus, the agent develops an assortment of complementary goods, products that satisfy related needs but cannot displace one another and that can be distributed through the same wholesale and retail outlets.

3. *Export management companies.* Formerly called *combination export managers*, these firms are the most original of the export agents. Export management companies contract to serve as the exclusive export outlet for their client and function like the manufacturer's own export department. The export management company combines the principle of complete and exclusive distribution rights (characteristic of the selling agent) with the principle of a complementary or noncompetitive product line (characteristic of the manufacturers' agent). A new version of this type of firm has shifted its objective from the long-term continuation of relatively

routine trade to the creation of new export opportunities and capabilities for its client manufacturers.

4. *International brokers.* The activities of the international broker closely parallel those of the pure trader, except that the broker does not actually buy or sell but only mediates the transaction.

Export Buyers   The next major type of export institution is the export buyer, who buys in one country for an entity in another country. There are two main types. The *export commission house* (often known as the *indent house* in the ex-British areas of the world) is a resident buying organization for foreign firms. Because its primary affiliation is with the foreign firm, it can seldom be anything other than a supplementary outlet for a manufacturer's export business. However, small firms in many countries rely solely on this export channel.

Resident buyers are offices of governments or industries maintained in another country to procure supplies that must be imported in substantial quantity. Resident buyers form a minor segment of the export structure except in some smaller countries that trade heavily with the Communist bloc.

Legal-Advantage Organizations   International business has been subject to special legislation in all countries. These laws frequently provide for special types of business organizations to be employed under certain circumstances, generally to promote export trade or enhance the strength of the country's enterprises vis-à-vis international competitors. While it would be impossible to present a global survey of such organizations, we can outline the two types found in the United States.

1. *The Webb-Pomerane association.* The Export Trade Act of 1918, sometimes called the Webb Act or the Webb-Pomerane Act, permits cooperative export activities among U.S. companies. The law grants conditional exemption from certain parts of the Sherman Antitrust Act of 1914 and from Section 7 of the Clayton Act to associations of business firms organized for the exclusive purpose of export trade as long as the activities of the association comply with three conditions; (a) they do not restrain the export trade of any other company; (b) they do not raise or lower prices in the United States; and (c) they do not restrain trade within the United States in any other way. These associations benefit primarily the manufacturers of staples and raw materials, because the products are standardized, they are sold primarily on the basis of price, and marketing techniques are simple to define. These associations have declined in importance as the patterns of manufacture and export have shifted toward complex products and more sophisticated marketing practices.

2. *Domestic international sales corporations (DISCs).* In the fall of 1971 Congress authorized U.S. companies to set up special subsidiaries called DISCs to handle foreign sales of American-made goods. The aim was export stimulation through tax incentive. DISCs can be established only for the purpose of trade; these subsidiaries are not allowed to undertake any manufacturing. In practice, most DISCs are paper corporations, consisting of a legal charter and a separate chart of accounts, while actual trading is carried out by the parent firm. A panel

convened by GATT in 1976 declared DISCs and similar devices in Belgium, France, and Holland to be disguises for export subsidization.

The Import Subzone

The institutional framework of import activity, although not a mirror image of export activity, is quite similar; naturally, import and export structures must form a functional whole if their joint objective—the flow of international trade—is to materialize. We are not concerned here with whom these institutions belong to or whose specific interests they serve, but with how the apparatus for trade is constructed. The import structure embraces three main categories of institutions: import merchants, import representatives, and consumer-owned import establishments.

Import Merchants   Full-function *import houses* with a general line of merchandise, which dominated the U.S. wholesale trade in its early days and up to World War I, have all but disappeared from the scene. Extreme protectionism and the depressed conditions of the 1930s severely weakened the competitive position of the general import house, already strained by challenges from the revolution in American marketing headed by large-scale retailing organizations. When World War II started, all these adversities were further aggravated, apparently wiping out the general import house as an international wholesaler in the United States. This type of institution still exists in some other countries, but everywhere the trend has been toward the limited-function import trading company.

The *import trading company*, like its export counterpart, specializes both in terms of the distributive functions it undertakes and in terms of the products it will import. Typically, it concentrates on a narrow range, either one line or a combined assortment geared to a demand pattern of a specific group or to the requirements of a particular domestic distribution channel.

Import Representatives   As indicated earlier, the broker who is active in the export business is often also engaged in import activity, so most should have been classified as *international brokers*. While some brokers do limit their activity exclusively to export transactions, this author has no knowledge of exclusive import brokers. However, two types of import representatives exist.

1. *Commission houses.* Unlike the export commission house, the import commission house is strictly an agent that buys abroad on behalf of a consumer, makes all arrangements in the name of its principal, and acts in all respects strictly in compliance with the authority given it by the principal. It assumes no financial responsibility for either the foreign supplier or the domestic consumer.

2. *Resident representatives of foreign exporters.* To avoid direct investments in overseas sales offices or distribution branches, exporters of all types have long utilized resident representatives in different foreign markets to handle the export selling

function, i.e., to generate import orders from the agent's country to the exporter. This representative can be either an agent or a merchant.

Consumer-Owned Import Establishments   In importing, as in exporting, the shift has been toward direct control over the process and over establishments carrying it out. Manufacturing firms that use foreign materials or components have come to rely on their own import unit if this is the only foreign activity of the company or have transferred the procurement function to an international division if a variety of multinational operations is involved. The import department, where it still exists, resembles the export department, except that it ususally has a product-based organization.

Large retail stores—department stores, chains, and supermarkets—have set up their own import units, which deal directly with foreign sources or export intermediaries. Smaller retailers (such as independent department stores and local chains) have created *cooperative buying groups*, which usually function as a suborganization to their cooperative buying organization. Both these retail import entities have shown vigorous initiative in having their own resident buyers in the source countries and in seeking direct contact with potential merchandise resources for new products and product ideas.

STRUCTURAL MODELS OF MNCs

This three-zone pattern evolved in the last century and provided the basic model for international business until about 1950. It was a model of institutional specialization, the firms in each zone performing only their special part of the international trade process, none assuming responsibility for the entire process. Such specialization met well the requirements of a world in which very little trade crossed international borders.

The growth of MNCs in the 1950s and thereafter created several alternative structural models to the three-zone pattern (see Figure 12.2). In a general sense, these alternatives reflect the stages of growth from a UNC with exporting activity to a fully integrated international corporate structure. Lately, however, there has been an increasing tendency to skip the intermediate stages and move directly from alternative A to D, E, or even F.

The International Division Model

When domestic business firms start developing foreign operations, a typical problem they face is the lack of management expertise in international matters. Their managements have not had any experience in operating under foreign conditions. The firms' managers have made their mark in the domestic setting. Foreign countries are truly foreign to them. Their perceptions of risk and uncertainty in foreign markets are inflated by ignorance and their propensity for action lowered by fear of failure. The decisions they do take turn out to

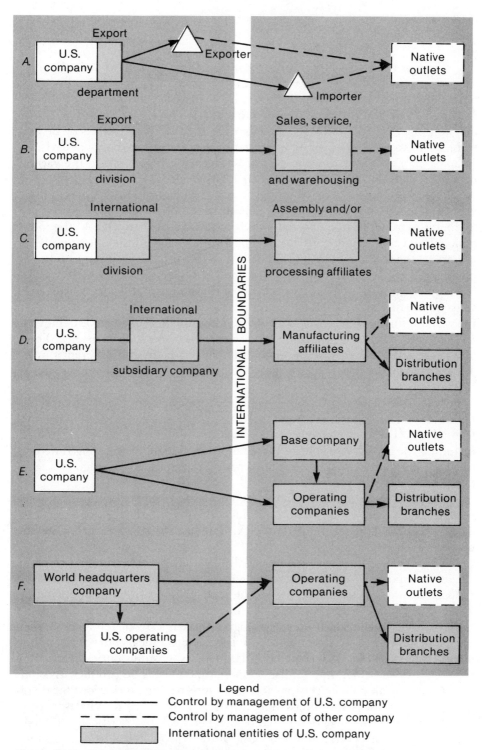

Figure 12.2 Types of Relations Between Parent Organizations and Their International Entities

be erroneous due to their inept identification of the real risks. Experience and expertise in international and foreign situations are very scarce skills for these firms.

There is no easy solution to this problem. Management style is the most important asset of any firm. A wholesale replacement of managers is, therefore, out of the question. Retraining the entire management cadre is equally infeasible in any realistic time frame. What is left is to gather together all the bits and pieces of international expertise that the firm may possess or be able to hire and to create a separate organizational unit, an international division, to house it. From here these scarce skills are then rationed out to the various operating divisions on the basis of their relative needs.

The international division model is shown in Figure 12.3. Part A is more typical in companies that are divisionalized by product line, while Part B can be found more often in territorially divisionalized firms. In Part A, the international division mainly supplies technical competence in the operating level; in Part B, the international division does that and also has an input into policy making.

The main purpose of the international division is to put the international skills of the firm to most effective use. For a fledgling MNC these skills form the weakest link in the management chain. How are these skills to be deployed? And how will the international division relate to the operating divisions? These questions have no standard answers; different companies do different things. Their behavior in this respect is largely dependent upon the characteristics of their products and markets.

Product-based divisionalization is typically associated with technological differentiation. Each division is required to master a significantly different product technology. The management of each division possesses a separate identity, including the capacity to control the vital production and marketing functions of the product lines. Mangement power is rooted in the knowledge of a technologically complex product.

Territorially divisionalized companies put market complexities ahead of technological complexities. Either the products involve relatively simple technologies or the markets are highly complex. The line managers must master the market.

The international division is essentially a variant of the territorial principle. As such, it poses fewer problems for companies already using territorial divisions. In product-based companies the introduction of the international division creates more serious problems. Since the corporate command structure is built around the product line technologies, there is a strong tendency in such companies to regard the international division as a technical entity for handling technical tasks—letters of credit, consular invoices, customs duties, translation of foreign documents, and similar support functions. The product divisions tend to reserve all policy decisions regarding international operations for themselves. This reduces the international division's influence on vital strategies and policy decisions, where international expertise is most critically needed.

No perfect structural solutions exist for these problems. The nearest thing to a satisfactory solution is the model depicted in Part B of Figure 12.3. Even

A. *EXECUTION-ORIENTED*

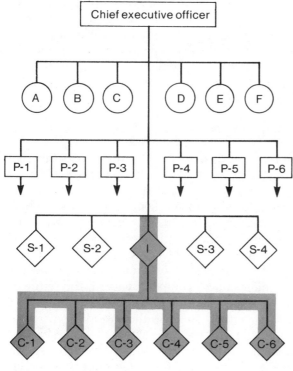

1. Headquarters level: centralized activities of corporate intelligence, strategy, policy, planning, control.

2. General staff units and functional specialists, each a different specialty such as research, manufacturing, finance, legal.

3. Operating level: relatively autonomous product divisions, each representing a different product.

4. International operations: international division functions as a service division (S-1 to S-4 indicate other service divisions.)

5. Foreign sector: foreign-based affiliates organized under country or area managers but in technical matters working closely with product divisions, each representing location in a different country.

B. *POLICY-ORIENTED*

1. Same as 1 in A.

2. Same as 2 in A.

3. International operations: international division functions as a semi-autonomous organization with cross-divisional jurisdiction over international activities of the company.

4. Same as 3 in A.

5. Same as 5 in A.

Figure 12.3 Alternative Structure for the International Division

here, the international division, although under the protective eye of top management, remains in many ways dependent upon the product divisions. This is particularly true if foreign factories use the manufacturing or engineering services of the domestic plants. How well or poorly the international division functions in the product division setting always depends, therefore, on the cooperation and support it can get from the product divisions. Horizontal communication channels and interdivisional personal relations are thus crucial.

The International Subsidiary Company Model

Creation of an International Subsidiary Company   The difficulties inherent in the divisional model have compelled business to seek other structural solutions to its international problems. The international subsidiary company, a separate headquarters for foreign activities of the firm, has been used by a number of firms. At one time it was the most prevalent form of MNC organization. More recently, it has yielded to the world company model.

The international subsidiary company may be conceived of as the lifting of the international division out of the domestic corporate structure and elevating it to the status of a legally independent company with all the statutory organs, charter, and officers of an autonomous firm. Customarily, the word *international* has been used in the name to distinguish the subsidiary from the parent—Boeing International, General Electric International, Weyerhaeuser International. Its separate legal status qualifies the subsidiary for some special privileges under statutes and regulations covering taxes, foreign trade, foreign aid, and some other government controls. However, the primary reasons companies adopt this organization are the strategy advantages and operating efficiencies that it offers.

The international subsidiary company model goes beyond divisionalization. Its scope is not limited to the domestic structure, nor are its operational capabilities subordinated to domestic divisions. Although it may serve the objective of diversification of both products and markets, it is not limited to this or to any other objective of the domestic divisions, nor is it reducible to a routine service unit to the latter. Rather, the subsidiary is an international headquarters prototype, a structural system for the administration of multinational foreign operations in the broad sense: corporate holdings, asset producing activities, marketing, operating facilities, research, personnel, and organizational subentities.

A Galaxy of Companies   The international subsidiary headquarters may or may not be directly involved in operational activities. In large corporations, it is often a company of companies, the central headquarters of a variety of operating companies scattered throughout the world, whose only commonality may be the fact that they all are located outside the United States. In smaller companies, it is typically a hybrid between a holding company control center for different foreign affiliates and an operating headquarters for managing the day-to-day operations of the affiliates.

Where it is fully developed, this model possesses a self-contained head-quarters structure in most respects, including trade and transfer arrangements among the affiliates and supply arrangements with domestic subsidiaries of the parent.

Figure 12.4 shows the structure of the international subsidiary model. It creates two separate structures, one for domestic management, the other for international management of the firm. The two structures are linked on top in the office of the chief executive officer, who heads both companies. The operational synchronization between the two is carried out by a special staff unit in the parent company headed by a *contact officer*, who is a vice president

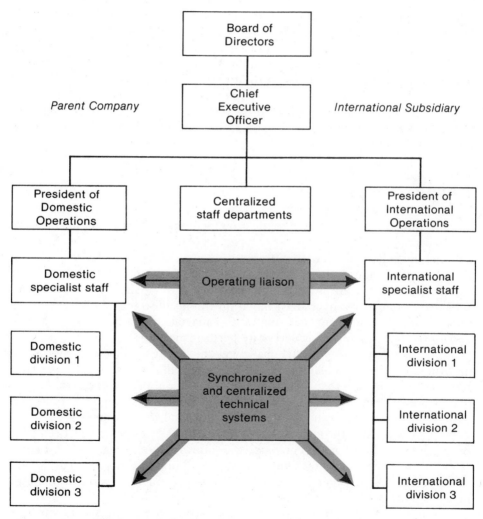

Figure 12.4   The International Subsidiary Company Model

or of equivalent rank. For greater effectiveness, the contact officer may sit on the boards of directors of both companies.

Internal Structure   The international subsidiary's internal organization may take on a compound structure, where some product organization may be superimposed upon the geographic principle. For example, within one diversified company there exist three subsets of operating subsidiaries: one for heavy equipment, one for scientific instruments, and one for consumer products. Although in each country and world region there are appropriate corporate organs with general jurisdiction in the territory, the product groups have a high degree of autonomy and are in many countries really subheadquarters for their own specialized subsidiaries or other types of affiliates. In larger firms the international structural design often takes on a resemblance to a galaxy, with multiple centers, differentiated communication channels, and multiple levels of managerial jurisdiction.

The distinction between the international division and the international subsidiary company is often difficult to discern. In many firms the heavily overused word *division* remains in the title of the organization long after its substance has been converted to an international subsidiary company. This semantic difficulty has misled some observers to rate the divisional organization as the most common among U.S. companies. Actually, the subsidiary is much more prevalent.

The World Company Model

Organizational accommodation to the growing impact of international business upon corporate strategies has not stopped with the development of the international subsidiary model. It represents, however, a turning point. To this point, all the stages in the development of international organization—the export department, the international division, and, finally, the international subsidiary company—have been based on the premise that the separation of international management and domestic management leads to higher managerial proficiency and better corporate performance.

The world company model challenges this premise. The challenge is not motivated by the parochial naiveté, "What is good at home is good abroad," but by the realization that the more discriminating approach, greater intellectual awareness, and more cosmopolitan orientation that are required in international management, can also sharpen and revitalize the domestic sector of a company by raising the levels of social and cultural awareness and by reducing provincialism and other psychological rigidities resisting organizational adaptation to the ever-increasing tempo of change. Thus, the slogan could almost be reversed, "What is good in international management is good in domestic management."

Figures 12.5 and 12.6 (on page 234) show two versions of the world company model. In its simplest form, its command structure rests on the geographic

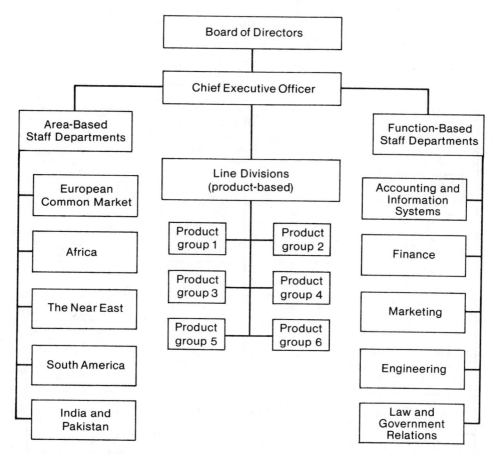

Figure 12.5   Product-Centered World Company Model

principle, with area specialists occupying the key line positions. To this basic structure can be added elements of product organization as well as functionally specialized units. In technology intensive firms, the line structure would be represented by product groups and areas and functional expertise assigned to staff positions.

The world company model makes no distinction between the domestic and the foreign. This does not mean that the model is insensitive to territorially changing variables, such as cultural, economic, or political factors. Its principal aim is to place no structural limitation on either the scope or degree of adaptation of the organization to the realities of different localities. Such adaptation is possible on both an international and intranational basis whenever the existing conditions make it desirable. Since the nature and extent of adaptation needed are determined by territorial variations in conditions, the degree of adaptation in any particular aspect of the organization must be greatest in the localized activity areas and in functions that are directly related to any locality. Consequently, most of the ability to adapt is required on the lower levels of

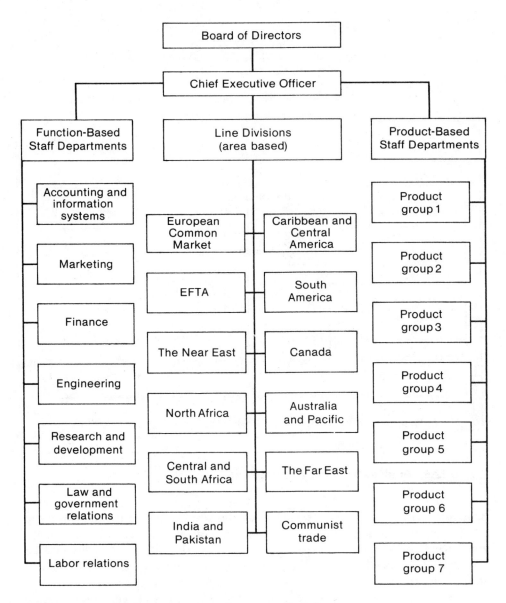

Figure 12.6 Area-Centered World Company Model

the organization structure, and the need to adapt decreases along the vertical axes of the organization.

The world company model compels headquarters executives to view their management responsibilities from a global perspective and to cultivate structures and objectives that enable maximum growth and profitability to occur in a worldwide context. The headquarters of the world company is, thus, concerned not just with national or international affairs, but with world affairs.

Its orbit is the globe and, in the future, conceivably also the moon and outer space. Management problems peculiar to individual countries or to certain groups of countries belong primarily to lower level jurisdictions. In theory, there is no nation centeredness at all at the top management level. However, since under existing political realities the headquarters of a company must be domiciled in some country, there is always, in fact, a home country whose environmental constraints are an inescapable reality to the headquarters managers of a world company.

Monocentric and Polycentric Structures

Entry into each new country compounds the environmental diversities of a MNC. How top managment can best deal with these diversities is a persistent issue of MNC organization. A well-designed organization must provide the structural basis for the most effective distribution of decision making power, as determined by the conditions and constraints that vary from country to country or from one world region to another.

Different host economies represent competing environmental systems, all of which have power over the MNC and each of which is vying for predominance over other host countries. The United States wants all MNCs to behave according to U.S. norms, not only in the United States, but also in all countries where it has affiliates; similarly, Japan would like them to behave according to Japanese norms everywhere. No MNC can comply with such conflicting expectations; rather, it must choose among them. The choice made by each MNC is determined by its management's assessment of the most probable course of least resistance. Since there are no concrete standards to measure the different host government reactions, the assessments vary with the outlook and biases of top executives.

In a monocentric MNC (Figure 12.7A, on page 236), all top management powers (strategies and major policies) are centralized in the world headquarters. The affiliates' autonomy is limited to putting the headquarters' decisions into practice, that is, to making operating decisions only. The monocentric model is appropriate when the MNC has affiliates in just a few countries that are relatively similar.

As the number of host environments increases, the need arises for dividing the MNC's operating territory into geographic zones and establishing a zonal subheadquarters, sometimes called a base company, for each. Such a polycentric model is shown in Figure 12.7B. The base company can be utilized in either the international subsidiary model or in the world company model.

Centralization Versus Decentralization

Because it is highly heterogeneous, the environment of an MNC is inherently hostile to uniformities in both initiative and response of the corporation. An effective interplay between the MNC and its environment can result only from

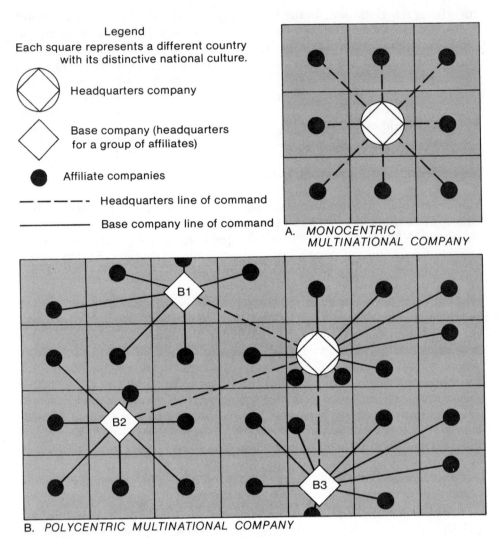

Legend
Each square represents a different country with its distinctive national culture.

Headquarters company

Base company (headquarters for a group of affiliates)

Affiliate companies

– – – – – Headquarters line of command

———— Base company line of command

A. *MONOCENTRIC MULTINATIONAL COMPANY*

B. *POLYCENTRIC MULTINATIONAL COMPANY*

Figure 12.7   Monocentric and Polycentric MNCs

a structure that is capable of a variety of simultaneous initiatives, responses, and other types of organizational behaviors. This argues for decentralization.

In a typical MNC, there is an advantage to a central clearinghouse of information about the gross situation, but decisions and execution require more minute local data. Deciding in headquarters means relying on information that is cumulatively abstract and to a greater or lesser degree irrelevant. Also, the line of command execution must apply standards and procedures that cumulatively do not fit the specific local situation. This is true because the central headquarters is by its nature first of all an accumulator and assimilator, sometimes also a synthesizer, and only secondarily a dispenser of what it has accumulated, assimilated, and synthesized from the total corporate realm. In mathematical terms, the headquarters functions as a producer and dispenser of analyses. The problems in different parts of the realm, however, depend upon specifics and can therefore be resolved only in terms of specifics.

The maxim that a society that distributes power widely is superficially full of conflict but fundamentally strong and stable applies to the MNC perhaps even more than to political bodies. With their own peculiar abilities, aspirations, and criteria, each affiliate, country, continent, and professional grouping in the MNC can increase its contribution to the company if there is a closer alignment and freer interchange among the different parts of the corporation on one hand and between the various parts and their environments on the other hand. The recent shift among MNCs toward polycentrism is propelled by this dual objective. How a firm adapts to its various national environments determines whether it has smooth or stormy relations with host governments. We shall explore this relationship in Chapter 15.

SUMMARY

MNCs alter the competitive environment for UNCs as well as for the MNCs themselves. Each MNC is a highly complex organization, and each is different from all others in numerous specific ways. In broader terms, some MNCs share certain common features that others do not. Studying the commonalities and differences among them has enabled researchers to construct different structural models of the main organizational characteristics of MNCs.

Companies in an early stage of multinationalization tend to model themselves after the export-import firms by setting up execution-oriented international divisions. With continued growth, the firm elevates the international division to active participation in strategic planning and policy formulation. The policy-oriented international division may or may not subsequently be given an independent juridical status by converting it to an international subsidiary company. The latter became the dominant structure for large MNCs during the big push period of the 1950s and 1960s, when the rapid rate of creation of foreign affiliates combined with the scarcity of educational programs in international business to create serious shortages of international managers. Separation of international management from domestic allowed maximum use of international management expertise. As this scarcity started to ebb, the world company model evolved. This combines the international and domestic management responsibilities at the top management level. Today many MNCs are patterned on this model.

Territorially divisionalized firms have generally had a relatively smooth adaptation of their organization to multinational diversities. The same cannot be said of product divisionalized firms, whose adaptation to international expansion presents difficult problems of duplication and conflicting authority of product and area managers.

Many MNCs have been torn between requirements for adapting to different conditions in different world regions and the need for streamlining decisions and information systems through centralization. The larger firms seek to balance these opposing forces by creating subheadquarters or base companies in different regions of the world. The subheadquarters adapt operating policies to the environmental peculiarities of their respective regions.

FOR REVIEW AND DISCUSSION

1. Define the following terms as referred to in MNC organization: informal, formal, de jure or statutory, de facto or managerial.

2. Would it be appropriate to divide the management of trade among the affiliates of MNCs into the same three stages or zones as the management of export and import business of UNCs? Explain.

3. Organizationally speaking, all MNCs are actually composites of many companies rather than one firm. Comment.

4. How important is it to distinguish clearly between the international division and the international subsidiary? Are there variables that make the distinction more or less important?

5. If you were the manager of a product division of a firm, would this bias you in any way regarding the organizational models available to your firm in its international growth?

6. How many different ways can you conceive of for a firm to bring the expertise of territorial and technological specialists to bear on its management decisions? What are the risks and tradeoffs in this process?

7. Is it reasonable to project that all MNCs will adopt the world company model as time goes on? Why or why not?

8. Which factors promote polycentric structures? Consider both external and internal factors.

9. Deciding in headquarters means relying on information that is cumulatively abstract and to a greater or lesser degree irrelevant. Comment.

10. Why are certain departments (such as transportation and computer systems) usually centralized while others are not?

13

Foreign-Based Affiliates

*H*ow each of the foreign entities of an MNC are organized is first of all a matter of law. To gain entry to a particular country, a company must comply with all the legal provisions applicable to it. Since the laws of no two countries are identical, the legal aspects of establishment must always be handled as special cases.

Generally speaking, visas for corporate entry into a country are subject to more restrictions than are those that apply to people, goods, or capital. To meet these requirements, MNCs have relied mainly on four alternative approaches: a branch license, a subsidiary company under the laws of the host country, a joint venture with one or more indigenous companies, or a licensing agreement with an indigenous firm. In more recent years three additional alternatives have been added: management contracts, production sharing arrangements, and technology transfer agreements.

FOREIGN BRANCHES

From a legal standpoint a branch is not a separate juridical entity but a physical offshoot of the parent firm. As long as both the branch and the parent are in the same country, they are subject to the same national jurisdiction. Since the branch does not have a juridical personality of its own, the parent company remains responsible for any legal action taken either by or against the branch. If, however, a branch is located in a different country, the parent's legal umbrella cannot cover it. Each is in a different national jurisdiction.

Lacking its own juridical personality, a branch will not be licensed by a host country unless it is first domesticated by having a national of the host country serve as its legal custodian. The custodianship must be based on a formally executed *power of attorney*, by which the parent company conveys to the foreign citizen or firm complete legal rights over the branch. Since such an arrangement creates subtle problems and additional uncertainties, foreign branches of MNCs are uncommon.

The foreign branch has other weaknesses. Business licenses may be of short duration, and frequent renewals involve considerable expense. Also, regulations and government surveillance may be tighter. For example, the branch may be required to patronize local suppliers, not compete with local industry, or refrain from employing nonnationals. Finally, the taxable base may be defined so that the branch becomes taxable not on the basis of its own earnings or assets but on the basis of the total profits or capitalization of the MNC.

FOREIGN SUBSIDIARIES

To avoid such discriminatory treatment, most MNCs prefer to organize their affiliates as indigenous enterprises under the laws of the host country. Although the legal forms of enterprises have over the years become relatively similar, significant differences still exist. The most important of these is the existence of organizational forms other than the corporation that have juridical person-alities separate from their owners and in which the owners' liability is limited to their investments in the enterprise. For example, German law provides for a limited liability company (G.m.b.H.) that resembles the U.S. corporation in all features essential to management yet enjoys much greater freedom of action than does the German equivalent of the corporation. Thus, the U.S. term *to incorporate* is often as misleading as is the popular notion that the various national affiliates of a multinational company are corporations. Many are not. Some others should not be. With the growth of the MNC the legal differences and the various organizational opportunities that the laws of different countries provide have become better understood by U.S. business.

DUAL ORGANIZATION

De Jure Structure

In most countries, the law requires that a certain number of directorships or other positions in the firm be staffed by local nationals. Compliance with this requirement produces a statutory or de jure administration that most MNCs find unsuitable for the actual management of the affiliate. MNCs limit the functions of these officers to the very minimum required by law: holding an annual meeting; signing necessary forms, tax returns, and annual reports; sanctioning legal contracts; representing the affiliate in court litigations. To safeguard itself, the parent company must fill these positions with people of unquestionable integrity or, more commonly, counterbalance their official powers with contractual constraints such as leasing the assets to the de jure administration with the proviso that the officers delegate the operational re-sponsibilities to individuals appointed by the lessor.

Another typical host country requirement is local participation in equity ownership. Sometimes more than half of the capital invested in the affiliate must be controlled by local businesses. In countries in which such restrictions exist, the MNC usually either buys part ownership in an existing foreign concern or induces a foreign firm to coinvest with it in a new venture. The latter practice has become popular in recent years, especially among makers of technical products such as machine tools and other factory equipment, who need technical personnel to help install and to service the products they sell.

To enable the local coinvestors to contribute the legally required share of equity capital, the parent company may permit the coinvestors to turn over existing assets such as buildings, machinery, sites, production processes, and even goodwill. Monetary values can be assigned to all of these by mutual agreement. Thus, the need for a cash contribution by the local concern is minimized. How far an MNC is willing to go in this respect depends upon the alternatives available to it and the profit potential of the particular market.

De Facto Structure

The de facto management of foreign-based affiliates is often different from the de jure administration. No standardized interrelationship between the de facto and de jure managements exists; each company develops its own formula. In some companies the two are completely divorced. In others they are quite closely interwoven, with most titular officers serving as operating executives. In the great majority of cases the actual management is in the hands of people other than the legally prescribed directors and officers.

The complete separation of de facto and de jure administrations is illustrated by the organizational structure of a large U.S. company that operates affiliates in a number of Latin American countries. Each of these affiliates is incorporated under the laws of the respective country, but none of them functions as a separate administrative unit. Instead, they "buy" their management from a *management services corporation*, a subsidiary of the parent company, organized exclusively to manage all the activities of the company in the Latin American area.

The de jure and de facto structures of foreign-based affiliates have become more integrated in recent years, as MNCs have started to hire more local managers and as they have generally raised the level of sophistication of their managers by setting up executive development programs emphasizing international problems. Where such training programs have been in existence for some time, the results are most encouraging.

JOINT VENTURES

A *joint venture* is a business enterprise in which two or more business entities from different countries participate on a permanent basis. The participation is not limited to equity capital but normally extends to control of the undertaking through manufacturing processes, patents, trademarks, managerial know-how, or other operationally essential factors.

Most joint ventures are bipartite. The traditional model calls for a foreign majority partner and a local minority partner, the former providing the management and the latter serving to anchor the venture in the indigenous economy. In the past the insistence on majority ownership and undivided managerial authority by U.S. partners limited multipartite venture formation, since local partners regarded fractional shares of minority ownership too small for any real influence.

Majority and Minority Positions

Increasingly, host country objections to and legal restrictions against foreign domination of joint ventures, especially in the developing countries, have started to foster a growing acceptance of minority positions by U.S. firms. Experience has shown that majority position does not exclude host government interference—it sometimes causes or compounds it—nor is minority position necessarily synonymous with lack of influence and management control over the venture.

Host governments guard jealously against overt foreign control. Power, railroads, port facilities, hospitals, public service facilities, and other aspects of the infrastructure constitute the hard core of the industries very closely watched by government authorities. Resource-oriented industries, such as mining, tropical agriculture, and lumber, where majority positions or complete foreign ownership used to be the rule, are now required by many host countries to have majority control by local nationals, sometimes a government corporation, and to limit foreign equity to 49 percent or less. Refusal of some companies to comply with this requirement has led to expropriation of their properties by host governments.

The acceptance of minority position and willingness to enter into partnership with state enterprises have removed two corporate taboos that have blocked the formation of multipartite joint ventures. Now the way is open. Although the tradition-bound, older MNCs, as well as many overly centralized ones, are still wary about the new flexible approach, the newer MNCs are already enmeshed in multipartite ventures. Since they require greater cross-cultural sophistication and more adaptive decision making processes than the old bipartite arrangements, multipartite ventures are likely to grow only to the extent to which the expertise of international management advances to equal this new option.

Types of Joint Venture Enterprises

A joint venture may take several forms, depending upon the identity of the partners and the extent of the ownership by each partner (Figure 13.1). Re-

Comments	United States	+	Partner	=	Joint Venture
Foreign partner from a third country	National Steel, Inc.	+	Luxemburg Steel Corp.	=	National Steel of Brazil
Foreign partner a local firm; both partners in same industry	United Chemical, Inc.	+	Union Chimique Française, S.A.	=	United Chemical of France
Foreign partner a major customer of joint venture	U.S. Cement, Inc.	+	Indian Building Material Co.	=	Cement Company of India
Foreign partner a distributor in the field of joint venture	Imperial Auto, Inc.	+	Imperial Auto Distribution	=	Imperial Auto of Germany
Foreign partner a landowner or government agency	Tin Mining Company, Inc.	+	Thai holders of concession rights	=	Tin Mining Company of Thailand
Foreign partner a non-manufacturer	United Aluminum, Inc.	+	Canadian financial institutions	=	United Aluminum of Canada
Foreign partner a government	National Oil, Inc.	+	National Libanese Oil Agency	=	National Oil of Liban

Figure 13.1   Types of Joint-Venture Partners (All Names Fictitious)

garding partners, a firm has basically three choices: local companies (private enterprises), government agencies, or parties from a third country. Regarding ownership, the key decision is whether to acquire a majority position or to accept a minority position; subsidiary issues involve the degree of flexibility and adaptability that the particular proposition warrants.

Identity of the Partners   The early joint ventures were often associations among partners all of whom were alien to the country in which the enterprise was located. For example, a U.S. company combined with a British firm for oil exploration in Arabia, or French and Swiss companies joined efforts to mine phosphate in South America. In most cases, the advantage of a common enterprise arose from pooling the different resources and capabilities of the partners. One may have had the capital but lacked the experience or the political entree into a country, and the other firm may have possessed the latter. In highly speculative investments, spreading the risk was also an advantage.

Association with Local Private Interests   Normally, the local partner in a joint venture is a company of some significance in the field. As such, it can contribute production facilities, markets, distribution outlets, labor, and management to the new enterprise. The need for starting from scratch is thus eliminated, typical initial losses are minimized, the developmental period is shortened, and both the investment and the uncertainty about the foreign partner are reduced.

A joint venture may also be formed with a local partner operating in a related field. In India, for instance, the Tata Engineering and Locomotive Company (locomotives and heavy engineering products) has organized an automobile division with Daimler-Benz of West Germany; in the Philippines, the Intercontinental Hotels Corporation has formed a joint venture with a Philippine real estate firm. This kind of association is usually initiated by the foreign firm, which seeks out a local company for some specific reason. The more common reasons are these:

1. To gain entry into the country
2. To keep the dollar portion of the new investment under a desired limit
3. To achieve vertical integration of operations where either supplier-consumer or supplier-distributor relationships are involved
4. To gain access to natural resources, patents, or other valuable inputs that a native company may control

In some cases, joint ventures are formed by partners who have no industry connection or functional relationship. For instance, Monsanto Chemical holds 40 percent of the stock of an Italian company, Sicedison S.p.A., a diversified manufacturer of organic and inorganic chemicals, for which the native partner and majority owner is Societe Edison, a large Italian hydroelectric company.

Other local partners in joint international business ventures include financial institutions, such as commercial banks, which in many countries are main owners of factories and trading firms. Life insurance companies, too, may act as joint venture partners.

Association with Public Enterprises or Government Agencies Joint ventures are not confined to private capital. Governments have been taking an increasing interest in this type of international business organization. Direct participation by official agencies such as ministries in equity joint ventures, though existing to some degree in the underdeveloped countries, is likely to remain an exception. The typical format for government participation in joint ventures is through government owned business corporations set up for this purpose. They bear such titles as Corporacion de Fomento de la Produccion (Chile), Nacional Financiera (Mexico), Industrial Development Corporation (Pakistan), and National Development Corporation (Lesotho).

The main activities of such public corporations are investments in manufacturing and other sectors considered essential to a country's economic development. They also boost lagging industries for a better overall economic balance. Such development corporations assist in the promotion, financing, and organization of new industries; broaden the opportunities for private investors; and help governments to fulfill planned economic goals.

In some countries, participation by the public corporation is essentially a temporary booster operation that continues until an enterprise achieves a desired maturity. At that point the government corporation withdraws from the venture and is succeeded by private investors.

In other countries, the government corporation gradually increases its share of the joint venture equity and at some designated date becomes the sole proprietor. In the meantime, the foreign company provides the technology and management for the joint venture. Presumably, the private partner will move on to some new joint venture when turning over the old one to its government partner.

In an increasing number of countries, certain sectors of the economy are blocked out for government control and development. This is true not only in developing nations such as India, Egypt, or Algeria, but also in a number of industrial countries such as Italy, Great Britain, Sweden, and France.

Doctrinaire Opposition   Private investors in the United States have in the past opposed partnership with branches of foreign governments. The main reason has generally been a doctrinaire adherence to the classical free enterprise concept. Investors believed that mixed companies are retarded by government participation and therefore less profitable than wholly private operations. They also feared that the government corporation would use political pressure rather than administrative efficiency to guide the mixed venture. In light of recent experience, this danger has been exaggerated.

There is increasing evidence that the purely ideological barrier to entering a mixed ownership joint venture is being broken down by private enterprise and that a more flexible point of view is gaining currency. This is especially true in the raw materials sector. In many countries mineral resources belong to the state; hence, raw materials production is directly dependent upon state participation in one form or another. If U.S. business wants access to these resources, its options are limited to working with or for the government of the host nation.

Joint Venture Strategies

Companies using the joint venture structure as their main vehicle for international expansion may pursue different strategies. One is the *spider's web* strategy, used by Volvo of Sweden. This firm has established a network of joint ventures by (1) forming a group of truck manufacturers in Europe (including KHD of Germany, Soviem of France, and DAF of the Netherlands); (2) teaming up with Garret, Mack Trucks, and KHD in the United States to make gas turbine engines; (3) starting a joint venture with Peugeot and Renault in France for automotive parts and service business; (4) joining with International Harvester for production of tractor components; and (5) maintaining a separate joint venture with DAF of the Netherlands for multiple purposes. Through these joint ventures Volvo has been able to tap into the production and marketing networks of several other MNCs whose centers of strength lie outside Volvo's previous reach.

Another growth strategy is the *go together and split* joint venture. As the phrase implies, two or more firms form a joint venture for a given number of years, after which the venture may be liquidated or reorganized. The advantages of this strategy are cooperation during periods of urgent need for external resources, such as rapid growth, exploratory activities in untested markets, meeting a common competitive threat, and greater control of each partner in choosing its own direction after the joint venture contract expires. Government corporations of developing countries frequently opt for this strategy but, as the record shows, they seldom really split. Instead, they are liable to extend the arrangement for long periods.

Successive integration is a third joint venture strategy. It implies a weak interpartner relationship at the start and a progressively greater involvement as the venture matures. In some cases it may ultimately lead to complete merger of the partner firms. Since the change in the relationship is part of the initial plan of the successive integration venture, this strategy has proven particularly successful in allowing adjustments to environmental changes.

Sociopolitical Advantages of Joint Ventures

Compared to wholly or majority owned subsidiaries, a joint venture enjoys a number of significant advantages that derive from its sociopolitical image as an indigenous member of the host economy. Unlike the subsidiary, the joint venture is seldom discriminated against by the host nation. Discrimination against foreign firms is inherent in the concept of a sovereign nation, which, in terms of its own logic, must promote and defend the interests of its citizens in preference to those of other people. Association with a native enterprise in a joint venture also helps the affiliate to achieve positive relief from burdensome domestic regulations. That is, through joint venture status the affiliate gains access to the full scope of the host country's government services.

Host Country Preferences   Government attitude is crucial for any affiliate, especially in countries in which central planning, socialization, and public regulation of business activity are dominant. Import licenses, foreign exchange controls, business and professional taxes, and work and residence visas for engineers, technicians, and managers are routine controls by which a government can straightjacket a foreign firm's operations. On the positive side are tax exemptions, tariff protection, low-interest loans, and other special privileges used by many countries as incentives for stimulating investment and industrial development.

For the host government, joint ventures offer opportunities to local capital to participate in profitable and productive undertakings. Foreign companies are likely to seek out the most rewarding opportunities; through *cofloatation* (the shares or other securities issued jointly by the partners), local capital will be directed into the most productive fields. Second, joint ventures are presumed to transmit techniques and managerial know-how more effectively than wholly foreign-owned enterprises. Third, joint ventures eliminate host government worries about undue domination of industry by foreign investors. Valid or not, the distrust of wholly owned subsidiaries is encountered throughout the underdeveloped world. Fourth, some host countries prefer joint ventures as a means of strengthening their balance-of-payments position through minimizing dividend transfers and repatriation of foreign capital.

For these reasons, some governments strongly encourage local participation in foreign ventures in key sectors of their economy. However, the enforcement of such policies has been quite flexible. In some sectors, local capital may be unavailable or insufficient, and in others the need too pressing to wait for it to become available. Nevertheless, the screening by governments of foreign-investment proposals has become increasingly thorough in most host countries to ensure that foreign capital is channeled into sectors acceptable to the host government. In particularly sensitive sectors, the foreign investor may be prohibited by law from investing in certain industries except on a joint venture basis. In Burma, for instance, the law requires 60 percent Burmese control in any corporation that exploits minerals, forests, fisheries, coal, petroleum, or other natural resources. Similarly, Mexico has a constitutional provision that limits foreign control to a maximum of 40 percent in corporations engaged in agriculture, radio or television broadcasting, motion pictures, publishing, advertising, fishing, transportation, and a number of other activities.

In highly nationalistic countries, the joint venture format is often the most feasible if not the only avenue of MNC activity. As citizens in those countries identify a joint venture with their own society, their antiforeign sensitivities become neutralized. A favorable public image is especially important for the consumer goods industries, since it directly affects the acceptance of their products. The same could be said about service firms, such as banks, insurance companies, hotels, and common carriers.

Labor Relations   In labor relations, the joint venture enjoys three important advantages. It can bargain with unions without being vulnerable to anti-U.S. or antiforeign attacks or other political vicissitudes that may beleaguer wholly owned affiliates. The joint venture escapes the issue of wage statistics which include all affiliates of all MNCs, statistics that lend themselves to misinterpretation and ideological demagoguery. Last, studies in industrial psychology show that employee morale tends to rise after local capital enters a previously all-foreign enterprise, no less among the white-collar staff than among the blue-collar laborers. In the developing countries, where political leadership is supersensitive to national identity and citizens are subjected to intensive indoctrination in nationalistic ideology, the gains in morale can be very important.

Management Systems of Joint Ventures

Wherever individuals from different national, economic, ethnic, and cultural environments join in a common effort, there is a high probability of conflicting views and value judgments and of different ways of looking at problems in general. The history of allied military campaigns, church organizations, and political movements offers centuries of testimony to this fact. Interpersonal friction in the multinational management group must, therefore, be regarded as a basic but normal problem of managing a joint venture enterprise. Like similar problems, it requires methods and policies specifically designed to deal with it.

Coalition Management If the parent companies wish to prorate management control among themselves according to their ownership shares in the joint venture, they are committed to a *coalition administration* of the venture. The resultant management group not only is imbued with the different national, ethnic, and cultural norms of the factions assigned to it from each country but, since they are representatives of different firms, they will also bring to the joint venture management their own parent companies' points of view, objectives, and managerial practices.

The compounding of the cultural and managerial differences makes a coalition joint venture management a highly conflict-prone proposition. In addition to the cultural contrasts, the coalition must cope with a number of other causes of dissension. First, there are environmental constraints. One partner may be operating only in its own country while the other has international commitments. This may mean, for example, that the local partner is taxed by its government only, while the multinational partner is subjected to tax obligations in several countries; or that the local partner, being attuned to its uninational environment, views any deviation from its own organizational and managerial behavior as undesirable, while the multinational partner, being subject to different influences in other countries, regards such a point of view as highly parochial.

Second, there are the general difficulties of nonunified management. Each partner is faced with the problem of explaining and justifying to the other or others, as the case may be, its headquarters' decisions and actions in respect to the operations of the joint venture. Hence, administration is more difficult and psychologically demanding. Related to this are conflicting objectives and implicit differences in ethical standards. For example, family-controlled companies, typical in many foreign countries, confront their nonfamily-owned U.S. corporate partner with demands to make executive appointments from among the family membership, to pay frequent and high dividends, and to divert company resources to the family's other consumptive needs. How serious these differences are depends upon the particular partners and countries involved.

Autonomous Management The alternative to the coalition is to endow one of the joint venture partners with the sole responsibility for day-to-day management. The other partner's managerial involvement is limited to long-range strategy decisions, such as product line selection, major investment expenditures, and other nonoperational goals and policies. Within this broad, long-range framework the managing partner will have complete autonomy in all operating decisions. In newer joint venture agreements, the provision for a managing partner or, alternatively, for managerial autonomy of the joint venture is expressly provided.

The experience with noncoalition joint venture management has been generally better than with the coalitions. It has eliminated many of the sources of dissension.

FOREIGN LICENSING

Characteristics of Licensing

A unique affiliate in the MNC structure is the *licensee*, a foreign firm franchised to produce and sell the parent company's (licensor's) products. Licensing makes available to a foreign firm some intangible industrial property, such as a patent, a manufacturing process, or a trademark, for the purpose of cultivating the licensee's market. This obviates the licensor's need to enter the market through export trade or capital investment. It also provides an inexpensive means of exploring and testing a company's growth potential in a particular area before any irretrievable investment is made. In return for the property rights transferred to it, the licensee pays royalties, which are normally based on its output or sales of the licensed product.

Licensing agreements entail greater risk than normal export operations but considerably less risk than direct investments. For this reason, licensing is frequently used as a transitional phase between export and foreign manufacture in a company's international expansion process and is succeeded by a more extensive commitment. *Royalty* and *stock participation agreements* are specifically designed for gradual conversion from licensing to equity operation. They provide for a low or declining royalty plus a stock purchase commitment to succeed the licensing arrangement. The licensee acquires a partial ownership interest in the successor company through the stock purchase agreement. Such arrangements permit equity financing from the proceeds of the very product for which the equity was intended.

Licensing has sometimes been defined as the exportation of technology and know-how. Government owned corporations of developing nations have recently started to use licensing agreements for such limited purposes. Normally, however, licensing goes beyond technology transfer; it involves a continuous cooperative relationship between the two business firms for their mutual benefit. For this reason it is more correct to classify licensing as a *nonequity joint venture* in which pooling of resources among the partners is the overriding characteristic. It is not to be equated with direct investment; the industrial property rights are not sold outright but are leased or loaned for a given period, and the proceeds are royalties, not dividends or profits.

The Licensing Agreement

Common Terms   A licensing arrangement is always formalized in a written agreement that stipulates which property rights are being transferred, the royalties or other considerations paid, where and how the rights are to be utilized, under which circumstances the rights are to revert back to the licensor, and the degree of participation the licensor is to have in the licensed operations or in the marketing of the licensed products. The contract may further cover the period of time, the size of the territory, the methods of control and payment, the applicable law in case of conflict, and the method of arbitration to be used in case of disputes.

Licensing is a flexible working arrangement that can serve the international needs of many different partners. The simple licensing agreement is limited to a patent or trademark. A complex licensing agreement may involve not only scores of patents and brands but also comprehensive manufacturing and distribution systems, active participation of the licensor in the management of the franchised enterprise, and possible ownership affiliation. Between these two extremes is an infinite variety of legal arrangements that transfer property rights, industrial know-how, and business services to organizations abroad. The common element of all licensing agreements is the permission given by the licensor to the licensee to use an industrial property right in return for a royalty.

Intracompany Licensing   In the past, foreign licensing agreements were used between companies that had no ownership ties. In recent years, formal agreements have become popular between parent companies and their foreign affiliates; the headquarters companies authorize their branches, subsidiaries, and joint venture companies, like any other licensee, to obtain the parent's property rights or services in return for regular royalty payments. Similar arrangements are now developing among affiliates of some MNCs. Among affiliates the usual royalty arrangement is often replaced by a *cross-licensing clause* under which one property right (trademark X) is exchanged for another (trademark Y), and both parties are simultaneously licensors and licensees.

Triangular Arrangements   A special case is presented by the triangular relations among a licensor, its foreign licensee, and a foreign joint venture company owned by the two. A rather common arrangement in such a situation is the royalty and stock participation agreement, from which the licensor can derive several important advantages: greater total return, by combining royalties and dividends, than through straight royalties; greater continuity of return, as the dividends do not cease if the agreement is terminated; and greater control over the licensee through the joint venture.

Reasons for Licensing

The advantages inherent in any cooperative international venture, such as the saving of capital and management resources and the favorable attitude of local government, apply also to licensing arrangements. In addition, there are at least four major motivations for foreign licensing.

Added Revenue from Industrial Property Rights   Licensing of industrial property rights is a source of income that has little relation to the licensor's previous manufacturing and marketing operations. This is particularly true for markets that are not covered and for unused patents and processes. Some companies use licensing only for such purposes.

The added income obtained from licensing may cover research costs or maximize returns from research and know-how. For instance, some of the large U.S. oil companies regularly license European producers to use patented processes that they have developed in the United States. In these cases, the oil company is not interested in the foreign markets as such but primarily in the royalties it receives, which partially offset the costs of discovering and perfecting the new processes.

A Marketing Tool   Licensing has often helped a company build goodwill and popular acceptance for its products abroad. This has been true even when only one of several products is licensed. As the local people become familiar with the company's brand through the licensed product, other products exported to the country share in this acceptance.

For high tariff countries, licensing provides more effective access to the market than exportation does. The same argument applies to countries with other import restrictions. For technical products that require service in connection with sales, licensing offers the only viable alternative to equity investment.

Protection of Patents and Trademarks   In some countries the only way to protect a patent or a trademark is to work it. A licensing arrangement will not only prevent the piracy of products, trademarks, or patents by a local concern but also yield a royalty to the firm.

Reciprocal Benefits from Foreign Know-How   Reciprocal rights to new technology and new products developed abroad by the licensed concern are included in the licensing contract or handled as another, parallel link between the two partners. Some companies report that such reciprocal rights are of greater value than the royalty payments received under the licensing arrangement, since the foreign research talent is obtained at a comparatively low cost.

Other Advantages   Licensing agreements can also be used for accumulation of capital for direct investment, for testing the potential of a market, and for meeting the needs of parent-owned foreign manufacturing plants that depend upon U.S. equipment.

COMPOSITE STRUCTURE

Most companies pursue multiple objectives in their ownership of foreign affiliates. They may have a wholly owned subsidiary in one country, a majority controlled venture in another, and a license arrangement in a third, depending upon the circumstances of the particular country or the venture in question.

The actual power structure of an MNC is a composite of management requirements, formal juridical organizations, and ownership ties among its national components. The popular notion that power is primarily a function of ownership is more often false than true, except, possibly, in wholly owned affiliates. Usually, the key criterion is management efficiency. To achieve its objectives, management must be able to exert its will over the various national entities of the complex. Accordingly, a management hierarchy, however simple or complex, must be constructed to satisfy this fundamental requirement.

SUMMARY

The creation of affiliates by MNCs is circumscribed by host country laws and regulations. In many countries the entry of foreign enterprises is restricted in some sectors and encouraged or even subsidized in others. Typical host country restrictions prescribe that a given percentage of equity ownership belong to local nationals and that certain officers of the affiliate be citizens of the host nation.

The kind of a charter an affiliate receives also depends on the host country laws. Some countries have legal provisions for various types of limited liability companies in addition to the corporate charter. Thus, the MNC has alternatives other than the corporate form of organization. To choose from among them the firm must fully understand the business implications of each. The organizational format prescribed by host country laws may or may not be suitable for efficient operations. If it is not, the MNC must establish a de facto or managerial structure to manage the affiliate.

In the past the MNCs have shown a strong preference for organizing subsidiaries. More recently, joint ventures and foreign licensing have started to increase in importance. The joint venture model can serve the common interest of a variety of different partners, but its management presents special problems that the subsidiary model avoids. Licensing is particularly appropriate for firms with limited capital resources but strong production, technology, or product reputations. As an MNC grows it usually acquires a variety of different affiliates, due to specific conditions and opportunities.

FOR REVIEW AND DISCUSSION

1. Branches are the most typical multiunit UNCs but are very rare in MNCs. Why?

2. If MNCs were not able to set up a de facto organization that differs in any way from their de jure structure, would their economic performance increase or decrease? Give reasons.

3. Why is it inadvisable to lump joint ventures and partially owned subsidiaries together?

4. Under what circumstances would you prefer the joint venture format over other types of affiliates? Why?

5. Joint ventures between private firms and publicly owned enterprises have grown rapidly in recent years. Why may this trend continue or reverse itself?

6. Why is coalition management usually conflict-prone?

7. Do you think that licensees should be regarded as foreign-based affiliates? Why or why not?

8. Does it make sense for affiliates of the same MNC to enter into licensing agreements with one another? Under what conditions?

9. Some companies have started with foreign licensing, passed through the joint venture stage, and ended up with subsidiaries with no export of capital from headquarters at any time. How can this be explained?

10. Though many MNCs have a stated preference for a specific type of affiliate, the organization of most is a composite of many types. Is this due to managerial inconsistency or are there other explanations?

SUGGESTED READINGS FOR PART FOUR

Alhashim, D. D., and Robertson, J. W. *Accounting for the Multinational Enterprise*. New York: Bobbs-Merrill Co., 1978.

deBodinat, H. *Influence in the Multinational Corporation: The Case of Manufacturing*. New York: Arno Press, 1980.

Choi, F. and Mueller, G. *Introduction to Multinational Accounting*. Englewood Cliffs, N.J.: Prentice-Hall, 1978.

Davis, S. M. *Managing and Organizing Multinational Corporations*. New York: Pergamon Press, 1979.

Farmer, R. *Multinational Strategies*. Bloomington, Ind.: University of Indiana Press, 1975.

Fayerweather, J. *International Business Strategies and Administration*. Cambridge: Ballinger, 1978.

Heller, K. H. *The Impact of U.S. Income Taxation on the Financing and Earnings Remittance Decisions of U.S.-Based Multinational Firms with Controlled Foreign Corporations*. New York: Arno Press, 1980.

Hood, N., and Young, S. *The Economics of Multinational Enterprise*. London: Longman, 1979.

Kolde, E. J. *The Multinational Company: Behavioral and Managerial Analysis*. Lexington, Mass.: D. C. Heath, 1974.

Kolde, E. J., and Hill, R. E. "Conceptual and Normative Aspects of International Management." *Academy of Management Journal*. 10:119–28, 1967.

O'Connor, W. F. *An Inquiry into the Foreign Tax Burdens of U.S. Based Multinational Corporations*. New York: Arno Press, 1980.

Raveed, S. *Joint Ventures Between U.S. Multinational Firms and Host Governments in Selected Developing Countries: A Case Study of Costa Rica, Trinidad, and Venezuela*. New York: Arno Press, 1980.

Vernon, R. *Sovereignty at Bay: The Multinational Spread of U.S. Enterprise*. New York: Basic Books, 1971.

Part Five

MULTINATIONAL COMPANIES IN WORLD SOCIETY

*M*uch of the technology, capital resources, and management talent of the world's economy are in the possession of MNCs. MNCs make or significantly influence decisions as to the allocation of resources, the types of financial controls, the organizational structures of major production systems, and the pace of international trade and investment. Their pervasive impact has made MNCs a most perplexing problem. They have provided not only a new focus for international economic relations, but also raised issues of intense importance in domestic affairs. The societal costs and benefits of MNC activities are often matters of conflicting interpretations: all factions see the MNCs differently; ideological, parochial, and national prejudices compound the confusion.

How to deal with MNCs has become a concern to all governments, yet there has been no common response. After a series of temporary measures, the United Nations set up its Center for Transnational Corporations as a permanent agency to further research and consultation on the subject, but its influence on government regulatory actions has remained minimal to date. Each nation has acted, or failed to do so, independently. The exponential growth of conflicting regulations places MNCs in increasing peril of multiple jeopardy, being simultaneously right and wrong in several different countries for a given reason. In the industrial West, recent actions have shown a convergent trend, at least in terms of general principles, as to the mutual rights and responsibilities of MNCs and host countries. In the developing world, important divergences continue. Many developing countries welcome MNCs as potential suppliers of capital, technology, management, expertise, and labor skills; others have erected various restrictions on MNCs.

How to analyze and resolve conflicts between MNCs and national societies objectively remains an urgent problem. The organizational and juridical complexities of the MNC require that nations' traditional regulatory practices be replaced by more sophisticated methods that are capable of being coordinated and synchronized on an international scale.

The three chapters in Part Five tackle the problems of the interaction between the MNCs and world society in a logical sequence: Chapter 14 studies the topic in the home country context; Chapter 15 shifts the focus to the host country; and Chapter 16 develops analytical approaches and techniques for resolving MNC-society conflicts.

14

MNCs and Home Societies

MNCs have become a major force in the world economy. They have stirred nationalistic emotions and created perceptions of threat to domestic well-being in both home and host countries. The mounting fears and the inappropriateness of existing laws and regulations have intensified the search for new public policies and new international arrangements that would enable governments to control their growing powers. Of particular concern to society as a whole has been the fact that MNCs, due to their multicountry structures, may be able to evade the jurisdiction of any government in certain respects. These possibilities are inherent in transfer pricing, taxation, and other activities of MNCs discussed in this chapter.

The relationship between MNCs and society is a reciprocal one. The MNCs cause changes in national business systems and their linkages to one another, and laws and policies cause changes in the MNCs. Trade agreements, exchange rates, regulation of direct investment and technology transfer, all affect MNC activities; political tensions such as the demise of détente after the Soviet invasion of Afghanistan or the growing assertiveness of developing nations exert indirect influences on the MNCs. The mutual interdependence between society and the MNC poses perplexing problems. Many of the issues and relationships involved are so new that neither experience nor research has fully exposed their ramifications; others are highly complex and defy any indisputable explanations (see Figure 14.1).

Public attitudes toward MNCs are biased by a nation's position as a home or host country. Historically, home countries have perceived MNC activities as desirable extensions of their domestic business systems. Conversely, host countries have viewed MNCs as agents of foreign influence and exploitation. This historic dichotomy is now shot through with conflicting perceptions of the MNCs. Different segments of society, such as labor, investors, consumers, traders, and farmers, see their self-interests affected in different ways. As a result, a multisided controversy about the societal merits and demerits of MNCs has grown in both host and home countries.

In this chapter we will examine the MNC's conflicts with society mainly

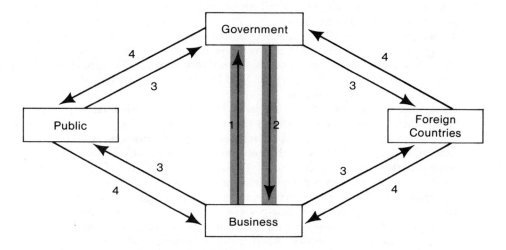

1. Direct corporate influences on legislative and regulatory behavior:
   Lobbying   Campaign contributions
   Recruitment of officials   Government contracts
   Advice and consultation

2. Direct government influences on business behavior:
   Laws   Public policy
   Regulations

3. Indirect corporate influences on government

4. Indirect government influences on business

Figure 14.1   Business-Government Interactions in the United States

from the perspective of the home nation. In Chapter 15 our focus will shift to the host countries.

HOME COUNTRY CONFLICTS

The most aggressive challenge to the traditionally supportive home country policies toward MNCs has come from organized labor. In the United States, by far the largest headquarters country, the AFL-CIO, in cooperation with other unions, has mounted a relentless campaign aimed at severely restricting multinational business activities. Other anti-MNC groups support labor's campaign either to protect their ideological biases or their own economic interests.

Critics charge the MNCs with the following detrimental effects to the U.S. economy:

1. Investment depression. The MNC foreign investments deplete capital resources needed for domestic investment, which undermines economic growth and new job creation in the United States.

2. *Technology drain.* The MNC exports U.S. technology in order to exploit low cost foreign labor, depriving the U.S. worker of his or her rightful opportunity to share in the utilization and rewards of this technology. Through technology transfers and foreign investments the MNC replaces U.S. workers with foreign workers; that is, it exports jobs.

3. *Export displacement.* The MNC displaces U.S. exports with foreign produced goods, thereby decreasing domestic employment and payrolls, causing the U.S. trade balance to deteriorate, and depressing economic conditions at home.

4. *Low wage imports.* The MNC substitutes imports from its U.S.-affiliates in low wage countries for U.S.-made goods. These imports undermine U.S. wage standards, cause unemployment, and idle plant facilities.

5. *Tax evasion.* The MNC evades taxes by deferring profit repatriation, manipulating transfer prices, and circumventing government regulations. The revenues lost to the national treasury result in a higher tax burden on the general public.

6. *Payments disbalancing.* The MNC's activities have inflicted the United States with chronic balance of payments deficits, fueled inflation, debased the dollar as a stable currency, and contributed to international monetary disorders.

To remedy the situation, organized labor has lobbied for legislation to regulate MNC operations. It has called for (a) the creation of a federal investments commission to license and supervise transnational capital transactions; (b) restriction of outward transfers of technology, by subjecting patents to export licensing and prohibiting foreign production of a patented product; and (c) extension of U.S. tax liability to all foreign affiliates of U.S.-based MNCs, by eliminating the foreign tax credit and the deferred tax status of the affiliates' profits.

MNC EFFECTS ON HOME COUNTRY TRADE AND PAYMENTS

The mounting criticisms of MNCs has produced a flurry of research projects aimed at determining how the creation of foreign affiliates by U.S. companies affects the U.S. domestic economy. Several of these studies have been conducted to support some group's special interest or ideological assertions; however, sometimes the truth is better reflected by what the researchers failed to find rather than by what they did find.

Harvard Case Studies

A research team at the Harvard Business School, headed by Robert B. Stobaugh, studied direct investment projects of nine MNCs.[1] The projects were

---

1. Robert B. Stobaugh et al., *Nine Investments Abroad and Their Impact at Home* (Cambridge: Harvard University Press, 1976).

selected from industries that allegedly were exporting jobs, namely, chemicals, electrical goods, food processing, machinery, petroleum, primary and fabricated metals, rubber products, and transportation. Each company's case was scrutinized in great depth. The findings show that in seven of the nine projects the foreign investments caused no displacement of U.S. exports, nor had they in any way added to U.S. imports. These firms had faced the choice of either making the investment or losing the market to a foreign competitor. Exporting from the United States was not a feasible alternative because higher costs made the products noncompetitive.

In the two remaining cases the issue is not clear-cut. The companies had "jumped the gun," acting on educated guesses as to what their major competitors' next moves would be rather on than factual information. One of these cases involves a U.S. rubber company, which built a tire factory in Canada in order to gain control of the market and to forestall Michelin of France from moving in. Michelin came in anyway and soon afterward invested in another tire plant in South Carolina, right on the home territory of the U.S. firm. The pre-emptive strategy had failed. In retrospect, the U.S. company might have been better off not to have built the Canadian factory, which was never able to achieve optimal output due to Michelin's capture of a large share of the market. Had the company tried instead to supply the Canadian market through exports from the United States, it is doubtful that the Michelin factory would have been able to completely expel the U.S. product. Thus, whatever volume of exports survived the Michelin offensive could be presumed to have increased U.S. exports.

In drawing this conclusion, however, we are applying hindsight rather than foresight. When the investment was made the objective was to capture the growing Canadian demand for indigenous production. That indigenous production did, in fact, materialize. Had Michelin backed off or had it not had a superior product, the U.S. rubber company's investment strategy might very well have paid off handsomely. As things turned out, Michelin grabbed a large enough share of the Canadian market to keep the U.S. company's production at a suboptimal scale.

The other case involved the establishment of a radio factory in Taiwan by a U.S. manufacturer. The company's strategy was to head off a Japanese invasion of the U.S. car radio market by finding a low cost source of supply. The U.S. firm jumped the gun in that the Japanese needed some five more years before they were ready to assault the U.S. car radio market. It is plausible that for this five-year period the radios could have been manufactured in the United States, though at a higher cost, instead of having been imported from the Taiwanese plant. While we can criticize the timing of this investment, there is no question that the investment itself was the right response to the anticipated competition of Japanese imports.

As in the case of the tire factory, the critics have the advantage of being able to study the record of an investment that has been in place for some years. The managers who make the investment decisions must rely on predictions of future events. They never have the real facts, only educated guesses. Intelligence about foreign competitors' moves is particularly difficult to obtain and assess.

Stobaugh's study draws two conclusions. First, U.S. direct investors rarely have the choice either to export or to invest in foreign production capacity; normally the decision not to invest abdicates the market. Second, the nine investment projects in aggregate increased U.S. trade and contributed to its domestic employment and balance of payments surplus.

Industry Studies

Other studies have reached similar conclusions. Lipsey and Weiss made a study of the pharmaceutical industry's foreign investments; their conclusion was that the foreign affiliates of U.S. based MNCs give rise to large exports of pharmaceuticals from this country.[2] The DuPont[3] and Union Carbide[4] companies have each commissioned exhaustive analyses of their international investments. Both studies document by product and by country (a) how investments in foreign production capacity generally promoted exports from the United States; (b) where host country requirements for local content fostered indigenous growth that increased imports from the United States; and (c) where exceptional host country measures forced local investment that induced divestment by U.S. MNCs followed by a decline of U.S. exports.

A case in the DuPont study adds a behaviorist dimension to the subject. When the company announced its plans to invest in a given country, U.S. exports soared, though the plant was yet to be built. When the investment decision was subsequently reversed, U.S. exports dropped abruptly. DuPont researchers have no convincing explanation for why the potential host country market reacted in this manner.

U.S. law requires that the Overseas Private Investment Corporation (OPIC) assess the economic effects of all foreign investment projects that it insures. These assessments cover the effects on trade, employment, and balance of payments. OPIC also evaluates whether the investment could be made in the United States instead. With a large number of critical investment cases, with full factual documentation of each, the OPIC information bank is both broadly based and factually complete. The OPIC concludes that MNC investments in their foreign affiliates in aggregate are favorable to U.S. employment and its balance of payments.

Another broadly based study was conducted by the U.S. Department of Commerce. Its main finding was that MNCs have generated more exports and imports than the rest of the U.S. economy and that MNC foreign trade has

---

2. Robert E. Lipsey and Merle Yahr Weiss, *Exports and Foreign Investment in the Pharmaceutical Industry*. Working Paper No. 87 (Washington, D.C.: National Bureau of Economic Research, 1975), p. 29.

3. *Positive Effects of Manufacturing Abroad on Domestic Employment in the DuPont Company* (DuPont, 1972, with update in 1975).

4. *Union Carbide's International Investments Benefits the U.S. Economy* (Union Carbide, 1975).

been characterized by an export surplus while UNC trade has not. The study was made before U.S. oil imports reached their overpowering magnitude.

Comprehensive Studies

Research by E. J. Kolde has kept a sizable group of MNCs under close observation since 1959.[5] The initial survey covered 104 MNCs with 533 affiliates. Though the main objective has been to chart the behavioral and managerial evolution of MNCs, the information collected covers both trade and investment activities of the companies studied. These data reveal that:

1. In general, direct foreign investment tends to increase trade. Decreases of trade caused by investment are rare exceptions.
2. The relation between investment and trade varies from industry to industry, dependent mainly on product characteristics. Relatively simple mass production items (automobile tires, fabricated steel, kitchen utensils) show the lowest potential and complex high technology products the greatest potential for increased trade resulting from foreign investments.
3. The trade induced by an investment varies with the age of the affiliate. A new affiliate is often marketing oriented and performs but limited production operations (packaging, repair, partial assembly); its marketing prowess creates a greater pull of parent company's exports to the host markets. As the affiliate matures, its manufacturing functions increase and its dependence on parent firm supplies tends to diminish.
4. If the MNC's affiliates make only duplicates of or market-adapted substitutes for the parent company's products, as is the case with tires, kitchen utensils, and fabricated steel products, the advancing independence of the affiliate may at some point lead to export substitution.
5. If the MNC's production organization provides for specialization by country of component manufacture and integrates the affiliates as well as the headquarters company through mutual exchange of inputs, the aging of the investments will not lead to any decreased potential for trade. On the contrary, the investments represented by the specialized affiliates keep triggering new trade as the international integration of the system evolves.

Since the lion's share of U.S. foreign investments belongs to the technology intensive producers of complex components, statement 5, above, far outweighs the alternative, statement 4. Some traditional economists have countered these findings by arguing that U.S. exports would not necessarily shrink if MNC investments were restricted; being denied the investment option MNCs would come up with new methods of serving their foreign markets with U.S. exports.

In addition, exporting does not provide a host country with the services that a direct investment provides:

Another point is that a modern American manufacturing corporation does

5. E. J. Kolde, *The Multinational Company: Behavioral and Managerial Analysis* (Lexington, Mass.: D. C. Heath, 1974).

much more than produce commodities. It recruits and trains workers, researches and develops products, seeks out new customers through advertising and other marketing activities, finances and distributes its products, provides technical assistance to users, and maintains repair, service and spare-parts facilities for old customers. . . . Recognition of these ancillary activities is critical.[6]

TRANSFER PRICING

Since each MNC affiliate is subject to a different national jurisdiction, business transactions among them require prices, like those among independent firms, showing the value of these exports and imports. Though foreign trade for the host nations, interaffiliate transactions are but intracompany transfers for the MNC. How the transfer prices are determined is of great significance to the company as well as to the country of origin and to the country of destination.

Zero Sum Trade-offs

The country in which the transaction originates is benefited by a high transfer price, as this assures high profit for the local affiliate, which translates into a high tax base for the country. The host country of the affiliate to whom the shipment is destined is in the opposite position. Its interests are best served by a low transfer price, which reduces the cost for the affiliate in its jurisdiction and thereby helps to increase taxable profits in this country. If its import tariffs are high, the country of destination will be faced with a trade-off between tariff revenue and tax revenue, one being benefited by a high transfer price, the other by a low one.

If the transfer is between two foreign affiliates of a U.S. MNC, the U.S. tax authorities may view the transaction according to its potential effect on the parent company's tax liability in this country. They would be particularly vigilant if Subpart F income is involved (see pages 269–70 for an explanation of Subpart F).

The MNC itself will have to consider a number of objectives in setting transfer prices: (a) maximizing utilization of existing plant capacities as conditions change, (b) reallocating assets in response to inflationary trends or political risk, (c) providing criteria for measuring the profit performance of affiliates, (d) increasing the size of the market, (e) strengthening the ability of the MNC to compete, (f) attaining economies of scale, and (g) reducing the effect of domestic and foreign restrictions. To deal with all these variables, MNCs typically rely on a systems approach in arriving at the optimal transfer prices.

6. C. Fred Bergsten, Thomas Horst, and Theodore H. Moran, *American Multinationals and American Interests* (Washington, D.C.: The Brookings Institution, 1975), p. 68.

MNC Alternatives

A transfer price is optimal when it contributes the most to the MNC's overall objectives, taking into consideration their relative priorities at the time. Thus, the optimal price is not necessarily synonymous with the most beneficial price from the viewpoint of any specific affiliate or of any particular host country. As far as the various objectives of the MNC as a whole are concerned, only the headquarters management has knowledge of their specific nature and the facts behind them. Governments, labor unions, and other outsiders lack this knowledge. They depend on the information that the MNC is willing to share. Since knowledge is power, the outsiders feel threatened by the MNC's knowledge. As a counterweight, government authorities challenge the MNC's transfer prices in order to force the firm to issue more details in defense of the transfer prices used. The challenges not only keep the MNC on its guard but also enable the governments involved to obtain additional data from the firm.

The MNC may also have the power to choose from among different pricing methods, each yielding a different price for intrafirm exports and imports. It may choose from among various accounting methods of allocating headquarters expenses; use equity or debt in meeting an affiliate's capital needs; charge various rates of interest on different interaffiliate loans; levy fees for research and development, patents, and trademarks; and influence the affiliates' sales by pricing and marketing strategies of the finished goods. All these are complex matters that do not yield to simple right or wrong solutions. Rather, they have multiple solutions, each correct in terms of the particular method used to determine it.

Preplanned Distribution of Profits to Affiliates   The more complex the pricing situation, the greater is the MNC's range of alternatives from which to pick its transfer price. Having at its disposal a range of justifiable transfer prices gives the MNC a powerful tool for shifting its income and reallocating its resources internationally. Differences in host country tax rates, if large enough to outweigh other factors, may become an incentive for the MNC to set the transfer price so as to minimize its global tax burden. This would call for high in-transfer and low out-transfer prices to high tax countries and low in-transfer and high out-transfer prices to low tax countries. As a result, profits would be predistributed among the affiliates according to the headquarters plan. However, it is a rare occasion when the preplanned profit distribution is determined solely by tax considerations. Foreign exchange restrictions, purchasing power disparities of exchange rates, inflation, and pending revolutionary turmoil are often more compelling than tax differentials in preallocating profits.

Risk of Double Taxation   In terms of its internal economics, an MNC would ideally seek to reap its profits in markets where short-term earnings rates are the highest and distribute them to countries where the long-term risk of loss is the lowest.

This corporate ideal collides with the government goal of maximizing tax revenue under any given set of national policies. Each host country seeks to capture for its tax jurisdiction the largest conceivable share of MNC income. These attempts may lead to double taxation of affiliate profits. This happens when the tax authorities of both the exporting and importing nations require that the actual transfer prices used by the firm be recalculated for tax purposes so that all profits from the transaction would accrue to their respective ends. For instance, if the MNC's transfer price yields a profit of $2 in the country of origin and $4 in the country of destination, the tax authorities of both countries may insist on changing the price so that the total profit of $6 will accrue to their nations; thus, both will tax the MNC on $6, causing the MNC to pay taxes to both countries on same profit. Since in any direct confrontation the government power will prevail, the tax minimizing potential of MNCs through transfer price manipulation is relatively limited.

U.S. Tax Rules for Transfer Pricing   The U.S. tax law, as recently amended, requires that a "fair price" be used when any tangible property is transferred among related parties. A transfer price is regarded as fair if it is the same as that which two independent traders would use in an "arm's length" transaction. The tests of an arm's length price are: (a) existing open market price for the product transferred, (b) the resale price used by the recipient affiliate minus a normal markup, and (c) the cost of production plus an appropriate gross profit percentage.

If a transfer price fails to meet any of these tests, the U.S. tax commissioner is authorized to reallocate gross income, deductions, and credits among affiliated companies to reflect the full U.S. tax obligation of the MNC as a whole. Such retroactive allocation can cause serious complications for the firm. Since its affiliates have already been taxed by their host countries, the MNC has very little hope of having host country tax returns adjusted to the reallocation. Host governments regard home country reallocations of affiliates' taxes as external interference in their fiscal jurisdiction and reject company application to that effect as illegal.

THE TAX CONTROVERSY

Tax evasion is another charge levied against MNCs. According to critics, an MNC can escape taxes by shifting resources and activities from country to country and by transferring goods and services among affiliates at transfer prices designed to minimize the total tax liability of the firm. The manipulation of transfer prices is alleged to undermine domestic stability and to thwart national economic policies. As a high tax and high price country, the United States is singularly vulnerable to the loss of public revenue and the destabilizing effects of such MNC moves.[7]

7. *Ibid.*, pp. 73–74.

U.S. Tax Law

The reality is more complex than the critics' charge suggests. To begin with, U.S. tax law is based on equity or tax neutrality on a national basis. This principle requires that both domestic and foreign income of U.S. firms be taxed. Otherwise, a firm receiving foreign source income would pay fewer taxes than another firm with the same income but all from domestic sources. Equity on a national basis, however, creates inequities on an international basis. For example, if the tax rate in the U.S. is 50 percent and in Switzerland it is 20 percent, the Swiss branch of a U.S. company would be subject to a much higher tax burden than its Swiss competitors. Equity on an international basis requires that the subsidiary pay the Swiss tax—the source country rate—and no more.

To avoid double taxation, the U.S. tax law has a foreign tax credit provision that allows the headquarters company to deduct host country taxes from its U.S. tax obligation. Thus, the effective U.S. tax obligations of the Swiss branch referred to above would be 50 percent minus 20 percent, or 30 percent of its earnings. This does not work in reverse. If the foreign rate is higher, the headquarters company cannot charge the excess against its domestic tax obligation.

Another basic premise of the U.S. tax law has always been *juridical domicile*, the country of incorporation. Domestic corporations are taxed on their worldwide income; foreign corporations are taxed only on income earned in the United States. A domestic corporation is defined simply as one incorporated within the United States; a foreign corporation is one incorporated outside the United States.

If the foreign-based affiliate of a U.S. company is not a branch but a separately incorporated entity under the host country's law, its profits are not subject to U.S. taxation unless and until they are distributed as dividends to either the U.S. parent firm or its U.S. stockholders. This is the root of the MNC tax controversy. Under this rule the profits of foreign affiliates can remain immune to U.S. taxation for extended periods, if not forever, since only the MNCs themselves can decide when to repatriate the profits. It may be wiser for the MNC to take the profits of one affiliate to establish another subsidiary in some third country.

Subpart F Critics equate the deferral of profit repatriation to an interest-free loan from the U.S. Treasury to the MNC. This argument has gained enough support to induce Congress to modify the juridical domicile rule. The modification, called *Subpart F* of the Internal Revenue Code, obligates the headquarters company to add to its taxable income certain earnings of its foreign affiliates even though the earnings have been neither repatriated nor distributed to the parent. This obligation applies to three types of affiliate incomes:

1. *Foreign holding company income,* which includes dividends, interest, royalties, rents, and any other distributions received from the ownership of stock or securities in other foreign companies, for example, subsidiaries of the affiliate.

2. *Foreign base company sales income*, which is income derived from purchase and sales transactions between related parties (affiliated companies) where goods traded are both produced and sold (or bought) outside the legal domicile of the affiliate. For example, if an Italian affiliate of a U.S. company bought goods from a Spanish affiliate and sold them to an Austrian buyer, the Italian affiliate would be the recipient of base company income.

3. *Foreign base company service income*, which relates to income from services rendered outside the host country for an affiliated company or related person. It parallels base company sales income.

This puts all foreign-based affiliates that profit from trade in which three or more affiliates are involved under U.S. tax obligation, irrespective of in which country their profits may be. Only manufacturing affiliates who sell direct to third parties can claim immunity from U.S. tax authority as long as the earnings remain in the host country. However, such isolation defeats the inherent advantages of the international specialization and integration of MNC operations. Therefore, its impact is far greater than it may appear at first.

The inconsistency between the juridical domicile criterion and the Subpart F provisions is eliminated by the formality of deemed dividends. If an affiliate's earnings remain abroad the Subpart F income is deemed to be distributed to the headquarters company and must be included in its taxable income on an annual basis. Thus, by simply labeling affiliate earnings *deemed dividends* the law compels the headquarters company to pay taxes on income that in reality has never been legally signed over to the U.S. headquarters firm. The size of the deemed dividends is roughly related to the difference between the U.S. and the host country tax rates; the larger the difference the higher the distribution requirement. If the rates are nearly equal or the foreign rate is higher, no deemed dividend income is taxed by the United States.

Violation of Host Country Tax Sovereignty   Host countries strenuously oppose U.S. attempts to tax affiliates operating in their national jurisdictions. They regard the deemed dividend provision as an illicit means of taxing enterprises that are part of their economies, chartered under their laws and deriving profits from their markets. Developing nations particularly object, because the deemed dividends tend to induce a flow of capital from the poor to the rich countries. In addition, U.S. taxation of the affiliates nullifies the tax incentives that many developing countries offer to attract inbound investments.

Effects of Foreign Tax Credit

If the foreign tax credit was eliminated, the foreign investment climate for U.S. MNCs would also inevitably change. All foreign source income would thus become taxable twice, first by the host government and then by the United States.

A Brookings Institution research team has calculated that the actual taxes imposed by host countries on U.S. MNC affiliates represent an average of 40 percent of their pretax profits. The taxes consist of income plus dividend withholding tax collected by host governments when the profits are repatriated.[8] Both qualify for the U.S. foreign tax credit. Although tax rates vary from country to country, on the average the foreign source income of the MNCs has paid taxes quite comparable to taxes on domestic income.

Next the researchers used computer simulation to find out what the results would be if the foreign tax credit was eliminated:

> Our analysis indicates that U.S. manufacturing investors would not only stop sending new capital overseas but also repatriate substantial sums already invested. While the rate of new investment by overseas affiliates would be slashed by more than half, foreign operations would continue to expand, albeit at a greatly reduced rate, as long as the subsidiaries could tap local capital markets.[9]

The same researchers calculated what the elimination of foreign tax credit might do to domestic investment. Taking for granted that host countries will prevent massive repatriation of U.S. investments in order to protect their domestic stability and balance of payments positions, the higher U.S. taxes resulting from the elimination of the foreign tax credit would raise the total tax burden of U.S. MNCs by some 20 percent.

Such double taxation would sharply depress the MNC after-tax earnings and cause the domestic investment actually to fall. Since the return on investment in foreign affiliates has typically been higher than on domestic investments, the double taxation would tend to depress investment in general, reducing both domestic and foreign employment. It is well documented that the rate of new investment depends on after-tax earnings.

It is safe to say, therefore, that suppression of foreign investment through higher taxes bears no guarantee of greater domestic investment and employment.

SUMMARY

The growing influence of the MNC has created economic and political controversies in both home and host countries. Owing to their multicountry presence, MNCs enjoy operational options that extend beyond any single nation's jurisdiction. Public attitudes toward MNCs are in a state of flux. Whereas in earlier years, public opinion in headquarters countries was supportive of MNCs, recently this has changed. Labor unions and some other groups have become critical of MNCs. However, research findings tend to support the conclusion that the majority of MNCs make a positive contribution to the economy. How efficient and productive any particular MNC is may vary with both industry and the maturity of the firm.

8. *Ibid.*, p. 190.
9. *Ibid.*, p. 208.

Transfer pricing has been a major source of controversy. Since MNCs can use it to pursue a variety of different objectives, no simple cause-and-effect analysis can satisfactorily explain this phenomenon. By selecting the most advantageous accounting methods, MNCs can vary their transfer prices considerably even in the face of strict government regulations. Financial and political instabilities have induced MNCs to distribute prices among affiliates by predetermined plans to ensure their monetary security and convertability.

Taxation of MNCs is complicated by the many different sources of revenues as well as the host country accounting and tax laws. To pressure the U.S.-based MNCs to repatriate their foreign profits, Subpart F was grafted onto the basic tax law by Congress. It subjects interacting foreign affiliates of MNCs to current U.S. taxation regardless of whether they declare any dividends to the headquarters or not. Host countries regard the Subpart F provisions as an illegal method of taxing firms in their jurisdiction and, as such, interference in their internal affairs by the U.S. government.

FOR REVIEW AND DISCUSSION

1. In what ways are the interactions and tensions between society and the MNC different from those between society and a UNC?

2. Evaluate the validity of the six main criticisms that labor unions have levied against MNCs. Has their relative significance changed in the past decade?

3. What do the Harvard studies show?

4. To what extent do the comprehensive studies of MNC activities over many years support the critics of MNCs? The enthusiasts for MNCs?

5. Is transfer pricing used mainly to minimize the MNC's tax burden? Explain.

6. In the world of rampant inflation and political instability, all MNCs should use preplanned profit distribution among their affiliates and the headquarters. Discuss.

7. How would U.S. MNC taxation be changed if the United States switched its tax laws to the principle of equity on an international basis?

8. Does Subpart F encourage or suppress international specialization? Explain.

9. Would you support the elimination of foreign tax credit? Why or why not?

10. How are investments and taxation of MNCs interrelated?

15

MNCs and Host Societies

The presence of MNC affiliates is a profoundly significant reality in much of the world. Most host countries have wooed MNCs through investment incentives and many other means. To push back the tyranny of material wants, low productivity, and aversion to change, various countries have sought the cooperation and capabilities of MNCs. Even the Soviet Union and other communist countries have started to seek ways to entice MNCs to cross their previously ironclad borders. Thus, the push toward the propagation and growth of the MNCs has been global in scope.

Increasingly, however, the MNC has become a source of controversy, at times acute resentment, in many countries. Canada, France, India, Iran, and some African states are widely publicized sites of recent dramatic clashes between governments and MNCs. Similar conflicts have surfaced elsewhere throughout the world.

ADAPTABILITY OF MNCs TO HOST ENVIRONMENTS

All MNCs are not equally prone to cause friction and tension in their host economies. Some adapt with relative ease and become closely integrated with their host environment, both economically and socioculturally; others remain isolated and insulated, often forming alien enclaves in the host society. There appears to be a causal relationship between the MNC's organizational structure—that is, its organizational design as well as its underlying objectives and strategies—and its capacity for social adaptation to host country conditions.

In terms of inducement to social conflict, MNCs fall into three categories: home dominated, host dominated, and internationally integrated.

Home or Parent Dominated MNCs

These enterprises are organized and managed in such a way that the foreign-based subsidiaries and other affiliates, whatever their specific legal form, serve primarily in a complementary support role. Their function is to help the parent company achieve its business objectives in the headquarters country. The subsidiaries have an entirely dependent role. Their local interests and needs, including social adjustment, are subordinated to and, if necessary, sacrificed for the parent company's home operations. Highly centralized, run by absentee decision makers, and serving purposes external to the host countries, the home dominated MNC is highly prone to host country conflict. Its insensitivity toward host nation needs is compounded by its ethnocentric managerial behavior.

This type of MNC has been particularly, but not exclusively, characteristic of extractive industries and novice entrants into multinational operations. Increasing self-assertion of host country governments has put home dominated MNCs under increasing pressure to reform or divest.

Federated or Host Dominated MNCs

In its pure form this model is an MNC whose headquarters is set up more like a holding company than a management center. The actual management authority, except for general policy guidelines, is delegated to individual subsidiaries. The company is highly decentralized; the subsidiaries are managerially autonomous or very nearly so. Each subsidiary is run by executives who are local nationals, who rely on local methods and decision making processes, whose leadership style derives from the indigenous social norms, and whose personal standards and loyalties are identified with the host society. In brief, there is a tight integration of each affiliate with its host country.

The federated MNCs are the least prone to social conflict—they seem to be a sociologist's ideal. From an economic perspective they are far less perfect. The high degree of autonomy that each affiliate enjoys severely limits the MNC's ability to utilize its capacities as effectively as a more closely coordinated structure.

Internationally Integrated MNCs

These firms are organized to pursue objectives and activities that are worldwide in scope and concept. Their primary interests are not identified with the headquarters country or with any other particular nation. They are apolitical and anational institutions. To be sure, they must have nationality for the purposes of meeting statutory requirements as legal entities to be licensed to do business, but this is nationality only in form; in substance they are transnational or perhaps even supranational. Their primary loyalty is to the company itself rather than to any nation. Their purposes, behavior, values, and operational incentives all derive from their own multinational structure, not from home country or host country policies or patriotisms.

The substantive essence of such companies lies in international specialization and managerial integration, a process often called *international ration-*

alization. These MNCs specialize production according to the principle of comparative advantage: acquiring inputs from countries with lowest relative costs, that is, locating production facilities for each component in the country best endowed with the necessary resources, and distributing outputs in the markets where the rewards are greatest. Thus, they possess a competitive advantage, a productive superiority, over domestic or uninational firms in both developed or developing countries. This productive superiority derives from the wider range of strategic choices; they are always able to choose the least costly production alternative and to combine it with the most profitable marketing alternative.

Because of their greater productive efficiency and profitability, the globally integrated MNCs represent the fastest growing segment of international business. The growth is propelled in part by the expansion of these companies themselves and in an increasing part by the adoption of the globally integrated model by other companies. The process of conversion from other structural forms of international business to the globally integrated mode is only beginning. Much further growth is certain to take place in the next several years. Only a return to ultraprotectionist trade barriers could thwart this trend. Consequently, the integrated MNC is the most likely to demand attention in any search for solutions to the problems of social responsibility of multinational firms.

Conflicts between the globally integrated MNCs and host nations arise from the fundamental fact that the inner logic of such transnational enterprises is violated if identification of corporate interest with the national interest of any particular host state is imposed. The violation is the interference with the international optimalization process of the company, which tends to destroy its productive superiority, not to mention profitability.

AREAS OF CONFLICT

Although the MNC has no power over the host government, it may have considerable power under that government. By being able to influence certain factors, the MNC has the opportunity to help or harm national economies; in this sense, it may be said to have power against host governments. Critics of the MNC perceive these powers as potential perils to host societies.

The strategic aspects of a host country's national policy that are subject to the influence of the MNC include:

1. Planning and direction of industrial growth
2. National control of key industries
3. Financial policy
4. Export-import policy
5. Pricing policy
6. Research and development
7. Human resource policy

Planning and Direction of Industrial Growth

Host nations have viewed with concern the tendencies of many MNCs to centralize strategic decisions in their headquarters. For the host governments this signifies loss of control over industrial strategy to the foreign-based MNC. The MNCs' allegiances are geocentric; their overall objectives are growth and profits globally rather than in the host economy. These objectives require efficiency in the functional areas of management—production, marketing, finance, and so on. Many MNCs have sought greater efficiency through centralization, with headquarters domination of affiliates as the unavoidable result.

Risks of Excessive Centralization Empirical evidence indicates that a high degree of centralization tends to lead to inflexibility of parent company policies. Decisions are made in headquarters regarding the product mix for each affiliate, extent of interaffiliate sales of semifinished and finished products, export pricing, interaffiliate sales, input procurement, packaging, long-range planning, research and development, and, particularly, financial management. When the authority over these vital business decisions is located beyond their jurisdictions, local authorities counter with restrictions on affiliate activities. Clearly, centralization extracts a price from the MNC. A satisfactory method of calculating it is yet to be devised. When things are sorted out the price of centralization may well turn out to be far greater for many firms than the operational simplifications gained by it.

Government Goals Governments of all nations, particularly those of the less developed countries, are assuming more responsibilities for the achievement of economic growth and social goals than formerly. To be successful they need a fairly high degree of certainty in the business sector. The presence of affiliates managed from foreign-based headquarters introduces uncontrollable factors that interfere with the government's planning and policies of economic development. With substantial segments of industry owned and directed from abroad and with home country governments bent on perceiving the affiliates as foreign extremities of their economies, the host governments see a serious challenge to their ability to affect the desired goals.

The more responsibility for economic growth and stability the government accepts, the greater its direct involvement in business regulation and direction, and the greater the possibility that the MNC will be perceived as a potential agitator of the national plans. For example, the French minister of industry recently charged that foreign-owned affiliates in France were both unconcerned with objectives of the national plan and had means of avoiding its guidelines. Host governments see their planned goal achievement frustrated to the extent that the MNCs take their cues from the home governments or pursue geocentric goals that are divergent from the host nation's goals.

National Control of Key Sectors

The MNCs' technological power and their tendency to cluster in key industrial sectors has given rise to another fear in the host countries. By permitting foreign investors to control key industries, nations are in the precarious position of losing control over strategic sectors. In Canada, for example, the concentration is threefold: in major industrial centers, in key industrial sectors, and in the hands of a few companies. The fear of industrial domination is no chauvinistic fiction but in many instances an obvious truth.

Technology Gap The ability of the headquarters company to determine whether, when, and how the newest techniques are employed by affiliates has aroused fears in host nations of an increasing dependence on the MNC for technological progress. It has been argued that this dependence is attributable to a technology gap between the United States and other countries. A lesser commitment of European- and other non-U.S.-based companies to research and development is given as the cause of the gap. Researchers who have attempted to go beyond the expenditure figures discredit the technology gap theory by showing that technological inventions and innovations have come no less frequently from Europe than from the United States. Furthermore, the European inventions have tended to be major breakthroughs. The issue is by no means clear as far as Europe or Japan are concerned; however, there is no room for argument on this point in reference to the developing nations.

The necessity of relying on the home country's technology, in turn, leads to the fear of foreign control and ownership of industry. As a given industry sector becomes dominated by MNCs, the host country becomes dependent on the technological in-transfers of the foreign-headquartered MNC for its growth and product development. Once achieved, the dominant position of the MNC is believed to be self-perpetuating. Dominance itself provides the affiliate with resources to help perpetuate its role as the major innovator.

National policies aimed at greater independence in technology are a mixture of the desire for local research and development facilities and their ownership as well as the desire for technically advanced items produced locally. However, it appears that many countries have no feasible alternative to relying on foreign technology. They need MNCs in order to avoid a stagnated economy and bring about indigenous development.

Foreign Takeovers The strategy of some MNCs has been to place their direct investments in the host country into acquisitions of pre-existing indigenous firms. To the host country this strategy conjures visions of takeover by foreigners. In smaller or less industrialized countries the point is quickly reached when no nationally owned companies may be left in a particular industry. Thus, a foreign monopoly control is created. Larger nations, too, are sensitive to foreign takeovers. A rash of bills was introduced in Congress and the legislatures of various states when the U.S. public first learned that

Japanese companies had acquired some Hawaiian hotels, Kentucky horse farms, and Alaskan timber and mineral rights. An even greater reaction followed the news of Arab acquisition of U.S. businesses in the 1970s. France and Canada provide other illustrations of public apprehensions in major industrial countries about foreign takeovers.

A number of nations have reacted to such fears by restricting acquisitions to prevent the elimination of local competitors and to channeling foreign investments into the establishment of new firms that make a larger real contribution to the host economy and avoid the disturbance in the market that major acquisitions typically cause.

The possibility of the MNC eliminating indigenous competitors is real. With its superiority in resources (financial, managerial, and technical), the MNC is often at an obvious competitive advantage compared to the domestic firm. Oftentimes the MNC enters a host country in which it already possesses a strong market position built on imports. This makes it a much more formidable threat to local competitors.

Financial Policy

As a matter of financial policy the MNC can choose to invest its profits either in the host country or elsewhere. The host country government naturally prefers domestic investment, but the power lies with the MNC to determine where the profits will be allocated.

Balance of Payments The MNC may help relieve a deficit in the host country balance of payments. No conflict arises in this situation. The firm may also contribute to the worsening of the host country balance of payments. For example, an investment by a U.S. parent may produce a larger demand for U.S. capital equipment, thereby increasing the deficit. The MNC has been indicted for causing capital flows to fluctuate and even reverse. In addition, increased investment in the host economy very likely increases the market share held by the affiliate, which can conflict with host country interests. This makes the allocation of profits a very sensitive area. If the parent decides to transfer the profits outside the borders of the host country, the latter gains no benefits from the investment potential of the firm. If the dividends to the parent company fluctuate from year to year, the payments position of the host country may be destabilized.

Borrowing Power The source of borrowed funds can also create conflict. The MNC can borrow from local sources (the host economy), U.S. sources, third-country sources, or multinational sources. This enables the MNC to import much larger sums than a uninational company could. The potential threat to the balance of payments position of the host country is similarly greater.

Also, host government domestic monetary policy may be easily undermined by the countering efforts of the MNC. A typical example involves the MNC's extension of credit to a foreign subsidiary at a time when the host nation is attempting to dampen domestic purchasing power through import restrictions and exchange controls. Thus, the foreign-owned affiliate has the power, cash, and credit to avoid efforts by the state to constrain credit and investment.

Even though the magnitudes involved are not large in comparison to major elements in the balance of payments, and many countries have substantial earnings from overseas investments, these points are overlooked when attitudes toward foreign investment are formed within the host country. The exact impact of an inward foreign investment on a country's balance of payments is usually too complex to be easily explained.

Export-Import Policy

The export-import activities of the MNC can also affect the host country balance of payments. Exports from affiliates may be subject to decisions made in the head office that seek to fit the affiliate's trade into the international marketing scheme of the MNC as a whole. This means the affiliate's exports could go to the parent or other affiliates instead of to customers desired by the host government.

Another host country criticism of the MNC is that it may allocate export markets among its affiliates, thereby preventing them from exporting as they might otherwise and damaging the prospects for expansion of exports of the host country.

Importing policies may be similarly dictated by the home office. Affiliates may be directed to import from the parent itself or from other affiliates instead of using resources from the host country, thus further contributing to a trade deficit on the part of the host.

However much the MNC may contribute to economic growth and stability in the host country, the fact that the parent has the ability to alter the activities of the affiliates increases the uncertainty facing the host government. The fact that the MNC's decision center is outside the jurisdiction of the host government further compounds the uncertainty.

Pricing Policy

The controversial aspects of MNC pricing relate in part to intracompany pricing or transfer pricing and in part to pricing policies for customers outside the company itself.

Leakages Through Transfer Pricing   As discussed in Chapter 14, transfer prices can be calculated so as to shift assets among the entities of the MNC through intracompany (interaffiliate) sales, royalties, technical assistance fees, and the allocation of headquarters expenses. The potential significance of these flows to the host country balance of payments is indicated by the fact that remittances by foreign affiliates to the headquarters of MNCs have been consistently far greater than the flow of funds from headquarters to the affiliates.

Transfer pricing is capable of serving various other objectives unless it is prevented from doing so by effective government regulations. If the host countries employ foreign exchange restrictions, the transfer price may be designed to circumvent the restrictions. If a particular host country has high profit taxes, the transfer price may be used to reallocate the profits to a low tax country. When economic or political instability plagues a host country, transfer prices can be used to keep to a minimum the company's cash reserves in that country. Transfer prices can also be used to strengthen the competitive position of a company or to neutralize the competitive advantage of others. If used for these or similar purposes the transfer price becomes an obviously objectionable device.

Power to Undercut Local Competitors   In market pricing, local industry often fears the ability of the MNC affiliate to cut prices to any level necessary to achieve either a foothold or to increase its market share. It is possible for a large MNC to absorb sizable per unit losses on its sales in a small host country without sacrificing its overall profitability. Thus, there is reason for the local people in such countries to be on guard.

Some MNCs have established a global single price policy; that is, the same price applies all over the world. By doing so the MNC denies itself the ability to respond to the demands of individual country markets or to utilize to its maximum advantage the oligopolistic market structure of most host countries. The problem becomes further complicated when trade barriers and government regulations create inducements for differentiating prices among host country markets.

MNC affiliates have, at times, entered into price restraining agreements. Normally, affiliates of U.S. MNCs are not permitted by their parents to establish cartellistic relations because of U.S. antitrust laws. In countries where cartels are commonplace an affiliate's refusal to participate creates a gnawing doubt among local industrialists as to whether the U.S. affiliates will behave by the agreed-upon rules.

Research and Development

Research and development can cause a conflict of interests between the MNC and the host country in several ways. The first is the location of the research and development facilities. Most host countries urge MNCs to establish local research and development capacity. Having creative work going on helps to accelerate efforts in other areas of scientific research and innovation in the host society. MNCs, however, tend to concentrate research efforts in the home country. Of host countries the most advanced nations are preferred because of their educational institutions and scientific talent. Whatever the scope of the affiliate's research and development program, growth of such a department is dependent on the home office. And whatever the pattern of relationships concerning research within the firm, it is not one that eliminates the dependence of the host economy on the parent company's technological priorities.

Even if research is done by the affiliate in the host country, the issue of ownership rights over the findings can cause conflict. Should the company decide to use the results of the research in some other country, the benefit to the local economy is minimized.

In sum, the MNC usually helps the host country reach a higher level of technology, but not as fast as the nation wants, nor is the technology necessarily the type that the host government deems appropriate for its needs. Furthermore, there is the problem of who controls the results of the research. So long as domestic ownership and control over key sectors and key technology have not been achieved, national governments feel threatened. The conflict over ownership of technology is taking on new dimensions as MNCs expand their research bases to host countries and as more and more host countries assume the dual role of both host and home country.

Human Resource Policies

Home Country Expatriates   In the early stages of international growth, a firm tends to staff its foreign-based affiliates with headquarters country managers, that is, home country expatriates. The advantages here are twofold: first, simplicity of selection, appointment, and promotion, all of which can be done in a unilateralist frame of reference without disturbing the established practices and routines of the firm, and second, the relative uniformity of backgrounds of all managerial cadres throughout the multinational structure— everybody is the product of the same national and corporate cultures and has reached his or her position by playing by the same rules. U.S.-headquartered MNCs seem to be among the most committed to dependence on the expatriate transferee in their foreign-based affiliate management.

Third Country Expatriates   Another source of executive talent is the third country expatriate, who may be defined as a manager who is a citizen of country A and works in country B for a company headquartered in country C. Most of these are multilingual Europeans or Orientals with a European education. Many are refugees from communist countries. Third country nationals are reported to be more adept at integrating themselves into new situations and making friends in a foreign social setting than the unilingual U.S. expatriates.

A number of U.S. companies have expressed a definite preference for third country expatriates in overseas management positions. Burroughs Company, for instance, had only three U.S. citizens operating abroad in 1980; the rest of its overseas divisions were run by third country expatriates. The versatility of third country executives may indicate high mobility toward top management positions. For example, one established MNC, Nestlé of Switzerland, has long used non-Swiss in top corporate posts. Of the top eleven members of Nestlé's present board of directors, six are non-Swiss.

All expatriates are a potential source of host country conflict. The local society generally views them with mixed reactions. The upper classes may resist the expatriate because he or she is an influential outsider who threatens the local power and prestige structures. At the same time, they realize the expatriate brings new technologies and behavior patterns that benefit their country and themselves. The lower classes resent the presence of expatriates because they are foreigners and because they hold prestigious high paying positions. Racial or religious biases tend to compound the resentments further. Foreigners may be welcome as long as they are "not white," "not Hindu," or "not Asiatic," while members of the same race and religion may be perfectly welcome and acceptable in the neighboring country. The MNC must learn to sense and be guided by the strength of these nationalistic and xenophobic feelings. Host society reactions will range from slowing of permits and documents in government offices to acts of terrorism and destruction of property.

Host Country Nationals Established MNCs have come to rely heavily on host country nationals as the source of executive personnel. The reasons for this switch have been the following: the need for understanding the local environment, the rapid growth of overseas operations requiring speedy expansion of the management group, the increased ability to utilize individuals with different national backgrounds successfully in the corporate structure, and direct or subtle pressures by host country authorities to replace expatriate managers with indigenous employees.

While all host governments appear to favor their people strongly in executive assignments, they nonetheless can violently object to the salary policy of the MNC. In this area the MNC can be criticized if it holds fast to local salary standards, for underpaying local nationals in comparison with headquarters executives, and criticized if it exceeds the local standards, for undermining local firms and pirating their best people. This is a real dilemma.

Personnel Practices In the area of employment policies, there are several potential conflicts. One is the attempt to impose the home country's methods, mannerisms, and behavior patterns on the host society through the operations of the affiliate. For example, an Italian affiliate of one MNC scheduled two hours for lunch and a half day of work on Saturday, as is customary in Italy. Taking for granted that shifting the working hours and work days of the week would lead to greater productivity, the head office ordered the affiliate to drop the Saturday shift and to shorten the lunch time to 45 minutes. This change met such strong resistance from the Italian workers that productivity plummeted.

The hiring and firing policies of affiliates of most U.S.-based MNCs parallel those of the parent company; that is, firms shift management personnel, lay off redundant employees, and regroup and retrain labor to meet new tasks.

These dynamic and sometimes harsh policies are contrary to the social values of many foreign countries, where customarily both managers and labor receive more stable treatment by the firm and are tied to the firm for extended periods of time.

In the area of worker recruitment and training the MNC encounters several problems. In less developed countries, the most common problem is the scarcity of skilled people—workers, managerial personnel, research and development scientists, and technicians. If the firm imports the needed skills, the host country must forego both the training and the jobs for its own nationals; for the MNC to undertake the required training programs locally is often financially prohibitive.

In certain host countries manual work cannot be included in any training programs for supervisory personnel because of the strong social stigma attached to it. The same may be true of sales. There are difficulties in interesting educated nationals in sales positions in certain countries because in those countries sales work is low in social esteem.

Conflicts may arise also from the promotion policies of the MNC. Some countries have rigid social stratification in which on-the-job achievement and economic performance are not recognized. Merit-based promotion of the most competent or deserving personnel to management or supervisory positions, thus, flies in the face of expectations and notions of social propriety. Perhaps the best example of this problem would be the promotion of a member of a lower caste to a position of supervision over a member of a relatively higher caste in India. While less obvious, the same conflict is encountered in many other, particularly developing, countries in a more subtle context.

NATIONAL SOVEREIGNTY OF THE HOST COUNTRY

Erosion of national sovereignty appears to be the pervasive fear resulting from the expansion of the MNC. This loss may be the consequence of dependence on foreign technology, foreign industrial dominance, or the MNC's ability to affect its own desired results. Losing its sovereignty, the nation loses its power, and without power the existence of nationhood, even its identity, becomes problematic.

Excessive centralization and lack of managerial diplomacy help to feed such fears. For example, there was a strong French reaction to the closing of a French plant by Remington Rand. This reaction was not focused on what action had been taken, but rather on where and how the decision had been made. In this case, the decision was cabled from the U.S. parent, allegedly without prior consultation with either the management of the affiliate or with the officials of the host government. This is by no means an isolated incident. Much resentment is caused by the MNC's failure to communicate its intentions and motives to the host government and other local bodies whose interests may be affected. With the tendency of U.S. firms to centralize, such problems are increasing.

Differences in relationships among societies must be recognized by the MNC if the fear of loss of national sovereignty and identity is to be allayed. These differences may be economic—income structure, compensation structure, capital-labor relationships—or personal. Diversity of institutional settings is evident.

By increasing the international influences, the MNC may reduce choices open to the host government regarding the most appropriate means of guiding the domestic economy. The policies and activities of MNCs do affect the balance of payments, economic planning, competitive climate, development of technology, and many other aspects of host economies. Intensified by sensitized nationalistic sentiments, these effects reinforce the perception of peril to the host society. To alleviate host country fears, MNCs must learn to adjust their activities to the indigenous needs and sociocultural attitudes of host societies.

SUMMARY

The affiliates of MNCs have been a source of controversy in host countries since their inception. In the last few years the controversies have been complicated by the fact that an increasing number of host countries have started to acquire a dual status as some of their own firms multinationalize.

The most conflict prone are the home dominated MNCs, while the host dominated MNCs enjoy the greatest political tranquility. Neither can compete, however, with the internationally integrated MNC when it comes to productive efficiency and market power. Through international nationalization, MNCs locate their production facilities in the least cost countries and market their outputs in the most profitable countries.

Conflicts between MNCs and host nations often arise from differences between the internal structure of MNCs and the government of host nations. Other conflicts can be traced to the specific policies of MNCs, especially in highly centralized firms. Takeovers of local enterprises, financial policies, pricing, and export-import activities are typical areas of MNC government confrontations.

The employment of expatriate managers and technicians has met with increasing hostility in host nations. This has led to hiring and training of local nationals for management roles in affiliates. How to compensate and promote local nationals in light of pay scales and opportunities elsewhere remain controversial issues.

FOR REVIEW AND DISCUSSION

1. Describe the main factors that make the internationally integrated MNC a potentially more able enterprise than the other two types.

2. Centralization may decrease not only costs but also earnings of an MNC. Comment.

3. A number of MNC-host nation conflicts derive from central economic planning. Why?

4. Some MNCs expand by building new facilities; others by buying up existing firms. Which is preferable? Under what conditions?

5. Identify and analyze conflicts that arise from MNC financial policies and practices.

6. How do home country expatriates and third-country expatriates differ as sources of conflict?

7. If MNCs would employ local nationals exclusively all host country conflicts relating to management personnel would be eliminated. Discuss.

8. In which ways do the hiring and lay-off policies of U.S. firms run counter to indigenous values and laws in host countries?

9. If you were an executive of an indigenous company of a given host country, would you welcome or oppose U.S. MNCs? Would your answer be modified if you were in a different host country? In a different industry?

10. What are the dilemmas that host countries that are now becoming home countries also face?

16

Resolution of
Society-MNC Conflicts

*I*n the last two chapters we surveyed the conflicts between society and the MNC as perceived by home and host countries. Our focus was on the substance rather than the context of the issues. It was the nation versus the MNC, in a one-to-one adversary relationship. Such a simplifying abstraction is useful for developing a comprehensive overview of the unresolved problems surrounding the MNCs. In order to create solutions to the problems, we must place the issues in a more realistic context. The assumption of a one-to-one relationship between the MNC and a government is closer to fiction than to fact. There are not just two conflicting parties but many, and they more often cooperate than quarrel.

The MNC operates within several economies. It must interact and come to terms with all the host countries involved. Each country has its own perception of what its national interests and needs are and how these are best served. To assume that the interests of all host countries are synonymous is naive and unrealistic.

To understand a conflict we must understand not only the issues in dispute but the parties to the conflict, their objectives, their constraints, and their powers to act. Otherwise, we run the risk of drifting into the sphere of abstract issues and artificial actors.

PARTIES TO CONFLICTS

Who the actors are and how they relate to one another is shown in Figure 16.1. The figure includes only two affiliates and two host nations. In a typical MNC the number of both is much greater, and so is the number of conflict relationships and parties. A study of Figure 16.1 helps to underscore the fact that there are not two parties to disputes between the MNC and its host country but several parties, each of whom may have a real stake in the issues involved.

288

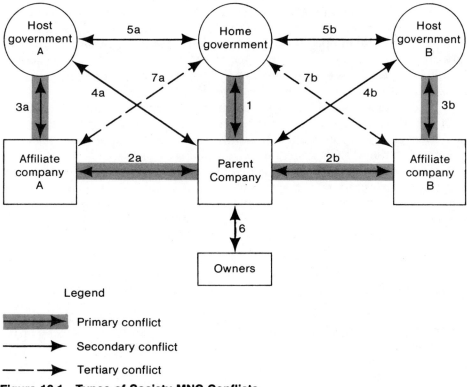

Figure 16.1   Types of Society-MNC Conflicts

Sources of Conflict

The source of disputes is the parties' conflicting objectives or interests. Particular issues are of greater concern to some parties than to others. There is typically a primary pair of adversaries in any dispute, but that does not necessarily exclude the other parties. For example, when the home government pressures the headquarters to repatriate more of the MNC's foreign earnings, the affiliates as well as the host country governments become parties to the conflict; or if headquarters restricts an affiliate's sales or other market behavior, the host government and home government both may see their interests threatened. Any single interaction or even the action of a single party may affect the interests of all others in some manner. Thus, the dispute settlement process often requires multiple participation.

Primary and Tributary Conflicts

As Figure 16.1 shows, there are three levels of conflict relations in the MNC. For the sake of simplicity they are referred to as primary, secondary, and tertiary. The primary axes for conflict run between the home country government and the parent company, between the host country government and the affiliated company, and between the parent company and the affiliated companies. From an operational point of view, it is along these axes that the principal conflicts take place. The secondary axes usually function more as amplifiers or catalysts than as operational channels for a continuous interaction. This is even more true for the tertiary relationships.

The types of issues from which the most frequent conflicts arise are shown in Table 16.1. To resolve any of these issues, it is necessary first of all to find out where the problem originates and then to trace its implications for other members of the MNC's system of relationships.

This analysis presumes the actual existence of a multinational structure for the company. It is not applicable to a new investor who has not yet established an affiliated enterprise in a host country. In such an initial phase the relevant channels would be the fourth level of relationships and possibly also the fifth and sixth levels.

TYPES OF CONFLICTS

For purposes of analysis, the disputes themselves can be divided into two broad categories, subjective and objective.

Subjective Conflicts

Subjective conflicts stem from human failings such as prejudice, ignorance, incompetence, corruption, or greed. Some manager makes a decision that is either legally or ethically wrong. The headline making scandals such as the ITT Chilean affair, the Lockheed briberies, and the Nestlé sales of baby foods in poor countries provide well-publicized illustrations of such misbehavior. In journalistic rhetoric the misbehaviors of a few become the normal behavior of all. If Lockheed resorts to bribery of high officials, that is taken to be sufficient evidence that all MNCs spawn corruption in governments; if Nestlé's marketing strategists erred when transplanting the promotional strategies used in the United States and Europe to less developed countries, it is taken to prove that the MNC disregards any potential for social harm that its products may cause; or if some ITT executive, true to the colonial tradition, uses corporate assets in support of political subversion in Chile, other MNCs are indicted by implication for the same folly.

In point of fact, multinational business is far less prone to misbehavior than is domestic business. By all accounts, the incidence of illegal and unethical actions per firm, per a given sales volume, or per investment have always been substantially greater in domestic business than in international business. Even in reference to the incidence of socially ignorant or purely technocratic decisions, decisions in obvious conflict with a country's indigenous social condi-

Table 16.1   Selected Conflict Issues[a]

Corporate objectives (2, 3)	Affiliate caught between pressures from parent company and host government
Ownership structure (2, 4)	Host government favors local participation
Organization (2, 4)	Host government regulations restrict corporate choices of organizational design
Management of affiliate (2, 3)	Host government demands that expatriates be replaced by local nationals
Training of employees (2, 3)	Host government pressures affiliate to develop training programs to foster advancement of nationals
Labor intensity (2, 3, 4)	Host government emphasizes employment over production efficiency, causing higher unit cost
Import controls (3)	Host government pushes use of local inputs
Export policies (2, 3)	Host government demands export expansion
Investment controls (4, or 2, 3)	Host government growth priorities rate MNC product low
Capital transfers (2, 3, 4)	Host government suffers balance of payments deficit and restricts outbound transfers of funds
Distribution of profits (2, 3, 4)	Disagreement over fair ratios
Transfer pricing (1, 2, 3)	Home and host governments require the firm to use different rules than its own best interest dictates; conflict is compounded by mutually contradictory requirements of different host governments
Infrastructure (2, 3, 4)	Disagreements over responsibility for building roads, electric power sources, water and sewer systems, and other infrastructure facilities
Research and development (1, 3)	Government dictates where and how new technology is to be developed and deployed
Technology transfer (1, 3)	Government requires affiliates to import nonprofitable technology or restrain the export of profitable technology to the firm's units in other countries
Specialization of facilities (2, 3)	Host government pressures MNC to broaden product line or to make more parts locally
National planning (2, 3, 4)	Host government plan weakens position of MNC
Income distribution (3)	Host government seeks to raise income of impoverished masses or tries to avoid the creation or growth of a highly paid elite of industrial workers
Extraterritoriality (1, 2, 3)	Home country dictates that parent company require affiliates to honor its laws and regulations if different from the laws and regulations of the host nation, a multifaceted and very troublesome phenomenon
Social behavior (2)	Different cultural and social norms in home and host countries; affects most seriously the communication and interactions between headquarters and the affiliate managers
Sovereignty (2, 3, 4)	Host government fear of dependence on or domination by the MNC
Taxation (1, 2, 3)	Host governments and/or home government seek to maximize tax revenues; they assign different values to the same transfer transaction, require different systems of accounts, disregard MNC's tax obligations to other nations

[a]Numbers refer to level of relationships, that is, to first, second, third, and fourth level relationships.

tions, MNCs have come out reasonably well compared with UNCs. This is probably due to the fact that the MNC is much more exposed to public scrutiny and that it typically employs more professionally educated managers than do UNCs.

Bad Press   Why, then, are the MNCs perceived to be more socially irresponsible? The answer lies in the relatively greater newsworthiness of MNCs than UNCs. In most host countries, MNCs are controversial institutions. Often they are also larger than UNCs. Therefore, MNCs command more attention than UNCs; they get more press coverage, and vastly more bad press. Consider the following incident.

On a recent lecture tour in India this author read in a Madras paper that the head of a local pharmaceutical firm had been found guilty of fraud for manufacturing and selling a worthless product under the false label of a well-known antibiotic. From Madras the author continued to Calcutta, Bombay, and New Delhi. In each city the audience was generally aware of the Lockheed, ITT, and Nestlé scandals, but not a single person in any of the three other Indian cities had ever heard of the conviction of the Madras pharmaceutical executive. Indeed, many people found it necessary to examine the newspaper to convince themselves that the story was true. No wire service had found the Madras case important enough to put it on a news wire, not to mention sending correspondents to Madras to cover the trial. If a Madras affiliate of an MNC such as Pfizer or CIBA had committed the same offense as the Madras UNC, would the Indian press have reacted with the same lack of interest? Hardly. The case would have been front page news all over India and the rest of the world, from the indictment to the conviction.

Due to ideological and nationalistic sensitivity, the MNC is closely watched by news media. Its actions get extensive press coverage. The surveillance by press and host government can hardly be ignored by MNCs. Any disregard in this respect is certain to inflict serious damage on the firm's image and future welcome in host countries.

Lack of Cross-National Sensitivity   Since subjective conflicts are caused by human error (managerial failures), they do not lend themselves to any concrete rational solutions. Each is a different case, with its own personality factors involved. The subjective conflicts can be prevented only to the extent to which the professional preparation of MNC managers can be improved. Their skills in cross-national and cross-cultural adaptations of business operations have been the weakest link. The level of international management knowledge is generally still low. We can reasonably expect substantial improvements in the years ahead. Correspondingly, we can expect a decline in the incidence of the conflicts of MNCs that arise from managerial failings of some kind, whether incompetence in international business or misassessment of foreign conditions.

Let us not expect too much. Faulty judgment and dishonesty occur in all walks of life. Even the most selective and highly policed professions, such as law and medicine, have their share of malpractice. We are thus assured a good measure of managerial misbehavior and its consequent conflicts between MNCs and host societies for years to come.

Objective Conflicts

The objective conflicts offer much brighter prospects. Since they arise from the rational pursuits of the conflicting parties, they lend themselves to objective analysis. Once the problem is fully understood by all parties, the way is open for tenable solutions.

The objective conflicts derive from the divergent goals of the host nations and the MNCs, as illustrated in Table 16.2. This is but a partial comparison. A number of other objectives that would reflect similar divergencies could be added. We cannot hope for perfect harmony between the host countries and the MNCs. Conflicts are inherent in their relationship, just as they are inherent in the relationships between domestic enterprises and government authorities. The conflict per se is not bad. It can produce laudable results—greater efficiency, better information, or removal of barriers. It is how the conflict is resolved that determines the final outcome—the result can be constructive, destructive, or neutral.

The overriding imperative for host countries and MNCs is to determine which resolutions provide the most constructive alternatives, keeping in mind that this is always a matter of trade-offs. The ultimate outcome can be a gain for both. This is known in game theory as the "win-win" model; it is predicated on constructive cooperation among parties in seeking solutions to conflicts. "For many, if not all conflicts, the need is to find a way to resolve them

Table 16.2 Selected Strategic Goals

Host Governments	Multinational Companies
Increase of national income	Return on investment and increase of corporate assets
Economic modernization	Competitive position
More and better employment	Efficient, low cost production
Broadly based development and dissemination of industrial skills	Selective hiring and training of employees
Diversification of economic activity	Specialization of production for efficiency
Avoidance of foreign takeovers of domestic firms	Acquisition of indigenous capacity
Development of domestic research capability	Location of research and development facilities in countries with best universities and other scientific institutions
Stimulation of investment in backward regions and rural areas	Location in large cities where infrastructure and labor supply are most developed
Balance of payments equilibrium	Free convertibility of currencies
Control over the pattern of economic development	Freedom of trade and investment
Maximization of public revenues	Minimization of tax burdens

constructively without eliminating the differences which led to the conflict. Differences and tensions often yield a productive outcome."[1]

Unfortunately, in practice the "win-win" method of conflict resolution is often sacrificed to the "win-lose" model, which presupposes one of the parties to win and the other to lose. The result is not a bargain but a capitulation. Obviously, such a prospect incites acrimony and discord rather than concili-ation and compromise. What is worse, the "win-lose" method shifts the focus of analysis away from the economic and social benefits and forces a political power play of "who has the last word" that is devoid of economic content.

NATIONAL OR INTERNATIONAL REGULATION OF MNCs

The relationships between the MNC and its host and home societies are never a matter of pure conflict or pure cooperation, but a process of simultaneous conflict and cooperation. Any equilibrium between the conflicting and coin-ciding tendencies derives not from any mechanistic adaptation, but from in-teraction, negotiation, and other processes of exercising the powers each side can apply. Unilateral resolution of conflicts between the nation and the MNC cannot produce rational results. If the state dictates the norms for corporate policy, or if the company seeks to counterpose its own strategy, including that of nonparticipation, to national policy, no true resolution of the conflict is possible.

That each nation must fight its own fires is beyond argument. Short-term problems and urgent issues cannot wait for international processes to run their course. However, the basic differences between the MNCs and host states represent long-term issues, the resolution of which requires not only thorough analysis and explication but also adherence to clearly articulated and inter-nationally accepted principles. Independent regulatory action by each indi-vidual nation is sure to lead to a chaotic maze of regulations reminiscent of the labyrinthian rules of foreign trade during the ultraprotectionist interwar period.

Commonality of Interests

Any action that one country takes in reference to the MNCs is likely to have some effect upon the MNC's operations in other countries. This is quite anal-ogous to the erection of trade barriers or the imposition of foreign exchange restrictions. A study of the various issues in Table 16.1 should provide ample illustration of this point.

Thus, regulation of MNCs does not lend itself to a permanent resolution through unilateral national action. It requires multilateral international action. If each country were to take the matter into its own hands, it would risk

---

1. Rensis Likert and Jan Gibson Likert, *New Ways of Managing Conflict* (New York: McGraw-Hill, 1976), p. 5.

retarding international investment and economic development in its own economy as well as exposing its neighbors to similar setbacks. This is to say, imposition of diverse and conflicting social requirements on the globally integrated MNCs jeopardizes their efficiency and productivity. Since these MNCs have become the major vehicle for direct investment, technology transfer, industrial development, and economic modernization, their demise would be detrimental to the economic future of the world, particularly the developing countries.

Rhetoric Versus Regulation

This is not to say that MNCs should have license to proceed without social accountability. To the contrary, public control over the MNCs is long overdue. Despite much rhetoric on the subject, there has been very little regulation. Governments have sought to make do with traditional trade controls and monetary restrictions, instruments quite obsolete for the purpose. As a result, the MNCs have often enjoyed the economic nirvana of a regulatory vacuum. As pointed out by Rainer Hellman, individual governments as well as trade unions and consumer groups are not in a position to establish the transnational organizational structures necessary to deal effectively with MNCs.[2]

Rationality dictates that the regulation of MNCs needs to be not only international in scope, to maximize the economic benefits that MNCs can contribute, but also comprehensive in coverage, to assure a fair and equitable distribution of these benefits among the host countries. Doubts and uncertainties about the distribution of the benefits has been the paramount cause of the increasing controversies surrounding the MNCs. Removal of these doubts, therefore, should be the central objective of any code of MNC behavior.[3]

AN INTERNATIONAL REGIME FOR MNCs

The growing urgency of social issues involving MNC activities has led to various projects aimed at creating an international regulatory regime for MNCs. One of the agencies involved is the United Nations Center for Transnational Companies, under whose auspices a code of MNC conduct is being developed. We should not expect this code to provide any quick cure for regulatory weaknesses. Even if a satisfactory code is developed, the United Nations has no machinery to enforce it. At best, it can serve as a set of guidelines that over time may promote commonality of national treatment of MNCs. Hellman argues that regional blocs such as the European Community and the Andean Common Market offer greater potential for unified action due to the similarity

2. Rainer Hellman, *Transnational Control of Multinational Corporations* (New York: Praeger, 1977).
3. Hellman, *Transnational Control*, p. 23.

of interests among their members. On another front, in an attempt to prevent government action, a number of industry associations have proposed their own codes of international behavior.

A recent Brookings study has proposed the following recommendations:

1. All home countries should harmonize their taxation of MNC profits earned by foreign affiliates; all should adopt a uniform system of foreign tax credit and treat domestic and foreign investment alike.
2. All countries should agree to limit the use of tax incentives for either outbound or inbound investments.
3. Common standards should be established for transfer prices and other methods of allocating tax revenues among all nations served by any given MNC.
4. Host countries should limit their use of government incentives for inbound investments; such incentives distort international capital allocation and cause conflicts between governments as well as between governments and MNCs.
5. Intergovernment cooperation should begin to work out concepts and procedures by which home countries can extend their antitrust (antimonopoly) laws to foreign subsidiaries without committing extraterritorial violations of host country jurisdiction.
6. A common safeguard mechanism should be established for restricting MNC activities if they cause adverse internal effects in a country.
7. Machinery should be set up for settlement of international disputes relating to MNCs such as expropriations and extraterritorial application of a given country's national policies.[4]

In addition to these permanent measures, the Brookings group recommends further international conventions to deal with some issues that may be self-liquidating in the long term, but that for the foreseeable future cannot be ignored, such as coordination of restraints on MNC activities in communist countries, promotion of MNCs in extractive industries to ease raw material shortages, and the treatment of "hot products," that is, the output of businesses taken over illegally or without proper compensation. In addition to these, international standards are needed for performance requirements that are levied on MNCs by many governments. Typical performance requirements include capital import or export quotas, minimum export volumes, requirements to increase or diversify the export mix, value added and indigenous content requirements, import substitutions, local ownership, and various job quotas for local nationals. According to the Brookings report:

> These requirements are often cloaked in the guise of more general policy objectives such as regional development schemes or general labor policies. It should not be permissible, however, to justify either investment incentives or performance requirements because "they are also available to domestic firms. . . ." The principle is not whether the discrimination is against or in favor of the foreign-based firm. The principle is whether the policy has the effect of exporting the host-country's problems to other

4. C. Fred Bergsten, Thomas Horst, and Theodore Moran, *American Multinationals and American Interests* (Washington, D.C.: The Brookings Institution, 1978), pp. 488–89.

countries; such measures should be barred except where justified under exceptions to the rules, and foreign retaliation should be authorized.[5]

SUMMARY

Conflicts between MNCs and countries with which they are involved derive from two basic sources, human failures and divergent goals. The first category may be called subjective conflicts, since they are caused by the subjective attributes of the decision makers involved. To resolve subjective conflicts, both MNCs and governments must raise the levels of international awareness, managerial sophistication, and professional ethics.

The second category may be called objective conflicts. These are inherent in all business and government relationships in which the objectives of the corporate interest and national interest differ. Though subjective factors may complicate such conflicts at times, they are irrelevant to their causes. The objective conflicts arise from the fully rational behavior of managers and government officials in pursuing their separate goals.

Effective conflict resolution requires that all parties to the conflict be identified and their interests in the conflict clearly understood; the headquarters company, the various subheadquarters, the affiliates, the host governments, and the owners, all may have a stake in the outcome. Therefore, MNC-society conflicts require multipartite participation to resolve them.

Differences among host country regulations have made many MNC activities controversial. This confusing situation is now being addressed by various world bodies such as the European Economic Community, the Andean Common Market, and the United Nations. Multilateral treaties to harmonize the regulatory rules of all countries in a major world region generally reduce the friction between MNCs and host nations.

FOR REVIEW AND DISCUSSION

1. Why is it misleading to treat MNC-society conflicts as one-to-one relationships?

2. If ten more host countries were added to Figure 16.1, would this increase or decrease the need to differentiate among primary, secondary, and tertiary relationships? Explain.

3. Contrast subjective conflicts with objective conflicts. Do both lend themselves to the same remedies?

4. If you were a news reporter, would you pay more attention to MNCs or to UNCs? Why?

5. Bergslen et al., *American Multinationals*, pp. 489–90.

5. Which three factors listed in Table 16.2 are the greatest potential sources of objective conflicts? Justify your choices.

6. What are some other divergencies between the strategic goals of MNCs and host governments than those stated in Table 16.2?

7. Give some illustrations of how the "win-win" and "win-lose" methods have been employed in resolving international disputes.

8. What has prevented host nations from regulating MNCs?

9. Evaluate the potential effects of national as opposed to international regulation of MNCs on business and governments?

10. If you were to draw up an international code of conduct for MNCs, what regulations would you include in it?

SUGGESTED READINGS FOR PART FIVE

"A Congressional Response to the Problem of Questionable Corporate Payments Abroad: The Foreign Corrupt Practices Act of 1977." *Law and Policy in International Business* 10:1253–1304, 1978.

Barnet, R., and Mueller, R. *Global Research*. New York: Simon and Schuster, 1974.

Bassiry, R. *Power vs. Profit: Multinational Corporation-Nation State Interaction*. New York: Arno Press, 1980.

Bergsten, C. F., Horst, T., and Moran, T. *American Multinationals and American Interests*. Washington, D.C.: The Brookings Institution, 1978.

Davidow, J. "Multinationals, Host Governments, and Regulation of Restrictive Business Practices." *The Columbia Journal of World Business* 15:14–19, 1980.

Doz, Y. L., and Prahalad, C. K. "How MNCs Cope with Host Country Intervention." *Harvard Business Review* 58:149–57, 1980.

Klein, J. "Entrapment or Opportunity: Structuring a Corporate Response to International Codes of Conduct." *The Columbia Journal of World Business* 15:6–13, 1980.

Kumar, K. *Transnational Enterprises: Their Impact on Third World Societies and Cultures*. Boulder: Westernview Press, 1980.

Vernon, R. *Storm Over the Multinationals*. Cambridge: Harvard University Press, 1977.

Part Six

ENVIRONMENTAL DYNAMICS: NORTH-SOUTH BUSINESS RELATIONS

*I*nternational businesses must function in a world of contrasts: old and new, primitive and modern, pious and agnostic, unutterably beautiful and sickeningly squalid, educated and ignorant, progressive and stagnant, sophisticated and naive, all in constant agitation. To interpret this volatile diversity, to make sense of this apparent chaos, we must try to identify the underlying forces, the prime movers, of global dynamics.

Two-thirds of the world's population live in countries that have yet to enter the twentieth century as perceived by the West. Many have yet to reach the nineteenth. These underdeveloped countries seek industrial development and social modernization but have not yet acquired such preconditions as an infrastructure of public facilities, an acquisitive psychology, technical capacity, and stable government.

The success or failure of any foreign business enterprise in a developing area rests heavily on its ability to cope with the lack of infrastructure and with the socioeconomic realities, which sharply differ from those in the developed nations. The major forces that shape economic decisions of the third world nations today are not only economic but also technological, political, social, and cultural. Failure to recognize or to reckon effectively with such noneconomic factors remains a major obstacle to international business in the third world.

The developing nations' struggle for self-assertion has ascended from self-government to the control of natural resources and further to a call for a new international economic order. Now a new frontier is being added, involving the flow of information in news reporting and the control of "cultural property"—the archeological artifacts and art objects that found their way to museums and private collections in the West during the colonial era. As a result, the environment for international business in the developing areas is not only changing but new dimensions and strengths are being added to its dynamics.

Chapters 17 and 18 contrast the environmental conditions for international business in the developing countries with those in the industrial and postindustrial countries and help us to grasp the realities and necessities of developing economies. Chapters 19 and 20 carry the analysis to the international and global levels, focusing on the pressing economic and political issues between the developing and the developed nations.

17

The Business Environment
in Developing Countries

*I*n popular parlance the global economy is viewed as a composite of three distinct worlds or socioeconomic systems. The *first world* includes the nations of Western Europe and North America, plus Japan, Australia, and New Zealand. All these are capitalist countries whose economies rely mainly on private enterprise and the competitive market system. The *second world* consists of the communist nations, with their centrally planned economies and state-run enterprises. The *third world* includes the less developed countries (LDC) of Africa, Latin America, and Asia. United Nations official nomenclature refers to these as *developing nations*, not as poor or underdeveloped nations, regardless of whether they are progressing or stagnating economically.

THE THREE WORLDS

Dividing Lines

The distinction between the first and second worlds is unmistakable; the former relies on the capitalist model, the latter on the Marxist-Leninist model. The distinctions between the third world and the other two are not as clear. Poverty and backwardness respect no ideological boundaries. Many noncommunist countries are poor, but so are most of the communist countries. Thus, if poverty and economic backwardness are to define the third world, much of the second world would have to be included. International analysts are inconsistent in their usage of the terms *third world* and *LDC*. Some include the poor communist nations, others exclude them. For most business purposes, it is better to treat all communist countries as members of the second world because of their entirely different economic systems and decision criteria. Business analysts, therefore, limit the third world to noncommunist developing nations.

The line between the third and first worlds is blurred by different notions of rich and poor, or developed and underdeveloped. Per capita GNP is the most commonly used indicator of a nation's relative ranking. However, neither per capita GNP nor any other version of income is a truly satisfactory indicator of a nation's development. For example, Table 17.1 (pages 306–7) shows that Libya outranks Finland, Austria, and Japan, and Saudi Arabia outranks New Zealand and Great Britain. Observing how people in Libya and Saudi Arabia actually live, we are struck by the primitive conditions, massive illiteracy, and industrial backwardness prevalent in both. In contrast, Austria, Finland, Japan, New Zealand, and Great Britain are all among the most sophisticated, educated, and industrialized countries in the world. Clearly, there is more to development than a high per capita income.

The Relevancy of GNP Data

Let us not discard the GNP per capita outright. Though less than perfect, it is actually a very useful indicator, in fact, the best single indicator under normal conditions. The illustrations above deal with abnormal conditions. Libya and Saudi Arabia belong to a very small group of countries whose GNPs have skyrocketed in a matter of a few years as the compound result of the world oil shortage and the creation of OPEC. Their sudden riches have come from the rapid escalation of oil prices rather than their own productive capacities; their fortunes are not too different from a speculator's windfalls.

If we eliminate the OPEC members and guard against any similar anomaly where a nation suddenly experiences a massive appreciation in value of its exportable commodities, the per capita GNP reflects rather well the general state of the nation's development. Cross-referenced with such qualitative indicators as literacy, life expectancy, university degrees, and occupational breakdown, the GNP figures can be modified to any desired degree, dependent upon the purpose of any particular study.

Even if we exclude the OPEC nations, we still face the question, At which point in the income continuum does poverty end and prosperity start? There is no objective standard or any international agreement on this point. What is rich for a citizen of Bangladesh or Rwanda is far below the official poverty line of the United States or France. Thus, we must rely on our own best judgment of where to draw the line.

In the 1950s the problem was considerably simpler. With the exceptions of Japan, Australia, and New Zealand, all African, Asian, and Latin American countries qualified for the third world. Today the matter is considerably more complicated. Since the 1950s the third world countries have developed at widely divergent rates.

The per capita GNP has passed the $1,500 mark in a number of third world countries, including Ireland, Singapore, Puerto Rico, Hong Kong, Trinidad, Portugal, Argentina, Uruguay, Brazil, South Africa, Panama, Jamaica, Costa Rica, Lebanon, Mexico, Chile, Taiwan, Turkey, and South Korea, in addition to the OPEC nations. Can these still be classified as third world nations? If not, where do they belong? A move is at present underway to create a new identity, *newly industrialized countries* (NICs) or *advanced developing nations.*

Table 17.1   GNP per Capita at Market Prices

COUNTRY	AMOUNT IN U.S. $[a]	COUNTRY	AMOUNT IN U.S. $[a]
Poorest Developing Countries—The Fourth World			
Bhutan	80	Afghanistan	180
Bangladesh	90	Tanzania	180
Mali	100	Pakistan	180
Ethiopia	100	Sri Lanka	190
Upper Volta	100	Sierra Leone	190
Nepal	110	Madagascar	200
Somalia	110	Guinea	210
Rwanda	120	Lesotho	210
Chad	120	Haiti	220
Burundi	120	Central Africa	240
Burma	120	Kenya	250
Zaire	130	Mauritania	250
Malawi	130	Uganda	250
India	140	Yemen	270
Mozambique	150	Sudan	270
Niger	150	Togo	270
Benin	180		
Moderate Income Developing Countries—The Third World			
Indonesia	280	Mongolia	830
Arab Republic of Egypt	280	Syrian Arab Republic	830
Yemen Arab Republic	300	Malaysia	830
Cameroon	310	Peru	840
Angola	310	Algeria	1,010
Ghana	370	Turkey	1,010
Thailand	380	Taiwan	1,050
Honduras	400	Chile	1,050
Nigeria	400	Mexico	1,060
Liberia	410	Lebanon	1,070
Senegal	410	Costa Rica	1,130
Philippines	420	Jamaica	1,150
Papua New Guinea	450	Panama	1,170
Zambia	450	Brazil	1,220
Bolivia	510	South Africa	1,340
Morocco	520	Uruguay	1,370
El Salvador	530	Iraq	1,390
Zimbabwe	530	Rumania	1,400
Congo	530	Argentina	1,580
Colombia	650	Portugal	1,660
Paraguay	650	Iran	2,060
Ivory Coast	650	Trinidad and Tobago	2,190
Jordan	650	Hong Kong	2,230
Ecuador	700	Puerto Rico	2,310
Guatemala	700	Bulgaria	2,460
South Korea	700	Venezuela	2,540
Nicaragua	770	Greece	2,570
Dominican Republic	790	Singapore	2,580
Tunisia	800	Ireland	2,620

Table 17.1 *continued*

COUNTRY	AMOUNT IN U.S. $[a]	COUNTRY	AMOUNT IN U.S. $[a]
Communist Countries—The Second World			
Cambodia	80	Yugoslavia	1,800
Laos	90	Hungary	2,280
Viet Nam	160	Bulgaria	2,310
China	410	U.S.S.R.	2,760
North Korea	470	Poland	2,860
Albania	540	Czechoslovakia	3,840
Cuba	860	Democratic Republic of	
Mongolia	860	Germany	4,220
Advanced Countries—The First World			
Spain	3,050	Australia	6,990
Italy	3,220	Belgium	7,020
Israel	3,920	Federal Republic of Germany	7,510
United Kingdom	4,180	Denmark	7,690
New Zealand	4,200	Norway	7,800
Japan	5,090	United States	7,880
Austria	5,620	Canada	7,930
Finland	5,890	Sweden	9,030
Netherlands	6,650	Switzerland	9,160
France	6,730		
Newly Rich Countries			
Saudi Arabia	4,500		
Libya	6,320		
Kuwait	15,480		

[a]Computed at 1976 prices.

Source: The World Bank Atlas (New York: World Bank, 1979, 1980).

On the other end of the spectrum are the nations whose economic growth has ranged from negative to negligible. These are the poorest of the poor. Over one-third of the world's nations belong to this group. Should these not be treated as a distinct group? Yes, says the United Nations, which has established a separate commission to deal with the economic and social problems peculiar to the landlocked and least developed nations.

From Three to Four Worlds

Some analysts have proposed splitting off the less developed group from the third world entirely to form a *fourth world*. To date, this proposal has not advanced much beyond academic discussion.

Regardless of which way the categorization is ultimately resolved, the underlying fact remains that the developing nations represent a highly heterogenous mass not only economically but also culturally. Any attempt to forge them into homogenous subgroups can at best achieve but partial success. The practical value to business of more homogenous categories will become clearer as we understand the realities of third world societies and how they are affected by the various development processes.

THE MEANING OF POVERTY

Although the developing countries differ in innumerable ways from one another regarding cultural, social, and political systems, they all share one very important problem—the need for raising the level of life. Poverty is the common economic denominator. To overcome poverty, to alleviate the deprivation and misery caused by material shortages is a socioeconomic dictate that no government, radical or ultrareactionary, can ignore.

Definitions of Poverty

Poverty in the developing world is both absolute and relative. By *absolute poverty* we mean below subsistence living, that is, inadequate supplies of physically necessary requirements for sustaining normal human life—not enough calories, not enough proteins, minerals, fats, and other nutrients; not enough drugs and medicines; not enough medical services; not enough housing; not enough means of avoiding malnourishment, exposure, and premature death. By *relative poverty* we mean a situation in which certain segments of society are considerably worse off than the majority. This underprivileged segment need not be below physical subsistence level—they need not actually starve, freeze, suffer in a physical or biological sense—but they suffer psychologically because they cannot live as normal members of the particular society.

Relative poverty may lead to absolute poverty due to the hopelessness, negative attitudes, and lack of motivation it may foster. The consumption expectations—decent or humanly acceptable standards—of relatively poor people are shaped by the standards and modes of living of their more affluent compatriots. There is a gap between what they can afford and what most of their fellow citizens actually consume. In the United States, the official poverty line at this writing is $4,250 for a single person and $5,950 for a two-person family. The advanced country poverty problem has no solution short of an equalization of income distribution, for the reason that the richer these countries become, the more the levels of aspiration of low income people increase. Hence, the perception of poverty may even increase.

Contrasted with the incomes in the third world countries, the incomes of the U.S. and the European poor look plush. The financial resources of the U.S. poor place them in the ranks of the very rich in the eyes of Africans,

Asians, and Latin Americans. This is not to say that the problem of poverty does not exist in the first world countries, nor that their poor do not suffer. Their feelings of failure, inadequacy, and hopelessness are real enough, but they are mainly psychologically rooted, not due to insufficient means to meet biophysical needs.

The poverty problems experienced in the third world countries are quite different. The homeless millions in India, the tribesmen of Africa, or the peasant populations in almost any underdeveloped country have no equivalent in the industrial world. For absolute poverty there is an unmistakable, absolute solution—higher real income.

The Closed Circle of Absolute Poverty

The reason so many developing countries have failed to break the grip of absolute poverty is graphically explained by the vicious circle of absolute poverty. As elaborated by Ragnar Nurkse, this self-perpetuating system is depicted in Figure 17.1, in which the arrows show the cause-effect relationship.[1]

To improve their lot, the absolute poor must somehow break this circle. That they realize this and have come to regard it not only as an economic imperative but as a political and ideological maxim is a fact that no government, old or new, autocratic or democratic, can any longer ignore. Indeed, the tide of political awakening that in recent past swept away what seemed invincible

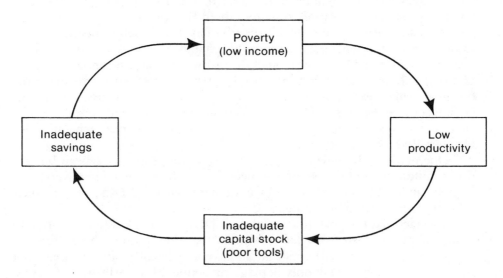

Figure 17.1   The Closed Circle of Absolute Poverty

1. See Ragnar Nurkse, *The Problems of Capital Formation in Underdeveloped Countries* (Oxford: Basil Blackwell, 1955).

colonial empires gained much of its immense force from the rising expectations that greater contact with the outside world brought to those people.

The Urge to Industrialize

The growing contact with richer nations has helped to point also to what the third world now accepts as the only answer to this problem, industrial development, with all that entails—capital investment, education, technology transfer, and sociopolitical modernization. The faith in industrialization is so deep-rooted and profound that it is often looked upon not only as the basic economic objective but also as a political ideology.

The urge to industrialize, to grow in economic strength and political stature, is the force that unites the underdeveloped world and propels it to mobilize its energies on a global scale, as happened at the U.N. Conference on Trade and Development (UNCTAD), the Law of the Sea Conference, and similar joint efforts. UNCTAD first met in 1964 to air third world grievances over international economic relations and GATT; its deliberations received wide publicity and strong enough support to make UNCTAD a permanent agency of the United Nations acting as the global forum for third world nations to discuss trade and development problems.

The Law of the Sea Conference started in 1974 and has held a series of extended sessions since. It is concerned with the task of working out a treaty that will create a new international regime for the world's oceans by (a) redefining the borders of territorial seas; (b) establishing principles and rules for the exploitation of oceanic resources (both fisheries and deep sea mining); (c) setting standards for an equitable distribution of the potential oceanic wealth among coastal and noncoastal nations; (d) establishing rules and standards to prevent pollution and contamination of the marine environment; and (e) fostering international cooperation in scientific research and technology to make the potential economic wealth of the oceans accessible to development.[2] As this book went to press, the new treaty was reportedly ready and was to become valid at the next session of the Law of the Sea Conference, scheduled for October 1981.

One need not become a prophet to predict that these have been but the first manifestations of the potential power that the brotherhood in poverty and in goals and aspirations is placing in the hands of the LDCs, despite their differences in many other respects.

The fact that the governments of the LDCs are irrevocably committed to industrialization at all costs does not mean that they possess the capacity to bring it about, nor that they all go about it intelligently. But they are not standing still. They are not only hoping, but acting, as we shall see in Chapter 19. Discontented with the slow pace of market processes, they are determined

2. Endel-Jakob Kolde, *The Pacific Quest: The Concept and Scope of an Oceanic Economy* (Lexington, Mass.: D.C. Heath, 1976), pp. 67–85.

to force the pace by government initiative and action, which often translates into central planning of the economy and setting up of state-owned enterprises.

INCOME DISTRIBUTION

Low as they are, the per capita GNP figures actually tend to overstate the standard of living for the majority of inhabitants in third world countries. As statistical averages, these figures hide the brutal fact that much of the national income accrues to the few at the apex of the income pyramid, leaving a considerably reduced amount of income available to the large masses at its bottom. The inequity of income distribution is much more pronounced in the LDCs than elsewhere. Two-thirds of the families, belonging to the poorest categories, receive less than one-third of total available income. In the upper group, the top 20 percent of families receive between 50 percent and 60 percent of the total income. To emphasize the inequality of income distribution, 5 percent of the wealthiest families take between 22 percent and 40 percent of total income in the LDCs as a group.

Another important deviation from Western patterns is the small share of income going to the middle class. In LDCs the middle three quintiles accrue less than half of total income, from 36 percent to 45 percent. This restricts the capacity to save almost entirely to the upper income group. In advanced countries the middle class is a major source of savings and investment.

A factor that leads to the understatement of income data of developing countries is the prevalence of barter. National income accounting is limited to monetary transactions. In the developing areas, vast amounts of informal barter take place for which no records are kept and which, therefore, are not entered into national income and product accounts. Much of the barter involves either homemade merchandise or agricultural commodities.

Another unrecorded activity of importance in a backward economy is breaking of bulk, that is, dividing "normal" packages into minute amounts and retailing these extremely small (by western standards) quantities of merchandise from roadside stands or shoulder baskets. Units of ten matches and teacups of salt are examples. The function of miniretailers is undeniably important in LDCs economies but, again, the difficulties of measuring the business volume are obvious. Although many LDCs, for example, Brazil and India, attempt to estimate the incomes of ambulatory traders and the values of agricultural commodities consumed by growers, these figures are generally rather crude.

NEITHER CAPITALISM NOR COMMUNISM

No theoretical model adequately describes the business environments of developing countries. They are mixtures of many contradictory and coexisting forces without any discernible pattern. In some respects they are capitalistic; in many other respects they are not. Often they exhibit feudal characteristics, but this model, too, is a very poor facsimile of the realities.

The governments of the developing countries span the entire spectrum of political ideologies. There are monarchs who reign by divine right, there are republics, and there are revolutionary rulers with new left leanings. Moreover, the ideological labels may be misleading. They do not necessarily reflect the degree of democracy, individual freedom, or political rights of individuals and business enterprises.

Many of the LDCs tend to lean closer to autocracy than to a free society. To a westerner who is dedicated to the democratic ideal this is a disheartening truth, but western ideals are counterposed by nonwestern realities of life, both ideological and material, in the developing world. To govern, governments must be able to cope with actual conditions, whatever they are, ideals or no ideals. The conditions in LDCs are often such that only very strong and forceful governments can effectively govern. Autocratic leaders and autocratic methods are, therefore, commonplace. Lack of internal cohesion, bitter factionalism, intertribal rivalry, lack of an educated electorate, and many other factors agitate against western democratic processes and institutions.

COLONIAL HERITAGE

With very few exceptions, the developing nations have a colonial past. In Latin America the postcolonial period has been longer and the experiences with independence and self-government are richer. In Africa, Asia, and Oceania, the colonial inheritance is still fresh and visible. Confused loyalties, weak identifications with nationhood, and a lack of internal cohesion are common to most of these countries.

When originally subjugated by colonial conquerors, these peoples were still in a prenation stage of development. The prevalent sociopolitical organization was tribal. Each tribe was more or less independent, with its own social and economic structures, based on its peculiar history, geography, and traditions. Under the colonial rulers the tribes were not integrated into nations but were kept in the tribal minisovereignties. To prevent the tribes from forming anticolonial coalitions, the colonial powers fomented and cultivated intertribe conflicts and rivalries.

Divided Nationhood

When the colonies finally gained independence it was nationhood in name but not always in substance. Tribalism still exists and creates disjointed values systems and social structures in most excolonial countries in Africa and Asia. Both government and business find this disjointedness a difficult challenge.

The problem is further aggravated by the fact that most colonial countries used *indirect rule*. They staffed only the superstructure of government with officials from the mother country and let the local government functions be carried out by the traditional tribal elders. Although many maharajas, sultans, and other tribal chiefs were opposed to the colonial rule, they were forced to act as agents of the colonial administration. As such, they became suspect in the eyes of the local people, and both their traditional authority and their leadership abilities were undermined. Many tribes are still suspicious of national governments and often distrust their own elders who hold transtribal (national or regional) office.

When the nations of Africa became independent, the political boundaries of countries were carved without due consideration for the tribal structures; however, tribal boundaries still transcend political boundaries. All this adds to internal conflicts and creates problems and instabilities in many border areas. To avoid becoming engulfed in these conflicts and problems, any business firm operating in the developing countries must be well aware of the local setting and its constituent elements.

Corrupting Bureaucracy

The use of native chieftains and community elders as agents of the colonizing authority reduced the respect given to native rulers, who came to be seen as representatives of the oppressor government. Thus, the traditional fabric of social authority in the tribal power structure was weakened. But this was not all. Introduction of western legal systems had a similarly disintegrative effect. Superimposing western legal systems on the tribal structure resulted in the breakdown of the disciplines of the indigenous society. Simple honesty and personal accountability, which in most primitive societies serve as the main means of order, were replaced with a multitude of regulations and legal technicalities.

Much of this was a matter of redefinition and relabeling. The indigenous system may have sanctioned witchcraft as legitimate; the imported western law declared it a crime. Gifts to traditional chiefs and elders were regarded in native culture as not only right and proper but often purifying and sanctifying; the imported law declared them bribes.

This was only part of the problem. The alien legal rules and judicial procedures, in sharp contrast with local customs and the local sense of justice, opened opportunities for profiting from ignorance and confusion. A class of lawyer-translators to serve as go-betweens between the western bureaucracy and the native people arose. Rather than facilitating integration between the government and the governed, as they had been intended to do, these interculture brokers found their own interests best served by disintegration. This assured that both the colonial officials and the native people had to depend on the lawyer-translators, who used their special skills and their connections with the colonial authorities against their simpler countrymen for the purposes of bribery and extortion. Knowing that the officials of the mother country were themselves inaccessible to the people, because they were so few and because they understood neither the language nor the culture, the native lawyer-translators usurped much of the actual government power.

When independence came, the colonial legacy was often a lawyer-ridden bureaucratic system deluged with favoritism and corruption. Highly repugnant to the native populations, this colonial inheritance greatly increased the difficulty of building confidence between the new national governments and the people.

In addition, with no local electorate to obey, the colonial authorities had often governed by expediency, utilizing traditional structures and leaders wherever convenient, and issuing decrees, backed by military force, when voluntary compliance was not forthcoming. This created public distrust of government. National authorities have had but modest success in restructuring this colonial legacy and in changing public perceptions of government.

ECONOMIC STRUCTURE

Sources of Livelihood

The logical place to begin an investigation of the economic structures of a country is with an analysis of the activities that support the society or that provide the people with their livelihoods. To demonstrate the contrasts between developing and developed countries, the data for three countries of each type are juxtaposed in Figure 17.2. One pair represents large countries, one medium countries, and one small countries. They were chosen from seventeen other pairs studied, any of which could have been used, as they all showed the same contrasts.

The various productive activities are grouped into four structurally different economic classifications. *Primary activity* consists of agriculture and other extractive industries (mining, logging, fishing, oil production); *secondary activity* embraces manufacturing, processing, and construction industries; *tertiary activity* includes wholesale and retail trade, transportation, and communication industries; the service sector consists of government personnel, professional people, and miscellaneous consumer services. Whether the service sector should be combined with tertiary activity or presented as a separate element is debatable. In economic literature, the two are often lumped together.

The employment patterns shown in Figure 17.2 correlate closely with the breakdown of national product by sectoral sources. Since people in secondary and tertiary activities earn more than those in agriculture, their relative contributions to the national product are somewhat greater than their percent share in total employment. The fact still remains that for most LDCs, a large proportion of the GNP comes from agricultural and raw materials production. To the extent that industry exists, it is generally in the area of light consumer goods. This means that a main part of the GNP is derived directly from the land-based activities, from production of agricultural commodities and live-

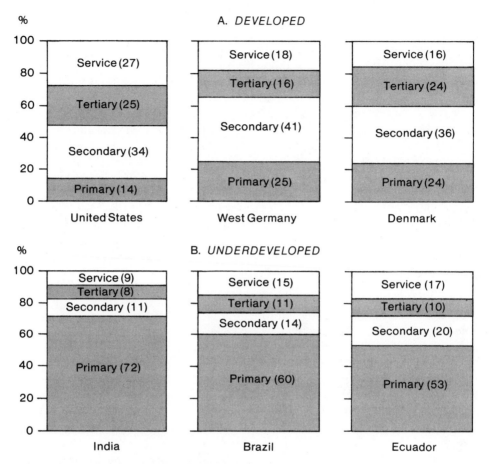

Figure 17.2 Employment by Activity in Developed and Underdeveloped Countries

stock, from the mining of minerals or drilling of oil, or from the processing of foodstuffs and textile fibers.

Another characteristic of developing economies is that they specialize in a small number of commodities. Such production is generally labor intensive and uses a large portion of the land in the production process. The narrow production base requires that exports be similarly specialized. For example, over 70 percent of Bolivia's exports have been in tin, over 70 percent of Colombia's in coffee. Petroleum has accounted for over 90 percent of Venezuela's exports and over 85 percent of Iran's exports. Cocoa beans have made up over 65 percent of Ghana's exports. On the other hand, for Mexico and Argentina, which are more developed, the percentages for any single commodity have been less than 25 percent of the total. We shall further analyse this problem in Chapter 19.

Land Use

Insufficient Utilization   Although land is of such decisive importance to third world nations, they utilize no more than one-quarter of their land for agriculture. In contrast, the United States and Germany utilize about half of their land areas for agricultural production. The main reason for the low percentage of usage is lack of capital and technology. In many LDCs, such as Brazil, much of the land remains inaccessible. It is impossible to cultivate the land if there are no roads, no equipment to clear the jungle, and no labor force and farm machinery to cultivate the crops.

In other LDCs, especially in Africa, much of the land is arid. Irrigation is often possible but requires capital and engineering not available from indigenous sources. In still others, agricultural production has been held back by an archaic marketing system that is incapable of distributing surplus production from fertile districts to deficit areas; for example, surplus grain has been left to rot in agricultural regions at the same time millions of people have been starving in urban centers and other regions of the country.

Inefficient Utilization   Along with this inability to use large portions of available land, the LDCs face problems with respect to the land that is in use. For most commodities, the productivity of agricultural land is generally much lower than it is in the developed nations. Crop yields in grains and cereals in Latin America, the Orient, and Africa rarely exceed one-half to two-thirds of what they are in North America, and in many cases they run far below one-half. For potatoes, yields range from less than one-third to just over one-half, and for cotton, from about one-fifth to about four-fifths of yields in the United States.

Such low yields are due in part to the limited extent to which modern farming methods and equipment are utilized. Nine-tenths of the tractors and three-fourths of the chemical fertilizers used in the world are used in first world countries.

The low yields are also due in part to the nature of land holdings in the LDCs. The vast majority of the rural population of third world countries owns either no land at all or only tiny holdings of a few hectares. Family incomes are near subsistence level, which constrains their ability to save for modernizing the traditional production methods. Agricultural practices date back for centuries, and implements are equally antiquated. Due to the very small holdings, modern farm machinery could not be effectively employed even if financing were available.

For example, in Thailand, the majority of farms range from 3 to 5 hectares. In Brazil, about 45 percent of the farms are less than 10 hectares and another 40 percent range from 10 to 100 hectares. In Latin America, almost 75 percent of the farms are 20 hectares or less in size.

Land Tenure   In Latin America as a whole almost 65 percent of the land is controlled by only 1.5 percent of the farmers, all of whom own over 1,000 hectares of land. In Bolivia the extent of large holdings is even greater; 6 percent of the farmers control 92 percent of the land. In Venezuela, 1.6 percent of the farmers control almost 75 percent of the farmland.

For historical reasons, the land of these large estates is the better land of the country. Absentee ownership is a common phenomenon, and labor for the farm is supplied by the *colono* system. Under this system, cash payment is not the general form of compensation for work; rather, the worker becomes a tenant farmer on a small parcel of land and, in return for this, works a certain amount of time on the large estate. The tenant farmers are economically discouraged from improving the land on which they work, for they will receive insignificant benefits from any increased production; the absentee owner neither knows nor cares, for his primary interests lie elsewhere. Under such a system the productivity of land is nobody's business.

Implications for Foreign Investors

Structural Biases Most of the industry in the developing countries is in light consumer goods and not in capital goods. Such industries can supply neither capital equipment nor the variety of basic goods an industrial enterprise requires. Thus, the costs of developing a new industry in these countries may involve not only the cost of setting up production facilities but also the cost of overcoming the present pattern of natural resource allocation and land use, which is heavily skewed in favor of a few primary commodities.

Small Market The pattern of land use also limits the size of the domestic market for manufactured goods. Agricultural production is based upon labor rather than upon capital intensive production methods. The land is often tilled as it has been for centuries, without much use of machinery and other industrial devices, such as soil additives, for increasing productivity. Thus, the demand for heavy machinery for agriculture remains low. A significant demand for capital goods can develop only after a country can supply its fundamental requirements for foodstuffs and textiles from indigenous sources and can utilize savings and exports for capital investments.

Shortage of Capital Up to the point of self-sufficiency, the light consumer industries can grow faster than demand because of the opportunity for import substitution. Capital requirements for such plants are lower than those for capital goods manufacturers. With the general shortage of capital in these countries, it is in this sector that most investment takes place. Therefore, the patterns of land use in the underdeveloped countries affect both the supply and demand considerations of industrial enterprises, limiting the supply of raw materials and capital equipment and limiting the markets for heavy goods once they have been produced.

THEORIES OF ECONOMIC DEVELOPMENT

Growth Theories

The forces that govern economic growth are not yet well enough understood to permit absolute understanding. There is much room for different theories and different approaches. Countries with very different theories have obtained very similar results, and countries with very similar theories have obtained very different results. The reason for the uncertainty is the complexity of the problem. Economic growth involves not only the whole economy (business, agriculture, trade, banking) but also the educational system, social life, and infrastructure.

Development theory can be reduced to two practical approaches. First is the *balanced growth theory*, which argues that economic development is possible only if it takes place in all sectors of the economy simultaneously. It implies that a country undertakes a well-planned and extensive development program. That program includes all business and economic activities. However, unless there are markets for all products and services, there will be little possibility of and incentive for creating growth-producing investment.

Second is the *unbalanced growth theory*, which argues that certain sectors of the economy or certain industries lead the growth and others follow. The implication of this is that government effort and economic planning should focus primarily on producing growth in the lead industries and that the rest of the business activities are to be left on their own. To put it in more academic language, unbalanced growth implies that differential growth rates in various parts of the business system create interacting pressures that lead to general economic growth and industrial development.

Since governments of many developing countries lack the financial means to pursue balanced growth, the prevailing tendency is to give more emphasis to the unbalanced approach. Governments are keen to encourage foreign investments in industries that they feel will lead to growth. They are equally prone to forestall those investments that might provide weak or negative linkages with the rest of the economy. In either case, business must be prepared to adapt to policies implemented by the government as the growth process advances and as the company itself becomes part of a country's internal economic dynamics.

Capital Infusions

When the African and Asian colonial empires collapsed and the new nations were born, the prevailing belief among theorists and aid experts was that capital shortage was the most critical problem of the new countries. This resulted in the so-called *big push policy*—a massive injection of capital into the developing economies to raise the ratio of capital to labor. The reasoning was something like this: In a subsistence economy there is no excess to be saved from production because everything produced goes to feed, clothe, and house the population. Since there are no savings, there is no source from which to derive investment capital. Without investment capital, improvement in the production system cannot be made because machines, tractors, factories, irrigation systems, and other modern production facilities all require capital investment. That capital, then, had to be supplied.

Foreign Aid and Direct Investments   The big push philosophy gave rise to various foreign aid programs and development loans. Private enterprise was encouraged to invest in developing areas. The policy was intended to bring about a massive flow of capital equipment into the developing countries and set in motion an upward moving industrial development spiral. The initial capital and technical aid were to come from the industrially developed countries, primarily the United States and European nations. The spiral would then start generating internal savings and thus create its own source for further investment. Sustained growth would follow. No important considerations were given to the structures of the economy. The question of balanced versus unbalanced growth was simply considered immaterial.

Waste and Corruption   After some fifteen years of massive aid and technical assistance, the big push turned out to be a disappointment. The postulated result did not materialize. Adding capital to labor and land did not result in an automatic output of goods and services. What is worse, the big push policy produced some negative results that had not been anticipated. Businesses in the granting countries, such as the United States and France, started jockeying for the aid funds, that is, trying to promote foreign aid especially earmarked for their industry so that they could turn the aid dollar into trade dollar for their profit. This had a tendency to subvert the real aims and to push the aid problem into partisan and self-serving politics in the industrial countries. In the recipient countries, aid produced corruption—diversion of aid funds and commodities to black market operations, speculation in aid programs, and various misappropriations.

Political Side Effects   Aid had also an inevitable political connotation; namely, whichever government was in power in the aid-receiving country benefited politically from the aid funds. The government could both claim credit for the benefits resulting from the aid and, at times, use the aid funds for purely political purposes, such as campaign expenses, to perpetuate its own power. Finally, the results of aid, even if they were real and substantial, were often difficult to demonstrate or measure. The public in the grantor countries, therefore, was left uncertain that the aid contributions had been productively employed. All this led to an ultimate abandonment of the big push and the capital infusion theory. We shall return to this problem in Chapter 20.

Human Resources

The next theoretical contributions focused upon the human elements. This theory postulated that the LDCs had a low capacity to absorb capital because they lacked educated and motivated people, the critical factor in progress. The implications of this theory were that education played a very fundamental role, and that government policy had to shift from direct business investment to educational human investments to build up human resources to make economic progress viable. We shall discuss the specific policies relating to human resources in Chapter 18.

SUMMARY

The unifying force for the third world has been absolute poverty. To break its grip, these countries have sought to internationalize and modernize their economies. This common commitment to economic progress has welded these diverse cultures and political systems into a global coalition to facilitate mutual assistance activities and to form a common front vis-à-vis the first and the second world nations.

Third world attitudes toward business still remain warped by colonial legacies. Tribalism, distrust of central authority, and top-heavy income distribution are common. Much of the economy is landbound. Dependence on agriculture and other extractive industries dominates. Land use is often governed by tribal traditions rather than agronomic considerations, and the productivity of land is generally lower than in the developed countries. The traditional patterns of land use limit the demand for agricultural machinery and technical services. The best developed manufacturing sectors produce light consumer goods, with durables on a rapid upswing in the more advanced LDCs.

Theorists have advanced a number of different models for achieving economic progress, but none has gained universal acceptance. Each LDC takes a different approach, mixing various theories and, in general, shifting from theory to increasingly pragmatic considerations. The most widely encountered policy debates relate to the balanced versus unbalanced growth theories and to the issue of priorities between investments in plant and equipment and investments in education.

FOR REVIEW AND DISCUSSION

1. Which of the three worlds do you find the least satisfactory as a classification? Why?

2. What are the shortcomings in GNP per capita figures for rating the developmental achievements of different countries?

3. Relative poverty often leads to absolute poverty. Comment.

4. How is it possible that LDCs with widely different and sometimes ideologically hostile political systems have been able to vote en bloc at the United Nations and to cooperate closely at other international conferences?

5. Does tribalism strengthen or weaken national economic policies? How?

6. How have attitudes toward business been affected by colonial legacies in LDCs?

7. Discuss the implications to international business of the economic structure that is typical to LDCs.

8. If you were to design a land reform proposal for an LDC, what objectives would you set for the reform? What means for achieving the objectives would you propose?

9. What factors determine the capital absorptive capacity of an economy?

10. Is there any evidence showing that the negative side effects of foreign aid have become progressively worse? If not, have they been eliminated?

18

The Human Environment in Developing Countries

*I*n the final analysis the prosperity of any nation depends on its people. The poor countries are no exception. Their populations harbor, on the one hand, great potential for progress and, on the other hand, great perils. In numbers of people and population growth rates, nearly all of them are richly endowed, but the masses remain on the periphery of the economy's productive process. Because of the overriding significance of people-related factors in developing economies, we shall devote this chapter to a review of the strategic aspects of the human environment.

THE POPULATION PROBLEM

The world population is in a state of explosive expansion. Throughout the milleniums of human history, population growth was slow. Diseases, wars, and other calamities left little room for growth. In 1775, when Adam Smith wrote *The Wealth of Nations*, world population totaled 750 million; in 1975 it had reached 4,000 million. The upturn coincided with the start of the Industrial Revolution. Since then, growth has been accelerating in a very nearly geometric, or exponential, progression, as prophesized by Thomas Malthus. By the year 2000 world population is projected to range from 6,000 million to 7,000 million. At least in most of the twentieth century, the exponential growth applies only to the developing countries' populations as the developed nations have experienced a more or less straight line growth (Figure 18.1 on page 324).

Low Food Supply

Malthus's other prediction was that the world food supply will grow only by an arithmetic, or straight line, progression, thus creating an everwidening gap between the requirements for and supply of food.

The first world countries have so far proven Malthus wrong. Taken as

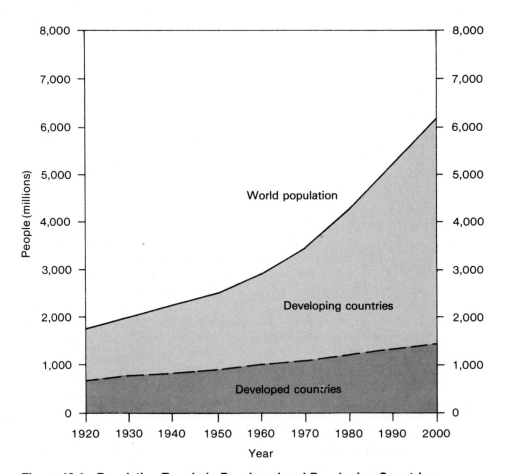

Figure 18.1   Population Trends in Developed and Developing Countries

Source: Demographic Yearbooks (New York: United Nations, 1970, 1976, 1979).

a group, their food production has not only kept pace but even outdistanced their population growth. In the third world countries the reverse has been true; food production has fallen progressively further behind. As a consequence, famine has become epidemic to scores of LDCs. According to the United Nations, over half of the population of the world's poorest nations have too little to eat, 50 million people starve to death each year, and some 250 million people in Africa, Asia, and Latin America suffer brain damage or blindness or become deaf-mutes because of malnutrition. Many more suffer from protein deficiency.

If present growth rates continue, the third world and the poor communist countries will have 80 percent of the world's population by the year 2000. Such a numerical disparity will have serious consequences for all nations. How to contain the population explosion is, therefore, a global concern.

The direct cause of the population growth in the third world is modern medicine. As diseases such as malaria, smallpox, and the plague are stamped out, millions survive who in prior times would have perished. Death rates have declined radically. Since birth rates have not declined, larger and larger increments have been added to the total population. To contain the growth, the birth rate, too, must be reduced, but this is a far more difficult task.

Birth Rate Rigidities

Many factors combine to perpetuate the high birth rate. For the impoverished masses large families not only symbolize virility, strength, and social importance but also provide a system of collective economic security. The larger the family, the better one's chances in illness, misfortune, and old age.

The status of women discourages family limitation. The traditional role of the female as child bearer and caretaker encourages a high birth rate. The woman confined to a domestic position is obligated to fulfill her function as a mother. This particular obstacle to family planning may be diminishing as women in LDCs gain increased freedom, but this is a perilous process, as the Iranian revolution has shown. In some societies children are wanted as additional workers. This is the case in tenant farming and in intensive agriculture, such as wet rice or small scale fruit production.

The extended family system, where close relatives live in a communal household, permits early marriage and makes it possible for adolescents to become parents, since the responsibility for feeding the children rests on the household.

Lastly, religious beliefs tend to reinforce high birth rates. Dogmas associating childbirth with Divine Providence and glorifying children and the poor frustrate efforts at birth control and undermine family planning. Cultural inertia, ignorance, and reluctance to change have similar effects.

The Politics of Overpopulation

If excessive population is to be prevented, the freedom to have children must be restrained. This inevitably involves government regulation of family life. Here logic and reason conflict with social values and sentiments. Rightists and leftists alike abhor any interference with family autonomy. Legislation regulating family life is, therefore, politically precarious.

Yet we cannot argue with the numbers. If nothing is done, the earth's present more than 4 billion people will increase to 25 billion in the next century. Their requirements for food and housing will far exceed any presently conceivable capacity of the earth's resources. The quality of life will necessarily deteriorate everywhere. When that happens, it will be followed by political turmoil, international strife, and terrorism. Amid mass frustration, violence and political chaos will thrive. Those who have will become targets of those who do not. We may, in fact, already be further down this path than any government or international agency is willing to admit.

Family Planning

To date, public policies to curb population growth have been limited mainly to family planning programs. In the developed countries they have been quite successful, in the developing countries, not so successful. To make them politically and theologically palatable, family planning programs have been based on voluntary participation. No compulsion has been used. The family planners' functions have been narrowly limited to educating couples in how to use contraceptives and to disseminating information on the advantages of smaller families, and they have had little impact on the galloping birth rate.

The LDCs must one way or another gain the political will to face this problem squarely. The traditional values must make room for present necessities. The rich countries must share the burden; in the long run, they have more to lose than the poor countries if the population increase continues.

EFFECTS OF POPULATION PRESSURES ON BUSINESS

The consequences of rapid population growth vary according to national circumstances. For the economically advanced countries, growth may mean greater markets and an expanding economy. For the nonindustrial developing countries, the effects typically are the opposite.

Productive and Nonproductive Population

A study of the population pyramids in Figures 18.2 through 18.5 shows that the age structure differs significantly in the developing countries, Brazil and Malaya, from that in the advanced countries, the United States and Sweden. For the former, the pyramids rest on a wide base, which is indicative of a high birth rate, and are characterized by concave sides, as mortality is comparatively high. For the latter, the pyramids take a beehive shape with a relatively narrow base and convex sides, which reflect longevity and low mortality.

Figure 18.6, in which aggregate figures of the underdeveloped and developed sections of the world are portrayed, indicates that these are not exceptional cases. The proportion of nonproductive age groups in the society is much higher in the underdeveloped areas than in the developed ones, a fundamental reason for the low national productivity and the widespread poverty in underdeveloped countries.

The adverse numerical ratio tells but a part of the story. The productive person in an LDC must in general not only produce for a greater number of the nonproductive youth and aged than does a productive person in an industrial country, but also do it with less capital, technology, education, and fewer tools.

The Escalating Crisis

The current population explosion is contributing to the disproportion between productive and nonproductive segments of the population, since the reduction of the death rate has been caused primarily by success in curbing the incidence of infant mortality. Consequently, population growth is taking place mostly in the broad base of preproductive young people, while the available work force remains the same as before.

It might be reasoned that this problem is temporary and will correct itself once the first generation of the infants raised with new medical care has reached maturity. Demographers generally discount this argument for two reasons. First, children who will marry and reproduce before reaching productive maturity will cause at least a serious delay before the productive cycle can catch up with the reproductive cycle. Second, the poverty, squalor, and hunger that characterize life in the LDCs will prohibit an average life span comparable with that in the industrialized world. In other words, those who manage to reach the productive years cannot be counted on to produce for as many years as workers in the advanced countries.

For business, the consequences of unfavorable age distributions are far reaching. The domestic market, because of the broad nonproductive base, is interested chiefly in meeting subsistence needs. The production and marketing of consumer goods is limited because of the overriding demand for food and clothing. The production of goods is further lessened by the shortage of mature workers. A large proportion of the population is below labor age, and, of those old enough to work, the vast majority must be employed in meeting subsistence needs. The demands of the nonproductive populace for food commodities and raw materials for clothing and housing lessen the availability of products for export trade and capital formation.

Constraints on Food Surplus

To feed their exploding populations the developing nations have two available means: (a) increase the efficiency of their agricultural resources through chemical fertilizers, insect sprays, hybrid research, and better farm implements; or (b) make more complete use of agricultural products by such means as direct consumption of grains, transforming indigestible crops such as soybeans into digestible products, and changing peoples' dietary habits.

Each of these methods is costly in terms of both capital and human resources. Each generally means the sacrifice of domestic industry and commerce. Urgently needed industrialization is further delayed by agricultural

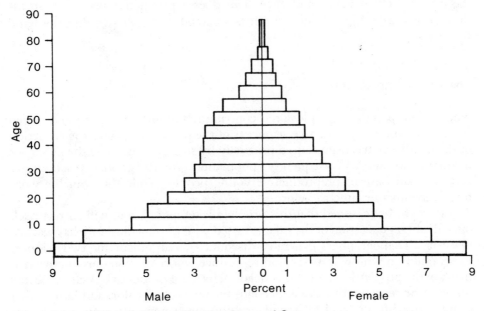

Figure 18.2   Malaysia, Population by Age and Sex

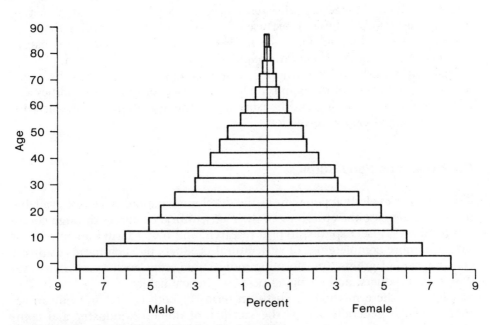

Figure 18.3   Brazil, Population by Age and Sex

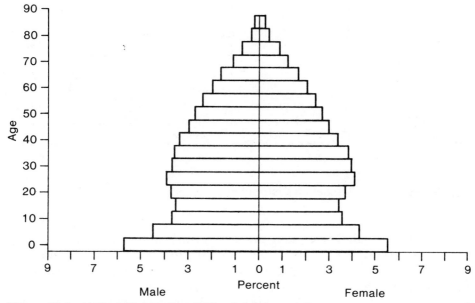

Figure 18.4   United States, Population by Age and Sex

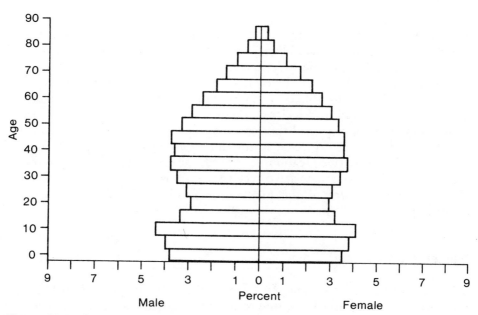

Figure 18.5   Sweden, Population by Age and Sex

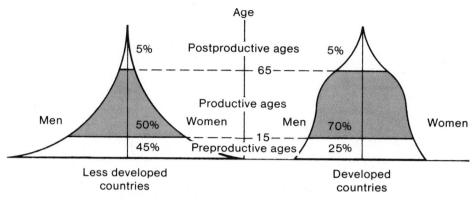

Figure 18.6   World Population Distribution

demands for capital. The existing domestic firms will have more limited markets, as consumers spend greater amounts for food, with less for consumer
items, and as government taxation (needed to supply capital for agricultural
investment) depletes the spending money of the populace. Foreign commerce
may diminish as agricultural investment makes exportable raw materials less
available, and as exportable raw materials become comparatively rare, the
country's ability to import is impaired.

DEVELOPING AND UPGRADING THE LABOR SUPPLY

The growth of manufacturing and other business activities, especially export
trade with advanced industrialized nations, requires technical training and
education beyond the elementary stage. Literacy alone, benchmark though it
is, does not suffice. The crucial weakness in the LDCs is secondary education.
For people to be employable by business and industry, or for that matter by
government, as clerks, technicians, foremen, or junior executives of various
kinds, they must have passed the secondary level. Unfortunately, secondary
education is too often neglected in the developing countries in favor of elementary and university education. In Africa, for example, it is estimated that
the number of persons who have received secondary educations is between
one-third and one-fifth of the number of existing jobs that require such
education.

Elementary Education

Inflated Literacy Data   Table 18.1 shows that although school enrollments
have been increasing in LDCs, they still lag far behind comparable figures for
developed nations. Statistical data usually overstate the educational progress,
especially in regard to literacy and to primary education. The illiteracy figures

Table 18.1 School Enrollment by Age Groups and Sex

AGE GROUPS	1960		1970	
Developed Countries	Male	Female	Male	Female
6–11	90.4%	90.5%	92.9%	93.2%
12–17	79.5	76.1	87.3	85.5
18–29	10.5	6.0	16.4	11.6
6–29	50.8	47.3	56.6	53.7
Developing Countries				
6–11	54.4	36.4	68.6	51.6
12–17	27.6	14.5	39.4	23.7
18–29	2.9	1.0	5.2	2.5
6–29	26.2	16.0	35.4	24.3

Source: UNESCO Statistical Yearbook (New York: United Nations 1974), p. 104.

are generally compiled during a population census, and the measurements used vary widely. In many countries the ability to read and write one's own name constitutes literacy, so that functional literacy is probably much lower than is shown in official statistics. The United Nations is promoting a standard definition of literacy: "A person is literate who can with understanding both read and write a short simple statement on his everyday life." Even this seems modest in light of business realities. Although the value of literacy in traditional, handicraft-agrarian cultures may be limited, for industrial enterprise and modern agricultural production it is imperative. Education and the transformation from peasant agriculture to an urban-industrial economy can only proceed hand in hand.

Quality of Schools With the exception of some elite institutions, the level of instruction is generally low in LDCs. Teachers lack adequate preparation and are usually overburdened with large classes. Although some countries, such as India, have issued government decrees limiting class size to a specified figure, such rules have had little practical effect.

The subject matter is often inappropriate. Traditional education in ex-colonial schools is modeled after its European counterpart. Even the independent nations of Latin America pattern their schools after those of Europe, primarily those of France. The curricula of the schools emphasize basic intellectual skills. Many classes are taught in the language of the old colonial power.

The result of this system of education has been an accumulation of unrelated and often, to the learner, irrelevant or unimportant material, which is quickly forgotten after the examination—a skill in reading that enables the student to recite aloud to the instructor but does not allow him to understand the words he reads, a general ignorance of methods for improving agriculture, a preparation for a higher education that very few are able to attain —in general, knowledge out of context and useless in the environment in which the individual must live. In short, it is an education devoid of domestic culture and its practical economic aspects.

Obstacles to Improving Elementary Education   Although most countries have compulsory education, the regulations are not well enforced in practice. The economic level of the population, especially in rural areas, is the primary obstacle. Children are required to work in order to contribute their share to the family income; to people on subsistence income, food is more important than education. Diseases and malnutrition also keep enrollment and attendance down.

The attitude of the population toward education is another obstacle to school attendance. Uneducated parents rarely see any benefit in learning to read and write. The children themselves may have a negative attitude if the education does not lead to foreseeable and desirable goals. Colonial and traditional schools have presented an image of hard work and vigorous discipline that discourages many. The fear of schools and the necessity of forsaking present satisfactions for uncertain benefits in the future result in a negative attitude toward school of any kind. Even if all attitudes are favorable, very few LDCs can afford to provide the teachers, schools, and books for mass education.

A problem seldom confronted by western educators is that presented by the variety of languages found in the countries of Asia and Africa. Margaret Mead suggests that ". . . A basic condition of successful literacy—on any large scale—is that it should be attained in the mother tongue." This condition makes education even more difficult and expensive. Again, this is a problem of allocation of scarce resources, and the returns from education, although great, are slow in coming. The necessity for mass education for economic development is obvious; the means to attain it are not.

Secondary Education

The secondary school enrollment ratios are more meaningful than those for the primary school, as they represent individuals who will probably remain literate.

The ability to attend secondary school is limited much more than the ability to attend primary school by the economic position of the individual. When a young man reaches the age for secondary school, he is generally expected to contribute a considerable share to the family income or to be economically independent. In some cultures a potential student may be blocked from enrollment by social position. In rural areas, secondary schools are even less accessible than the primary ones since distance and transport facilities become the ruling factors.

The quality of secondary education in LDCs is often higher than the quality of primary education. These schools are essentially aimed at preparing students for universities, and the standards are quite rigorous. However, here again there is a lack of relevance to everyday life. Those who do not finish secondary school or who do not go on to a university are trained to do little other than be a clerk and keep books. Technical, agricultural, and forestry training are typically conspicuous by their absence from the secondary educational programs of developing countries despite the fact that these are fields in which most graduates must earn their livings. The objective of the secondary schools is to teach an individual to appreciate literature and culture but not to prepare him for active participation in the productive processes of his society.

Higher Education

Higher education in underdeveloped countries is provided only for a select few. Although, as with primary and secondary education, the schools are often free, it is only the very wealthy who can afford to attend. Table 18.2 underscores the striking differences between LDCs and developed nations as to engineers, scientists, and other university educated professionals.

Higher education is very expensive to the state, resulting in an insufficient number of institutions and teachers. Entrance requirements are set very high to restrict the number of students. These conditions can be expected to improve with economic development and perhaps can be tolerated for the present. The basic difficulty is an antiquated university structure unable to cope with modern needs. A student who wants to study chemistry must take a full engineering or pharmacology curriculum; if he is interested in biology, he must enroll in the medical program. Designed to train the nineteenth century professions, such a university is ill suited for educating psychologists, market researchers, or technicians for such modern fields as automatic computation, aerospace, or electronics. Hence, those who do receive higher education are often trained for nonproductive professions or find little opportunity for applying their skills.

On the other side are individuals who are sent to European or U.S. universities and obtain professional, technical, or scientific education not tailored to the needs of LDCs. Upon return they often cannot find jobs in which to apply their knowledge. An LDC may not have companies that need engineers specializing in aeronautics, hydraulics, or low voltage electronics. Grad-

Table 18.2 Number of People per One University Educated Professional Person in Selected Countries

COUNTRY	RATIO	COUNTRY	RATIO
India	1:3,343	Uruguay	1:57
Ghana	1:410	Republic of Korea	1:36
Zambia	1:200	France	1:30
United States	1:76	Finland	1:14
Kuwait	1:75		

Source: UNESCO Statistical Yearbook (New York: United Nations, 1973), pp. 25–28, 504–7.

uates in business administration often find that what they learned at the U.S. or European university has very limited applicability because of the very different institutional and sociocultural systems in their home lands. The western universities and their faculties have failed to recognize the need to change their offerings for foreign students to make their studies more relevant. Ironically, therefore, the foreign educated elites are compelled to leave the LDCs to find employment in the developed countries.

Another serious deficiency of universities in LDCs is their relative lack of training in business administration and organization. This problem is being felt more and more as LDCs strive for economic development. Efforts are now being made to introduce managerial courses and even degree curricula in a number of LDCs. In others, recent statements of educational policy show that the problem is being recognized. Progress can be expected to be slow at best: the lack of qualified business professors is almost total. Any LDC citizen with such qualifications is quickly absorbed by business or government.

NEGATIVE IMPLICATIONS OF EXCESSIVE POPULATION GROWTH

The population problem in underdeveloped countries is interlaced with social, political, and economic issues. It is fraught with dogma and beset by counterclaims from nutritionists, agronomists, political realists, and social idealists. Its implications to business are mainly adverse. They can be summarized as follows:

1. Rapid population growth causes an expansion of the broad base of unproductive young people.
2. This expansion increases the emphasis on food production, at the expense of business and industry, and channels capital and workers to agriculture in order to feed the expanding population.
3. The quality of the labor force suffers as the country is pressed to provide education, food, clothing, and housing for additional millions.
4. To keep up with population growth, governments may be forced to appropriate for basic consumption needs resources that otherwise would go for investment in industry and in the infrastructure.
5. Increased family size lessens the possibility for individuals as well as for government bodies to accumulate the capital for expanding business and industrial activity. Large family size permits little saving and weakens the tax base of the nation.
6. Insufficient capital limits imports, and increased domestic demand lessens potential exports.
7. Social instability and inability to absorb foreign capital discourage investment by the firms of industrialized countries.

This list of the negative consequences of rapid population expansion obviously cannot be applied in its entirety or to the same degree in all developing countries. Business and industry expand in some countries regardless of growth rates. The presence of valuable resources attracts domestic and foreign development, and the availability of land, as in some South American nations, may counter the negative aspects of rapid growth.

The predictions of ill effects must be applied selectively, and they will vary in degree in different developing countries. No fixed rules relate population to business development, but the trends are significant. The indications are that business and industry will find great contrasts and paradoxical conditions for a long time to come in an underdeveloped country. Predictions of an early solution to the population problems are unsupported to date. The situation requires intelligent analysis and socially responsible action not only from governments but also from business enterprises.

LABOR UNIONS

Compared with labor organizations of the developed countries, the unions of the developing countries represent an economically weaker but politically more explosive force. To understand this force, we must understand the circumstances that condition union activity as well as the character and scope of the unions themselves.

Deficiencies of Unions

Generally, unionism in developing countries is a house divided against itself. Rudimentary education and lack of experience in industrial labor-management problems diffuse the efforts of the workers to express their protests and to realize hopes. In spite of the rapid growth of unions, effective unionism is rare. The greatest obstacle is the apathy of workers. Unemployment, underdevelopment, and an irregular labor supply often make the collection of union dues impossible and seriously undermine the union's economic position.

A multitude of small, independent unions view the business world from a feudal perspective. They form many rival federations, based on political affiliation, social ideology, or religious beliefs, which resist amalgamation into integrated labor movements. Union leaders are usually outsiders, middle-class intellectuals with doctrinaire philosophies who lay greater stress on ideological issues than on the practical problems of wages, working conditions, and productivity. As a result, most of the unions are tied to some political party or religious order and put its interests first. Another type of union leadership comes from the opportunist who capitalizes on the workers' predicament and discontent.

Collective bargaining is in its infancy in most LDCs. Workers do not understand it, and union leaders prefer to practice politics. Although most

LDCs encourage union growth, nearly all restrict collective bargaining by limiting the right to strike, enacting comprehensive labor codes, and providing for compulsory arbitration or labor courts.

In summary, the labor unions of LDCs are characterized by small size, financial weakness, reliance on outside leadership, interunion rivalry, absence of national organizations, inadequate use of the methods of trade unions, and inability to rely upon the strength of organized workers.

Industrial Wages

To be effective in wage bargaining, unions must be able to exert enough power to compel recognition and fair dealing from management. Theoretically, a perfect balance of power between a union and management should exist. In the industrial countries unions have generally acquired the strength to bargain with management and have often even become the dominant party because of labor legislation and labor-oriented public policies.

In LDCs, unions seldom possess the power to bargain effectively. Their financial resources are seriously limited. In addition, they are vulnerable to political action and economic recession. As a minority group, industrial workers find their interests sacrificed when they conflict with those of the nonindustrial majority. The impact of an economic downturn is felt with the greatest force in the industrial sector, yet the industrial worker is less able to cope with unemployment than are agricultural workers.

Lacking the strength and experience for effective bargaining, unions in the LDCs resort to disruptive tactics, such as riots and demonstrations, designed more often to get favorable legislation enacted than to influence the outcome of any particular wage settlement or of some other labor problem. Many union leaders still believe that the function of a union is to hurt the employers, no matter what the circumstances. This attitude is a relic of the struggle for independence, when disobedience of the ruling class, including managers, was regarded as patriotic and morally just.

Whether unions and other occupational groups are strongly or weakly political is partially a function of the existence of alternative means of political expression and influence. The overwhelming importance attached to trade union activities by the political parties in LDCs is a reflection of the importance of the labor movement and its capacity to influence social life.

The effectiveness of wages and salaries as incentives for productivity depends to a substantial degree upon the employee's assessment of the nonfinancial rewards and penalties connected with the job. The newly recruited worker may gain or lose social status, an important nonfinancial consideration. Any system of social stratification, even a complex multidimensional one, raises questions of equity since it rests on the differential functional importance of positions and on the differential talent of persons. Existing systems tend to transform inequality of position into inequality of opportunity. Thus, commitment to a system of reward based on merit and of mobility consistent with talent and training may still inspire the employee in an LDC to attempt to alter the system as well as his place in it.

Labor Efficiency

Through the efforts of the International Labor Organization of the United Nations and the International Conference of Trade Unions, regional training centers have been set up to develop indigenous cadres for labor unions in the LDCs. These centers aim to establish comprehensive programs tailored to the peculiarities of each LDC. A very sizable fraction of the trainees who have so far completed the programs have been recruited by government and business management for administrative positions.

Productive Efficiency   The trade unions play a very important part in improving productive efficiency within an industry. If the workers take interest in their work, they may suggest from their experience many practical ways of minimizing waste of raw materials, improving the distribution of the work load, and making minor technical adjustments. In the U.S.S.R. the *Stakhanov movement*, which contributed so much to the success of Soviet planning in the mid-1930s, was nothing more than a method of motivating workers to exceed their output quotas, reduce waste, find ways of increasing productivity, and suggest better ways to accomplish their tasks. But workers must be encouraged to offer such suggestions and must be assured that these will be given proper consideration. Joint production committees and work councils are valuable means of associating the workers with improvement in productive efficiency. The trade unions, as the natural leaders of the workers, may make such instruments of worker participation a reality.

Wasteful Labor Practices   Wages are generally low where labor is inefficient and where there is a labor surplus. Many factories in developing areas employ more labor than necessary. The prices of locally produced goods are relatively high because of insufficient capital equipment, poorly organized manufacturing processes, and lack of mass market. To tap the demand in export markets and to compete with imported goods, manufacturing standards must be raised. Only in this way can there be more jobs at higher wages. In the course of these adjustments technological unemployment occurs. Like the craftsmen and the sweatshop laborers in the first world countries, workers in LDCs resist technological change, first, because they are already suffering from serious unemployment, and second, because increasing productivity does not necessarily lead to higher wages, and when it does the wage increase tends to lag behind the productivity due to high unemployment. Also, the reallocation of the labor force as a consequence of technological change is much more difficult and painful in a developing area than in one already industrially developed.

MANAGERIAL RESOURCES

The industrial progress and vigor of any society depend on its leadership's ability to find, develop, and utilize natural, financial, and human resources effectively. Narrowly conceived as entrepreneurship in classical doctrine, this leadership in modern society is exercised mainly by managers of business enterprises.

LDCs are poorly endowed with managerial talent. Compared with capital, labor, and natural resources, management is typically most conspicuous in its scarcity. The historical causes for the scarcity can be found in the social organization and cultural norms. The traditional social hierarchy lacks space for the managerial group; it simply does not belong. The cultural norms repel managerial rank as a threat to the traditional order, undermining the village elders, tribal chieftains, or religious figures such as the mullahs in Islamic countries.

The school systems of the LDCs have as yet not produced enough industrial managers, partly because higher education or technical institutions are too few and partly because the cultural influences have caused the existing schools, until very recently, to neglect subjects helpful to entrepreneurial growth.

Sources of Management Talent

Managers emerge from seven background areas in LDCs: artisans, merchants, industrial families, workers in largescale industry, government service, the armed forces, and other professions.

Artisans are skilled workmen and apprentices. With a little capital through savings, they can extend their markets outside their immediate neighborhoods. In favorable conditions, an artisan can expand a small enterprise into a factory. According to Stepanek, this period of growth from small artisan enterprise to factory involves approximately two generations.

Merchants have generally shown a low aptitude for becoming managers of industrial enterprises. Their interests and skills are much better suited to arbitrage and speculative transactions aimed at producing quick profits than to long-range planning and supervision of complex corporate bodies. This judgment might not hold if the merchant has had adequate education and training in business administration, but at present few merchants in LDCs possess the experience to discharge management responsibilities in an industrial enterprise. Their main contribution is in the small business traditional to the particular country or region.

Industrial families could be expected to be the ideal source of managerial talent in the LDCs. To a degree this is true. Many outstanding executives have had their start in family businesses, but an even greater number of people with the same background have never come close to qualifying as executives in the professional sense of the term.

Most people, including managers, in LDCs are not motivated to change. They do not enjoy taking risks. However, for those individuals who do, methods must be devised to attract their attention, and perhaps in this way the more rapid development of entrepreneurship in LDCs can be brought about. In numerous cases, government loans to individuals who lack aptitude have failed to produce entrepreneurship through training. To take one example of many, in Burma, training of paper makers was nearly all wasted time. After much interviewing and testing of the individuals being trained, it was found that they were training for management positions only for prestige, not for performance.

A prerequisite for managerial development in the third world often is a change in the existing ideas and attitudes regarding the nature and role of management. Business executives are conceived as the entrepreneurs of classical and neoclassical doctrine; historically they have been synonymous with profit takers, lacking both interest and position in the society and its culture. Careers in government enjoy a unique position; the profit motive is replaced by the incentives of official privileges and social prestige. Therefore, the public image or, more correctly, misimage, of managers must change before widescale indigenous development of management resources can be expected.

Even if an LDC trains a certain number of qualified managers, they will not necessarily become available for managerial employment. Many individuals use the training credentials to gain entry to some nonbusiness occupation. Others use their newly acquired qualifications to seek employment abroad. The propensity to emigrate seems to be on a constant upswing among promising young people in all LDCs. Thus, the quality of indigenous management is not automatically raised by the introduction of business administration courses in the schools or by government aid for education at foreign universities. Steps must be taken to eliminate the exodus and to make opportunities in domestic business more attractive. The austerity of a brisk industrialization policy, with its hardships and forced savings, generally aggravates this problem.

Other environmental conditions and social structure characteristics restrict the number of persons eligible for management positions, even when they have adequate educational background. Entrance into higher level jobs is often controlled by family ties, by class or caste, by friendship, or even by political affiliations. This control has worked to the detriment of developing managers by restricting the range of experience accessible to persons with good potential and by placing in high positions persons with lesser abilities.

Further limitations on the development of a national pool of available managerial talent have been imposed by the geographic and social immobility evidenced in many of the developing countries. People are often tied to their immediate vicinity because insufficient communications cannot tell them where better jobs are; thus, management jobs are filled from among those persons immediately available. Also, custom sometimes ties people to the land even when they are otherwise free to go.

Development of Managerial Resources

Managerial resources may be upgraded for industrial management in four ways: workers may advance themselves, they may be provided with education by the community or the state, they may be trained on the job, or they may be aided by noncompany development facilities.

The first, self-education, can easily be dismissed except on a very rudimentary scale. A more constructive idea is that the community, the state, or the society should make the investment in advanced education and vocational training programs. To date, governments have concentrated their efforts in the technical sector. Only recently have national leaders started to appreciate the fact that the shortage of managerial skill and know-how is a serious obstacle to the growth of business and industry in LDCs.

Accordingly, government apathy in the area of management development is declining and a more positive attitude is gaining strength. Concrete manifestations of the change can be found in several LDCs, where departments of business administrations have been established at public institutions of higher learning. How successful these efforts will be depends ultimately on their faculty. Competent instructors of business subjects are very scarce in all third world countries. Much of the teaching is done by practicing managers as a sideline. In addition, there is very little capacity for business research. More research in developing countries' business problems is conducted by first world scholars than their own.

Company Development of Managers   Most MNCs are taking steps to shrink the role of U.S. expatriates in overseas management and to make more use of local executive talent. One key motive is to improve relations with foreign countries, especially the intensely nationalistic nations. Since the supply of local nationals capable of running a complex business operation is extremely limited, the MNCs must greatly expand their programs of training nationals for management jobs. In view of the lack of government assistance and of technical and business schools, the best source of high level manpower is usually the organization itself rather than the open market.

Obstacles to Company Development   Success in nationalizing management depends upon the industrial advancement of the host environment and upon the relative participation by home offices and by subsidiaries in decision making in the critical areas. It may be possible to use persons of lesser training and experience if the home office makes most of the decisions, the employees are well indoctrinated, and the subsidiary is well controlled. This is only a partial solution. The real questions are, What are the impediments to hiring nationals? What methods can the companies use to develop a national management force?

The two obstacles usually cited to the filling of overseas positions with nationals are the inherent inabilities of nationals and the scarcity of properly trained or experienced nationals. The first obstacle is itself a highly tenuous proposition, and the second can be overcome with long-range planning by the international enterprise.

The assumed inherent inabilities are these. Nationals have conflicts of loyalty to the country and the company. Nationals are not "company men"; that is, they lack the requisite domestic company experience. Lastly, nationals are disqualified by general national character weaknesses. The conflict of loyalty is, of course, an argument of doubtful validity, and the preference of MNCs for company men is of doubtful desirability. The accepted national stereotypes that some claim as character weaknesses cannot be substantiated. Different character traits (that many U.S. companies consider undesirable because they are different from the "right" U.S. traits) do not disqualify foreign nationals from responsible positions; these traits only make them more valuable, as they possess the cultural empathy that many U.S. expatriates lack.

The scarcity of properly trained or experienced nationals is the most potent reason for the present abundance of imported management in the overseas subsidiaries. To overcome this shortage, most MNCs have established company-run management schools of various types, sent more promising nationals to the United States or to Europe for schooling at the companies' expense, or made financial contributions to indigenous educational institutions, often with the stipulation that some business-related courses or seminars be organized.

SUMMARY

Rapid population growth is an ominous yet pervasive characteristic of third world countries. Declining death rates combined with the continuation of high birth rates generate the growth. Attempts to stem it through family planning have yielded but minimal results.

The LDC's labor force is proportionally smaller than that of industrial nations because of the large preproductive age group. This demographic structure places on each individual in the labor force a higher average burden to support nonproductive consumers than is required from the productive members of industrial societies. To this demographic barrier must be added the economic factors of high unemployment and underemployment, which further reduce the ratio of productively active to inactive members of the society.

Since food production has not kept pace with population increases, many LDCs have become increasingly dependent on food imports from developed countries. However, the population growth undermines the LDCs' capacity to trade as it tends to eliminate surplus production in any sector; without such surpluses the nation lacks the means of acquiring external purchasing power. Population pressures also discourage foreign investments.

Though unskilled labor is overabundant, skilled labor and managerial resources are scarce. This is due to the lack of educational opportunities and standards as well as to the lack of exposure to industrial production systems. LDCs have been trying to upgrade their labor forces through better education, but this is a long-term process.

As entities of a free market, labor unions in LDCs are severely restricted by massive unemployment and lack of skilled cadres. They, therefore, depend heavily on political action and ideological appeals.

Professionally trained managers are very scarce in LDCs. Neither the economy nor the educational system prepares people for modern managerial tasks in adequate numbers. This scarcity ranks among the most critical factors preventing progress. Some governments are addressing the problem by setting up departments of business administration and engineering at universities. MNCs have been experimenting with different types of management development programs.

FOR REVIEW AND DISCUSSION

1. Why have birth rates and death rates followed different paths of change in LDCs? Is it realistic to expect a better balance between the two in the future?

2. Explain the meaning and economic implications of the statement that young people in LDCs may become reproductive before they become productive.

3. Because of the demographic makeup of their populations, LDCs require greater amounts of capital and technology per person than the developed nations to attain the latter's standard of living. Explain.

4. Which aspects of business are affected by population pressures? How?

5. Compare educational systems of the LDCs with those of the developed nations from a managerial point of view.

6. Why do third world students who study at the universities of the first world countries often end up emigrating from their native lands after getting their degrees? What effects does this have on the LDCs? On the developed nations?

7. How do the activities and influence of labor unions in LDCs differ from those of U.S. unions?

8. Despite widespread unemployment and underemployment, manufacturers often find a shortage of labor in LDCs. Comment.

9. What factors might be responsible for the relatively low aptitude of LDC merchants to make good industrial managers?

10. If you were to set up a business in an LDC, how would you select and train your managers?

19

North-South Dialogue: Commodity Trade and Economic Structure

*E*conomic progress is an overpowering necessity in all LDCs. Subsistence existence—life at the periphery of biological survival—is no longer a viable political alternative. Radio, television, and motion pictures are mainly responsible for the change. The standards of living in the affluent countries that the modern communications media portray have had an irresistible impact upon the peoples in the developing world. Even the most fatalistic cultures have not remained untouched. The ignorance that isolated these peoples for centuries is yielding to an awareness of their comparative backwardness and a growing conviction that life need not be as bad as it is, that destitution, squalor, and hunger are social ills for which there are remedies, and that the goods and services that can turn earth into paradise already exist in other parts of the world.

This new awareness has set in motion a shock wave of social discontent, aptly labeled the *revolution of rising expectations*, that no government can ignore. Thus, governments of all LDCs are committed to economic development. This common commitment guarantees no common approach, but the common concern with development does act as a bonding agent, unifying these otherwise diverse nations into a powerful block that has started to reshape the world economy.

To stem the rising tide of discontent within their borders, the LDCs depend on the outside world. On the consumer level, it is mainly the industrial countries who are able to produce the kinds of goods demanded by the sudden burst of "new needs" until indigenous industries grow. On the industry level, the LDCs must import the key ingredients of industrialization: machines, technology, and management know-how. They also depend on the outside world for many of the means of sociopolitical modernization: scientific and professional education, an efficient civil service, legal concepts needed in complex organizations, infrastructure investments, and a great many other capabilities that determine the pace of economic progress.

Consequently, the LDCs' need to import is enormous. However, their ability to generate external purchasing power—foreign exchange—has been grossly inadequate to pay for such massive imports of developmental inputs.

344

How to deal with the mammoth gap between the LDCs' needs and capabilities has become a major problem of global relations. Since what the LDCs need the most—capital, technology, and markets—is obtainable only from the industrial countries located mainly in the northern hemisphere, the issues and arguments relating to the problem have been labeled the *north-south dialogue*.

DEMAND FOR A NEW SYSTEM

Controversies over international economic issues are not new. What is new is the global polarization of positions. The scope of issues involved is also unprecedented. The LDCs call for no less than a complete new system of international economic relations, a new international economic order (NIEO). The economic and legal principles, rules of business conduct, and institutional arrangements of the present system are to be scrapped completely or thoroughly overhauled to promote the economic and social progress of the LDCs.

The present system, according to the LDCs, is biased in favor of the developed nations and, as such, is a cause of the backwardness and slow growth of the LDCs. To eliminate the biases of the present system and to make it possible for the LDCs to bridge the gulf between their import needs and export capabilities, the LDCs demand a series of fundamental changes, which may be summarized as follows:

1. New rules of international trade establishing commodity agreements for LDCs' primary exports, increasing preferential treatment of imports from LDCs by developed nations, and indexing LDCs' report prices to their parities charged for their imports by developed nations
2. Increased foreign development assistance from rich countries
3. Expanded private financial flows to LDCs, increasing MNCs' and other private investments and creating more sources for bank lending
4. Debt relief in the form of cancellation or postponement or repayment obligations of LDCs' external debts
5. Accelerated flow of technology to LDCs
6. Recognition of LDCs' rights to all properties within their national jurisdictions
7. Greater weight to LDCs' interests by changing the decision making rules in important organizations such as the International Monetary Fund, the World Bank, and international bodies concerned with trade and investment

These demands were formalized in a series of resolutions passed by the United Nations. A resolution in 1974 put the NIEO officially on the world economic agenda.

To the first world countries, the call for NIEO is both a challenge and a threat. They recognize the problems and support the LDCs' aspirations for accelerating their development, but they reject the notion that a systemic change will help. To them the NIEO is wrought with grave uncertainties and possible harm to all. The basic battle lines are clear, but on specific issues the positions of the North and South are often entangled.

Before we take up the specific issues of this dialogue, it is useful to study the factual record of the international economic performance of LDCs. Since the ultimate measure of a nation's ability to pay for inbound transfers of resources is its capacity to export, we must understand the LDCs' export trade and its sources to interpret the NIEO meaningfully.

EXPORT TRADE

Taking the LDCs as a group, the long-term trend of the aggregate exports declined from about 31 percent of the world total in 1950 to 16.4 percent in 1972. Between 1973 and 1980 it regained a good deal of the loss. However, the apparent turnaround is misleading. It occurred primarily as a result of steep increases of oil prices by OPEC and secondarily as a result of a rather spectacular emergence of export manufacturing in a few rapidly developing LDCs. If we exclude these two exceptions, the growth of LDCs' exports has continued to lag behind that of the developed nations. The average annual growth rates of exports have been 7.5 percent for the developed countries and only 5.9 percent for the developing countries.

Figure 19.1 shows that LDCs' exports are heavily dependent on the mar-

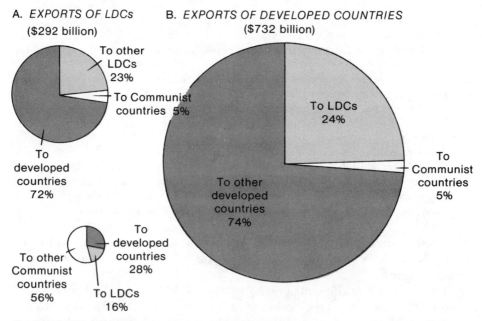

A. *EXPORTS OF LDCs*
(\$292 billion)

To other LDCs 23%

To Communist countries 5%

To developed countries 72%

B. *EXPORTS OF DEVELOPED COUNTRIES*
(\$732 billion)

To LDCs 24%

To Communist countries 5%

To other developed countries 74%

To other Communist countries 56%

To developed countries 28%

To LDCs 16%

C. *EXPORTS OF COMMUNIST COUNTRIES* (\$107 billion)

Figure 19.1   Trade Among the Three Worlds (1977)

Source: Yearbook for Trade Statistics (New York: United Nations, 1978).

kets of developed nations. But this dependency is not reciprocal; the developed nations sell but 24 percent of their exports to LDCs—most of their trade takes place with other developed countries.

As to commodity composition, LDCs' exports have come mainly from extractive industries. Excluding the OPEC nations, ten core commodities heavily dominate the LDC trade. In order of value these are coffee, sugar, copper, cotton, rubber, cocoa, jute, tin, tea, and sisal. Seven other commodities account for much of the rest: beef and veal, iron ore, bauxite, bananas, rice, wool, and wheat.

Since the output of these commodities depends directly on specific natural resources, the export mix of any individual LDC is necessarily limited by its resource base. Some LDC exports are dominated by a single product (Table 19.1); other LDCs depend on three or four (Table 19.2).

Table 19.1   Single Commodity Dominance in Selected LDCs' Exports

COUNTRY	COMMODITY	PERCENT OF TOTAL EXPORT
Zambia	Copper ore	91
Sudan	Cotton	61
Zaire	Copper ore	61
Ghana	Cocoa	60
Sri Lanka	Tea	59
Uganda	Coffee	59
Colombia	Coffee	58
Panama	Bananas	57

Table 19.2   Three Commodity Dominance in Selected LDCs' Exports

COUNTRY	COMMODITY	PERCENT OF TOTAL EXPORT	
Brazil	Coffee	36	
	Iron ore	8	49
	Cotton	6	
Argentina	Corn	15	
	Beef	14	36
	Wheat	7	
Philippines	Lumber	22	
	Sugar	19	59
	Copper ore	18	
Mexico	Sugar	9	
	Cotton	7	22
	Coffee	6	

Fluctuations in Export Prices

Excessive specialization in a very few primary commodities renders a country vulnerable to fluctuation in world demand and export prices. In the developed countries, no single commodity dominates the export mix. If one product suffers, another may prosper; the losses in some are offset by the gains in others. The LDCs lack this stability. World demand for the few dominant commodities decides it all. The vulnerability is further aggravated by the fact that the demand for primary commodities fluctuates more violently than that for manufactures.

Plantation Agriculture

For the agricultural and forest products, the fluctuations are caused by both supply and demand forces. On the supply side, uncertainty is introduced by natural factors such as droughts, storms, floods, and the weather in general. Thus, the physical output varies from year to year. Prospects for a bad crop induce a rapid inventory buildup in consuming countries. Prospects for a bumper crop have the opposite effect. Both aggravate supply and demand disbalances and add to price fluctuations on the world commodity markets.

An LDC's output of agricultural commodities does not lend itself to administrative control. Plantation products such as coffee, tea, cocoa, and rubber are the least responsive to either government policies or market fluctuations, except in the very long run. The reasons for this stem from the economies peculiar to plantation agriculture.

Take for example, coffee. When the demand exceeds supply, prices are high. Anticipating the high prices to continue, growers put raw land in production. This may involve investments in jungle clearing and other land preparation. After the new land is seeded it takes six to seven years of care and cultivation before coffee bushes start growing beans. If in the interim prices have fallen or if the added output from the new bushes leads to declining prices, the growers will not discontinue the new plantations. They cannot afford to—the planting represents a cost that can be recovered only by selling the coffee. There is no alternative. Therefore, the lower price will not cause any reduction of output. On the contrary, the growers may actually increase the output to try to offset at least some of the loss in sales revenue due to the price decline. Naturally the growers' success in this respect is limited by the cost effectiveness of extra fertilizer, watering, and so forth. The tendency is unmistakable, however; the supply is elastic when prices go up but inelastic or even reverse-elastic when prices decline.

Mineral Products

For mineral commodities, the supply is more readily controllable. When the demand declines production can be cut back to maintain price stability. However, the sociopolitical conditions of LDCs seriously limit management's freedom to vary the supply in the interest of market equilibriums and prices. In countries such as Zambia or Zaire, the mines are the heart of the economy. They not only support the nation's balance of payments but also provide the bulk of nonagricultural jobs. With a meager tax base, the government lacks the means to pay unemployment benefits or to support other welfare programs. Labor unions are equally indigent. To protect the miners, the mines are not allowed to lay off workers without government approval. It usually takes a major crisis in the export market before that approval is granted. In addition to the legal limitations, the mining industries in LDCs have been brought more directly under government control by nationalization, that is, by converting private mining firms to state-owned enterprises.

Demand for minerals fluctuates widely in response to business conditions in the industrial countries. Because of the accelerator principle, the magnitude of these fluctuations often surpasses the variations in industrial activity. The constantly shifting market requires countervening adjustments in supply. For the reasons discussed above, however, the LDCs' mining output as well as exports of minerals can respond very slowly and meekly, if at all. The stickiness of the supply is again more serious in the case of falling prices than rising prices. As a result, the world minerals market is plagued by perpetual but largely unpredictable swings between shortages and oversupplies.

TERMS OF TRADE

The terms of trade (the ratio of export prices to import prices) have generally worsened for the LDCs, except for OPEC and a few manufacturing LDCs. Since the products that the LDCs export have declined in value compared with the products they must import, a larger quantity of exports is required to maintain any given import volume. This requirement is often difficult to fulfill. On the supply side, the natural resources for further expansion of production may be limited or the entrepreneurship and capital may be lacking. On the demand side, the world market may be near saturation and any attempts to increase the supply may depress prices and fail to improve the export earnings.

The prices received by the developing countries for their exports have lagged behind prices received for exports by the developed countries because the increase in demand for primary commodities has lagged behind the increase in demand for manufactured goods for extended periods. Since the LDCs have had to import mainly manufactures (of which capital goods have constituted 30 percent to 40 percent), the shifting terms of trade have deterred their ability to trade. Furthermore, the demand for primary commodities has been relatively inelastic both in reference to price and income changes. Neither the rise of incomes nor the reduction of prices has been met with greater consumption.

Synthetics

LDCs' export prices have been undermined by a growing number of synthetics that are substitutable for primary commodities. The onslaught has been greatest on agricultural fibers, such as silk, cotton, wool, jute, and sisal. Rubber has fared but slightly better. Inventing synthetic substitutes for minerals has been more difficult but not impossible. Plastics stronger than steel already exist, although they are still costlier to produce. In less demanding uses, plastics and plastic-reinforced materials have been substituted for metals. Their use is certain to widen. In many instances, new technologies have reduced the consumption of minerals per unit of output. Only petroleum has enjoyed a relative immunity to synthetic substitutes, but even this is about to change. The oil crisis has stimulated serious research to end the dependency of the industrial world on oil.

Indigenous Manufacturing

A popular scenario to change the terms of trade in favor of LDCs calls for the development of their own industrial capacities. When they industrialize more and more of the raw materials will be consumed where they are produced. This leaves less for exports and intensifies competition among industrial countries for the scarce supplies. Prices will go up. In addition, as its industry grows an LDC can shift its export base from raw materials to manufactures.

Although such tendencies have been discernible in recent years, they are not likely to cause revolutionary changes in the trade relations between the LDCs and developed nations. First, the LDCs supply only about one-third of world exports of nonfuel raw materials; two-thirds come from the first and second worlds. Second, only about one-half of the LDC primary exports consist of commodities that are not available to industrial countries from their own resources.

These commodities might be regarded as trumps in the LDCs' hands, but their significance should not be overemphasized. The monopoly is more apparent than real. The supplies of most of these commodities are dispersed among several LDCs, and coordinated action is by no means easy. Also, synthetics and near-substitutes of natural products give the first world's countries more flexibility than trade statistics would reflect.

PROPOSED TRADING RULES UNDER NIEO

The present system of international trade is based on the principles of market competition, nondiscrimination, and reciprocity in tariff reductions and other concessions among nations. Monopolistic practices violate the rules. The main deviations from principles have been in the preferential (nonreciprocal) treatment recently granted to imports from LDCs by industrial nations and inter-government commodity agreements that, with the exception of OPEC, have generally failed.

The LDCs contend that these rules hamper their trade. Since their traders lack the resources and managerial sophistication of Western firms, they cannot conclude a fair bargain under the competitive system. As a result, the gains from north-south trade accrue mainly to the industrial countries. In addition, the wide fluctuations in the demand for primary commodities, on which the LDCs depend, expose them to far greater instability of exchange earnings than industrial nations.

To correct these biases of the trading system, the LDCs propose:

1. Production cartels along the lines of OPEC
2. International commodity agreements to regulate prices and quantities
3. Indexing of export prices to prices paid for imports of manufactures
4. Extension of preferential treatment by developed countries

The first three proposals aim to raise and stabilize the earnings from commodity exports to LDCs and to assure stable supply for the consuming nations. The fourth proposal is to assure LDCs' manufacturers access to Western markets while protecting their domestic markets against foreign competition.

Control of Commodity Trade

The essence of the commodity control proposals is to conclude a network of international agreements covering all aspects of control of primary commodities in which the LDCs have an interest. The agreements would be binding to exporting and importing countries alike. A price range would be fixed for each commodity and maintained either by a quota scheme or by buffer stocks, depending upon the commodity.

Quota Agreements A *quota agreement* assigns to each producing nation the maximum quantity of any given commodity it can export. If an internal surplus occurs, the government of the country involved is obliged to intervene in its national market to prevent any leakage to the work market beyond the quota. If demand for the commodity is inelastic, this scheme can maintain prices at high levels, but only for short periods. When it is extended over longer periods, difficulties arise because individual producer countries, attracted by higher prices, may refuse to join on the premise that it is more profitable to enjoy unlimited volume, or they may find the leakage of domestic surpluses to the world market uncontrollable.

The greater the differential between the internal and the maintained world price, the greater the inducement to the domestic supply to escape. On the demand side, the user nations are encouraged by the artificially high prices to develop synthetics and other substitutes for the commodity. A further disadvantage to the producing countries themselves is that by allocating output and fixing prices abnormally high, governments may be subsidizing inefficient producers at the expense of efficient producers.

Buffer-Stock Agreement   A *buffer-stock agreement* establishes an international organization empowered to buy the commodity whenever its price drops below the fixed range and to sell when the price exceeds the range. The purchases increase demand when supplies are in excess and stockpile them for further use; the sales increase supplies when the consumption exceeds current exports.

The buffer-stock scheme is best suited for nonperishables that can be stored for extended periods, while the quota scheme can be used for any commodity. However, since the buffer-stock agreement centralizes control, it is functionally superior to a quota agreement, which must rely on the enforcement compliance of each participating country. To be fully operational, either type of commodity agreement requires near global adherence. If some significant producer refuses to join, the whole scheme is jeopardized.

Difficulties   To negotiate such agreements is not easy. The producing countries differ as to their price ranges, adjustment procedures, and enforcement methods. The consuming countries fear increases in the cost of their future imports and, in the case of buffer-stock agreements, the substantial investment in the facility. The biggest barrier to buffer stocks is the initial setup cost, which the United Nations estimated to be $10.7 billion in 1975; due to inflation it must have risen considerably since. This figure was calculated on the assumption of a simultaneous intervention in the eighteen major commodities; it can thus be regarded a worse case figure, as simultaneous surpluses in all commodities are improbable unless the prices are fixed abnormally high.

In addition to the steep initial cost, the buffer-stock facility would involve storage costs, estimated at 3 percent to 4 percent, and interest expenses on its stockpiles, which would vary with bank rates unless they were subsidized in some manner. To cover these current expenses, the facility would require a wide margin between its buying and selling prices. Under 1980 interest rates the margin would have to exceed 23 percent, which is entirely unrealistic. Unless the prime interest rates drop radically, say, to the neighborhood of 5 percent, no global buffer stock could be self-financing.

Indexing of Prices

As a rational alternative to market pricing, which they take to be dominated by industrial countries, the LDCs demand that the prices of primary commodities that they export be indexed to the prices of manufactures that they import. In support of indexation, the LDCs have argued that due to inflation the real purchasing power of commodity prices quickly deteriorates if fixed in nominal terms only, and the objective of stabilizing their export earnings is defeated. The prices of manufactures are selected as the standard for indexation because it is the manufactures that the LDCs must buy with their exports. Therefore, linking these two sets of prices protects the LDCs' terms of trade. However, many LDCs want more; they want improved terms of trade, to have the nominal money prices of commodities increase more than the prices of manufactures. This makes the indexation issue very controversial, both economically and politically.

Problems   How the index for manufactures would be computed and kept up to date on a worldwide basis is a practical problem that has yet to be solved. More fundamental objections to indexation relate to its economic effects.

As proposed, indexation would virtually terminate market pricing of commodities. The indexed price would not respond to variables that might cause the real price of a commodity to change in a free market. For example, when the real cost of producing a commodity declines due to improved technology or other reasons, the producers would reap a windfall. Backed by a buffer stock the excess profits could go on indefinitely, leading to massive stockpiles and misallocation of resources. Since the disposal of the surpluses would no longer be a country's responsibility, neither its government nor its producers would be motivated to cut back output. Since the overproduction would not be salable on the world market, it would accumulate in massive stockpiles unless destroyed by the buffer-stock authority or converted to nontrade use.

Effects of Indexing   That high commodity prices would affect adversely the import bill of industrial countries is self-evident. They would also hurt the resource-poor LDCs, who must also import the commodities. These are mainly the fourth world nations, the poorest of the LDCs. Though their present import needs in this regard may be limited, their prospects for future industrialization would be seriously dimmed. On the other end of the spectrum, the resource-rich developed countries, such as Canada, Australia, the United States, and U.S.S.R., would share in the windfall. As an ironic result, the power and influence of the two superpowers would be further increased.

The dangers of such perverse distributional effects of indexing could be reduced by appropriate clauses in the commodity agreements. Since the market mechanism would be inoperative, however, administrative adjustments to the real price would be difficult even if the commodity agreements were subjected to annual or biannual review.

FIRST WORLD RESPONSE

The industrial countries insist that any modification of world commodity trade be geared to the market forces. They are committed to the proposition that a free market is the best model for economic prosperity. They reject commodity cartels, price fixing, and other distortions of market forces. They argue for making the market system more effective by ensuring that market economy principles cannot be broken, as they often have been in the past, for the detriment of the LDCs, and by addressing the institutional problems that cause hardships for the LDCs.

Compensatory Financing Proposals

Their original counterproposals called for some *compensatory finance facility* from which the LDCs could draw swing credits when their export earnings were low and pay back when earnings were high. In 1975, the United States put forth the Kissinger Plan, which proposed a *commodity credit facility* under the auspices of the International Monetary Fund, for the purpose of stabilizing LDCs' export earnings by annual loans of up to $10 billion. The plan contained provisions for converting the loans into grants in hardship cases.

The first Lome Convention, in 1975, between the European Community and its 59 associated LDCs of the African, Caribbean, and Pacific regions, set up the STABEX mechanism, a fund of 375 million European units of account, from which the associate LDCs could draw interest-free loans when their export earnings are down; 36 of the poorer LDCs are exempt from repayment obligation.[1] The associate LDCs hailed the STABEX as the beginning of a new era in North-South relations. Whether future events will validate their optimism remains to be seen.

Following the EC's lead, the IMF subsequently established its own compensatory financing facility. It differs from STABEX by being open to both developed and developing member countries of the IMF and requiring that a nation have an overall balance of payments deficit to qualify. Under STABEX balance of payments, shortfalls are calculated separately for each export commodity of a member LDC; the nation is entitled to draw the aggregate of all shortfalls. In addition, the IMF facility requires repayment regardless of a nation's developmental state, whereas STABEX transfers are in the form of grants. The LDCs regard the IMF facilities as a token measure far short of their expectations.

MNCs and LDC Sovereignty

The NIEO envisages the legal and industrial structures of international business to be remolded by calls for:

- Affirmation of LDCs' sovereign rights to all property and resources within their boundaries
- Adoption of structural policies in the developed countries to promote industrialization of LDCs

The first point—affirmation of the LDCs' sovereignty—is mainly an aftermath

---

1. The name STABEX comes from the mechanism's role of *stabilizing exports* earnings in developing countries.

of the 1950s and 1960s, when a number of LDCs were struggling to get control over foreign-owned mining, plantation, and petroleum companies organized in the colonial days. These companies were legally well fortified. They had not only corporate charters granted by the colonial regime, but also long-term or open-ended contracts assigning them some key resource for exclusive exploitation.

Behind this double shield of documents, the companies invoked their prior rights to the natural resources. If the LDC government moved against them, the companies summoned their home government to intervene or took the host government to court under international law. Misguided legislation in the industrial countries, as exemplified by the Hickenlooper amendment (which disqualifies an LDC from receiving foreign aid if it nationalizes a U.S. subsidiary without paying full compensation), elevated the conflict to the diplomatic arena. Despite legal maneuvering and diplomatic threats, and sometimes because of them, the LDCs ultimately took the actions, including expropriation, that they saw fit. "The solemn inviolability of contracts" could not forever obstruct the consolidation of a nation's economic structure.

The big battles between the LDCs and the colonial resource companies are now a matter of history, but the battle scars are not. The bitter confrontations indicted the companies in public opinion with being agents of colonial exploitation and foreign domination. This image is yet to fade, even though those few MNCs that originated in the colonial era have now thoroughly purged their executive cadres and shed their colonial arrogance.

The diplomatic war over legal rights continues. The LDCs' involvements with multinationals are far greater now than ever before. The modern MNCs, particularly the new generation of nonownership-based MNCs, require vastly more complex contractual agreements than the raw material ventures. Thus, it is in the best interests of both the developed and developing nations that mutually acceptable principles and rules be adopted on the validity of contracts and on a due process for the adjudication of contractual disputes.

The LDCs want two things: (1) that legal disputes between MNCs and host firms or host country citizens or government be settled under the host country law; and (2) that major economic issues be settled by commercial treaties between the home country and host country governments rather than by contracts between individual MNCs and host governments. This is to say, the LDCs want an explicit recognition of their government prerogatives over private firms by the industrial countries as well as by international law. Anything less they find an abridgment of their sovereignty. This position is clearly reflected in the Charter of Economic Rights and Duties of States adopted by the United Nations.

The issues surrounding direct investments were discussed in Chapters 14 and 15. The NIEO proposals add one significant dimension—a call for a deliberate restructuring of domestic investments in the developed countries so as to facilitate the transfer of some industries to the LDCs. If the industrial nations stopped manufacturing products that could be made in LDCs either by MNCs or indigenous firms, the industrialization of LDCs would be accelerated and their exports increased and diversified.

How the industrial countries would bring about such restructuring of their investment flows is obscure. Some form of official coercion is implied. Increasing the international division of labor is an objective supported by many in the West; however, in the Western view any restructuring should be based on comparative efficiencies and not government declarations.

The willingness of firms to divest at home and to invest in LDCs depends to a large measure on the conditions that the LDCs offer for MNC operations. The desired flow of industrial investments will occur only if the objective conflicts between MNCs and host nations are recognized and an acceptable code for multinational business operations are incorporated into the LDCs' legal frameworks.

Preferential Treatment of LDCs' Manufactures

The NIEO calls for an extension of preferences granted by developed nations to LDCs' exports. Though this demand is not new, it is backed with increasing vigor and unanimity by the LDCs. To put it into its historical context we need to take a brief backward look.

To channel inbound foreign investments into the most critical areas of national economic need, the policies of import substitution became prevalent in the 1960s. The theory behind these policies postulates that by shutting off imports, two growth generating results will be achieved: foreign exporters will be compelled to establish factories within the country to serve their markets, which will get new industries started, and the inbound investment capital will create the needed inflow of desired technology, which will foster indigenous technological progress for further industrial growth.

Mixed Results   In some cases the import substitution policies have shown satisfactory results. This is mostly true in textiles, simpler household appliances, and other manufactures that are characterized by low technology and small production units. In industries requiring more sophisticated technology and management know-how, import substitution has been a mixed blessing. The automobile industries in India, Indonesia, and Malaysia provide illustrations. Although the immediate economic objective of getting a domestic automobile industry started was achieved, the long-term objectives of stimulating economic growth and technological development have failed to materialize. In addition, the automobiles produced are often of low mechanical quality and costly to operate, although they usually cost two to five times more than U.S., Japanese, or West European automobiles.

What went wrong? What caused the technological stagnation and even regression where progress was predicted? One answer is that the protection against imports removed the pressure and incentives for efficiency and improvement. Whether public corporations or private companies, the automobile producers have enjoyed near-perfect protection against import competition. There has been a built-in premium for the enterprise to maintain the status quo. A side effect has been a severe restraint on the most dynamic element in the industrialization of a society, namely, the development and dissemination of industrial skills, both in blue-collar and white-collar sectors.

This pattern of relative stagnation has not been limited to the automobile industry. It has repeated itself with regularity in other industrial sectors where import substitution has been applied as a protective blanket.

The import substitution policies have been further complicated by efforts to pry loose the technology from capital imports as such. Expropriation and nationalization offer tempting shortcuts to growth objectives, but their reach is limited to existing foreign firms. Since the takeovers act as the strongest possible disincentives for new foreign investments, they are self-liquidating policies.

Reappraisal Because of the disillusionments, LDCs are shifting emphasis from import substitution to export expansion in their manufacturing sector. To export their manufactured goods, they need products able to compete on rich nations' markets and access to those markets. To develop the manufacturing capability, the LDCs are emphasizing technology imports, which we shall discuss in Chapter 20. To gain access to the markets of developed countries, they are pursuing a strategy of nonreciprocal treatment in tariffs and other trade controls, under the generalized preference system discussed in Chapter 5.

This system is to yield dual results to the LDCs. It is to provide protection against foreign competition to their manufacturers so that they can take maximum advantage of the economies of scale; and it is to allow their goods to enter the developed nations without duties or quota restrictions that are applied to similar goods coming from other developed economies.

SUMMARY

The United Nations program for NIEO was introduced to redress the economic imbalance between developed and developing nations. It envisages revised international structures and mechanisms that would allow a more equal sharing of the benefits of international business and increase the influence of LDCs on international organizations. The program also seeks to harness the MNCs for the developmental purposes of LCDs by seeking global recognition of the host country's right to compel compliance by MNCs with national laws, regulations, and public policies.

FOR REVIEW AND DISCUSSION

1. Who are the principle trading partners of LDCs?
2. Describe the composition of trade of LDCs. What are its implications?

3. Are the reasons for price fluctuations of mineral raw materials and plantation commodities the same or different? Why?

4. Compare and contrast the buffer-stock and quota agreements.

5. Is it reasonable to expect that raw materials prices will outpace the prices of manufactured goods? If so, will the proposed indexing work for or against the LDCs?

6. How would commodity credit facilities such as STABEX or the IMF facility affect LDCs? Other nations?

7. Do you think the LDCs' demand for international affirmation of their sovereign rights to all property and resources in their territories has any real substance? Who else could have any such jurisdiction in their territories?

8. If the president of the United States wished to comply with the LDCs' demand for a restructuring of industrial investment in this country, what steps should and could he take to bring it about?

9. For what reasons have the LDCs been backing off from their import substitution policies in recent years?

10. Why is the role of synthetics certain to increase in future trade relations?

20

North-South Dialogue: Resource Transfers

*I*n addition to attempting to restructure trade and investments mechanisms, the new international economic order (NIEO) attempts to restructure technology transfers from the developed to the developing nations. The pivotal demands are two: to accelerate the transfer of technology to LDCs and to increase official development assistance—foreign aid—from the rich nations.

TECHNOLOGY TRANSFER

Technology is a new variable in the equation of economic relations. Traditional theory assumes that all nations have equal access to technology and, therefore, that there is no need to transfer technology from one country to another. Recent research findings have invalidated this assumption. In addition, they point to technological differences as a primary cause of international inequalities in economic achievements. To reduce the inequalities, technological capabilities of the backward nations must be strengthened. The quickest way to do so is to transfer technology from the developed to the developing nations.

How to bring about the necessary international technology transfers is an urgent but labyrinthine problem. There is no body of accepted literature on the subject, and although the problem has incited massive amounts of research in recent years, the inherent complexities of technology transfer are not yet fully understood.

Inconsistencies of Definition

Technology is an elusive concept. In its narrowest sense, technology is any device or process used for productive purposes. In its broadest sense, it is the sum of the ways in which a given group provides itself with goods and services, the group being a nation, an industry, or a single firm. Neither of these definitions, which delimit the range of possible definitions, offers a satisfactory working definition. One is too narrow to be meaningful, the other too broad to yield to analysis.

In practice, technology has been taken to be limited to science-based means of production or machine systems using inanimate energy such as thermal or electrical power. Much of the literature on technology transfer is based on this narrow definition. From a scientific point of view, this may be an acceptable definition, but from a social point of view, it is insufficient.

To be useful, any equipment must be capable of productive use; that is, it must be capable of converting inputs into consumable outputs and of doing so at costs that are competitive or otherwise socially acceptable. The economic essence of technology is not its physical or chemical configuration but its productive capability.

If technology is to be objectively valued and priced, as it must be if it is to be traded, the price must be determined by its productive capability. Purely cost based pricing of equipment and facilities is arbitrary. Many of the conflicts over technology transfers stem from the fact that a scientific rather than an economic concept of technology has been used.

To be productive, technology must be applied. No piece of machinery, no factory, no farm can function without being operated. Human participation is inherent in the productive capability of any technology. The terms *know-how* and *state of the art* have been used to distinguish the human aspect of technology from its scientific aspect. Perhaps a better terminology would be *hard technology* and *soft technology*, analogous to the hardware and software in the electronic computer industry. Whatever the terminology, the critical point is that unless accompanied by the managerial know-how to use it effectively, no technology is marketable.

There is still another fundamental characteristic of technology that demands clear recognition. Quite unlike commodities and capital, technology is not depleted or its supply diminished when it is transferred or used. It is usable but not consumable. Once created, technology is inexhaustible until it becomes obsolete. Therefore, export of technology need not cause the source country to reduce its use of the technology. Indirectly, the decline may result if the recipient country creates an industry large enough to change the global supply and demand equilibrium of the goods produced by the technology involved. For most technologies sought by the developing nations this is not the case.

Sources of Technology

Contrary to the classical assumption, technology is not a free good but a valuable property, nor is it evenly distributed around the globe. That is to say, the supply schedules differ widely from country to country. To obtain new technology, a nation has three alternatives:

1. Produce the technological capability at home
2. Import it from abroad
3. Import goods containing the desired technology

For most LDCs, home production of technology is often uneconomic. Since much of what they are seeking already exists in the industrially advanced areas, they can fill their needs by importation. Normally, the importation can be effected at savings over the domestic cost of research and development (R & D). R & D expenditures devoted to projects duplicating existing know-how are obviously wasteful. Thus, economic rationale requires that LDCs concentrate their home production of new technology on any unusual require-ments that cannot be met from import sources.

The access to technology depends on its ownership. *Nonproprietary tech-nology* belongs to the public. It is there for the taking, but it is not free. The taker must have the ability to gather it from libraries, public research insti-tutions, or wherever it may be found. To locate the sources and to sort out what is usable and unsuitable for any given application may involve consid-erable cost, which might be called the assembling and packaging of technology. Consulting firms specialize in this type of service. They very rarely produce any new technology but instead act as intermediaries between the sources and consumers of technology.

Proprietary technology is privately owned. It consists of patents, trademarks, and secret processes. The most efficient and profitable technology, often also the newest, belongs in this category. Access to proprietary technology is at the owner's discretion. It may or may not be for sale. If the sale creates potential competitors, the owner's interest is served by not selling it unless the expected loss from new competition is less than the price for which the technology can be sold.

Much proprietary technology is not for sale. It can move only with in-vestments of the owner firm. This is *embodied technology*, as distinguished from *disembodied technology*, which can be transferred without the original owner's investments. All nonproprietary technology is disembodied.

Modes of Transfer

Since technology defies delineation as a discrete variable, the analysis of its transfer is encumbered by such other factors as capital investments, economic organization, labor resources, entrepreneurship, and even sociocultural sys-tems. Lacking disaggregated data, different analysts have used different com-posites as proxies for data on technology flows. Many economists treat direct foreign investments and licensing agreements as synonymous with international technology transfers. Others tabulate scientific and professional conferences, technical assistance programs, exchanges of educators and students, plus many other kinds of information flows. Obviously, all of these have some technology content, but few are pure technology.

Due to these inconsistencies, any quantitative measurements of technol-ogy transfers based on proxy data such as direct investments must be treated with caution. Attempts to treat technology as an undifferentiated or homo-geneous phenomenon have caused intellectual confusion and economic misapplication. Technology is a composite term; its essence consists of a multitude of specific technologies, each with its own sources, uses, and transfer characteristics.

Importing Nonproprietary Technology   Nonproprietary technology can be transferred from one country to another in any number of ways. Technology in pure form can be imported if the transferee possesses the capacities to collect and employ it. LDCs may rely on indigenous enterprises or on foreign firms to do the importing. Since LDCs often lack indigenous firms who can affect the transfer, they rely heavily on foreign consultants.

Another way for a LDC to obtain nonproprietary technology is by importing the hardware required and then either implementing a training program for its use or dispatching managerial personnel abroad to study how to use the hardware. Experience tends to favor home-based training programs, initially with expatriate instructors from developed countries and later with indigenous instructors, over the alternative of sending people from LDCs to learn abroad. The advantage is twofold:

1. The home-based program ensures better adaptation of the technology to local conditions.
2. Fallout from the program is minimized by reducing the risk of "brain drain," which has ravaged many foreign-based programs.

Importing technology intensive goods is the third method of obtaining new technology. In many cases such goods can serve the same functions in an economy as locally produced goods but often at lower cost. As a general rule, the most technology intensive goods are capital goods required for factories.

Importing Proprietary Technology   An LDC's access to proprietary technology is far more complicated. To acquire embodied technology it must attract direct investments by the desired industry. The direct cost of such acquisition is any special incentives that the country is required to offer to interest the potential investor, who may have more profitable investment alternatives elsewhere. If the incentives offered exceed the investor's opportunity cost of foregoing its other alternative, both parties, the LDC and the MNC, benefit. The LDC has no concrete way of assessing the MNC's opportunity cost: it lacks both the necessary data and the expertise. This gives the MNC a strategic bargaining advantage and a wide latitude for its demands for incentives.

Proprietary technologies that are readily for sale can be transferred by exporting turnkey projects, licensing patents or trademarks, selling formulas or blueprints, organizing training programs, or dispatching experts. The choice depends again on the seller's preference—which serves the MNC's objectives best. Owner willingness to sell proprietary technologies varies widely. Some technologies, such as that of the latest IBM computers or Coca-Cola syrup, are absolutely nonnegotiable. At the other extreme are the so-called shelved technologies, for which their owners are anxious to find any takers at all.

The shelved technologies are mainly by-products of corporate R & D activities. For example, in the process of seeking improvements in aircraft and spacecraft technologies, Boeing researchers have discovered numerous patentable techniques and compounds for which the company has no anticipated use. It actively seeks to market these. Other companies with major R & D programs are in a similar situation. What are the shelved technologies worth? Nothing, until someone finds a productive use for them. This may occur long after the technologies have passed to the public realm, or never.

Between the nonnegotiable and shelved technologies lies a continuum of market abilities. In this proprietary continuum are the strategic issues of North-South dialogue on technology transfer. These issues involve the technologies that are the most productive and profitable and, therefore, the least available for purchase. For LDCs they are also the most critically needed technologies. Since they are inaccessible through the market, LDCs have turned to political means to acquire them.

The Market Model

LDCs' comparative technology deficiencies require access to technologies that belong to private firms. The governments of developed nations can facilitate the international transfer process, but they cannot force the transfer to take place without expropriating private property. LDCs' requests for treaty obligations or other official commitments by industrial nations to guarantee an expeditious and inexpensive transfer of technology is, therefore, largely a misdireted rhetoric. Only communist countries can contract to transfer technology by a government commitment such as a treaty. From democratic societies the outflow must be induced mainly through market forces. However, it is doubtful if an international market for technology exists in the normal sense of the word.

Any operational model of an international market must integrate the supply, distribution, and consumption phases of technology. This the international debate has failed to do. The issue has been often regarded as being limited to the cross-boundary transfer processes. What is worse, the transfer itself is viewed as a semimechanistic process that is assured if only the proper sets of rules and regulations are enacted. This has led to oversimplification and misconceptions.

Unlike markets for goods or capital, the technology market has no institutional structure of its own. There are no counterparts for banks, stock markets, export merchants, or import houses. The nearest things to a marketing institution in the international trade of technology are the consulting firms to which we referred earlier. Though they may make some technical adaptations, their function is mainly that of a sophisticated broker.

Right and Wrong Technology

Any manufacturing process can usually be set up using alternative configurations of equipment. In selecting the optimal equipment configuration, we must look beyond the general goals of low cost and high productivity and consider each configuration's demands for labor skills and attitudes, supervision, industrial engineering for tools and manufacturing techniques, materials and supplies, maintenance, product scheduling, inventory controls, and quality control procedures. Each of these ingredients is directly affected by the environment. The economic environment affects costs and availability of workers; the political environment establishes what is acceptable for a plant to make and how. Thus, it is imperative that a technical strategy be derived in part from a realistic assessment of the total environment in which it is to operate.

LDCs are usually traditional societies. Their tradition-based values are threatened by the changes technology may cause. For example, a very important cause of the Islamic revolution in Iran was the Shah's and his U.S. advisors' insensitivity to the fears of the illiterate and semiliterate masses and of the Islamic clergy. Technology infusion and cultural change must move together if social upheaval is to be avoided.

Since the society in LDCs is usually ill prepared to absorb the most advanced technologies, deciding what is appropriate for a given need is often controversial. There are no general formulas for such choices; they must be based on the specifics of each case. The LDCs have been clamoring for simpler, labor intensive technologies instead of the capital intensive technologies that are used in the West. They criticize the MNCs for leaning too much toward mechanization and automation and deemphasizing labor intensive processes. The emphasis placed on the capital intensive technologies is explained in part by six factors:

1. The strong engineering orientation involved in equipment decisions
2. The tendency to copy processes proven in developed countries
3. The lack of time and impetus for innovative study of the problem, for often the headquarter's executives who are responsible for equipping new overseas plants have not had enough personal involvement and first-hand field experience to understand fully conditions in the host country
4. The argument that cheap labor will not actually be cheap because of the sacrifice of quality and efficient output levels, leaving higher mechanization as the best means to assure both high quality and high production
5. Trends toward increased automation in developed countries
6. The prestige attached to the most modern methods for both the importer and the host country

MNCs are generally ill equipped for *reverse engineering*, that is, for redesigning their products and processes to make them less sophisticated and more consumptive of low-skill labor. It is up to the LDCs to convince the MNCs that reverse engineering can be profitably employed in their markets. Failing this, the technological adaptations will have to come through the LDCs' own firms.

Nationalism

Technology supply of LDCs is powerfully influenced by the policies of public authorities. Some groups in developing countries oppose technology imports and insist on indigenous production of new technology. They argue that since technology and growth are closely linked, those nations who are behind in the production of technology are destined to perpetual backwardness. This is false reasoning.

The principle at issue is this: Is the host country likely to develop faster by importing technology from the industrial world or by allocating its limited resources to duplicating that technology? As gratifying to the national ego that a domestic knowledge industry may be, the price it extracts from a developing economy is often prohibitive. The best investments for LDCs would seem to be reverse engineering and projects limited to the adaptation of existing technologies to problems peculiar to their economies.

FOREIGN AID

Since exports and foreign investments do not suffice to meet the needs for capital, LDCs must depend on foreign aid for low-interest (subsidized) loans and outright grants. The NIEO charter calls for an increased flow of foreign aid from the developed countries. This is not the first such appeal. Foreign aid has been a perennial subject for international debate since the 1950s. It is a multifaceted problem. At its heart lie the incompatabilities of goals of LDCs and donor countries, who have difficulties in agreeing on the uses and distribution of aid.

The Politics of Foreign Aid

The donor countries regard foreign aid as part of their foreign policies. Early aid was almost entirely a function of political commitments. Such countries as the United Kingdom, France, and Belgium directed most of their aid to former colonies. The United States gave a substantial amount in the 1960s and 1970s to Vietnam. A substantial amount is still given to support political friends such as Israel. There are no objective criteria for foreign aid. It may be given for military assistance, political impact, international or domestic economic reasons, or humanitarian help. The relative weights of the different objectives vary with time and donor.

Aid as a Political Instrument   The LDCs want to divorce aid from foreign policy. They are threatened by the potential of aid to be used by donors as a means of rewarding or punishing recipient countries, dependent upon their political leanings or choices of friends. The donor nations have yet to establish any common standards as to how much weight political factors should be given; each follows its own path. Only West Germany has made an unequivocal statement that it has no intention of imposing its ideas concerning social and economic values on partners in the third world who receive financial and technical aid, although it will continue to give more support to those countries with democratic systems.

Aid to undemocratic LDCs is a point of wide disagreement. The proponents of human rights argue that since any effective cooperation is practically impossible with undemocratic LDCs, where human relationships are overshadowed by injustice, intimidation, and physical threats on the part of those in power, they should be denied foreign aid. The proponents of political realism give other factors greater emphasis. Since these political realists have dominated U.S. policy, a very large share of U.S. aid has gone to highly autocratic regimes, including outright dictatorships.

Control of Use   The industrial countries like to be assured that their aid grants are used productively. They, therefore, favor *functional* or *project aid*, that is, grants restricted to a predetermined project such as irrigation, a hospital, or a power station, over *general aid*, that is, unrestricted grants that the recipient government can use as it sees fit. The LDCs prefer unrestricted grants, which give them the flexibility to deploy the funds where the need is greatest. On the face of it, this seems reasonable enough, but since the aid is to the government, it has political implications in both the LDC and the donor country.

Corruptive Side Effects   As a general rule, aid boosts the position of the government in power in the recipient country by placing additional resources at its disposal, to the relative detriment of rival political groups. The government gets credit for whatever is accomplished for the public good with the aid, but the government can also gain in other ways. It can divert the aid to finance political campaigns to keep itself in power or to reward loyal officials. Though all aid has spawned corruption, the record is especially dismal for general aid.

Political Base for Aid   As democratic societies, donor countries must be able to satisfy their publics that the appropriation of tax revenues for foreign aid serves a greater good than domestic expenditures. In the case of general aid, this is difficult to do; there are few concrete indicators. Project aid, on the other hand, is amenable to concrete performance criteria, such as new jobs created, megawatts of generating capacity added, or acreage irrigated. Unless public support for aid can be enlisted in the donor countries, all requirements of the LDCs come to naught.

In addition to the North-South controversies, there is the issue of whether aid should be based on economic or humanitarian considerations. The prevalence of starvation and diseases in the poorer LDCs elicits strong emotional support for aid to alleviate the suffering. Such aid goes for current consumption, not for investment; it does not promote economic development. To the contrary, it may actually retard capital formation by reducing available funds.

Economics of Aid   From a purely economic standpoint, aid should be allocated according to its relative productivity. The LDCs who can invest the capital most productively should be ranked first, and those who lack productive investment opportunities should be ranked last. The poorest LDCs, where current consumption leaves little for investment, would be disqualified for aid as the overall productivity of the aid transferred to them would necessarily be low. The economic argument draws further support from the theory that once a nation reaches a given level, the takeoff stage, it will be able to maintain a self-sustained growth and thus transform from an aid receiver to an aid donor.

In the world of scarcity, the progression from the most productive toward the least productive recipients of aid represents the best possible hope for an ultimate eradication of underdevelopment, as LDCs closest to the takeoff stage would be boosted, one after another, into the self-sustained growth level. In the meantime, the poorest countries have to make do without foreign aid.

Somehow the economic and the humanistic priorities must be synchronized. This is more likely to be achieved by ad hoc compromises rather than by adherence to some immutable model.

The Management of Aid

To divorce aid from politics, bilateral aid must be replaced with a multilateral system of aid. If the donor and recipient countries deal directly with each other, political considerations are difficult to exclude. Bilateral aid arrangements lead to international discrimination and favoritism. An ideal aid system would pool all aid donations to supranational arbitrators, who would distribute it according to a consistent policy. Both donors and recipients would be subject to objective criteria, as illustrated in Figure 20.1. The World Bank has started to assume the role of supranational arbitrator, but most of its collections and distributions remain largely on an ad hoc basis.

The present aid structure is totally voluntary. The volume and terms of aid are dictated by short-term political goals of the rich countries. Long-term trends are unpredictable. This makes development planning hazardous for LDCs. The nearest thing to an international standard now in existence is a U.N.-sponsored consensus setting 1 percent of GNP as the target for rich country donations.

Communist Aid

Communist countries have refused to participate in any multilaterial aid programs and have opted instead for strictly bilateral aid arrangements. In ag-

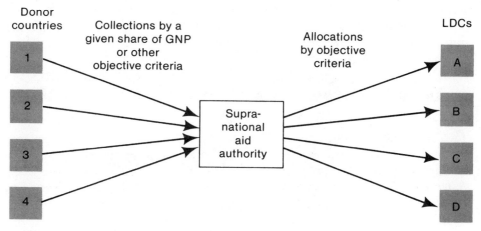

Figure 20.1   Multilateral Aid Model

gregate, aid from communist countries to LDCs has been extremely small. The total for all aid from communist nations over the quarter century between 1955 and 1980 was roughly equivalent to 5 percent of the total for first world nations; in other words, the aid of communist nations over the 25-year span has been roughly equal to one year's aid of the first world countries.

This does not mean that the communist countries are not eager to court the third world; rather, their strategies are different. Their aid has aimed to win privileged positions in carefully targeted LDCs. Both Moscow and Peking, with other countries on their respective coattails, have effectively orchestrated projects of high political visibility and national prestige, such as sports stadiums, cultural centers, and the Aswan dam. At times, the U.S.S.R. and its COMECON (see Chapter 22) allies have provided some general aid, but this has been mainly limited to propping up Marxist regimes such as Cuba and Ethiopia or to helping left-wing factions gain the upper hand, as in Angola and Zimbabwe.

Comparatively modest aid has brought the communists very good returns, as shown by the fact that they have won privileged positions in a number of LDC capitals and have struck counterbalances to Western influences in most others. However, their refusal to contribute financially to the NIEO has started to draw increasing criticism from LDCs. As President Shangari of Nigeria has said, "The time has come for the Soviet Union to reassess its historic refusal to lend assistance to non-communist developing countries" (press release 1980).

The Kremlin has maintained that the noncommunist LDCs are not entitled to assistance from communist countries because communist countries were not responsible for the decades of colonial rule. This reasoning is no longer acceptable to third world leaders. President Shangari of Nigeria has referred to this as an "escapist posture" and has called upon all developed countries to join in assisting the third world nations.

There is no room for doubt that if LDCs' needs are to be met a much greater contribution must be made by the communist countries. A more orderly system of burden sharing and a much greater degree of automatic aid transfers than now exists remain other unfulfilled goals of NIEO.

POTENTIAL EXTENSIONS OF NIEO

Two potentially significant additions to the NIEO program are at present under debate. One, the *International Development Strategy* (IDS), is trying to establish a coordinated program of world development. The other, the *International Program for the Development of Communications* (IPDC), is designed to establish standards of news reporting.

The Internationalization of Decisions

The IDS is intended to provide a long-term blueprint for efforts on the part of governments and international institutions to promote economic and social development of LDCs in the 1980s. It attempts to establish economic and social goals, objectives, and specific targets to be achieved over the course of the decade in order to accelerate the development of third world countries as well as to sustain global development. The IDS also contains specific policy measures designed to implement its objectives and targets.

If approved, the IDS will create a global forum for negotiations about the most difficult international business and economic issues affecting both North and South. These global rounds should "reflect the mutual benefits, the common concerns, and the responsibilities of all parties," according to the draft of the IDS. For the developed countries, such collective decision making in an international forum requires considerable abrogation of their sovereignty over international business relations and subordination of domestic policies to collective international decisions. They have, therefore, shown no great enthusiasm for IDS.

International traders and MNCs have taken a wait and see attitude toward the IDS. They generally favor global rules for business and some standards for host country responsibilities to international business, but they are fearful of rigidities and additional bureaucratic entanglements that the IDS may create.

The Management of News

The IPDC is a complex document designed to set standards for international news reporting. The impetus for it derives from a growing concern in third world countries over the power of the news media of the developed North. LDCs criticize Western media for emphasizing negative news, such as corruption, atrocities, ignorance, and wars, but leaving unnoticed economic and social achievements and original contributions to cultural developments. They further assert that the Western media has overwhelmed the third world public to such an extent that many people unconsciously have adopted U.S. and European attitudes. This they reject as an insidious subversion of indigenous loyalties and values.

Western governments are in general supportive of a free and independent press. They argue that an unregulated flow of information is essential for LDCs' economic development and social modernization. Soviet bloc nations advocate "the leading role of an informed elite" to direct the development efforts, since ordinary citizens are ideologically unprepared to make "correct choices." They regard news reporting based on nonofficial information as a source of confusion and counterrevolutionary tendencies. They, therefore, advocate government surveillance over all news reporting by any country's nationals, whether they are individuals or corporations. Third world countries also propose upgrading and protecting news reporters by establishing international guidelines for reporters behavior and requiring national governments to assure that reporters possess proper qualifications before they are permitted to practice journalism. This implies government licensing of reporters. To Western news organizations this represents a threat to the journalist's right to report and the public's right to know.

The implications to international business of any restrictions on information flows are far reaching. As private organizations, business firms as well as the management profession would be indirectly excluded from the market of ideas and any active role in the formation of public opinions. Such censorship could be particularly devastating to public relations, advertising, and other promotional activities of business.

SUMMARY

In addition to the restructuring of trade, NIEO envisages greater transfers of technology and foreign aid to LDCs. Unlike goods and capital, technology has no market as such. Most transfers of technology are embodied in MNC activities, such as foreign investments, turnkey projects, management contracts, licensing, or trade transactions. LDCs' indigenous capabilities to produce technology are very modest; most of what they need can be imported more cheaply than produced at home.

Since any given technology has an inexhaustable supply, the pricing of technology transfers lacks any objective standard. For nonproprietary technology, the price tends to reflect the cost of gathering and packaging it; for proprietary technology, the price may vary widely, dependent on the relative processes and expectations of the parties involved.

LDCs assert that MNCs tend to supply them with wrong technologies, disregarding their abundant labor resources and scarcities of capital. They would like MNCs to simplify the processes and products used in the industrial countries before they are imported into LDCs. Western firms have very little experience with such reverse engineering and are hesitant to comply.

Foreign aid, too, is a multifaceted issue. The LDCs regard it as a necessity to make up the deficit between their total export earnings plus inbound investments and their total need for new capital. The donor countries regard foreign aid as a foreign policy tool to be used as their national interests dictate. Apart from bilateral politics between donor and recipient nations, aid remains controversial also because of conflicting priorities of humanistic and economic approaches to LDC problems. If all aid were channeled through some supranational agency on a multilateral basis, objective criteria and explicit policies would have to be established. This would eliminate many of the disputes now surrounding this subject.

FOR REVIEW AND DISCUSSION

1. Discuss the inconsistent definitions of technology as they relate to objective analysis.

2. Evaluate the relative importance of different sources of technology.

3. Why is the most productive technology usually private property?

4. Under what conditions is it wise for an LDC to invest in indigenous technology creation?

5. What is meant by proxy data of technology transfer? How useful are such data?

6. How may technology be imported by LDCs? Does it make any difference whether it is proprietary or nonproprietary technology?

7. Describe and discuss the issues relating to the appropriateness of technology.

8. Explain the procedure by which the aid dollar becomes a trade dollar.

9. What are the motivations of foreign aid donor governments? Of recipient governments?

10. In what respect would international relations be changed if the management of aid were turned over to a supranational aid authority?

11. Do you agree with the humanist or with the economist in selecting which LDCs should be granted aid and which not? Why?

12. What do you think of setting standards for international news reporting? How might this affect business communications?

SUGGESTED READINGS FOR PART SIX

Frank, I. *Foreign Enterprise in Developing Countries*. Baltimore: Johns Hopkins University Press, 1980.

Hunter, J. M., and Foley, J. W. *Economic Problems of Latin America*. Boston: Houghton Mifflin, 1975.

Kindleberger, C., and Harrick, B. *Economic Development*. New York: McGraw-Hill, 1977.

Kolde, Endel-Jakob. *The Pacific Quest: The Concept and Scope of an Oceanic Economy* (Lexington, Mass.: D. C. Heath, 1976).

Kumar, K. *Transnational Enterprises: Their Impact on Third World Societies and Cultures*. Boulder: Westernview Press, 1980.

Meier, G. *International Economics of Development*. New York: Harper and Row, 1968.

Meier, G. *Leading Issues in Economic Development*. New York: Oxford University Press, 1976.

Munoz, H. *From Dependency to Development—Strategies to Overcome Underdevelopment and Inequality*. Boulder: Westernview Press, 1981.

Nemmurs, B. H., and Rowland, T. "The Generalized System of Preferences: Too Much System, Too Little Preference." *Law and Policy in International Business* 9: 855–911, 1977.

Olson, R. *U.S. Foreign Policy and the New International Economic Order*. Boulder: Westernview Press, 1981.

Reubens, E. *The Challenge of the New International Economic Order*. Boulder: Westernview Press, 1981.

Souvant, K. P., and Hasenpflug, W. H. *The New International Economic Order*. Boulder: Westernview Press, 1977.

Shaw, T., ed. *Alternative Futures for Africa*. Boulder: Westernview Press, 1981.

Stewart, F. *Technology and Underdevelopment*. Boulder: Westernview Press, 1977.

Part Seven

ENVIRONMENTAL DYNAMICS: EAST-WEST BUSINESS RELATIONS

*O*ver one-third of the world's population lives in communist countries. The world's two largest nations—the U.S.S.R., the largest territorially, and China, the largest demographically—belong to the communist system. The framework of the communist economy poses many managerial problems that are very different from those encountered in free market economies. The businesses of noncommunist countries can share in the communist markets only if they change their operations, strategies, negotiating tactics, and organizational structures so as to agree with the communist economy. This presupposes an ability to identify correctly the incongruencies between the communist and capitalist systems.

The communist system first emerged in Russia from the Bolshevik Revolution in 1917 and has since been recognized as being different not only from capitalism and democracy but also from Western absolutism and tsarist autocracy. Political theorists have labeled the Soviet order *totalitarianism* and have defined it as a system with a total concentration of power—political, economic, and cultural. The center of the concentration is the Communist Party, which prescribes a single set of all-inclusive values, preferences, and beliefs and which demands overt compliance from the entire population. The system can be conceived of as a nationwide corporation owned by the Communist Party; with the head of the party as the chief executive officer. Every citizen is a state employee with a specialized function. All aspects of business are politicized, and no clear distinction can be drawn between managerial and government responsibilities.

The three chapters in Part Seven review the evolution and characteristics of the communist system in the U.S.S.R. and the People's Republic of China, explain their institutions and strategies of international business, and analyze their business relations with the outside world, with special emphasis on relations with the United States.

21

The Business Environment in Communist Countries

What sets the communist countries apart from the Western world is their totalitarian ideology, which aims at integrating all aspects of life under a central authority, the Communist Party. The Communist Party prescribes, through various and at some times roundabout processes, a single set of goals, values, and behavioral norms. It orchestrates the political, sociocultural, and economic spheres of the society into one system.

CONTRASTING SYSTEMS

Business transactions between the communist countries and the United States, or other noncommunist nations, are greatly complicated by the sharp contrast in their economic systems. The usual methods of international trade, investment, and multinational enterprise are either entirely inapplicable or require modification. How the methods should be changed can be articulated only if we understand the incongruities between capitalist and communist economies.

The purpose of this chapter is to explain the inner workings of the communist economic system, its conceptual and institutional framework, its coalitions and factions, its processes of allocating resources, rewards, and penalties within the economy, and the criteria for success and failure. In Chapter 25 we shall build upon this knowledge as we discuss international business linkages between the communist and capitalist economies.

THE BASIC MODEL OF THE COMMUNIST ECONOMY

The communist economic model rejects the fundamental features of the capitalist or market economy. Private ownership of business firms, financial institutions, land, and natural resources is abolished and replaced by state ownership and management: "The nationalization of factories, banks, transport, land and natural resources enabled the Soviet Union to put an end to production anarchy and become . . . a single national economic organization."[1] The market mechanism, too, is abandoned, and in its stead a central planning system allocates both material and financial resources. This eliminates competitive pricing of all goods and services, whether they are consumer goods, raw materials, wages, or interest rates. Profits are also eliminated, and in their stead planners and administrators determine the criteria for success. All individuals, from a lumberjack to a cabinet minister, are state employees, with their wages and working conditions determined by the state. Thus, the communist model eliminates the diffusion of decision making to individual citizens and firms that characterizes the market system; it also eliminates the profit motive and the factor mobility that profit generates. Any individual's ability to accumulate wealth is limited strictly to personal savings from the state-regulated remuneration for work. All business income accrues to the state. There are no private fortunes, no wealthy individuals or families in our sense.

With the motivating forces of the market system abolished, what makes the communist economy work? How does the system hang together? Where are its controls? These are questions we must be able to answer if we are to do business with communist countries. The communist countries, especially the U.S.S.R. and East European nations, have long been training their negotiators in expertise on capitalist countries. Unless Western managers and trade officials become equally knowledgeable about the communist economy they will continue to fall victim to their own misconceptions.

Beginnings of the Communist System

The communist state was born in the Russian revolution in 1917. It espoused Marxism as its theoretical foundation. Karl Marx argued that the upper classes, the aristocracy and the bourgeoisie, lived at the expense of the masses. Their power to exploit the lower classes stemmed from ownership of the means of production—land, natural resources, factories, and other capital assets—since what Marx termed *surplus labor*—that above what the worker needs to exist—goes to the owners of property.

The first goal of the revolutionary leaders was to wipe out the old imperial order of the tsars and to ensure absolute power to the Bolshevik faction of the Communist Party. *Totalitarianism* had been invented. Replacing the wreckage of the old regime with a new society proved much more difficult. Marx had visualized the conversion from capitalism to communism in two stages. He postulated that after the overthrow of capitalism there would be a period of socialism under the dictatorship of the proletariat. During this period earnings from property would be eliminated and the economy geared to the maxim, "From each according to his ability, to each according to his work." Society would be cleansed of the decadent (egoistic, antisocial) values of the capitalist era and a new social consciousness, a higher morality would take their place.

1. Nikolai Nekrasov, "The Starting Point," in *Soviet Union*, No. 5 (350), 1979, p. 6.

The ennobling of the values system would reduce the need for government and cause it to "wither away" as communism arrived and its ideal, "From each according to his ability, to each according to his needs," defined the economy.

How long these stages would take Marx did not say. All Marxist governments claim to be still in the socialist stage. This has created a semantic ambiguity: the leaders of these countries are communists while their societies are socialist. What is even more confusing, the term *socialism* is also used to denote democratic welfare states such as Sweden or Norway.

Evolution of the Communist Economic Model

How the Marxist theory was to be put into practice presented a major problem to the Russian revolutionaries. Marx had preoccupied himself mainly with the ills and ultimate collapse of capitalism and left no blueprint of how the proletariat would erect its new society, except the sine qua non that there must be public ownership of the means of production.

Lenin's newly installed government faced two strategic problems: (a) whether industry or agriculture should be given the first priority in economic development, and (b) how the economy should be organized and managed. The original approach to the first problem was to place equal weight on both sectors; progress was expected to be spontaneous. As the economy continued to regress, a policy that substituted concrete targets for spontaneous development was adopted; a centrally planned economy started to take shape. The planning proponents theorized that industrialization of largely preindustrial Russia was the only way to save the revolution. Since foreign aid was yet to be invented and loans from the industrial countries were out of the question, due to their open hostility to the Soviet government, the leap forward was to be financed from indigenous sources. This led to the introduction of harsh measures to restrict consumption, generalize forced savings, transfer underemployed rural labor to industrial and infrastructural projects, and to institute compulsory work or output quotas for individuals, factories, and farms.

Ruthless rules favor ruthless rulers. As failing health confined Lenin, the powers of leadership were usurped by Joseph Stalin, who, in retrospect, was destined to outdo Adolf Hitler and Attila the Hun, and outfox Franklin Roosevelt and Winston Churchill one against two. Though posthumously charged with inhumanity toward his fellow citizens and a paranoid aggrandizement of his own infallibility, his personality became the undisputed organizer of the Soviet economic system and its sordid shadow—the Gulag Archipelago, a Siberian empire of forced labor camps and political exile to which millions were banished. After Lenin's death, Stalin became the personal embodiment of the totalitarian state.

Economic Organization

All-Union Industries   The basic structure of the Soviet economy is monocentric; all production and consumption is subordinated to a central command structure in the government in Moscow, which is presided over by the Communist Party.

The degree of centralization varies with the relative importance to the nation of a particular productive entity. The most important economic activities are assigned to *all-union ministries*. These include capital goods, weaponry, automobiles, electronics, pulp and paper, shipbuilding, agricultural machinery, and petroleum, along with several other manufacturing activities. Foreign trade, too, is managed by an all-union ministry. In 1980, there were thirty-one of these ministries, each forming a separate vertical sector of the economy.

Union-Republic Industries   Economic activities that do not rate the highest priority or are inherently localized are classified as union-republic industries. Although the ultimate control over these industries is exercised by Moscow, through the *union-republic ministries*, the actual managerial responsibilities are delegated down the line to the individual Soviet republics. There are further gradations: the more important segments (agriculture or coal mining, for example) are managed by a ministry in each republic, while less significant activities (millinery or bread baking, for instance) are delegated still further to the subdivisions of the republics, more or less similar to the counties and municipalities in the United States.

Collectivization of Agriculture   Stalin's design called for the abolition of private farming in order to place agriculture under government control and to increase the efficiency of food production. Agricultural enterprises were and still are organized in two parallel schemes: large state farms, called *sovkhoze*, whose workers are paid money wages, and large collective farms, called *kolkhoze*, whose workers are remunerated in kind, that is, the state deducts delivery quotas from their annual production and the remainder of that production is distributed among the workers for their own consumption or for marketing, at a state-fixed price. In recent years, there has been a tendency to monetize the kolkhoze farms and put them on the same basis as the sovkhoze.

Collectivization of Service Businesses   Artisans and service establishments such as barbers, tailors, cobblers, and cabinet makers are also collectivized, usually on a communitywide basis, and operate in *artels* that, like the kolkhoze, are cooperatives in form but state enterprises in substance. All decisions regarding production, budgets, and individual member welfare are made by government planning authorities rather than by the artel's own membership.

The basic organization of the Soviet enterprise system is shown in Figure 21.1 on page 382. For the sake of simplicity only one union republic is used. Other communist countries duplicate the same structure.

Planning

Thus, the mechanism for the allocation of resources and for the distribution of goods and services is the planning system: "National economic plans have

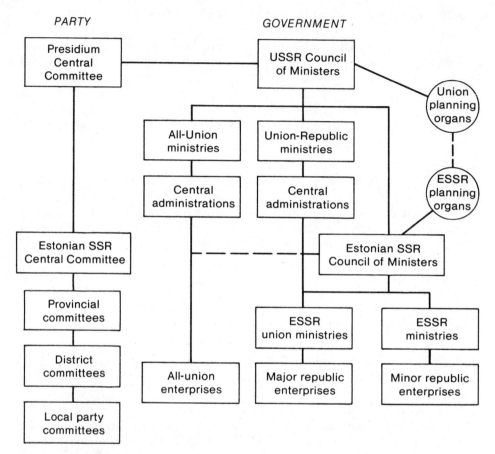

Figure 21.1   Institutional Structure of Soviet Republic's Economy

Source: Endel-Jakob Kolde, "Structural Integration of Baltic Economies into the Soviet Union," *Journal of Baltic Studies,* Vol. 9, No. 2 (Summer 1978), p. 166.

become the main instruments to carry the Communist Party's policy into effect . . . the building of socialist society, unprecedented headway in science and economics, and the attainment of major socio-economic objectives."[2] The economic objectives of the country are established by the highest political organ, the Central Committee of the Communist Party (see Figure 21.2). The primary objectives are limited for any particular planning period. The national planning agency, *Gosplan,* translates the general objectives into specific production and consumption goals and quota allocations to different sectors and production units.

The basic format of the plan is an input-output matrix that is worked out

Source of Figure 21.2 (opposite): Joint Economic Committee of Congress, *Soviet Economy in a New Perspective* (Washington, D.C.: U.S. Government Printing Office, 1976), pp. 11–17.

2. Nekrasov, "Starting Point," p. 7.

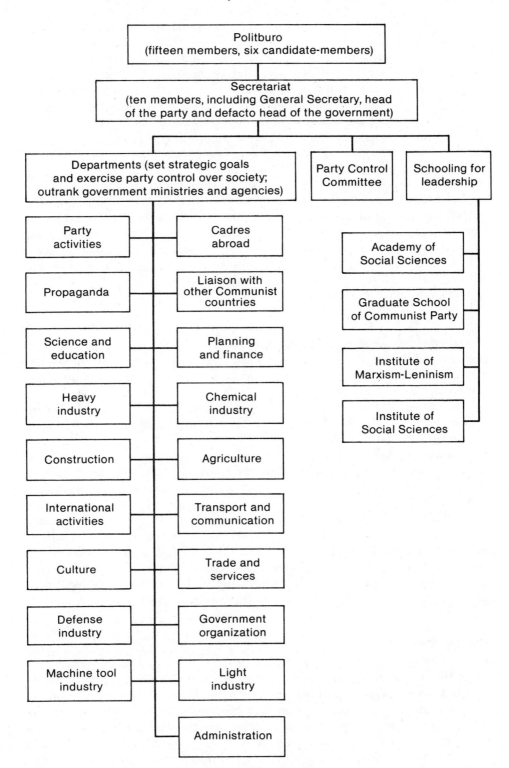

Figure 21.2   Organization of the Communist Party of the U.S.S.R.

both in physical terms, the *materials plan*, and value terms, the *financial plan* or economy-wide budget. The main factor of the plan consists of the targets of physical output and consumption in the all-union sectors. The union-republic industries are fitted into this structure through the active participation of the various republic planning organs.

The financial plan is worked out in cooperation with *Gosbank*, which serves both as the central bank and as a commercial bank, with nationwide branches. The bank monitors expenditures and revenues to assure that they comply with the plan. The plan incorporates a series of objectives from long-term growth objectives to quarterly and monthly quotas. The short-term plans are subject to a review and detailing as they approach implementation.

The result of the plan is to specify for each sector and enterprise not only output but also inputs available to meet the output quotas. No enterprise is free to choose its own objectives, not to mention its own product line, size, or location. An approved plan is not a guide or a goal, as in capitalist economies, but an official order that all production units and administrators must obey. Although all orders are not plans, all plans are legal orders. Thus, the principal task of Communist executives is to fulfill the plan.

Managerial Motivation   All managerial behavior in the Communist economy is structured by the plan. On the enterprise level, a manager's decision making authority is confined to operational and procedural aspects. This does not mean that clever managers do not try to influence policy decisions by various means, but by so doing they are, in effect, subverting the system. The policy decisions are made by the ministries, the Gosplan bureaucracy, and ultimately by the Communist Party.

Exceeding the plan brings honor, privileges, promotions, and monetary bonuses. Failure to fulfill the plan has the opposite result. Hitting the target means average or good performance, depending on how other managers are doing at the time. The rewards are on a scale assigning plus and minus points according to the size of the deviation from the planned output. The greater the deviation, the greater its positive or negative consequences, to the individual, department, or enterprise. In 1962, Professor Evsey Liberman of Kharkov introduced a plan to improve managerial incentives through greater autonomy of enterprises. In the Western press, this was often falsely interpreted as restoring the profit motive to the Soviet economy.

Worker Motivation   Hard work is recognized as valor on the battlefield. Like military heroes, superior producers are awarded titles such as "distinguished mechanic" (or actor or engineer). An exceptional performance merits a medal or a prize. On the more mundane level, the high performers qualify for vacations at seaside and mountain resorts or excursions to major cultural centers. Opportunities for such recreational pleasures are rationed out by trade unions on a strict merit rating system. Other material rewards, including a car, a larger apartment, or a hunting license, are similarly tied to one's production record. On the negative side, absenteeism, negligence, and damage to equipment or premises are punishable offenses.

Monetary bonuses have been introduced in recent years. They accrue primarily to enterprises and are distributed in part to a discretionary reserve of its managing director, in part to members of work brigades or departments based on their performance.

Socialist Competition   Perhaps the most ingenious incentive is a technique known as *socialist competition*. It works as follows. The employees of an enterprise, call it the Kalinin Lokomotive Works, are called to a meeting organized jointly by the local Party secretary, the head of the plant's trade union, and the managing director. The urgencies of increasing production are extolled by the three leaders. A motion is made that everybody volunteer to increase output by a given percentage and that the plant challenge another enterprise, say, the Red Star Textile Mill, to match its contribution. The deal being prearranged by the Party, the acceptance of the challenge is assured. In no time at all the race is on.

THE CHINESE EXPERIENCE

The Communist Party came to power in China in 1949. Mao Zedong started with the same theoretical premises as Lenin, but his prolonged struggle and the developments in the Soviet Union had tempered his views. In addition, his power was rooted in the countryside. He recognized the importance of adapting revolutionary principles to existing realities.

The Soviet example held great promise for China. Only through the establishment of industry would China be able to break out of the poverty level at which it had lived for centuries. Industrialization was the first priority, and the U.S.S.R. provided the blueprint. Central economic planning and the command economy became the mechanisms for the modernization of China. Through a high rate of savings and direct allocation of investment resources into capital goods industries, China would be able to grow. As in Russia, the sacrifices in China would have to come from the masses, since help from the industrial nations was out of the question. However, help from the U.S.S.R. could be counted on. In great contrast to Stalin's brutality, Mao succeeded in a peaceful collectivization of the peasantry; his rapport with his rural followers was successful in persuading the peasantry to stake its future on agricultural communes—Mao's version of the kolkhoze.

Balanced Growth Policy

Mao believed that the U.S.S.R.'s unbalanced economic growth strategy would not work in China. For sustained economic development to occur, the incomes of all sectors of society would have to be raised simultaneously. The goal of balanced growth became, therefore, the guiding principle of Chinese central planning. Another goal of great importance to Mao was the erradication of interregional inequality that prevailed in China. In this, too, he differed with Stalin, who used interregional differences for political purposes.

The period of the first five-year plan in China saw national economic planning much like that in the U.S.S.R. The priority industries (most producer goods, all large-scale modern enterprises) were under the aegis of the state, controlled by ministries at the center. These ministries were responsible for planning, output, investment, and product distribution. Transportation and communications were also under the central government. Low priority production, including agriculture, municipal utilities, local industry such as handicrafts, and local, more traditional, transportation, was left to local governments.

Need for Reform

In the late 1950s pressures arose to change the planning system. They stemmed from several sources. First, there were inefficiencies in the highly centralized planning system. Commands from central planners, because they were based on aggregated information, often did not match with local conditions. Lack of horizontal coordination among vertically planned sectors encouraged duplication and waste.

Second, there was the increasing realization that the Soviet model was not well suited to China's economic conditions. Emphasis on capital intensive techniques at the expense of labor intensive techniques did not take into account the relative abundance of labor as a factor of production. Emphasis on industry rather than on agriculture did not address needs of the rural majority. With population growth high, China's agriculture could not produce a surplus over its food needs for the industrialization effort without increases in investments in modernization. Food output could not be increased without modern methods. It had reached the limit of traditional technology.

The pressures for change were exacerbated by the Sino-Soviet split that developed in 1956. To maintain independence, any hopes of continuing aid from Moscow were over. China now had to go it alone, underscoring the need for a development policy better attuned to Chinese realities. A strategy was developed that recognized the priorities of agriculture and the need for industrial production on a smaller scale, using more labor intensive techniques. As agriculture had always been under local government control, these new priorities meant greater decentralization.

Regional Influences

As could be expected, there was much local dissatisfaction with the central command and its intentional disregard of local concerns. There was also Mao's personal interest in reducing the role of the central government and in stimulating local initiative. These political pressures were very important in the decisions to shift some of the planning and management functions from the central authorities to the regional authorities.

In 1958 the planning system was changed. Many of the operational decisions were transferred to regional governments, although Beijing retained the strategic decisions concerning the structural and equity goals of Maoist policy.

The reform has not decentralized ultimate control. Much greater coordination of economic activities within a region is undertaken now by local authorities, and more enterprises are under local administration, but Beijing still controls the output plans for high priority agricultural and industrial sectors, still establishes output targets of provincial plans, and still retains the right to intervene in any enterprise. Equally as important, the central government still allocates the most important producer and agricultural goods and has a virtual monopoly over investment policy for each region as well as between regions.

The decentralization of administrative planning and management has helped to eliminate the waste of the earlier centralized system while keeping its essential function, which is to dictate and assure the pattern of economic growth and to foster interregional equality.

It is appropriate to stress that the decentralization is in no way market socialism. The decision of what to produce still comes from above in the form of commands and plan targets. The supervising authority is simply a regional rather than a central one. Under *market socialism*, the decision to produce is an autonomous one in which the enterprise manager looks at signals, prices that reflect planners' demands and conditions of supply, and then decides what to produce. This is a decentralization option that no communist state has yet chosen.

ORGANIZATION AND BEHAVIOR OF INTERNATIONAL BUSINESS ACTIVITIES

Foreign trade and other international business activities of a communist state are planned as supplements to the domestic economy; their basic goal is to help fulfill the national economic plan. International business has at times been used by communist nations for purely political reasons, but when that occurs the objectives of the central plan as well as the plan itself are adjusted accordingly. The fundamental fact remains that all international business in a communist state is governed by the central plan.

Strategic Objectives

International business serves only as a complement to the domestic economic plan. It is a subordinate sector. Within the central plan there is a subplan for international business. This plan spells out what the country needs from foreign sources and how it is to satisfy these needs. Inbound transfers, such as imports of goods, are the primary factor. They are based on two considerations: what is needed for socialist development, and what can the nation itself sufficiently and efficiently produce. The difference is the amount to be imported, no more, no less. The needs are expressed in real terms. Maximizing neither the monetary gains nor the volume of trade is the purpose for which a communist nation trades.

The import plan indicates possible export opportunities for business firms of other countries. For example, the current Soviet plan seeks imports of sophisticated technological equipment, grain, and consumer goods. The Chinese require industrial and agricultural equipment.

Exports and other out-transfers are the function of the planned export requirements. The volume and prices of exports are planned to generate the necessary amount of external purchasing power. Actual rates of exchange are unimportant; only the marginal utility—the relative trade-offs among domestic goods—is important. Those commodities having the least marginal utility in the economy are to be exchanged abroad for those with a higher marginal utility. To calculate the domestic trade-offs, the planners use the prices that have been administratively fixed for domestic transactions. There are no domestic market prices. Only abroad do the communist planners and traders have to deal with market prices.

Centralization of Trade

Operationally, international business is completely separated from domestic economic activities. In the U.S.S.R. all international business is the exclusive jurisdiction of the Ministry of Foreign Trade, an all-union ministry. A similar supermonopoly exists in other communist countries. Individual enterprises, ministries in charge of domestic sectors, and even the governments of different Soviet republics are prohibited from engaging in international business on their own. Their needs are incorporated into the master plan. China has recently started to shift some foreign trade decision authority to ministries in charge of major sectors, but they must still coordinate their trade with the Foreign Trade Ministry.

The Foreign Trade Ministry carries out the international business activities through foreign trade monopolies, state trading corporations, which are set up by product line. They are the traders with whom Western business must deal. Their managers, like other communist managers, are charged with the responsibility of fulfilling the plan, that is, of acquiring the planned quotas of imports with the resources assigned for the purpose. They are to buy cheap and sell dear. This seems deceptively similar to capitalist trade, yet it is entirely different.

U.S. and other Western firms are in international business for private gain, to make a profit; the communist trading monopolies are in international business for a social gain, to fulfill the national plan. Our theory assumes that the traders' pursuit of private profits will yield more benefits than costs to the nation and thus indirectly produce a social gain, but there is no direct connection between private profit and social gain. A very profitable private transaction may involve a social loss; for example, exports subsidized by agricultural support programs or Export-Import Bank credits. Other international transactions profitable to private enterprise may cause unemployment or add to inflationary pressures. A communist trading monopoly will never trade if an overt social loss, as defined by the central plan, would result.

High officials of the Foreign Trade Ministry have often stressed the contrasting motives of communist and capitalist foreign trade. While business enterprises in the West engage in exporting and importing for the purpose of making a profit, the Soviet trading companies function as integral components of the centrally guided national economy. Their export and import activities are not guided by the profit motive, but rather by the economic needs and priorities of the nation as defined by the centrally formulated plan and as administered by the Ministry of Foreign Trade. Trade officials further emphasize that Soviet scientific, technological, manufacturing, and economic potentials have now grown to the point that they no longer depend on foreign trade (particularly trade with capitalist nations) to furnish needed materials and manufacturers. In their view, the Soviet economy can now produce everything or almost everything it needs to meet the goals of the plan. Thus, the Soviet response to U.S. threats of trade embargoes is an assertion of self-sufficiency.

Another important contrast relates to the role of government. Under the capitalist system, private firms can enter international business unless the government restricts them; under the communist system, the trading monopolies enter no international business unless the government orders them. The capitalist firms' international costs and prices are linked to their domestic costs; in a communist country trading monopolies are insulated from domestic costs and prices. Any such linkage is a matter for the planning authority to establish; it may give the linkage greater or lesser weight in finalizing the international business plan, as the particular circumstances may demand. The trading monopolies have no bargaining relationship with either their domestic suppliers or consumers. This fundamental fact must be understood by U.S. managers and the U.S. business press.

Its organizational isolation makes international business a highly specialized activity in communist countries. Personnel are trained in specialized institutions and their careers are devoted exclusively to some facet of international business. They are lifelong professionals with all the language and foreign area expertise necessary to the job. This is in sharp contrast to the Western practice, where the same executives may handle both domestic and international functions either simultaneously or periodically, where formal preparation for international responsibilities is either subordinated to domestic training or completely lacking. This disparity in education and experience helps to explain the frequent failures of U.S. business firms in dealings with the communist foreign trade monopolies.

In sum, international business of a communist economy is a separate yet subordinate sector of the centrally planned economy.

SUMMARY

The economic system of the U.S.S.R. is a command economy that rejects the basic elements of the capitalist economic model and utilizes compulsory central planning as the means of directing all productive organizations and activities. Important industries are managed directly by all-union ministries in Moscow; less strategic sectors report to member republics who, in turn, must comply with directions of union republic ministries.

The central plan is designed to fulfill the overall objectives set by the Communist Party. The Gosplan bureaucracy translates the overall objectives into specific physical and financial targets applicable to different republics, districts, and enterprises. Achieving the planned target is the most important indicator of performance. To stimulate productivity various nonmaterial incentives are widely used.

The People's Republic of China has adopted this model with minor modifications, due to different conditions and disagreements over the true interpretation of Marxist theory.

International business of communist countries is planned as a supplement to the domestic economy. The basic strategy calls for importing the products that have the highest marginal utility and paying for them by exporting the goods having the least marginal utility. Organizationally, international trade is separated from domestic business. It is carried out by state trading monopolies under the Ministry of Foreign Trade.

FOR REVIEW AND DISCUSSION

1. Juxtapose the main components of the communist and capitalist economic models and explain the relevance of each to business activities.

2. What are the differences between older forms of dictatorship and a totalitarian communist state?

3. Describe the different categories of economic enterprises of the U.S.S.R.

4. A Russian immigrant has characterized the U.S.S.R. as "a huge dinosaur with a very small head but armed to its teeth." Is this an apt description?

5. What is the relationship between physical and financial planning in the Soviet system?

6. If you worked for an enterprise in the U.S.S.R., how would you need to rearrange your professional values and priorities to be successful?

7. The Soviets claim to put greater emphasis on the dignity of work than the capitalist countries by rewarding high performances with prizes, titles, and other indications of distinguished achievement. Do you agree or disagree with this claim? Why or why not?

8. In what respect and why did the Chinese change the Soviet model?

9. Why have communist nations centralized international trade?

10. On what basis are export and import objectives established in a communist economy?

22

Soviet-U.S. Business Relations

*E*ast-West international business relations have been shaped by two primary variables: international political tensions and the import requirements of communist countries. In this relationship, politics has always overridden business. When the two countries are at odds politically, business is sacrificed; when political tensions ease, restrictions on business do the same. Politicization is the most profound characteristic of Soviet-U.S business relations. This remains as true in the 1980s as it has been in the past.

Before World War II the fear of dependency on capitalist countries led the Soviets to the concept of *autarky*, or economic self-sufficiency. It was also the capitalist nations' hope of "starving out the communist menace" that helped to politicize business relations with the Soviets.

THE COLD WAR

The United States and the U.S.S.R. emerged from World War II as unprecedented superpowers. Constructed on mutually antagonistic ideologies, each set out to fill the vacuums created by the war and to mold the international structure in its own image. As the tensions grew, business relations between the two became completely perverted, serving destructive rather than constructive objectives; to hurt rather than to aid the other superpower.

With its comprehensive command structure, the U.S.S.R. enjoyed a systemic advantage. To prevent trade with the United States, it had only to do nothing. The failure to act assured the result. The United States, on the other hand, had to resort to stringent government controls to restrain its firms from doing business with the U.S.S.R.

Major Legislation

The Export Control Act of 1949 was passed to regulate U.S. export trade. In it, Congress declared that the policy of the United States was to use export controls to protect the domestic economy from any excessive drain of scarce materials, to reduce the inflationary impact of abnormal foreign demand, to further the foreign policy of the United States and help in fulfilling its international responsibilities, and to protect the national security. Under this law, the U.S. government barred all exports and imports to the People's Republic of China and Manchuria, North Korea, North Vietnam, Inner Mongolia, and Cuba (except for food and medicine to Cuba). It also barred the export of arms and strategic and critical materials, but not other items, to the Soviet Union, Outer Mongolia, and most of the communist countries of Eastern Europe (with slightly fewer restrictions on Poland and Rumania). It placed no restrictions on exports to noncommunist nations or to Yugoslavia.

The Mutual Defense Assistance Control Act (Battle Act) of 1957 embargoes the exports of arms, ammunition, atomic materials, petroleum, and several other products to Communist nations. Any country disregarding the U.S. embargo disqualifies itself for U.S. economic and military aid. The Export-Import Bank Act forbids banks to guarantee, insure, extend credit, or participate in any way when the purchase or lease of a product is by a communist nation or when the product is for the principal use of a communist nation although the purchase or lease is negotiated by a third country.

The Trade with the Enemy Act requires all persons trading with communist countries to obtain first a license from the U.S. government. It also prohibits the transfer to certain communist countries of any interest in property subject to U.S. jurisdiction.

Additional Restrictions

A number of other laws and regulations have restated and further expanded these restrictions. The most important additional provisions include:

1. The withdrawal of most favored nation (MFN) treatment from all communist countries in 1957, although Poland and Yugoslavia have since been reinstated
2. Complete embargo on imports from mainland China, partially lifted in 1971
3. Miscellaneous specific restrictions, ranging from U.S. government funds not being used to purchase school laboratory equipment made in communist countries to the exclusion of Soviet turbines for the Grand Coulee hydroelectric project.

At the same time, the U.S. government continued to use indirect suasion to discourage business with the Soviet bloc. The most conspicuous success was the Ford Motor Company's reversal of its intent to build a truck manufacturing plant in the U.S.S.R. at Moscow's invitation.

No doubt these restrictions did not help the international business of the communist nations, but they did not hurt very much either. In most cases, like the truck plant, companies in other industrial nations were happy to get the business. The Soviets may have had to pay more, but they got what their plan prescribed. The U.S. embargo was ineffective.

DÉTENTE

In the 1960s cold war tensions started to relax. A movement began within the U.S. business community, which campaigned against the embargo as an economic folly. To refuse good business deals that the communist countries could at any rate close with European or Japanese companies seemed not so much the carrying out of U.S. foreign policy as self-denial on a national scale. Communist officials as well questioned the inimical policies that had been so economically costly.

Both the United States and the U.S.S.R. saw a huge mutual market because of size, industrial capacities, and economic diversities. The political climate, too, started to warm. The policy of détente was officially endorsed on both sides. It was no treaty of friendship, only a cessation of the cold war and the beginning of the process of normalizing relations. Since the main battlefield had been international business, in that area détente made its greatest impact.

Relaxation of Trade Restrictions

The first U.S. move to liberalize East-West business came in 1966, when an East-West Trade Bill was proposed. Although it failed in Congress, its modified version, the Export Administration Act, was passed in 1969. This Act did not abolish controls but decreed that controls should be abolished in instances where it could be shown that the U.S.S.R. could purchase the goods from other Western countries or Japan, except when U.S. security was threatened. The Department of Commerce has since removed over 2,000 items from the control list. The Act also allowed for presidential approval of Export-Import Bank financing of sales to communist countries.

In the 1970s, the trends from the late 1960s gathered momentum. The Export Expansion Act of 1971 raised the ceiling on all Export-Import Bank financial activity from $13.5 billion to $20 billion. In April 1971 export restrictions on wheat were rescinded, and the first of the big wheat deals was made in November 1971. Export controls were generally loosened, with $88 million in machine tools for the giant Kama River Truck Plant and $1 billion in automotive equipment being approved by the end of 1971. The Equal Export Opportunity Act of 1972 freed 1,500 goods from controls, indicating that the Department of Commerce's job would be to facilitate rather than inhibit exports to the U.S.S.R. This Act provides the current legal framework for the export control process.

In 1972, the two countries concluded the U.S.-Soviet Agreement on Science and Technology. That same year, the United States created the Commodity Credit Corporation to provide credit for Soviet purchases of U.S. grain.

Soviet Shortages

Similar changes of attitudes took place in the Soviet Union. The structure of import requirements changed so as to increase the desire to trade with the United States. Although the Soviets had proven themselves in heavy industry and metallurgy, they were deficient in the areas of electronics, chemicals, computers, and sophisticated forms of assembly line production. The new emphasis on science and research and development stressed these more sophisticated industries, but the Soviet system proved to be too ponderous, with its weak links between research institutions and industry, to respond. By the early 1970s the Soviets found themselves falling behind. They had seen what Japan had done with U.S. technology and equipment. Sensing the changing views in the United States, the Soviets periodically tested the U.S. market until finally, in 1972, they proposed resumption of negotiations on their lend-lease debt remaining from U.S. loans in World War II.

Legal Groundwork

In 1972 the Joint U.S.-U.S.S.R. Commercial Commission was created, which negotiated the U.S.-U.S.S.R. Trade Agreement in October 1972. In this, settlement of the Soviet Lend-Lease Debt was reached. The Soviets in the past had refused to offer over $300 million, and the United States had refused to accept less than $800 million. It was finally settled at $722 million, including interest. This payment by the U.S.S.R. was tied to U.S. extension of MFN treatment to the U.S.S.R., which was to be suspended in 1975 if payment was not forthcoming. The agreement by the U.S.S.R. to settle the debt made it possible to eliminate Johnson Act limitations on U.S. credits. Under the credit agreement, the Export-Import Bank could supply both direct credits and guarantees to U.S. citizens exporting to the U.S.S.R. via the Foreign Trade Bank (Vneshtorgbank) at terms granted elsewhere. The Trade Agreement also provided for expanded government commercial facilities in each country, expanded private business facilities, and third nation arbitration in the case of trade disputes.

The Fiasco of the Emigration Amendment   In 1974 Congress approved the MFN clause and extension of credits in the form of the Trade Reform Act, but it did so with the Jackson-Vanek Amendment attached, which made these extensions contingent upon liberalization of U.S.S.R. emigration policies. This amendment caused the agreement, so laboriously put together over a period of years, to be annulled by the Soviet Union as an interference in its internal affairs. The rejection set the stage for a period of uncertainty in U.S.-U.S.S.R. trade relations.

Other Soviet Objections   There were several other factors that led to the Soviet rejection of the Trade Agreement:

1. The value to the U.S.S.R. of the agreement had been reduced after 1972 because of the rise in the price of gold and the quadrupling in the price of oil as well as a rise in the price of gas and other raw materials. This led to a windfall to the U.S.S.R. of $3 billion per year in the value of their exports. With $3 billion in hard currency earnings every year, the U.S.S.R. did not need to make such significant concessions.
2. The Trade Reform Act included clauses that limited Export-Import Bank credits to the U.S.S.R. to $300 million over a four-year period unless there was further congressional sanction. This Stevenson Amendment detracted from the Trade Agreement because: (a) the U.S.S.R. was more interested in credits from the United States, especially Export-Import Bank credits, than it was in the lowering of tariffs through MFN treatment, because its prime interest was in large-scale projects with multibillion dollar credits; and (b) it was only a partial application of the MFN principle because it denied equal treatment by limiting credits.

These two factors robbed the Trade Agreement of much of its potential economic value to the U.S.S.R., and the emigration amendment required a demeaning political concession that strained the limits of linkage politics to the breaking point.

Constructing Conduits Between the U.S. and U.S.S.R.

Even though the Trade Agreement did not enter into force, both countries did abide by much of it. Among the provisions implemented were third-party impartial arbitration; the establishment of an official Soviet trade representative in Washington, D.C., and an official U.S. commercial office in Moscow; and reciprocal availability of business facilities and general trade promotion. In other words, at least there was now a structural framework to facilitate U.S.-Soviet business transactions.

Establishing Facilitating Bodies Another element in the structural framework within which private firms could more effectively pursue trade opportunities were a number of new international organizations. Of these, the most important official mechanism for commercial dialogue between the United States and the U.S.S.R. was the U.S.-U.S.S.R. Joint Commercial Commission, which was set up in 1972 to work out the details of the Trade Agreement. Still functioning, it works on a number of important problems relating to patents, licenses, copyrights, taxation, and joint ventures. Sometimes its enthusiasm for trade has even exceeded the hopes of executive departments in the U.S. government and ministries in the Soviet Union.

This official committee worked so well that a similar organization at the nongovernment level, the U.S.-U.S.S.R. Trade and Economic Council, was created. This council provides contacts of a different nature, as it is a binational council that aims at strengthening ties and economic relations between U.S. businessmen and Soviet foreign trade officials: 200 U.S. corporations and over 100 Soviet economic foreign trade organizations are represented.

Within the U.S. bureaucracy are several, even competing organizations, including the Bureau of East-West Trade, organized as a unit of the Department of Commerce to assist in the orderly development of trade between the United States and communist countries. The East-West Trade Policy Committee, which was especially influential under Secretary of State Henry Kissinger, reviews all major transfers of technology, evaluates government credits of over $5 million, and submits quarterly reports to Congress. The Council on International Economic Policy also takes part in policy decisions.

Soviet committees to facilitate international business include the U.S.S.R. All-Union Chamber of Commerce, which is engaged in trade promotion, and the State Committee on Science and Technology, which has linked up with U.S. firms for extensive research and development projects. Also available to assist U.S. firms in dealing with the Soviet Union is Amtorg, the Soviet buying agency in New York, and the Kama Purchasing Office, located in Pittsburgh.

Soviet Bilateralism   On the international level, the U.S.S.R. has always opposed the framework of GATT. Ideological views prohibit it from joining what it sees as a "rich man's club," even though Poland, Rumania, Hungary, and Yugoslavia are all members of GATT. Its strategy has been to obtain the benefits of GATT membership without joining the organization, preferring to operate via a network of bilateral trade agreements.

The U.S.S.R. was very successful in the 1960s in working out a series of bilateral trade agreements with Western European nations. Its Program of Industrial Collaboration with Industrial Countries was begun in 1966, and by 1972 eleven European countries and Japan had signed agreements, and other countries were looking into joint industrial projects in the U.S.S.R.

Successful Ventures Between Capitalist and Communist Enterprises
More illustrative of the progress of trade relations between the United States and the Soviet Union than the new commissions is the real evidence of trade growth. By 1977, more than 200 firms were engaged in trade with Soviet organizations and 26 U.S. firms had received accreditation to establish offices in Moscow. The agreements concluded provided for technological cooperation and equipment deliveries for a number of large Soviet construction projects, including complete plants such as the Kama River Truck Project, worth $192 million, in which more than 80 U.S. firms took part.

Among prominent U.S. business leaders promoting Soviet-U.S. trade have been Donald Kendall of Pepsico and Armand Hammer of Occidental Petroleum. Kendall arranged a barter deal with the Soviets in which Soviet officials agreed to match their Pepsi-cola purchases with sales of Soviet vodka in the United States by a Pepsico subsidiary. Kendall also serves as deputy chairman of the U.S. delegation to the U.S.-U.S.S.R. Trade and Economic Council. Armand Hammer has long been willing to barter, a favored method of trade for the Soviets. His company has a twenty-year agreement with the Soviets for an exchange of superphosphoric acid for ammonia, urea, and potash from the U.S.S.R.

Types of Soviet-U.S. Business Arrangements

Seven different vehicles for trade between the United States and the U.S.S.R. have been developed. Starting with the forms that involve less extensive and less complex cooperation and progressing to the forms that involve more extensive and more complex cooperation, they include the following:

1. *Science and technology agreements.* These agreements are signed by U.S. firms with the U.S.S.R. State Committee for Science and Technology. They generally call for exchanges of scientific and technical information, production samples, and seminars, as well as for joint efforts in research and development.

2. *Licensing agreements and turnkey projects.* Most Soviet purchases of U.S. licenses are the results of turnkey projects or purchases of machinery and equipment. A substantial number of U.S. firms have signed contracts to provide equipment and technology for complete plants to be constructed in the Soviet Union. Soviet enterprises have not constructed turnkey plants in the U.S., but they have registered 450 patents with the U.S. Patent Office and sold licenses to undetermined numbers of U.S. firms.

3. *Leasing agreements.* Under these arrangements, a U.S. firm owns the equipment and the Soviet enterprise uses it, making lease payments. At the end of the lease, the Soviet enterprise has the option of purchasing the equipment for a nominal amount, usually a dollar. Prohibition against Western ownership in the U.S.S.R. has prevented this relationship from being more widely utilized.

4. *Compensation arrangements.* These differ from straight barter deals in that Soviet goods do not directly pay for the imports of U.S. plant and equipment. They consist of at least two concurrent but unlinked sales contracts with attendant financing agreements. Frequently, the Soviet counterdeliveries consist of goods produced by the U.S.S.R. facility built with the U.S. machinery and technology.

5. *Joint tendering.* This involves an agreement between a U.S. firm and a Soviet enterprise to engage in the construction of a manufacturing facility, usually in a third country.

6. *Joint equity venture.* This is the most extensive form of industrial cooperation. In the U.S., there are two: the U.S.-U.S.S.R. Trade and Economic Council, Inc., in Washington, D.C., and the U.S.-U.S.S.R. Marine Resources, Inc., in Seattle, Washington. The U.S.S.R. does not permit such ventures in the Soviet Union.

SOVIET BUSINESS METHODS

Instead of cash purchases, the Soviets prefer barter. One barter arrangement is the *barter and switch arrangement.* This allows them to carry on foreign trade without a depletion of hard currency and to circumvent financial restrictions placed on trade by the United States or other parties. It also establishes markets for Soviet products in the West. This has been one area in which the Soviets have had difficulty, due to the lack of service centers, spare parts, and general knowledge concerning distribution and marketing. However, in these types of arrangements, the Western partner, with an already established market position, assumes the marketing task.

The most important centers for this type of trade arrangement are London and Vienna. The U.S.S.R. Foreign Trade Offices engage in three basic kinds of barter:

1. An offer to the Western participant of the commodity produced by the Foreign Trade Office with whom the firm is dealing
2. An offer of a list of products that are not limited to the particular Foreign Trade Office with whom the firm deals, a popular offer with most Western countries
3. A counterpurchase by which each partner specializes in the production of certain parts or items and then exchanges with each other to complete the product or product line

Cooperation agreements are a form of barter and switch that the Soviets have increasingly favored. These agreements may extend over several years, with repayment to be made by production from Soviet facilities that Western companies have helped build. One such agreement involves Soviet production of machine tools designed with West German assistance. The West German firm produced the initial prototype and subsequently supplied the Soviets with equipment required to set up production in the U.S.S.R. The West Germans will take production from these facilities in repayment. Some potential Western partners have shied away from such deals because of uncertainty over the quality of Soviet-produced products and over the inability of Soviet producers to service the products abroad.

The U.S.S.R. has a strong preference for balancing its international business transactions on a bilateral basis. It enters commercial treaties or agreements

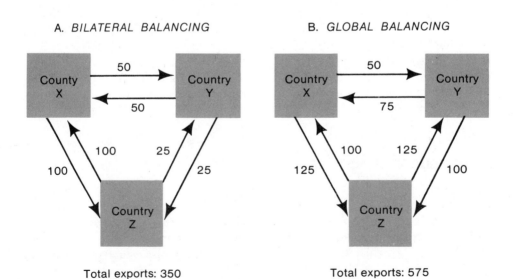

Total exports: 350   Total exports: 575

Figure 22.1   Trade Volume Under Bilateral and Global Balancing

that call for the other country to import from the U.S.S.R. an amount equal to its exports to the U.S.S.R. Typically, such a bilateral treaty calls for setting up clearing accounts in both countries' central banks. When the actual trade transactions take place, the exporter gets paid by its home country bank from the clearing account in its domestic currency, and the importer pays to its bank in that nation's currency, to be deposited in the clearing account. If all works the way it is originally planned, the trading balance at the close of the period is zero. If a deficit develops in the Soviet account the Soviets insist that the trading partner increase its imports. This may or may not work.

LDCs have usually complied more readily with the Soviets than the advanced nations in this respect. This is due partly to their weaker bargaining power, partly to their less discriminating consumers, and partly to the relatively greater importance of state-owned enterprises, which the LDC government can influence.

PRICING IN SOVIET TRADE

The iron law of communist trade is that exports must pay for imports. Since their currencies have no recognized international value, nearly all nonbarter trade takes place in convertible foreign currencies or in gold.[1] To meet the import requirements, the volume and prices of exports are varied so as to generate the necessary amount of foreign exchange. This is the overriding objective of pricing policy.

Domestic Prices

The Soviet export price need not bear any direct relationship to domestic prices or costs. In domestic pricing, the authorities pursue two courses. First, retail prices for consumer goods are set so that the planned output will be cleared, that is, equal to available consumer spending in a particular sector; this is the nearest to supply and demand that Soviet pricing ever gets. Second, wholesale and producer prices are determined by averaging the cost of all producers over a given reference period (by necessity, a past period) and adding a planned markup. The markup is varied by authorities to make things come out right.

Export and Import Prices

Since neither of these domestic pricing policies is readily adaptable to the competitive conditions in the world markets, the Soviets rely on a negotiated

---

1. Because the exchange rates are set administratively by the state, rather than established by market forces, the official rate does not equal the actual purchasing power of the currency.

price rather than a prefixed or planned price in foreign trade. The world market price, if one exists, is used as the basic standard. Otherwise, either the Soviet wholesale price or the trading partner's domestic wholesale price provides the starting point of the price negotiations. The managers of the trading monopolies are required to drive hard bargains with foreign firms and are awarded special bonuses if they succeed in realizing particularly favorable prices for the U.S.S.R.

Most exports and imports of communist countries are priced very near to the two basic standards: the world market price or the wholesale price in the country of origin. All are not, nor is there any compelling reason they should be. The concentration of control over international trade in the Foreign Trade Ministry creates a supermonopoly that can manipulate export prices and products in ways that are unthinkable under the free enterprise system.

For example, suppose a communist country needs an automobile plant and decides to import it as a turnkey project. Three foreign firms offer to build the plant: a U.S. firm for $60 million, an Italian firm for $68 million, and a Swedish firm for $72 million. The U.S. company is the lowest bidder, but it asks for payment in dollars or gold. The communist country's foreign exchange reserves are too small to meet these terms. If it bought the plant from the Italian or Swedish companies, it could receive long-term credit or pay in kind with raw material exports. Suppose further that the Foreign Trade Ministry finds a U.S. airline anxious to buy from it four supersonic aircraft, if they are priced at $15 million instead of the $16.2 million they cost to produce. By selling the four aircraft at a $4.8 million loss, the Ministry can save $8 million on the turnkey project (the difference between the U.S. and Italian offers) and record an overall profit of $3.2 million.

This is awesome power, although the Soviets have to date used it sparingly. Capitalist enterprise, where each individual firm must break-even to survive, has no counterforce to neutralize this advantage. No amount of rhetoric about the superiority of competition and the market mechanism over centrally planned economies helps, except perhaps as a tranquilizer. If the superiority of competition has not won in the past, when the communist countries were underdeveloped and weak, it is certain it will not do so in the future. How to come to grips with this disparity in pricing power is a fundamental problem to which U.S. government and business must jointly seek a solution. It would seem that certain cherished ideals of competition in this country will have to be viewed from a new perspective before such a solution can be contemplated.

INTRABLOC TRADE

Once a monolithic colossus ruled from Moscow, the communist countries no longer formed a solid bloc. Separatist tendencies have produced a polycentric power structure in which both Peking and Belgrade challenge the Kremlin and many other capitals vie for greater self-assertion. The loosening of political control has been followed by more independent trading policies.

China's own trade epitomizes the shuffling directions in intrabloc trade. In precommunist days, only 5 percent of China's foreign trade was with communist countries. After the communists gained power, the direction of Chinese trade was shifted toward the U.S.S.R. and other communist countries, and in 1955 their share was 77 percent. Since the Sino-Soviet split in 1960, their share has dropped to around 25 percent. Yugoslavia's experience is similar.

In the other East European countries, the U.S.S.R.'s dominance has weakened somewhat but still remains decisive. Through COMECON (the Council for Mutual Economic Assistance), the trade policies of Bulgaria, Czechoslovakia, East Germany, Hungary, Poland, Rumania, and the U.S.S.R. are subject to centralized supranational coordination. This quasi-common-market arrangement has been used by the U.S.S.R. to impose its control on the trade relations of the other members. However, resistance to this control has become increasingly apparent.

The stated goals of COMECON include:

1. An increase of intrabloc trade
2. Development of more optimal allocation of resources among member countries
3. More equal per capita production and consumption standards in the bloc nations

The first objective has become increasingly illusive in the last few years. As to the second objective, a violent disagreement has erupted about the type of specialization the U.S.S.R. has sought to impose on the other members. Rumania, particularly, has protested against being relegated to an agrarian role that it considers less prestigious and less rewarding than industrial development. The need to work out an acceptable theory of international economic integration and intrabloc trade has been emphasized but remains so far unmet. That leaves political negotiations and relative power positions as the only means for settling the issues. Incomparably larger than all the other countries combined, the U.S.S.R. can be assured of continued dominance of the COMECON trade.

NEW INHIBITIONS TO SOVIET-U.S. BUSINESS

We observed earlier that Soviet-U.S. business relations are a joint product of Soviet import requirements and political tensions. The two variables may either compound or counteract each other. When Soviet import requirements are small and tension high, business comes to a standstill; when the needs are great and tension low, business booms. The latter was the environment that produced détente.

The Politics of Linkage

To integrate business and politics, both sides have used the linkage policy approach toward the other, that is, trying to integrate a broad range of issues so that progess in one creates movements in another. In making specific decisions the strategic aspects of all issues that are affected are to be considered. From the U.S. side this is to prevent the United States from ending up by cooperating with the Soviets where it is strong and competing with them in areas in which it is weak.

The U.S.S.R. also connects politics with business. In the words of Leonid Brezhnev:

> Politics and economics, diplomacy and commerce, industrial production and trade are interwoven in our foreign economic relations. Consequently, the approach to them and to management must be integrated, combining the efforts of all departments [and combining] our political and economic interests.[2]

There are competing factions in the Kremlim, some totally opposing any U.S.-U.S.S.R. trade, some favoring trade on a limited scale, and others seeing large-scale trade with the West as a means of solving economic problems.

Linkage politics force the development of a uniform overall policy, with a high foreign policy of security issues, which must be worked out at high government levels, providing a framework within which companies operate at the process level or the level of low foreign policy of trade issues. In other words, what is good for Occidental Petroleum or Control Data may not be the best for national interests.

U.S. success with linkage politics has been questionable. Efforts to dangle benefits for good behavior before the Soviets has often tended to cause more tension than relaxation of barriers. The Jackson-Vanek Amendment is a case in point; it boomeranged and became a serious obstacle to East-West business.

The Demise of Détente

Iranian Militants   The Islamic revolution in Iran started a downturn of U.S.-Soviet political relations. The revolution offered irresistible political temptations to the U.S.S.R.—an opportunity to dislodge the U.S. from its position in the Near East could not be let slip by unattended. When Iranian radicals sacked the U.S. Embassy in Tehran and held its diplomatic personnel hostage, the Soviets tried to play both ends against the middle: they went along with U.N. Security Council's condemnation of Iran's violation of diplomatic immunity, but at the same time Soviet radio was broadcasting Farsi-language propaganda programs into Iran, which not only gave tacit support to the holding of American hostages, but also attacked U.S. policies with highly inflammatory rhetoric. When the Security Council in early 1980 took up economic sanctions against Iran, the Soviet Union vetoed the resolution.

This series of events greatly angered the Carter Administration. Détente was in danger, but no overt actions were taken to destroy it.

---

2. "U.S.S.R.: Outlook for U.S.-Soviet Trade Is Improving." *Business America* January 1, 1979, p. 27.

Afghan Invasion In 1979, Soviet troops invaded Afghanistan. This jarred the very foundations of U.S.-Soviet relations. President Carter ordered pending business deals cancelled and called for the boycott of the Moscow Olympics. It was an open break, a full-blown crisis involving the high policy issues. Détente froze over.

To experienced observers the Soviet takeover of Afghanistan was not entirely unpredictable. In April 1978 there had been a Marxist coup. After that the Soviets had been building their obtrusive presence: Soviet advisers were placed in all Afghan government ministries and military units down to the company level. When Muslim tribesmen and disgruntled nationalists started to pose an increasing challenge to the Soviet-backed Marxist regime, Moscow ordered its tanks to roll.

Both the U.S. and the U.S.S.R. embarked on a far-reaching reassessment of détente. As we noted before, the economic value of détente to the Soviets had been seriously limited by the Jackson-Vanek Amendment and President Carter's critical stance on the human rights situation in the U.S.S.R. The U.S., from its side, had suffered increasing agony as it watched the Soviets, either directly or through allies, decisively eroding the American position in Vietnam, Ethiopia, Angola and South Yemen. Stunning as the Afghan invasion was to the officialdom, the American public was already questioning the continued viability of détente.

SUMMARY

East-West international business relations have been highly politicized. As the political tensions ebb and flow, business activities expand and contract. The cold war was fought mainly with destructive economic pressures. Détente started a process of dismantling the restrictive laws and regulations, but new political tensions continue to jeopardize liberalization.

Reliance on the linkage policy has complicated matters by compounding business considerations with a variety of nonbusiness issues. Nevertheless, numerous capitalist-communist business ventures have been organized and Western business circles have shown increasing interest in business opportunities involving the U.S.S.R. and other communist nations.

FOR REVIEW AND DISCUSSION

1. Cite any evidence you can find to prove or disprove the statement that East-West international business relations have been shaped by international political tensions.

2. What are the cold war legacies to international business relations?

3. Is détente dead? Why or why not?

4. What intersystem differences are there between the United States and the U.S.S.R.? Why are U.S. negotiators unaware of them?

5. How do the Soviets use barter in international business?

6. Why have the communist nations remained strict bilateralists?

7. Can the capitalist countries neutralize the power of the Soviet Foreign Trade Ministry to offset losses in one sector with profits in another? If so, by which measures?

8. Is COMECON comparable to the European Economic Community? Why or why not?

9. Explain the meaning and implications of linkage policy.

10. Identify some recent business ventures of Western firms involving the Soviet Union. How do these ventures differ from similar business ventures in noncommunist countries?

11. Should the U.S. government control the sales of grain and other foodstuffs to the U.S.S.R. by private traders? Why or why not?

23

Trade with China

Although China has existed longer as a cultural and political entity than any of the other major powers, it is in some respects a new nation. Until very recently, it has not played an influential role in the modern interstate system nor exerted an international influence commensurate with its size and population.

This situation began to change when the Chinese Communist Party achieved power in 1949 and established the People's Republic of China. The new Beijing regime rapidly unified the country and established a strong political apparatus. It built up the country's military strength, initiated an ambitious economic development program, and started to play a more active role abroad.

In the late 1950s, however, China turned inward, toward angry isolationism, especially during the Cultural Revolution of the 1960s. China was at odds with all of the largest nations involved in Asia, including the Soviet Union, India, the United States, and Japan. For a brief period it had only one ambassador stationed anywhere abroad, in Cairo.

After the Cultural Revolution, Chinese leaders began to look outward again. Since 1971, there have been dramatic changes in China's policies, its international situation, and its role in the world. By 1975, it had established formal ties with over 100 nations, more than double the number in 1968. Its relationships with third world countries increased spectacularly. In addition, in 1971 the People's Republic finally replaced the Chinese Nationalists in the United Nations, becoming one of the five permanent members of the Security Council and acquiring the power of the veto. Since then, as a member of the most important bodies affiliated with the United Nations, with the notable exceptions of the World Bank and the International Monetary Fund, the Chinese have been heard on virtually all major international issues.

China's foreign trade and other economic relations have steadily increased during this period. Although its trade is still relatively small, especially in per capita terms, today China is an important importer of technology and capital goods of all kinds, and it promises to become a significant exporter of petroleum and other primary commodities. The important compromises that China has made in its militantly isolationist stance reflect not only its pressing domestic needs but also a general willingness to involve itself in the international community somewhat more than in the past. Like other countries, China's international economic policy is an integral part of its foreign policy.

INTERNATIONAL BUSINESS POLICIES UNDER MAO

Since the inception of the People's Republic, China has been governed by two guiding principles, self-reliance and egalitarianism. The aim of egalitarianism is to abolish the different classes in the traditional feudal society in China, while self-reliance is to develop China into an independent, self-sufficient nation able to protect itself from foreign attacks and exploitation.

The meaning of self-reliance has changed over time in response to changes in political and economic conditions. In the 1950s, when the Chinese economy was heavily dependent on the Soviet Union, self-reliance took the form of relying mainly on its own efforts and making external assistance subsidiary. When the Sino-Soviet split began to surface in 1960, China had diplomatic relations with only a few industrial countries in the West. Self-reliance became more inward-looking and narrower in scope. The goal at that time was maintaining independence, keeping the initiative, and relying on itself.

In the early 1970s, when the Chinese economy began to grow rapidly, China's diplomatic and trade relations, particularly with major Western countries, became more open and expansionary. The concept of self-reliance was more liberally interpreted. For example, Deng Xiaoping told the United Nations General Assembly in 1974 that, "Self-reliance in no ways means 'self-seclusion' and rejection of foreign aid." Thus, phrases such as "Learning from other countries" and "Making foreign things serve China," which were coined by Mao Zedong in the 1950s but fell into disuse were once again widely used in the Chinese media.

The changes in the interpretation of self-reliance have paralleled the changes in China's foreign trade policies during the last three decades. Generally speaking, a narrower interpretation of the principle has meant less foreign trade and vice versa. When the concept of self-reliance was applied to foreign trade it became a mixture of mercantilism and autarky. Self-reliance never meant complete autarky, but rather a deliberate pursuit of an import substitution and minimization policy. It meant avoiding any form of indebtedness, paying cash for all purchases, and never becoming dependent upon any single supplier.

As a result of this policy, China isolated itself from the rest of the world, especially in terms of science, technology, and industrial developments, during the 1960s. In addition, China also cut itself off from the world's capital markets and from access to either short-, medium-, or long-term loans. Under the impact of this policy, imports were scaled to the amount of foreign exchange available from export earnings and, hence, were kept to a minimal level.

Beginning in 1970 China's foreign trade policy took another turn. Partly because of China's sudden realization of its economic and political backwardness, and partly because of the perceived military threat from the Soviet Union, China began to resume trade with many Western countries on a larger scale. This led to an increased amount of imports, especially for capital goods such as plants and equipment.

INTERNATIONAL BUSINESS POLICIES IN THE POST-MAO PERIOD

After the death of Mao in 1976, the new government under Premier Hua Guofeng and Vice-Premier Deng Xiaoping began to restore order in economic planning and management and to adopt more liberal economic and foreign trade policies.

The Four Modernizations

Beijing began a "New Long March" toward a modernization of (a) agriculture, (b) industry, (c) national defense, and (d) science and technology by the year 2000. These ambitious targets are known as the Four Modernizations. In February 1978 these modernizations became part of China's constitution.

Specific Goals of the Modernizations   The main goals of the program can be summarized in a few points. The agricultural modernization was meant to accomplish five main objectives:

1. Gross agricultural production value should increase by 4 to 5 percent per year up to 1985.
2. Food output should reach a total of 800 billion catties (400 million tons) in 1985, up 45 percent from 1977.
3. Agricultural mechanization should be completed by 1985, with at least 85 percent of major farm work mechanized.
4. Water utilization should be expanded by 1985 to ensure an average of 1 mu (733.5 square yards) of dependably irrigated farmland per farm, meaning that effectively irrigated areas should total about 800 million mu (125 million acres).
5. Twelve commodity food bases should be established by 1985 and supply volumes should double or triple.

Modernizing industry can be summed up in the following six points:

1. The gross industrial production value should increase at least 10 percent a year through 1985.
2. Development of infrastructure industries should be accelerated, particularly in power generation, fuel production, raw materials manufacturing, and transportation, to stimulate the growth of light industry and defense industry.
3. All-out efforts should be exerted in geology and mining to meet the needs of infrastructure industries.

4. In the initial years, production increases are to be achieved on the existing infrastructure. Thorough examinations must be undertaken and steps taken to reform and renovate existing enterprises.

5. Construction of major new industrial facilities should produce fourteen diversified industrial bases of considerable strength throughout the mainland, focusing on steel, non-iron metal, coal, oil, power generation, railroad trunk lines, and ports.

6. The industrial structure should be organized into six regional economic systems (Southwest, Northwest, South Central, East, North, and Northeast) supplemented by a huge strategic service base in the interior.

Defense modernization plans include the development of modern weapons systems, including missiles and nuclear arms and improvement of military personnel. Finally, to make the achievements of agricultural, industrial, and defense modernizations possible, emphasis on science and technology becomes necessary. This emphasis produced the following goals:

1. Elevation by 1985 of certain important science and technology sectors to a point at or near the most advanced levels of the 1970s elsewhere.

2. Boosting the number of trained full-time scientists and technicians to 800,000.

3. Establishment of a number of modern science experimentation centers.

4. Completion of a national science research system.

Acting in accordance with the goals, the Chinese are taking steps, such as consolidation of research setups, assurance of positions for intellectuals, school reform, formulation of rules governing students abroad, recruitment through invitation of Chinese scholars from overseas communities, and enhancement of scientific and technological exchanges with foreign sources.

In fact, the Four Modernizations also call for rapid expansion of imports and exports. To overcome the negative impact on economic growth of the time lost in training and research during the decade of the Cultural Revolution and its aftermath, Chinese planners seem to have adopted a strategy of relying more heavily than in the past on imports of capital goods and industrial techniques, since technology and equipment imports typically provide the quickest and perhaps most economical way of promoting rapid growth in an underdeveloped economy.

Reassessment of Maoist Values   Three major issues—self-reliance, the impact of foreign technology on China's indigenous technology, and the ability to finance imports of technology—have been involved in Beijing's decision to increase technology acquisitions. With respect to self-reliance, current ideology holds that advanced techniques and experience are the common wealth of the working people throughout the world, and that every country as it develops is bound to absorb and make use of, to a greater or lesser degree, scientific and technological achievements of other countries. Self-reliance is not self-seclusion and rejection of foreign trade and technological transfer; "learning from other countries" and "making foreign things serve China" are both proper and helpful to China's economic modernization. To avoid technological dependence on any given country, China diversifies sources of supply and is highly selective in its choice of suppliers. Only those plants, products, and techniques that will eventually make China less dependent on external suppliers are imported.

In regard to the impact of foreign technology on China's indigenous technology, current leadership regards foreign technology as not inimical to the development of Chinese technology, providing such technology is properly used. The purpose of importing advance technology and equipment is to learn from them in order to promote Chinese inventions. The technology of foreign countries is to be applied analytically and critically, according to the principle of "First, use; second, criticize; third, convert; and fourth, create." By adhering to this maxim, China can assimilate foreign technology while reinforcing domestic capabilities.

New Objectives   The new leadership seeks the following objectives:

1. Greater stress on production than on politics
2. Greater authority to managers
3. Improvement of workers' standard of living
4. Encouragement of capital accumulation
5. Purchase of essential technology abroad
6. Stress on the role of scientists and technicians
7. Emphasis on scientific research and expertise

There are warnings that foreign equipment and technology must be carefully and economically purchased. Buying more technology than China can use serves to increase domestic consumption and limit products for export.

The extent of financing available for technology imports depends on the need to import grain and other agricultural products with foreign exchange earnings and on a willingness to accept credit and other trade arrangements. If Chinese agricultural development is successful and imports minimized, then the size of foreign exchange earnings will become the principal determinant of the level of plant and technology imports. To promote such earnings, current Chinese efforts are focused on four product areas: oil, coal, labor-intensive industrial products, and agriculture. In addition, China is making an effort to expand traditional export commodities. Greater attention is being given to design, quality, labeling, style, and packaging. To improve export earnings, current policy also calls for the adoption of more flexible trading practices, such as importing foreign raw materials and component parts for further processing or assembly and subsequent re-export.

Institutional Structure of International Business

The international sector of trade in China, like that of other communist nations, is an appendix to the domestic economy. Its scope and composition are determined by the central plan, and all international transactions are strictly reserved for the Ministry of Foreign Trade, the state's supermonopoly with product-based trading corporations analogous to the model used by the

U.S.S.R. The Ministry of Foreign Trade is composed of bureaus and institutions, trading corporations, and service arms. The bureaus divide foreign trade by geographic area. In addition, one bureau provides inspection and testing of foreign trade. The International Trade Institute also is a branch of the Ministry of Foreign Trade; its function is to train personnel for the state trading corporations and the Ministry of Foreign Trade.

The next level in the ministry is composed of trading corporations and service arms. The trading corporations deal with specific product groups, such as cereals, oils, and food stuffs (Ceroilfood), light-industrial products (Industry), machinery (Machimpex), native produce and animal byproducts (Chinatushu), technical items (Techimport), and textiles (Chinatex), as well as arts and crafts, chemicals, metals and minerals, and publications. The service arms include corporations for chartering, transportation, export commodities, packaging, and turnkey projects.

Regulatory Agencies   Other important agencies involved in some aspect of international business are listed below:

Organization	*Function*
Financial and Economic Commission	To strengthen unified leadership over financial and economic work
Foreign Investment Control Commission	To approve foreign investments in China, including joint ventures, 100 percent foreign-owned investments, and some compensation trade projects
Import-Export Control Commission	To supervise imports and exports, in order to strengthen the management of imports and exports, keep foreign exchange in balance, and introduce the most up-to-date foreign technologies, according to *Beijing Review;* the real function of this Commission remains somewhat of a mystery
China International Trust and Investment Corporation	To coordinate use of foreign investment and technology, also to work out details of joint ventures with foreigners and find appropriate Chinese partners
General Administration for Industry and Commerce	To register joint ventures before they start operation under a license
State General Administration of Exchange Control	To supervise the Bank of China's activities, to unify China's foreign exchange control, examining and supervising the commercial and non-commercial foreign exchange balance of payments

Banking   The People's Bank functions as the country's central bank, with 33,000 commercial branches throughout China. It also controls a dozen commercial banks in Hong Kong. The bank's new power comes from its ability to override local party officials in matters concerning economic policy. The People's Bank plays a major role in monitoring industrial performance, encouraging savings, deciding on new projects, controlling prices, and pushing factories and enterprises to maximize their export earnings.

To gain foreign exchange, the Bank of China has started selling travelers checks denominated in *renminbi* for use in China. It is also encouraging foreign banks and Chinese people in foreign countries to deposit money in time deposit accounts at competitive interest rates.

A recent important change was the separation of the Bank of China from the People's Bank. The Bank of China is now under the direct control of the State Council, China's cabinet. This puts the Bank of China on even terms with its domestic counterpart, the People's Bank.

Evolution in Trading Practices

Flexibility   As China pursues its modernization program, it is making significant changes in foreign trade practices. In contrast to previous years, China has agreed to use customer-provided designs, raw materials, and equipment in manufacturing commodities for export, and it has agreed to use customers' trademarks on commodities. It has accepted more flexible pricing, that is, closer adherence to international practices and trade terms, and it has shown a greater willingness to comply with foreign regulations. These changes are believed to have yielded good results. For example, one woolen textile factory in Beijing received 156 foreign sales contracts in 1978, double the number for 1977.

At the same time, China is experimenting with other flexible approaches, including arrangements in which the Chinese will process imported materials or assemble components according to the specifications of contracting firms and re-export the finished product. These arrangements have taken several forms. One arrangement is for China to accept raw materials or components supplied by foreign firms and to receive processing fees. In another form of arrangement, foreign firms supply some of the materials or parts with China providing the remainder. In a third variation, foreign firms also supply equipment, which China will eventually own through deducting its costs from processing fees over an agreed-upon period. In 1978, China signed more than 200 such contracts with companies from Hong Kong, Macao, and six countries, including Japan and the United States.

Compensation Trade   In addition, the People's Republic has become more interested in *buyback compensatory trade arrangements*. Under such arrangements, the Chinese provide the factory shell and raw labor, and foreign firms supply raw materials, training, designs, know-how, equipment, and possibly some supervisory personnel in exchange for part or all of the finished products. By the end of 1978, there were 38 such arrangements, mostly with local firms in

Hong Kong and Macao. A number of foreign firms, including a major British toy manufacturer and an internationally known Japanese fashion designer, also participate in Chinese compensation projects. Compensation project negotiations under way could lead to an additional $400 million in business each way between China and Great Britain.

China's compensation trade has found its widest application in the manufacture of light industrial projects such as knitwear, garments, plastic flowers, leather products, electronic watches, and processed food. Compensation trade seems to have a great appeal to China since it enables the Chinese to import equipment, technology, and expertise without having to pay the full cost in the valuable foreign exchange, of which China is so short. Yet the method is not without difficulties. In recent negotiations, for example, foreign partners had problems in obtaining the Bank of China's guarantee on foreign bank loans for equipment destined for compensation trade projects. Further, there are difficult problems for foreign partners with respect to the quality, pricing, and marketing of finished products.

In both export processing and compensation trade arrangements with foreign companies, a key role is played by local governments. In ten Chinese provinces and municipalities where these arrangements have been made, local authorities negotiated contracts directly with foreign firms. It appears that China is in the process of setting up export processing areas, with local governments mainly responsible for their development.

Barter Although Beijing has traditionally steered clear of pure barter contracts, the idea of barter is of increasing interest to U.S. companies doing business with China. Barter trade usually involves two-way trade of commodities using a single contract, as opposed to countertrade, in which goods may be exchanged for technology under separate contracts. With China itself pressing foreign companies to find ways of exchanging product for product, barter may be ready to play a role in China's international trade.

Joint Ventures with Capitalist Firms

In 1979 Beijing removed the "great wall" excluding foreign equity investments, when the National People's Congress passed the Joint Venture Law. This statute extends China's international business to include direct investments and joint ventures. The law is more a general framework of principles than specific rules. Its main purpose is to attract foreign capital, technology, and management expertise. The Chinese party to a joint venture may be a government ministry, a regional agency, or an individual enterprise. All types of businesses are entitled to joint venture operations; no sector is excluded.

One area of difficulty is the requirement that contributions to the joint venture by both (or all) parties be expressed in monetary terms. Since the Chinese currency is not truly convertible and since indigenous prices are set by planning authorities, the partners have no certain way of fixing comparable

A. *STRAIGHT BARTER*

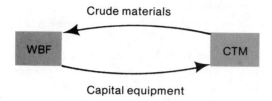

Crude materials

Capital equipment

Two variations:
a. Value of exports balanced with value of imports.
b. Cash paid for each shipment, with total payments for exports and imports balanced (bank may act as intermediary).

B. *TRIPARTITE BARTER*

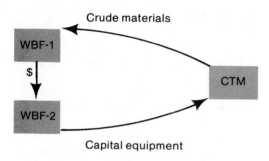

Crude materials

Capital equipment

CTM balances WBF-1's account against WBF-2's. Payment goes directly from WBF-1 to WBF-2.

C. *INDIRECT BARTER*

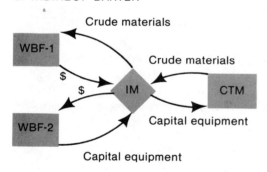

Crude materials

Crude materials

Capital equipment

Capital equipment

IM balances CTM's export and import shipments and serves both WBF-1 and WBF-2 as a trading company; IM typically specializes in trade with either the U.S.S.R. or China.

Legend

WBF   Western business firm
CTM   Communist trading monopoly
 IM   Inter-merchant

Figure 23.1   Types of Barter Arrangements

monetary values for their contributions. Similar problems are faced in the distribution of the joint venture profits. Chinese law requires that the net profit of a joint venture be distributed on a pro rata basis, each partner's share of the profits being determined by its share in the investment. However, the law is silent on various costs that greatly affect the size of the profit, such as depre-

D. *SYNDICATED BARTER*

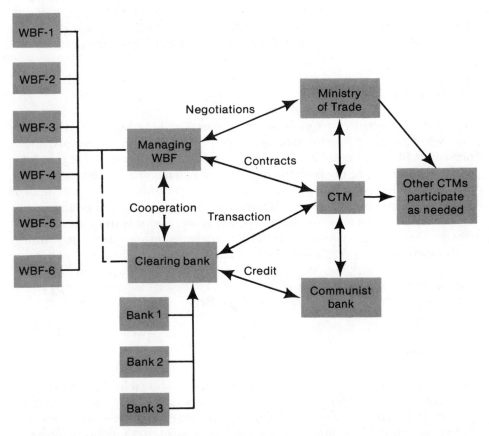

Necessary in major projects requiring several WBFs as supplier. The Communist country barters a large volume of one or two commodities to pay for imports; the managing WBF spearheads the project, setting policy and exercising supervision, with its bank acting as a financial clearinghouse.

Figure 23.1 *continued*

ciation, workers' bonuses, and pension funds. The applicable accounting principles must be mutually agreed upon. These uncertainties are counterbalanced by tax benefits guaranteed to joint ventures involving advanced technology or significant export earnings.

The management of the joint venture is its board of directors. By law, the chairperson of the board must be appointed by the Chinese partner and the first vice chairperson by the foreign partner. These provisions apply regardless of the respective investments of the partners; even if the foreign partner holds a majority position in equity, the chairmanship still belongs to the Chinese partner.

Although the general vagueness of the law has received much critical comment in the Western press, business firms have literally swarmed into China with joint venture proposals. In the first year after the law was promulgated, Chinese authorities reported that over 200 foreign joint venture agreements had been concluded or were in the process of active negotiation. The foreign partners are mainly Japanese, U.S., and West European firms.

The Hua Qiao Program

As a further incentive to inbound investments, China has offered *hua qiao* (overseas Chinese) opportunities for direct private investment that are not at present available to non-Chinese foreigners. The most dramatic of these opportunities so far are the investment companies, which have precursors in the pre-Cultural Revolution hua qiao investment corporations, in the provinces of Fujian and Guangdong. The Fujian organizations are capable of issuing stocks to and handling investments from hua qiao, accepting loans from hua qiao and foreign firms, engaging in compensation trade, entering into joint ventures with hua qiao, accepting enterprises run and financed by hua qiao of foreign entrepreneurs in appointed export-oriented zones in Fujian provinces, and contracting to construct buildings and highway projects abroad either by themselves or together with hua qiao or foreign firms.

Advertising

Above all, flexibility in China's trading practices is shown in the increased use of advertising. The Shanghai Advertising Corporation, restored in the latter part of 1978, is responsible for advertising Chinese export commodities abroad. It has established business relations with more than 100 foreign newspapers and magazines, and has begun to accept foreign advertising for display in Chinese publications and on Chinese radio and television.

The ongoing reorganization of all aspects of the foreign trade structure reflects Beijing's efforts to improve the efficiency of conducting international business.

CHINA'S RELATIONSHIP WITH THE UNITED STATES

During 1950, two-way trade between China and the United States totaled $191 million, with China exporting almost three times as much as it imported; the U.S. share of China's total foreign trade was 22.5 percent. When Chinese troops entered the Korean War, however, the Department of Commerce embargoed all U.S. exports to China under authority of the Export Control Act of 1949. Shortly afterwards, Beijing assumed control of all U.S. property in China. On these somber notes, all relations between the two countries came to a virtual standstill, although some Chinese imports continued to reach the United States until 1953.

The first indication of U.S. desire to change its policy toward China did not come until 1969, when U.S. tourists and residents abroad were permitted to purchase up to $100 worth of goods originating in China. In 1971, the Treasury Department announced the removal of all controls on the use of dollars or dollar instrumentalities in transactions with China and its nationals. Finally, the Shanghai Communique of 1972 signaled the resumption of Sino-U.S. diplomatic relations, which had been dormant for more than twenty years.

Passage of the Trade Act of 1974 brought into law a variety of requirements that had the potential of affecting the newly developing Sino-U.S. trade by adding to requirements China would have to meet if full normalization of commercial relations was to occur. Under the act, the president is authorized to extend nondiscriminatory tariff treatment (most favored nation treatment) as part of a bilateral commercial agreement to nonmarket economy countries not currently receiving such treatment. Such a bilateral agreement is precluded, however, if the president determines that the country impedes its citizens from exercising that right or opportunity to emigrate. The president is authorized to waive these conditions for a period of 18 months if the waiver will substantially promote the free emigration objectives.

In 1979, the Sino-U.S. Trade Agreement was signed in Beijing. It incorporates mutual granting of MFN status and a provision to facilitate the availability of Export-Import Bank credits. Key points of the agreement include:

1. Recognition that China is a developing country, clearing the way for possible granting of duty-free treatment through the Generalized System of Preferences (GSP), if China joins the IMF and the GATT
2. A framework for allowing the Bank of China to operate in the United States and for U.S. banks to operate in China
3. Chinese protection of patents, trademarks, and copyrights equivalent to that accorded by the United States
4. Termination of the agreement if the president's waiver of the Jackson-Vanek Amendment is not renewed in future years

CHINA'S IMPORT CAPABILITIES

In striving for modernization, China must import a wide range of capital equipment and technology, some of which can be obtained from the United States on competitive terms. In many ways, the United States and China complement each other economically. China's rich resources of coal, oil, minerals, and hydraulic power need exploration and development, and the United States has advanced technology in these areas. The Chinese system of construction and plant management is well below world standards. This is an area in which U.S. architects, engineers, engineer-contractors, and management advisory and consulting services could play a major role.

Agriculture is another area in which the two countries complement each other economically. Chinese agriculture is relatively backward, and some U.S. agricultural techniques are among the most advanced in the world. China imports grain and cotton, and the United States has a surplus of these agricultural products. China is interested in acquiring food processing plants and technology that U.S. industry has to offer.

Paying for this great expansion of imports will require a substantial increase in China's hard currency earnings. A major drive is now underway to expand production of export products and to improve their quality and competitiveness in Western markets. Crude oil and nonferrous minerals are both expected to become major sources of export income. However, in view of the shortage of capital and technical manpower in China, the development of these industries will have to rely heavily on foreign capital and technology.

China's large import requirements but limited export capabilities will likely cause expenditures to rise more rapidly than earnings. Exports for 1979 through 1985 are estimated to be $95 billion to $105 billion, at 1978 prices. Thus, for the seven-year period, a trade deficit ranging from $10 billion to $35 billion is expected to be generated.

To reduce deficits, Beijing also has begun a major effort to expand hard currency earnings from remittances by overseas Chinese, from a return on investments in Hong Kong, from shipping operations, and from tourism. In an effort to attract additional foreign exchange, China is setting up other international ventures.

The Chinese approach to international trade and finance now seems to be aimed at minimizing trade deficits while attempting to achieve an overall balance of payments over the plan period. The major imponderables in this formula are (a) the success China has in coping with its agricultural problems, (b) the speed with which oil and nonferrous mineral resources can be developed, (c) the amount of foreign exchange that can be generated through invisibles, especially tourism, and (d) the success China has in new undertakings such as export processing projects, compensation trade, and joint ventures.

SUMMARY

The People's Republic of China remained in a self-imposed isolation until the early 1970s. Its economy was based on the principles of self-reliance and egalitarianism. Foreign trade was minimized and foreign ideas excluded.

After Mao's death, China embarked on a vigorous program of promoting both its political and business interests in the international arena. Membership in the United Nations, the signing of the Sino-U.S. Trade Agreement (1979), and the subsequent passage of the Joint Venture Law, which opened China to Western companies, are in sharp contrast with the old isolationism.

Many international business ventures are already established in China or are negotiating with the government. Despite its immense population, China suffers from serious limitations in its ability to reciprocate with exports, hard currency, or other internationally acceptable means of payment.

FOR REVIEW AND DISCUSSION

1. How do you interpret the emphasis on self-reliance and egalitarianism by China?

2. What was Mao's foreign trade policy?

3. What significance should we attach to the change of Maoist values?

4. If you wished to export a product to China, to whom would you have to sell your idea and with whom would you have to negotiate about the price and other terms?

5. Which countries are most likely to benefit from China's compensation trade? Why?

6. How would you assess the usefulness of the hua qiao program?

7. Why have Western firms shown such extreme readiness to enter China's market under the Joint Venture Law of 1979?

8. Are we justified in regarding the 1979 Sino-U.S. Trade Agreement as a major breakthrough? Why or why not?

9. How would you rate the present status of Sino-U.S. business relations? Are there any new developments of significance?

10. Why can China increase its imports only to the extent it is able to increase its exports?

SUGGESTED READINGS FOR PART SEVEN

Armstrong, J. *Ideology, Politics and Government in the U.S.S.R.* New York: Praeger, 1978.

Eckstein, A. *China's Economic Revolution.* New York: Cambridge University Press, 1977.

Gregory, P., and Stewart, R. *Soviet Economic Structure and Performance.* New York: Harper and Row, 1974.

Katsenelinboigen, A., and de Vine, H. "Some Observations on the Plan-Market Relationship in Centrally Planned Economies." *Annals of the American Academy,* Vol. 440 (1978), 186–198.

Leeman, W. A. *Centralized and Decentralized Economic Systems.* Chicago: Rand McNally, 1977.

Mathias, W. C., ed. *Common Sense in U.S.-Soviet Trade.* Washington, D.C.: American Committee on East-West Trade, 1979.

Pipes, R. *U.S.-Soviet Relations in the Era of Détente.* Boulder: Westernview Press, 1981.

Nove, A. *The Soviet Economic System.* London: Allen, 1977.

Starr, R. F. *Communist Regimes in Eastern Europe.* Hoover Institute Press, 1977.

Stuart, D., and Tow, W., eds. *China, the Soviet Union, and the West: Strategic and Political Dimensions for the 1980s.* Boulder: Westernview Press, 1981.

Thernton, R. *China: A Political History, 1917–1980.* Boulder: Westernview Press, 1981.

Uppel, J.S. *Economic Development in South Asia.* New York: St. Martins Press, 1977.

Wagley, C. *An Introduction to Brazil.* New York: Columbia University Press, 1963.

Wilcynski, J. *Economics of Socialism.* London: n.p., 1977.

Part Eight

INTERNATIONAL INTEGRATION

*I*nternational integration had its beginning in the 1950s in the formation of the European Coal and Steel Community, which was the predecessor of the European Economic Community. The central ideas of this movement seriously challenge the accepted ideas of the supremacy of the nation state and the primacy of national independence.

From Europe, integrationist ideas have spread to all parts of the world, causing major restructurings of markets and national economies. They have become a global dynamic generating ongoing changes in the environment of international business.

In Part Eight we shall study first the European experience, in Chapter 24. Integration schemes in other world regions are surveyed in Chapter 25. These factual reviews provide the basis for an analysis of the conceptual issues relating to international integration, which are discussed in Chapter 26.

24

International Integration of European Economies

The 1950s marked a turning point in European political ideology. Until then the inviolable and overriding goal had been national separatism. The prevalent aspirations were absolute sovereignty and national independence through policies aimed at self-sufficiency and subordination of the interests or independence of others. Interdependence was avoided and minimized.

Since World War II the tide has turned. National separatism, though still in evidence, has been superseded by pan-Europeanism. Rapprochment, based on international cooperation and the mutual interests that followed, released what have become self-sustaining forces for a closer and closer commercial and industrial interdependence of European nations. The principle of supranationalism has emerged as the conceptual vehicle for and the political objective of new ideology. Under supranationalism, sovereign nations are bound by decisions that are independent of national control.

The reasons for the decline of nationalism and the rise of supranationalism go back to the ultraprotectionist economic policies of the interwar period, especially those of the depression-ridden thirties, when trade and currency restrictions, bilateral agreements, and other forms of international discrimination perverted trade and investments by substituting political criteria for economic criteria. The disintegration climaxed in World War II. When the hostilities ended, international trade and payments had reached a state of total paralysis, Europe lay in ruins, and the economies of most of the belligerents were utterly devastated. There were no victors, only the vanquished; all European participants in the conflict had suffered unimaginable destruction of life and property.

REALIGNMENTS

A way out of this catastrophe became the overriding priority. The search for it soon revealed that, despite the hostility and bitterness of the war, the European peoples had retained the strength and integrity to rise above vengeance and to unite their efforts for the benefit of all. As a result, the political forces in Europe were realigned, and pan-Europeanism emerged.

In the Soviet Union's design, postwar Europe was projected as an addendum to the communist orbit. The political disorganization and economic instability provided ideal conditions for debasing democratic institutions and introducing communist control. The Iron Curtain moved swiftly westward, enveloping Eastern European countries, one by one, from the Baltic to the Balkans—Estonia, Latvia, Lithuania, Poland, Czechoslovakia, Yugoslavia, Hungary, Bulgaria, Rumania, Albania, Eastern Finland, and East Germany, all were converted to communist rule. In other countries, too, communist activism thrust forward unmistakably. Although communist aggression, constituting a common threat, added impetus to the Pan-European unity movement, it is highly unlikely that any part of the continent could have survived as a democratic nation if the United States had not come to the rescue.

The U.S. reaction to the devastation of Europe was a massive injection of capital into West European economies to rebuild the industrial base and to repair the damage to infrastructure and agricultural production; it was called the Marshall Plan. The Marshall Plan gave $11.4 billion of U.S. economic aid to European countries with the condition that an international agency be set up by the aid recipients to administer the allocation and use of the funds. The Organization for European Economic Cooperation (OEEC) was established for this purpose. Under OEEC stewardship, the Marshall Plan was remarkably successful in rehabilitating the domestic European economies.

In the international sphere, the program was slowed by two competing views regarding the concrete actions that would best serve the economic interests of Europe. One group, dominated by the United Kingdom, advocated global free trade based on conventional economic notions. The other group argued that a global free trade scheme was beyond the powers of the OEEC to achieve and that, although it might serve as an abstract ambition to be pursued in the very long run, in the shorter run it should be subordinate to concrete measures designed specifically to deal with the existing European crisis. Its action orientation and progressive approach made this group the prime mover in the European integration movement. France emerged as its principal spokesman. The two factions could not be reconciled within the framework of the OEEC.

In 1950, the French government proposed that the coal and steel production of France and West Germany be pooled to form "common bases for economic development as a first step in the federation of Europe," with a supranational authority set up to govern the pooled industries. Nothing similar had ever before been attempted. Not even a theoretical model had envisioned international mergers of entire countries by voluntary action. The proposal led to the establishment of the European Coal and Steel Community (ECSC), with six members—France, Belgium, West Germany, Italy, Luxembourg, and the Netherlands.

The ECSC was a success. It did, indeed, establish common bases for economic development for its participant nations. Whether by design or by default, it served as a critical experiment, the pilot operation for all the other international integration schemes to follow.

THE TREATY OF ROME

After intensive consultation and negotiations the six member countries of the ECSC signed the Treaty of Rome in 1957, establishing the European Economic Community, later renamed the European Community (EC). The Treaty embodies a comprehensive plan of international economic integration. It rests on the premise that integration depends on the international mobility of goods, capital, people, and enterprises among member nations. Accordingly, the primary objectives are to create conditions conductive to this mobility by eliminating international barriers and by neutralizing environmental differences. Table 24.1 shows the basic outline of the EC. (EC membership was enlarged to ten by admission of the United Kingdom, Denmark, and Ireland in the 1970s and of Greece in 1981.)

Customarily, the administration of a treaty is handled by the foreign ministries or existing government department of the countries involved. The Treaty of Rome creates its own administrative machinery, patterned after the U.S. federal government. This supranational government has four main organs.

The European Commission

The Commission is the executive branch of the Treaty of Rome administration. The commissioners serve as heads of departments similar to those in the U.S. Cabinet: foreign affairs, agriculture, labor, and so forth. The president of the Commission is the chief executive of the European Community.

The Commission is a supranational body, not to be confused with an international body. In an international body each member is a delegate representing the interests of his own nation state. This is not the case with the Commission of the European Community. The commissioners and the commission staff are not delegates of their native countries but executives of the EC, whose duties and powers derive from the Treaty of Rome. Their allegiance is not to their home countries or the constitutions of their home countries; their allegiance is to the European Community.

The Commission is the most vital organ of the EC. It prepares the supranational laws that are to be passed by the Council and Parliament; it administers the EC's finances and prepares its budget; it also initiates policies and programs that in its judgment are necessary to attain the goals of the Treaty of Rome. The Commission is headquartered in Brussels.

Table 24.1   Integration Scheme of the Treaty of Rome

*(1) FREE MOVEMENT OF
GOODS*

To be obtained through

1.1 Trade liberalization	Successive elimination of tariffs, quotas, turnover taxes, excise duties, and all other forms of restrictions on the movements of goods among member states
1.2 Common agricultural policy	Common prices, subsidies and support programs, stockpiling and carry-forward arrangements, standards for importation and exportation, unified market organization for agricultural commodities
1.3 Common transport policy	Unification of freight rates and harmonization of shipping practices and regulatory standards of rail, highway, and inland water carriers; regulation of air and ocean transporation on Community-wide basis also if deemed advisable

*(2) FREE MOVEMENT OF
CAPITAL*

To be obtained through

2.1 Convertibility of currencies	Progressive abolition of all exchange restrictions and discriminatory treatment of capital transfers among member states based on nationality or place of residence
2.2 National-treatment principle	Opening the domestic capital market and credit system for Community-wide investment and credit transactions on a nondiscriminatory basis
2.3 Monetary cooperation	Consultations among central banks of member countries regarding rediscount rates, reserve requirements, open-market policies, and major monetary changes

*(3) FREE MOVEMENT OF
LABOR*

To be obtained through

3.1 Right to resettle	Abolition of any discrimination based on nationality regarding employment, remuneration, and working conditions; right to move about freely in all member states, to actively seek employment, and to take up residence in the country of employment
3.2 Common social policy	Equalization of remuneration for equal work in all member countries, establishment of common units of measurement for work performance and compensation; close collaboration among member governments regarding social legislation and policies including employment, labor laws, vocational training, social security, pensions, industrial safety and hygiene, laws relating to trade unions, collective bargaining, and general social welfare

Table 24.1 continues on page 430.

Table 24.1 *continued*

---

(4) FREE MOVEMENT OF
  ENTERPRISES

To be obtained through

4.1 Freedom of establishment | Right to engage in and carry on business activities, to acquire real property, to set up and manage enterprises, agencies, branches, or subsidiaries in any member country under the same conditions as its own nationals; abolition of any obstacles—legal or administrative—to the freedom of establishment by all member governments

4.2 Freedom of service | Progressive removal of restrictions affecting the industrial, commercial, artistic, and professional services supplied for remuneration by residents of other member states; right to relocate service personnel and facilities; liberalization of banking, insurance, and transport services according to common policies

(5) HARMONIZATION OF
  INTERNAL CONDITIONS

To be achieved through

5.1 Common rules of competition | Prohibition of restrictive business practices harmful to the consumer, including collusive price fixing; monopolistic limitation of production, markets, technical development, or investment; dividing markets or supplies; stifling competition through dominant bargaining strength, contractual arrangements, or any other means; requirement that companies operating in the EEC register all agreements covering more than one country

5.2 Common rules of aid | Any state aid to business which distorts competition is incompatible with EEC; aid of social character is permissible (to consumers, to disaster areas, and to depressed areas); aid to business may be approved by EEC authorities if intended to promote economic development of underdeveloped regions, to promote projects of common interest, or to remedy serious disturbances

5.3 Approximation of laws | EEC institutions issue directives for alignment of laws and governmental regulations which affect business enterprise in the Community

(6) UNIFICATION OF
  EXTERNAL RELATIONS

To be obtained through

6.1 Common custom tariff | Internal integrative links are protected by a uniform tariff system applying to all imports from nonmember countries; no national tariff schedule different from the common tariff is permissible

6.2 Common commercial policy | Foreign economic relations are structured in terms of Community-wide interests and executed in close collaboration with its supranational institutions; in tariff and trade matters the member countries act as a supranational body

---

The European Parliament

The European Parliament is a consultative rather than a legislative body; that is, it can recommend but not legislate. The actions of the European Parliament do not have a binding power on the Commission or on other EC organs. Despite this limitation, the Parliament does have a great deal of prestige, and its recommendations amount to legislation in fact if not in theory. When it passes a resolution or submits a recommendation, all organs and officials of the EC listen very carefully and try to comply with what the Parliament proposes.

Each member country elects its designated quota of members to the European Parliament, which meets alternately in Strasbourg, Luxembourg, and Brussels.

The Council of Ministers

The ultimate power to legislate is left to the Council of Ministers composed of one representative from each member country. The Council passes on all new policy matters that are not part of the Treaty or that require new legislative action. Unlike the Commission, the Council is an international organization; the nation state still holds the upper hand over the supranational system.

The Court of Justice

The judicial branch of the European Community is the Court of Justice. All disputes arising from the implementation of the Treaty of Rome are referred to the Court of Justice for adjudication; they cannot be litigated by national courts. This not only gives the Community a judicial authority for testing the legality of its policies and actions within the constitutional framework of the Treaty of Rome, but also keeps national courts from encumbering the EC with divergent interpretations and biases.

The popular belief that the Court is inaccessible to nongovernment litigants is unfounded. Private companies and individuals are permitted to bring proceedings directly to the Court if the Treaty of Rome or EC regulations are concerned. This direct access is particularly useful to multinational firms in combating restrictions of the member states. Any EC language can be used in legal proceedings before the Court of Justice.

THE EUROPEAN MONETARY SYSTEM

The Treaty of Rome contained no concrete provisions for a common currency and central bank. These matters were considered too politically sensitive at that time. People in all countries have a great emotional investment in their own monetary unit, regardless of whether they are rich or poor. However, it was always understood that sooner or later a complete monetary union will be required if the objective of a supranational economy is to be fully realized. But how this was to be brought about was a matter of conjecture for there was no precedent to follow.

The initiatives toward monetary integration by EC in its early years were quite modest. Europe was enjoying rapid economic growth and general prosperity, and there were no serious payments problems. In 1968 and 1969, however, the EC was jolted by a severe monetary crisis that pitted its two most important currencies, the German mark and French franc, against each other. Although the problem was ultimately resolved without the widely anticipated revaluation of the mark and devaluation of the franc, both governments had to resort to drastic measures to salvage the situation. From that point, the EC carried on an uninterrupted debate on monetary integration, commissioning six major studies[1] and scores of smaller projects to serve as agendas.

A formal plan of monetary integration was launched in 1979, when the Council of Ministers approved the establishment of the European Monetary System (EMS), with the European Currency Unit as its central instrument.

The *European Currency Unit (ECU)* is not a currency in the traditional sense. It is a unit of account and a means of financial control but not a medium of exchange; it is not traded or held by private parties. However, any debts, private or public, can be denominated in ECUs. The value of the ECU is based on a market basket index of the EMS currencies. The original amounts of each currency in the ECU were as follows:

West German mark	0.828	Danish krone	0.217
French franc	1.15	Dutch guilder	0.286
Belgian franc	3.66	Irish pound	0.00759
Luxembourg franc	0.14	Pound sterling	0.0885
Italian lira	109		

These shares are subject to change by unanimous vote of the EC member governments.

To calculate the value of the ECU in any single currency, it is necessary to convert the fractions of each component currency in the ECU into the desired denomination. For instance, the German mark value of the ECU is 0.828 plus the mark value of 0.217 kroner, plus the mark value of 1.15 French francs, plus the mark value of 3.66 Belgian francs, and so forth. The dollar value of the ECU is found by converting its component amounts of each currency into dollars and adding the results. The conversions are made by representative market rates of exchange.

---

1. Barre Report, Werner Report, Schiller Plan, Second Barre Report, Second Werner Report, and Fourcade Plan.

Since it is a composite, the value of the ECU in terms of any component currency fluctuates as the exchange rates fluctuate. For example, if the German mark appreciates against the other currencies, those currencies will convert into fewer marks. Adding those in the ECU sums of marks to 0.828 yields a smaller total than before the appreciation; conversely, the mark will buy a larger number of ECUs. The reverse applies if a currency depreciates against the other currencies.

The ECU varies less in value than do its individual constituent currencies. This relative stability recommends it as the unit of account for bonds and other international credit instruments. European central banks use the ECU both as the unit of account and as a reserve asset to be used in settlement of international balances. For instance, if the British central bank borrows francs from the Belgian central bank, its debt will be denominated in ECUs at the prevailing franc-ECU rate. If the German Bundesbank buys liras in the market, its claim on the Italian central bank is denominated in ECUs of the prevailing lira-ECU rate. The books of the Bundesbann would show no lira claim but an ECU claim; conversely, the books of the Italian bank will show no mark indebtedness but a debt of ECUs. The EMS central bank maintains ECU-denominated deposits at the European Monetary Cooperation Fund, which is administered by the Bank for International Settlements. This facility enables the banks to make necessary international payments in ECUs just as easily as in their respective currencies. If a country's ECU reserves do not suffice, the deficits can be paid by the equivalent amount of regular currency.

At present the EC governments are studying a proposal to strengthen the EMS by adding to it a European central bank. This bank would assume authority over exchange rate policy, liquidity, and international settlements within the EC framework. If this superbank materializes, the national central banks of the member nations will be placed in a role comparable to the regional reserve banks in the U.S. federal reserve system. That this will not happen without intense resistance seems a safe assumption.

THE IMPACT OF INTEGRATION ON EUROPEAN BUSINESS

Integration of the nine countries has profoundly changed business and its environment in the European Community. Instead of nine small markets, there is now one market of nearly 200 million people, with incomes and living standards among the very highest in the world. It has effectively removed the limitations the small national markets imposed on many industries.

Company Size

On the production level, the scale is no longer restricted by the limited ability of any one country to consume but can be increased many times if mass production raises productivity and reduces costs. Since the advantages of mass production vary from industry to industry, the gains from integration are more pronounced for some industries than for others. However, all industries are affected significantly, partly because most European companies were small not only for economic but also for historical and institutional reasons and could, therefore, gain from an increase in size, and partly because new production technologies such as automation and computerization have been pushing the production-cost curve further and further to the left, making it necessary to increase the production scale accordingly in order to enable a plant to enjoy optimal costs.

Figure 24.1 provides a graphic explanation of the changed outlook in the cost-output relationship caused by integration. Companies in the fields in which production techniques have remained stable have benefited as shown in Part A, by sliding down the cost curve from the national cost level, which was dictated by the limited ability of the national market to absorb output, and by adjusting their output as near to the optimal per unit cost as competition and other market forces permit.

For companies in the fields in which mechanization and automation have replaced labor, the opportunities for cost reduction have been twofold, as shown in Part B: by sliding down the curve, as in Part A, and by shifting from the old to the new production technology, as illustrated by the right-hand curve, and by reducing production costs to the new optimum level. It is difficult to imagine any industry that has been completely immune to new techniques.

To a greater or lesser degree, therefore, all productive sectors have been affected by integration. That all companies have not exhibited equal ability to adjust to the changed conditions is a fact that needs no documentation. There have been casualties and glittering successes. The process continues. In some industries productive assets age quickly and rejuvenation of plant occurs after relatively short intervals; in others the life is longer not only because of the large initial investments involved but often also because the production cycle itself has a long duration. For example, in the aerospace field many products (aircraft, missiles, boosters) require seven or more years of engineering, prototyping, and manufacturing before the final product is available for consumption. Five- to ten-year cycles are not uncommon in other high technology industries. This means that the full impact of the integration on production cost takes a long time to run its full course. It can be argued that this process has only begun.

Meanwhile, the expansion of scale is being sought through modernization and new plant capacity and, more recently, through corporate mergers and cooperative industrial ventures. Thousands of firms are reported to have pooled their resources under a variety of legal arrangements. Company size has become the latest word in European executive jargon and is likely to remain so for the foreseeable future. Not only production costs but also such things as large cash flows, procurement advantages, research and development capabilities, and marketing strength preoccupy European industrialists.

A. BEFORE INTEGRATION

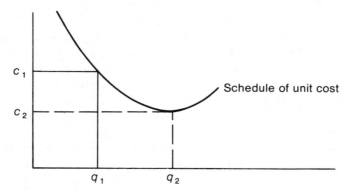

Schedule of unit cost

Legend

q_1 = maximum national output
q_2 = optimal output
c_1 = national cost per unit
c_2 = optimal cost per unit

B. AFTER INTEGRATION

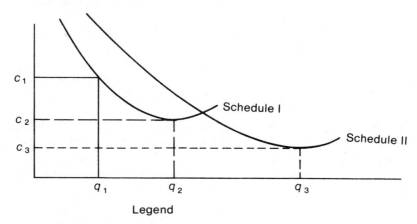

Schedule I

Schedule II

Legend

c_1 = national cost per unit
c_2 = optimal cost per unit
c_3 = optimal cost per unit for large-scale (optimum-size) plant
q_1 = maximum national output
q_2 = optimum output of existing plant
q_3 = optimum output for large-scale (optimum-size) plant

Figure 24.1   Impact of Integration on Production Costs

Competition

Mergers do not violate the Treaty of Rome so long as the common rules of competition are not broken. The official policy requires that the EC market satisfy two conditions: first, that there are enough independent companies to ensure competition and, second, that these units are large enough to handle research and marketing problems efficiently.

The EC regulations place no other limitation on company size. Rather, the test for legality is the effect a merger has upon the production and distribution of goods. If a merger contributes to efficiency of business operations, it is legal; if not, or if it obstructs the freedom of action or choice of consumers or suppliers, it is illegal.

The same interpretation has been adapted to most other aspects of cooperation among business firms, including cartels. In the EC conception, monopolies are just another form of economic organization. The EC antimonopoly code differentiates between bad and good cartels, something not possible under the U.S. antitrust statutes. An example of a good cartel is an agreement among small manufacturers of marine paint that was sanctioned by EC authorities. An official explained this action as follows:

> The marine paint market is shared by the big international groups and many small manufacturers. The big groups operate sales agencies in all major ports so that the purchaser can buy the same product everywhere, a selling point of great importance for paint repair work, for instance. This advantage is not available to small manufacturers, which restricts their ability to compete. Now, a number of small companies from several countries got the idea of offsetting the disadvantage by developing paint jointly, laying down quality standards, and selling under the same trade mark. This project, which transforms small firms of merely local importance into serious competitors for the international group, was authorized by the Commission since we expect it to stimulate competition.[2]

As this example shows, collusion among competing firms is not automatically outlawed under the EC code. The authorities reserve the right to assess the actual impact of a proposed cooperative arrangement among firms and then either approve or disapprove its implementation. It is the expected outcome that counts, not the legal form.

Marketing

Professionally managed, large-scale marketing institutions were few in pre-EC Europe. Those that existed were limited to major metropolitan centers. The marketing revolution that the United States experienced in the 1920s and 1930s had bypassed Europe. The concepts of mass merchandising, rapid inventory turnover, low per unit markups, self-service, and coordinated promotion strategies were generally unknown or neglected. Much of the retailing and wholesaling structure had resisted any change for generations. Brief descriptions of the French and German marketing systems illustrate the problems.

---

2. Personal interview.

The French Marketing Tradition   The French preintegration pattern was characterized on a retail level by extreme specialization by product. That system had developed when specialization was first discovered to be an important means of increasing economic efficiency, and the French went farther in this respect than anybody else in the world. This specialization on retail level was so extreme that, for example, to get the ingredients for an ordinary lunch it was necessary to go to six or seven different stores. You could not buy pork and beef in the same store, nor could you buy cake and bread in the same store. The same was true of other types of goods. Such a high degree of specialization requires different supply policies, inventory policies, pricing, promotion, and all other marketing policies from those used in multiproduct stores that are typical in U.S. retailing.

On the wholesale level, the French system was characterized by extreme geographic centralization. The center was Paris, and all the outer areas, the provinces, depended upon the Paris wholesalers. This centralization was almost absurd for agricultural goods and food stuffs. Though most of them were produced outside of Paris, they all were funneled to the Paris market and then redistributed back to the provinces. Such extreme centralization had far-reaching implications for marketing management. Paris was the decision making center, and the costs of shipping to and from Paris were the decisive cost elements. Physical distribution, transportation, brokerage fees, middleman profit margins, and all other standards were set in Paris and universally applied throughout the French wholesaling system.

The German Marketing System   German retailing was quite similar to the French, but not so extreme. The specialization by product line did exist, but it was not carried to such an extreme as in France. On the wholesaling level, the German system had a very high degree of functional centralization. In Germany it was not Berlin or any other particular city that was the wholesaling center. There were competing centers, and many large cities served as regional wholesaling headquarters. But functionally, the marketing system in its entirety revolved around the wholesaling firm. The wholesaler devised the strategy, set distribution patterns, determined prices, and dominated the entire marketing activity.

Figure 24.2 (page 438) illustrates how the initiative for marketing action flowed to the right to the retailers and through them to consumers and to the left to manufacturers and other suppliers. It was the wholesaling firm that took the initiative and had the power to push a product forward to the consumers and to induce the producers to desired action.

This dominance of the wholesaler helps to explain one of the basic characteristics of German marketing, namely, the relative passivity compared to U.S. business in reference to promotion, advertising, and salesmanship. There is much less of all that in the German system as well as in the French system, for wholesalers have felt that because of their dominant position they really did not need to promote, advertise, and sell aggressively. The other members of the marketing channel, realizing their dependent position, accepted the system.

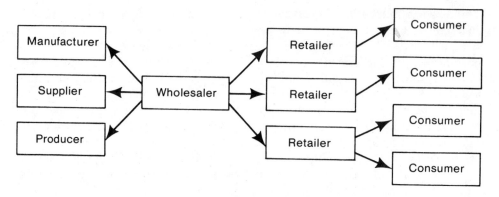

Figure 24.2   Initiative for Marketing Action in West Germany

Marketing in Other Countries   The marketing systems of the other original EC members were essentially variations of the French and German systems. Italy, Belgium, and Luxembourg fit closely into the French pattern, and the Netherlands into the German one. In many respects these marketing systems were utterly inadequate for the requirements of mass production and the expansion of industrial activity that the Treaty of Rome engendered. Family-based retail establishments, some of which had remained unchanged for four or five generations, and traditionally-determined marketing channels and pricing practices had acquired a social acceptance that repelled change.

Integration provided the impetus for a massive overhaul of the distributive system. The European marketing revolution is now at its final stage. The hard shell of traditionalism that for generations circumscribed European marketing has been forced to make room for modern approaches, merchandising methods, and wholesale and retail institutions.

Labor Cost

Despite increased mobility, labor has become increasing more costly relative to other factor prices. The increase is primarily due to the high level of investment and business activity, which has resulted in a scarcity of labor and has greatly increased the bargaining position of trade unions. In general, the rise in wages has outstripped the productivity inputs. When the Treaty of Rome was signed European wages were 30 percent to 40 percent of U.S. wages. At present the two are in an approximate parity. As a result, mechanization and automation have gained constantly as capital has been substituted for labor.

SUMMARY

Since World War II, pan-Europeanism has gained a growing following. Its most concrete expression is the European Community, which integrated the national economies of its nine member countries into a supranational economic system.

The integration model calls for unrestricted international mobility of goods, capital, labor, and enterprise within a framework of supranational politics. Most of these objectives have already been achieved. Supranational agencies have been set up to administer the integrated systems. The European Monetary System has also been developed.

Due to the integration process, European business has changed in numerous ways: the size of firms has increased, mass production has encouraged mechanization and automation, rules of competition and market behavior have been standardized, the dividing influences of traditional marketing practices have been reduced, and national statutes and regulatory codes have been harmonized to facilitate Community-wide business activities.

FOR REVIEW AND DISCUSSION

1. Describe the political and economic forces that contributed to the emergence of the EC.

2. Analyze the integration model of the Treaty of Rome presented in Table 24.1. Rate the relative significance of its different components, assess which aspects are the most difficult to carry out, and compare it with the theory of international trade.

3. In which respects, if any, is the EC already a supranational system? Consider trade and trade controls, investments, banking, monetary policy, transportation, travel, labor, and any other aspects that seem significant.

4. Why has international integration caused European businesses to grow in size? Why has the growth been greater in some sectors than in others?

5. How does the EC legislative process differ from a nation state's legislative process?

6. If you were designing an international integration plan, would you include a judicial body such as the Court of Justice or would you let the member countries' court systems handle legal matters? Why?

7. Compare the French, German, and U.S. marketing traditions.

8. Do you agree that monopoly power can be used either constructively or destructively? Elaborate.

9. What is the current status of the European Monetary System?

10. Would you recommend that the East European communist countries be invited to join the EC? Why or why not?

25

International Integration in Global Context

*I*nternational integration is a means, not an end. Though its immediate objective is to replace small national markets with a large supranational market, the long-term objectives are to facilitate specialization of production, economies of scale, increased rate of growth, and more trade. Since these benefits are anxiously sought by all nations, especially by the small and economically backward LDCs, the Treaty of Rome has become the model for a global movement from national economic separatism toward supranational integration. No part of the world, not even the communist countries, has been able to resist the promises of integration.

In this chapter we shall survey the dynamics, not so much of the legal and formal aspects as of the economic and political aspects, of this ongoing transformation of world markets and international business relations.

INTERNATIONAL INTEGRATION IN LATIN AMERICA

Initially, international integration in Latin America took two parallel forms, the Latin American Free Trade Association (LAFTA) and the Central American Common Market (CACM). Subsequently, the Andean Common Market has been added. These are not mere imitations of the European Community. The impetus for closer economic cooperation among the Latin American countries has come from the grave economic problems that have retarded the economic development and social modernization of the nations of this continent.

The Latin American Free Trade Association

LAFTA was established by the Treaty of Montevideo, signed in 1960 by Argentina, Brazil, Chile, Mexico, Paraguay, Peru, and Uruguay. Colombia, Ecuador, and Bolivia joined LAFTA later. The objectives of the Treaty of Montevideo can be classified as short-term, intermediate, and long-term goals.

441

The short-term objectives of the Treaty are the expansion of present markets and trade and the gradual elimination of barriers to intracontinental trade. The intermediate objectives call for maximum utilization of available production factors, more effective coordination of the development programs of the different production sectors, and aid to members with the least advanced economies. The long-term objectives of the Treaty are progressive complementarity and integration of the national economies and gradual creation of the conditions necessary for a complete economic community patterned after the EC. A peculiar feature of the entire Treaty is that every step is left open for further negotiation and revision.

Provisions of the Treaty   The member countries are required to eliminate, with respect to substantially all of their reciprocal trade, the duties, charges, and other restrictions on imports originating in the territory of any other member. Unlike the Treaty of Rome, the Treaty of Montevideo has no concrete schedules. The elimination of duties and other restrictions is to be achieved by means of periodic negotiations.

The fact that a free trade area is the form of integration provided under the Treaty means that each nation retains its own national tariffs against third countries, and that there is no requirement to establish a common external tariff. The Treaty does, however, recognize the need for reconciling import and export regimes as well as the treatment accorded to goods, services, and capital coming from outside the area. The Treaty also provides for "progressively closer coordination of industrialization policies" and the negotiation of "mutual agreements on complementarity by industrial sectors," that is, for fostering international specialization and reducing duplication of industries in different member countries.

In sum, therefore, the signatories to the LAFTA treaty seek to create a free trade zone where goods produced in any signatory country may be traded anywhere within the zone. This freedom applies to MNCs and indigenous firms alike. Since MNCs tend to emphasize the economies of scale, it is hoped the mass market will attract foreign capital and technology to manufacturing industries. This hope has already been validated by experience.

Loopholes   The Treaty provides a number of significant escape clauses. A contracting party may impose provisional nondiscriminatory restrictions on imports originating in the area if such imports have serious repercussions on productive activities of vital importance to that country's economy. A country may also impose restrictions to correct an overall unfavorable balance of payments. Furthermore, agriculture is accorded special treatment to meet deficits in domestic production and to equalize the price of imported and domestic production. Normal supplies of agricultural goods are to be made available to consumers without disrupting regular production activities.

Promoting Complementarity   The principles of reciprocity and complementarity are central to the treaty. According to the *reciprocity principle*, each country should reduce import restrictions, with the expectation that concessions given and received will result in a more or less equal expansion of that country's imports and exports with the area as a whole. The underlying purpose is to avoid situations in which increased zonal trade gives rise to increased balance of payments deficits or in which a country receives benefits from increased export trade at the expense of the industrialization program of some other member.

The *principle of complementarity* aims at promoting balanced economic growth for the zone as a whole. It recognizes that many countries cannot widen the industrial base within the confines of national markets. Hence, industrialization requires broader supranational markets and specialization and complementarity within Latin America with respect to various industries. Complementarity is to occur by means of planning and negotiation rather than by means of market forces alone. Various countries will specialize in the production of various finished products and intermediate goods, selling them in the entire LAFTA zone.

There is a priority on cooperation and planned expansion of trade and national output and a de-emphasis on competition. There is a deep concern for the coordination of industrialization policies of the various LAFTA countries, for the promotion and protection of their industries, and little mention of the role of competition in promoting efficiency.

Administrative Structure   The Treaty creates two administrative organs, the Conference of the Contracting Parties and the Standing Executive Committee. The Conference is the supreme organ of the association and is charged with implementing the Treaty of Montevideo, laying down rules of procedure, promoting negotiations, appointing the professional staff, and making other administrative policy decisions. It is composed of delegations from each of the contracting countries; each delegation has one vote. The Conference may make decisions only if two-thirds of the contracting parties are present and no negative votes are cast.

The delegations making up the Conference are representatives of their governments and are subject to control by the latter. They are not delegates to a supranational body acting independently of their governments, as are the EC delegates to the European Parliament. Therefore, to the extent that governments are subject to the pressures of special interest groups, the Conference delegates are subject to these same pressures. Decisions made or not made by the Conference are very much the result of pressure politics of the member countries.

There is no machinery whatsoever for the enforcement of LAFTA provisions or decisions. The EC provides for the European Court of Justice; the LAFTA treaty does not provide any judicial structure. Hence, adherence to LAFTA policies is, in essence, voluntary, one reason its results have been far less than impressive.

The Standing Executive Committee, headquartered in Montevideo, is the permanent operating organ of LAFTA. It is responsible for supervising the implementation of the provisions of the present treaty and handles all house-keeping chores of the organization; it has no policy making powers.

The Central American Common Market

The General Treaty on Central American Economic Integration, the basic instrument of the Central American Common Market, was signed in Managua, Nicaragua, in 1960. This Treaty includes Costa Rica, El Salvador, Guatemala, Honduras, and Nicaragua.

Main Provisions The treaty provides for free intermember internal trade and for a common external tariff. The signatories are committed not to grant tariff concessions to countries outside the CACM on imported goods that are also produced within the CACM. Duties may be levied on commodities imported from within the CACM only if the goods are subject to internal taxation; the duty may not exceed the amount of the internal tax. Countries may not sell within the CACM at a price lower than the domestic price of the goods (antidumping or price nondiscrimination), and direct or indirect export subsidies are forbidden. The treaty provides for the construction and main-tenance of communication and transportation facilities and for the standard-ization of rates charged for their services; for nondiscriminatory treatment of capital investments made by nationals of any country within the CACM; and for industrial integration of the several economies.

The Governing Institutions The general administration of the CACM is carried out by three bodies: the Central American Economic Council, the Executive Council, and the Permanent Secretariat. The Central American Economic Council is the governing body for the coordination of the economic policy of the contracting states. It is composed of the ministers of economic affairs of the five countries. The Executive Council acts as the steering com-mittee of the Economic Council. Its function is to implement the Managua Treaty in conformity with the basic principles established by the Economic Council. This body is composed of one delegate and one alternate appointed by each of the contracting parties. Resolutions are adopted by majority vote. The Permanent Secretariat handles all operational business.

The Andean Common Market

The Andean Common Market was formed in late 1968 by five countries along the west coast of South America—Bolivia, Chile, Colombia, Equador, and Peru. The thinking behind Andean integration was that, as LAFTA had progressed at a moderate pace mainly because it had been difficult to achieve agreement between countries of such diverse economic strength as Argentina and Brazil on one end and Bolivia and Equador on the other end, the Andean countries, all being small and having more in common, could proceed more expeditiously.

Experience has proven this optimism justified. The ACM has, despite very significant economic variations among the individual countries of the group, outpaced other Latin American integration schemes. It has been particularly successful in promoting trade and establishing unified regulatory standards for MNC activities and technology transfers.

BASIC ECONOMIC PROBLEMS OF LATIN AMERICA

The economic integration schemes in Latin America should be regarded as a response to basic economic difficulties that have burdened the Latin American countries for decades. The most critical of these are balance of payments deficits and an inadequate rate of industrialization and development. The architects of the integration schemes hoped that development could be accelerated and balance of payments difficulties alleviated through the creation of supranational markets.

International Payments

Latin American countries face both cyclical and continuous balance of payments problems; that is, they have experienced great instability in their export earnings, and they have had great difficulties in achieving continuous growth of exports in terms of value.

The instability in export earnings is a consequence of the commodities that Latin America exports. These countries are primarily producers of food and raw materials (primary products), which comprise a very large percentage of their exports. Like other LDCs, many of the Latin countries are heavily dependent upon one or two commodities for export earnings. For example, exports of coffee and bananas account for about 80 percent of Central America's export earnings; crude oil accounts for about 90 percent of Venezuela's export earnings; and coffee accounts for about 80 percent of Colombia's export earnings.

Earnings of primary products fluctuate widely as a consequence of violent shifts in supply or demand or in both. All the disturbing factors that were discussed in Chapter 19 are at work. Demand for raw materials fluctuates because of business cycles in the industrialized countries. In periods of recession, demand for raw materials falls greatly, causing prices and export earnings to plummet. Demand for foodstuff tends to be less volatile, but supply depends on the vagaries of weather.

Effects of Economic Integration in Latin America

The rate of economic development is regarded as too low by Latin American policy makers. Although living standards in Latin America are on the average higher than those in Africa and Asia, they are still low relative to the Western industrialized countries.

Accelerated Growth   Not only is per capita income low, but the rate of population growth is extremely high, requiring high rates of economic growth in order to prevent per capita income from falling. Population growth for Latin America as a whole has averaged 2.5 percent per year. Again, there are substantial variations of rates among countries, with population in Costa Rica growing at 3.6 percent and that in Paraguay growing at 1.5 percent. But generally, if the people of Latin America are to enjoy a higher standard of living, income must grow in excess of the rate of population growth. To state the problem in another way, the rapid population growth makes rapid economic expansion imperative if living standards are to improve rather than deteriorate.

The integration of markets has apparently paid off in accelerated growth. Between 1960 and 1980 the GNP of Latin America virtually tripled. This was more rapid growth than that experienced by the industrial nations. As a percent of the combined GNP of the first world, Latin America GNP was 6 percent in 1960 and over 8 percent in 1980.

Enlarged Markets   A major factor limiting economic development has been the inadequacy of export earnings. The Latin countries must both satisfy demand for manufactured consumer goods and diversity production. When incomes rise, demand for imports tends to rise even faster. Without a commensurate expansion of exports, because of low price and income elasticities of demand for primary products, the terms of trade deteriorate and deficits undermine the balance of payments.

Historically, Latin countries tried to counterbalance export limitations by restricting imports. Like many other LDCs, they adopted policies of import substitution. By erecting tariffs and other barriers against imports they tried to stimulate the development of their own manufacturing. These policies were initially rather unsuccessful. The national markets were small and the protected manufacturers tended to use antiquated technologies to produce low quality but high price goods. In more recent years these problems have started to disappear. The integration schemes embodied in LAFTA, CACM, and ACM, have enlarged the markets and envigorated competition.

As a consequence, Latin industries have become more economic and cost efficient. Though they still encounter supply bottlenecks when they need imported inputs, they are doing much better than in the 1960s.

Formerly, export earnings were used mainly to import consumer goods. More recently, a growing share of the export earnings has been used to purchase the capital goods and intermediate inputs required for the manufacturing sectors. When the export earnings are at their low ebb, however, manufacturing production may have to be curtailed.

The Pro-Integration Argument

The Latin American economic integration schemes were designed to assist participating countries in overcoming their export and domestic market barriers to growth. In fact, they have significantly alleviated the problems. The schemes are now regarded as engines of growth and development. But there is still much disagreement over integration, especially concerning its future impact.

Those who see great potential in the integration schemes view them as sources of dynamic change. The major obstacle to industrialization in Latin America in the past has been the absence of a sufficiently large market to allow manufacturing industries to operate at a high volume, low cost capacity. Because of the market limitations, many industries never became established and others were unable to expand. The markets were limited both by the size and the low purchasing power of the individual nation's population. The industries that did exist were low volume, high cost operations that could not compete in export markets.

The supranational markets are changing that. The various countries can now specialize and cooperate in the development of different industries. This expands the flow of imports and exports among members and strengthens trade with the outside world. These trends reduce not only the countries' vulnerability to the vicissitudes of international trade but also their dependence on the export of primary products. As a result, their export earnings can grow and stabilize.

The Anti-Integration Argument

Those who prefer national separatism see little further potential in the supranational markets. Most Latin American imports come from the United States and Europe, not from other countries on the continent.

There are also a number of provisions in the LAFTA Treaty that are either contradictory to general trade liberalization or that allow the individual countries to avoid their commitments. Of particular importance is the provision that exempts agricultural commodities. Since these countries are overwhelmingly producers and exporters of agricultural goods, exemption of these goods from the free trade provisions excludes most of the economy from the supranational system.

The treaty allows LAFTA members to erect barriers to trade if increased interzonal trade causes serious harm to industries vital to the development of their economies. The countries are also permitted to erect trade barriers to correct serious balance of payments deficits. Capitalists in Latin America have historically enjoyed heavy protection, and many of the older industries have been viable only behind high protective tariff walls. Therefore, the probabilities are high that the escape clauses in the Montevideo Treaty will be invoked sooner or later.

Some of the more doctrinaire critics speculate that the supranational schemes will be more trade diverting than trade creating. In general, a country will gain if integration arrangements create additional trade, and it will lose if integration decreases trade or diverts imports from low cost to high cost sources. Since many Latin American industrial undertakings have been high cost operations, the free trade zones will result in the member countries buying more from high cost producers within the zone and less from low cost producers outside the zone.

Integration and Development

The success of Latin American integration is critically linked to the success of general economic development. If these countries are successful in their development efforts, they will not be so hesitant to participate in extended foreign trade. If their policies are not successful and their industries do not prove viable in international markets, then these countries may again retreat behind protective walls.

Balance of payments remains the most critical variable. The area has suffered a persistent deficit in its external transactions in goods and services. In recent years this deficit has increased, due primarily to the greater cost of oil, inflated prices of industrial inputs, and higher interest rates on external loans. The optimists predict that the industrial development that integration engenders will help export earnings to correct the payments deficits in the long run. The pessimists disagree.

In a very real sense, this is a circular condition in which success breeds success and failure feeds on failure, a highly interdependent situation in which successful development and favorable balance of payments enhance the chances for success, and successful integration efforts accelerate development. Successful economic policies in Latin America have been heavily dependent on export earnings, which come mainly from the industrialized countries. If the countries can maintain and build upon these markets their success is assured. If not, a spiral of deterioration will be set in motion. The most important aid that the industrial countries can extend to Latin America is to maintain cyclical stability and to buy more of their export products.

INTERNATIONAL INTEGRATION IN AFRICA

Africa is a vast amalgam of diverse peoples, terrains, and resources. The continent has been subjected to a wide variety of influences. Colonialism on the part of several European cultures has been a salient factor in African history. With resources that are both diverse and rich, Africa suffers from awesome underdevelopment that is only accentuated by the proximity of the wealthy European countries.

Africa is thus a fertile field for ideological conflict. There is a tremendous desire to emulate Western successes through economic progress; there is an equally powerful commitment to preserve African individuality. Can both these ideals be attained? Are modern industrial civilization and the indigenous cultures of Africa congruent or conflicting? These are the perplexing questions that give cohesion to the otherwise pluralistic societies and policies of African peoples.

African Nationalism

A most pervasive political force in contemporary Africa is nationalism. It affects all institutions, including international business enterprises. At a time when nationalism in the Western world is in decline, the strong emphasis on nationalism in Africa may seem strange. African leaders, however, see in a strong national awareness a rational means for important ends.

Internally, it is a means of nation building, of overcoming a lack of national identification among the tribally factionalized population. As such, nationalism is expected to supply the counterforce to the tribalism that still divides the loyalties of most Africans, and to give meaning to the irrational borders by which African independence was parceled out. The borders of most African countries mark nothing else than the previous colonial holdings of European countries. There is seldom any ethnic, cultural, or economic rationality to these borders.

Externally, nationalism is a means of eradicating colonialism; of removing the dominant influence of industrial nations and inspiring indigenous leadership and initiative. This is a costly ambition. Its price includes the loss of the technology, capital, and trade that has been the essence of the neocolonial linkage. Africans believe that international integration among African states will provide a superior alternative to the old linkage.

The Need for Integration

The importance to African nations of international integration derives not only from the basic economic factors, but also from political and social considerations that cannot be easily separated from each other. The basic motive on the economic level comes from the realization that for all but a few of the larger African countries, some form of international cooperation is an absolute prerequisite for economic development, due to the smallness of their economies.

Africa's political geography is conspicuous with its large number of small independent countries. Nearly all of these emerged from the collapse of colonialism after World War II. Their long subjugation to foreign rule, with its economic exploitation and social mistreatment, has left lasting scars on the continent's consciousness. Abolition of the remaining colonial influence and the prevention of its recurrence are, therefore, essential to any viable politics in African countries. This is a precarious requirement, for the point at which constructive international cooperation ends and undue foreign influence starts is not readily ascertained. Extremism against any non-African influence has at times already led to international isolation of some African countries. It is to be hoped that these are exceptions rather than indications of continental trends.

The Organization for African Unity

Integration in Africa has been developing along two main lines: pan-African schemes, which encompass most of the continent, and regional plans, which are limited to a few neighboring nations.

The Organization for African Unity (OAU) represents the main pan-African integration effort. It was created in 1963 by the Treaty of Addis Ababa, which was ratified by 39 African countries. The purposes of the OAU are:

1. To promote unity and solidarity of the African countries
2. To coordinate and intensify the countries' cooperation and efforts to achieve a better life for the peoples of Africa
3. To defend the countries' sovereignty, territorial integrity, and independence
4. To eradicate all forms of colonialism
5. To promote international cooperation, with due regard for the Charter of the United Nations and the Universal Declaration of Human Rights

To implement these goals, the charter provides that member states shall coordinate and harmonize their general policies, especially in the following fields:

1. Political and diplomatic cooperation
2. Economic cooperation, including transportation and communication
3. Education and cultural cooperation
4. Health, sanitation, and nutritional cooperation
5. Scientific and technical cooperation
6. Cooperation for defense and security

The charter also specifies a policy of nonalignment with any other bloc.

A valuable by-product of this cooperation was the creation of the African Development Bank. However, in other respects the OAU has little to show. There are no specific timetables for achieving the goals set forth in its charter. In fact, a realistic appraisal of the OAU since its inception shows that progress toward its goals has been almost negligible. The most tangible results have been the creation of study groups and of further meetings in order to discuss more concrete proposals for the future. The Organization has succeeded, however, in presenting a somewhat unified voice for Africa in the world forum.

Regional Integration

Within the continentwide objectives and principles of the OAU several regional integration plans have been attempted. In the 1960s it appeared that regional integration would soon overshadow the OAU as several integration plans came into being. The ex-colonies of France created the West African Customs Union but promptly broke into two rival factions, the Entente and the Central African Economic and Customs Union. The goals of both organizations are the elimination of trade barriers, equitable distribution of industrial investments, coordination of development programs, and common policies in dealing with nonmember countries.

The ex-colonies of Great Britain (Kenya, Tanzania, and Uganda) formed the East African Community; and the Arab states in Northern Africa set up the Arab League for political cooperation and the Arab Common Market to integrate their economies. Disruptions, political ferment, and frequent hostilities have caused repeated postponements, extended periods of dormancy, and even dissolution.

The fate of the East African Community (EAC) serves as a dramatic illustration. In its early years, the EAC showed remarkable results:

1. A common customs tariff was established.
2. All trade restrictions between members were abolished.
3. Monetary and exchange controls were standardized, and fiscal and monetary policies coordinated.
4. Three supranational public service corporations were set up (the East African Railway Corporation, East African Ports and Telecommunications Corporation, and East African Airways Corporation); these corporations provided nearly all transport and communication services in the EAC.
5. The East African Development Bank was set up to boost economic growth.
6. EAC-wide services were organized for tax collection, statistical censuses, and research.

This program was implemented through a close personal relationship among the three heads of state, Kenyetta of Kenya, Obate of Uganda, and Nyerere of Tanzania. The overthrow of Obote by Idi Amin reversed the trend. Political relations between Uganda and Tanzania deteriorated rapidly. Restrictions were reinstated on intra-EAC trade and financial transactions, community agencies were dissolved, and ultimately, in 1977, the EAC treaty itself was canceled. This was subsequently followed by armed hostilities and the removal of Idi Amin from power with the help of Tanzanian forces. The return of Obote to the Ugandan presidency in 1980 may have provided an opportunity to restart this integration effort.

Similar, though less drastic, political conflicts have plagued other African integration programs. Intertribal tensions have contributed to the instability. In Nigeria and Ethiopia full-fledged civil wars have been fought. In many other countries, including Zaire, Cameroon, Kenya, Rwanda, Burundi, and Sudan, just to name a few, outbursts of tribal tensions have seriously limited governmental options.

In Southern Africa, a customs union and a de facto currency union exist between the Republic of South Africa and the smaller states of Lesotho, Botswana, and Swaziland. The movement of labor from the lesser developed states to the more industrially advanced Republic of South Africa is permitted under these agreements. Aside from these factors, however, there is little desire among the nations involved to achieve any closer form of economic integration.

The Dynamics of Necessity

From a practical business standpoint, regional integration in Africa so far may have seemed rather illusory, much more smoke than fire. However, the relative lack of progress does not mean that the integration movement can be written off. Quite the contrary, the will to succeed appears to be stronger than ever. The ability to exercise the will, lacking in the past, is gradually being acquired. The balance between the factors that retard integration and those that promote it is shifting under the massive pressures for economic necessities and industrial development.

The internal forces that are working for integration among the nations of Africa include:

1. A consciousness on the part of African leaders that the relatively small size of many African nations, their uneven resource endowments, the small size of their markets, and the distortions in the pattern of economic activity inherited from the colonial period seriously inhibit attempts at development purely on the national scale, and that cooperation might lead to a widening of the horizon of such development
2. Political considerations, which take the form of a desire to present a collective African front in matters affecting the continent as a whole
3. A strong desire to replace the heavy metropolitan-colonial orientation in the cooperative ventures of the colonial period with increased cooperation among African nations themselves
4. The inclusion of timetables that allow the countries involved to make the necessary adjustments that integration efforts entail
5. Common monetary systems and provision for certain common services, such as transportation and communications systems

In the early years of independence, most African nations remained economically dependent on their ex-mother countries. Their economies were geared to the needs of the ex-colonial power. Their currency was tied to it, trade was limited to it, and even the schools remained as they had been under colonial rule. Although many of these characteristics are still detectable, they have had to yield to new trends and developments during the postcolonial years. Replacing the imported legacies of the colonial era with indigenous institutions, values, and practices is a high priority in all Africa. The breakup of the colonial rigidities clears the scene for more flexible and need oriented structures.

INTERNATIONAL INTEGRATION IN ASIA

Except for China and India (which are integrated systems—see page 456), international integration in Asia is still in the formative stages. A number of plans, agreements, and organizations have been established to promote regional cooperation and integration, but none has reached an operational stage. The more important ones include the Association of South-East Asia (ASA), the Maphilindo (RCD), the Pacific Free Trade Area plan (PAFTA), the Ministerial Conference for Economic Development of South-East Asia, the Conference of South-East Asia on Development, under the auspices of Japan, and the Association of South-East Asian Nations (ASEAN). In addition, business and industry groups from five Pacific countries (Australia, Canada, Japan, New Zealand, and the United States) have formed the Pacific Basin Economic Cooperation Organization for the purpose of providing private enterprise an international institution for overall economic development of the Pacific basin.

All these organizations reflect an increasing recognition of the need for integrating national economies in Asia. Progress, however, has been retarded due to lack of any organic relationship among the different organizations; none has the ability to go it alone without adequate political or financial support.

To provide a comprehensive organizational framework the Asian and Pacific Council (ASPAC) was formed. Its members include Australia, New Zealand, Korea, Japan, Taiwan, Malaysia, Thailand, and the Philippines, with a total population of about 290 million. Other countries of the region may join if they wish. Burma, Indonesia, and Singapore have already indicated interest in eventual membership. A major purpose of ASPAC is to work toward an Asian common market. Preparatory studies and negotiations to this end on both government and nongovernment levels have been going on for some time.

The fact that the membership includes both advanced and primitive countries greatly complicates the matter. In a detailed study of complementarity, special country bias, and intensity in trade flows between advanced western Pacific countries and selected developing countries in Asia and the Pacific, Drysdale reaches the conclusion that economic integration among Australia, Japan, and New Zealand would be particularly beneficial, since they already have a high complementarity of exports and imports. He further concludes:

> The developing countries in the Asian-Pacific regions are relatively much more important to the trade of these two countries than they are to the world at large. . . . Thus, there is a strong case for coupling any policy initiative by advanced western Pacific nations with the extension or adoption of trade policies specially designed to accommodate the needs of developing countries in the Asian-Pacific region.[1]

1. Peter Drysdale, "Japan, Australia, New Zealand: The Prospect for Western Pacific Economic Integration," *The Economic Record* 45:327–329, 1969.

FROM NATIONAL TO SUPRANATIONAL ECONOMIES

Where will international economic integration ultimately lead? Is the nation state and its sovereignty at bay? Has a new organization of the lands and peoples of the world started to replace what has been taken for granted for generations? Are we witnessing the end of an era and the beginning of another? Questions such as these surface with rising frequency as plans and programs for supranational systems proliferate. Though no one can profess with certainty the outcome of the international dynamic, raising these questions is not just speculation. The answers bear on the very foundations of the world markets and business systems in general.

If the integration of national markets and national economies signifies a reorganization of the global structure of markets and production systems, all aspects of international and, for that matter, domestic business will be fundamentally affected. The first to feel the impact are makers of long-term decisions, such as industrial investors and development planners, whose time frames extend into the future. Corporate strategists, lending institutions, and international carriers, too, must model the long-term future in time to prepare for its demands.

The Nation State: A Stage of Political Evolution

To say that the nation state may one day vanish may strike us as preposterous. Economic and political theories take the nation state system as something immutable, a fundamental fact of life. The possibility that this global framework may not be a constant or static system but a dynamic process is nowhere contemplated. In this, the theoreticians have ignored history.

Our nation state system is nothing but the latest stage of world organization, and its lifespan may actually turn out to be relatively short compared to others. Certainly, the feudal order from which the nations evolved lasted nearly ten times longer than the nation state has existed to date. The feudalistic system was composed of empires not of nations. Sovereignty rested in the ruler (king, emperor, czar), not in the people or even the state. The ruling dynasties were not necessarily nationalistic but belonged to international aristocracy (the King Bernadette of Sweden was a French nobleman, Catharine the Great of Russia was a German princess); there was no concept of nationhood in today's sense. The feudal empires were fractionized into near autonomous mini-empires run by nobility whose only due to the ruler were taxes, soldiers, and loyalty. The principalities of Monaco, Lichtenstein, Andorra, and Luxembourg protrude into the nation state system as living remnants of the feudal order.

World organization has never been static. It has always changed, but not at the same rate. In some periods the change has taken place within a given organizational design; in other periods the design itself has changed. It is a change of design that international integration may have introduced.

Emerging Global Reorganization

To attempt a projection of how the global markets and business systems may be restructured, let us start with a look at the forerunners of the European Community.

The United States of America The oldest integrated system is the United States. Although it has been labeled a nation state for the lack of any more appropriate model, it never really has been a nation in the sense that Sweden, France, Germany, or Spain are nations. It is a common market of 50 states, a suprastate economy.

There have been strong and deliberate ideological efforts to mold it into a nation, but, whether good or bad, such efforts never quite succeeded. Economically, however, the United States succeeded very very well, outdoing all its rivals. It is a combination of many states with free trade and a completely integrated business system. The United States did not come into existence by a plan like the Treaty of Rome, it just happened. It was a fortunate chain of historic events that formed the United States, the War of Independence, Napoleon's need for money, the Russian sale of Alaska. Thus, the first common market derived from random events.

The Union of Soviet Socialist Republics The same is true of the second suprastate economy, namely, the U.S.S.R. It, too, is a combination of several states; and it, too, came into being more or less as a result of random historic events. Nobody intended it to become a supranational economic system. The first World War had weakened Czarist empires; Lenin, who happened to be a Russian, was the foremost spokesman for the Bolshevik brand of communist philosophy at that time; the Germans, intent to undermine the Russian front through political and psychological subversion, extended financial support to Lenin (in exile in Switzerland), providing him safe passage to Russia and backing his Bolshevik revolution. They never dreamed of the Bolshevik armies one day occupying Berlin.

Of what might have been fifteen or twenty separate nation states, the Soviet system developed. The Soviet Union is now the largest country in the world in land mass and resources. There are many languages, many races, and many cultures: Kazakhs, Latvians, Lithuanians, Estonians, Ukrainians, Georgians, Armenians, Byelorussians, Uzbeks, and many others. The U.S.S.R., therefore, forms not a nation but a massive supranational society. Like the United States, the U.S.S.R. has evolved into a superpower. Both have the influence, ability, and resources to do things that no nation state in the world can match.

Global Impact The rise of the two superpowers placed European nation states in potential jeopardy. Though stronger than before, they had become second-rate countries in the modern world. It was no longer the nineteenth century, when the nation states were the most powerful organizations. The nation state had become relatively antiquated, compared to the superstates.

It was this emerging disparity that inspired the Treaty of Rome. The EC is the first supranational system that was designed to achieve the same benefits that the two superpowers had achieved through accidental developments.

China and India   In the Orient there are two other giants, India and China. Neither fits the nation state model. India covers a subcontinent. It is a collection of many peoples with many more languages (over 100 dialects) than the whole of Europe. In population, too, India exceeds Europe. China is a similar conglomerate of different peoples, all of Mongol race, who are a heterogenous mix of cultures and languages. China is the most populated country in the world. It is clearly a supranational society.

When these four countries are added to the integration schemes already discussed, the idea that world markets are indeed in a process of fundamental reorganization can hardly be dismissed. In Africa and Latin America, much of the legal structure for change is already in place. When there is greater readiness on the part of national governments to let supranational agencies assume strategic control of economic development, the national fractionalization of both continents could disappear rapidly.

The Japan-Australia Axis   Southeast Asia and Oceania remain the only two major regions of the world where international integration has not progressed beyond the planning phase. The most striking development in this area is the rise to dominance of Japan. Although Japan is geographically small, economically it is the third largest country in the world. In any foreseeable future, the Japanese influence is the dominant factor in that area. Part of the Japanese push comes from its critical need for raw materials. Its own reserves are very limited. Japan is also overcrowded, and there is not enough land for further growth. But Japanese society has the drive, the education, and the technology to accomplish things.

Japan has targeted areas having available unused land and natural resources. The largest areas of this kind are Australia and Canada. Australia is an underpopulated continent. Here we have the inevitable opposites: the overflow of Japan and the semivacuum of Australia. Sooner or later the overflow will gravitate to the vacuum. Japan is already the largest investor in Australia. The Australians have even adjusted many of their previous prejudices and legislation to facilitate, although grudgingly, greater Japanese contribution to their economy, especially the infusion of Japanese technology and industrial investment.

The choice for Australians is really not to have Japanese or to have nobody. It is rather whom to have. The pressure on Australia does not come from Japan alone. It comes also from many other overpopulated areas, such as Java, India, and Bangladesh. All these overpopulated areas are trying to push themselves into the Australian vacuum.

The choice for Australia is between the less educated poor of the other overcrowded areas or the Japanese capitalists. The choice is, of course, obvious. The economic axis between Australia and Japan, important as it is, falls far short of a full-fledged supranational system. However, anything in the way of integration in this part of the world is most probably going to develop around this axis.

Japan's other push has been into two other underpopulated and resource rich areas, Canada and Alaska. In Alaska today, Japanese investment is greater than the investment from the other forty-nine states of the United States put together. Japan is a heavy investor in mining, fishing, forestry, and other resource industries. Canada also has a large amount of Japanese investment, in the same areas as Alaska, and expects more. Japan has also had some success getting into Soviet Siberia, which has large forest regions and mineral deposits. The Soviets would like the Japanese to develop the infrastructure in order to open up the resources.

Indonesia   Indonesia is another potential giant. At the end of World War II it was a very backward and primitive country, but it has made impressive progress since the mid-1960s. Its resource base is one of the richest in the world.

How Indonesia and the rest of the Oceanic countries will link to the Japan-Australia axis remains to be seen. The economic leadership and force that makes the difference in this part of the world will come from the growing economic connection this axis provides. Whether Japan will opt for another supranational system with its own influence and the Australian participation, or whether it will work itself into some other group remains to be seen.

Implications for Business

Undeniably, the globe is changing in economic and business terms. The market limitations that so far have been so important in international development, and the small economies that have excluded large production and marketing systems and financial schemes, are being eliminated. It is not the limitation of the market or the limitation of the country that will determine what types of things will be done; rather, it will be the new systems, the new knowledge, and the new technology. Large business systems, whether they are government enterprises or private corporations, will dominate world economies. The small enterprise and the small competitive entrepreneur are probably condemned to relative insignificance.

To summarize, the consequences of international integration are many and far-reaching. Although their specific characteristics can be revealed only by the future, several implications are already clear:

- The integrated supranational systems replace small national economies with larger regional economies.
- The supranational economies create demands for products and technologies that are neither feasible nor workable in segmented national markets.

- Large-scale production and large-scale marketing offer inherent superiorities in the integrated environment.
- Cultural and ethnic pluralism of the supranational systems generate both diversity and dynamics to a degree much higher than any typical nation state economy has traditionally encountered.
- Growth in size and complexity of organizations and institutions necessarily results from integration.
- New skills and refined techniques for solving business problems are a primary prerequisite for successful operations.
- Money and capital markets must sooner or later be completely aligned with the integrated economies; currency convertibility within each supranational system and, ultimately, a single systemwide monetary unit are, therefore, realistic long-term expectations.
- The integration of national units into greater markets implies increased growth opportunities for the individual firm; this in turn invites keener competition and requires more aggressive strategies of growth.
- Since political integration inevitably follows, though not immediately or completely, the role of national governments tends to become that of sociocultural agencies, as the economic, technological, and military defense functions are gradually transferred to the supranational organs.

Since it is the statesmen of the nation states who preside over the process of international integration, the transfer of power to supranational organs will be neither swift nor uncontested. Nor will it be a matter of ideology. The decisive forces are economic and social processes that have outgrown the nation state system.

To what extent this integration process is likely to lead to more efficient systems of producing goods and services and to contribute to global welfare is a subject we will address in Chapter 26.

SUMMARY

International integration has become a global movement. Its long-term benefits are particularly important to small countries and to LDCs.

Attempts to imitate the EC in Latin America started with the creation of LAFTA. Though massive in its geographic scope, LAFTA has enjoyed only modest success. The CACM started out on a more promising note, but it has become ensnarled in political upheavals. The Andean Common Market, though the youngest, outranks the other two in both results achieved and future viability.

In Africa, the forces for international integration are extremely intense, but so are the disintegrative forces. The result has been friction and instability, although the balance has been shifting in favor of integration. In Asia, international business relations are more correctly characterized as international cooperation than as integration. Any supranational integration organization is yet to be formally established, although a number of studies and conferences have emphasized the need for integration in the Asia-Pacific region.

World organization has never been static. International integration represents a new dynamic that may signify a global restructuring of basic political and economic boundaries from nation states to supranational systems. As this reorganization progresses, new options and constraints for business are created.

FOR REVIEW AND DISCUSSION

1. Evaluate LAFTA in comparison to EC. Consider both design and achievements.

2. Why was the ACM established? How does it differ from the other Latin American integration plans?

3. Does CACM offer any realistic prospects as an integrated economy to MNCs or other investors?

4. What factors have propelled international integration in Latin America? What factors work against it?

5. Describe the nature and implications of African nationalism.

6. How and why is the balance shifting between pro-integration and anti-integration forces in Africa?

7. Why are business relations between Japan and Australia of strategic importance to the entire Asia-Pacific region?

8. Do you endorse the hypothesis that international integration represents the process by which the nation state system will be converted into a new global organization patterned after supranational entities such as the United States, the U.S.S.R., and EC? Explain.

9. How does international integration induce change in business organization and behavior?

26

Theoretical Issues of International Integration

Transformation from national to supranational is the essence of international integration. The nation state system that superseded the autocracies—principalities, kingdoms, and empires—has provided the basic blueprint for the present organization of the world. This has been the most remarkable epoch in man's economic and social achievements. In much of modern thought and action the nation state is not only taken for granted but also idealized as the epitome of self-determination and self-actualization of different peoples. Sovereignty, policy, economy, culture, and honor are but a few of the areas in which the nation state has molded modern conceptualizations. It is in this organizational framework that industrial and postindustrial societies have emerged. Thus, by all indications the nation state has outperformed, outranked, and overpowered all earlier political formats.

Ironically, it is the weight of its successes that is now overloading the nation state system. A wider and more flexible structure is the categorical imperative for a new epoch. The merging of separate nations into integrated supranational systems on a regional basis seems to be the format to meet this demand. Though of very recent origin, the international integration movement has already reached global dimensions. No continent, ideology, or nationality has escaped its effect. And this may only be the beginning.

All organizations are inherently conservative, especially when it comes to structural change. The nation state is no exception. As the most autonomous and complete of any organization so far devised, it does not readily succumb to pressures for reorganization.

It is, therefore, a gross oversimplification to say that international integration is running its global course with smoothness and ease. On the contrary, its path is uneven and full of perils. In addition to internal politics, East-West rivalries and the backwash of decolonization in the underdeveloped world obscure and retard its progress. But it cannot be stopped.

As science and automation push back technological frontiers, possibilities for better and richer life are created, but only for those countries that can amass the investments and absorb the quantities required by the expanding scale of the optimal plant. Neither small companies nor small countries can, therefore, qualify. Can any nation deliberately deny itself that which its large neighbors and integrated supranational communities can enjoy? Not for long. More than anything, the rising expectations of the consuming public everywhere are breaking the barriers that constrain growth and development.

Whether international integration will lead to an ultimate dissolution of the nation state is for the future to show. More likely, the nation state will be transformed into a state in a united states, an entity for limited local rule in a larger union. In this view, the existing super nations—the United States, the U.S.S.R., China, and India—are the forerunners of the emerging supranational systems. The fact that they came into being through revolution and force rather than voluntary collaboration marks a difference in the method of international organizational change but certainly not in its direction or ultimate goals.

STAGES OF INTEGRATION

International integration is a long-term process. The evolution of the supranational communities proceeds through a continuum in which at least six stages beyond the nation state have been identified. These stages are:

1. Free trade area: no tariffs or nontariff restrictions among member countries
2. Customs union: common external tariffs and consultation on trade policy
3. Common market: completely free movement of goods, capital, resources, and people among member countries, common external tariffs, harmonization of domestic policies, and coordination of international economic policies
4. Economic union: common currency, integrated domestic policies, and a common international economic policy
5. Political union (united states): complete unification of monetary, fiscal, social, and foreign policies, supranational system in fact replacing the nation-state as the source of sovereignty and security
6. Integrated supranational system: educational and cultural norms harmonized

This continuum allows us to define integration not only as movement along the continuum from a lower to any higher stage of integration, but also as an enlargement of an existing supranational business system by accepting new members into it. Thus, both the development of the Latin American Free Trade Association (LAFTA) into a customs union and the entry of Great Britain into the European Community (EC) are examples of integration. Similarly, a regression to a lower stage of integration or an exit of one or more members from a supranational business system constitutes disintegration.

Integration and disintegration may be simultaneous processes. Some supranational systems may be formed or expanded from the dissolution of others. For example, the expansion of European Community by the entry of Great Britain led at the same time to the scrapping of the European Free Trade Association. In Asia and Africa, where several integration plans currently vie for implementation, future integration will inevitably force many of these to disintegrate.

THEORETICAL PREMISE

International economic integration rests on the premise that there are economies of scale that cannot be exhausted within the limits of national business systems as autonomous economic entities, economies that can be achieved only in a larger sphere such as the EC, LAFTA, ACM, or some similar scheme. The prime purpose of international integration, therefore, is to increase the size of the market, which will in turn raise the productive efficiency of business firms to a higher level than similar firms can achieve without the integration of several national economies.

Consequently, any assessment of the effects of international integration must be formulated in terms of the proposition that there is a definite relationship between the size of a business system (economy) and its efficiency. Is there such a relationship? If so, what are its characteristics and ramifications? Answers to these and similar questions can be given only when the meaning of each of the variables is clearly understood.

Size of the Economy

The terms *economy* and *business system* are usually used to distinguish one country from another. Thus, there must be some dimensions that are common to both a nation and its economy. The size of a nation is expressed in either geographic area or number of people. Although both population and area are relevant to the concept of national economy, neither defines the essential aspects of the productive system as such.

The most generally acceptable measure of the economy is the gross national product (GNP), at least in concept, since it purports to embrace all goods and services produced during a given interval. In actual use the GNP is much less satisfactory than it is as a concept. As pointed out in other connections, GNP figures do not lend themselves to meaningful international comparisons; they are particularly misleading for countries in which much of the production is distributed without any recordable market transactions.

Another way to think of the economy is as a market. A market for what? The size of the market for goods differs from the size of the market for the factors of production. Density of population, existence and location of natural resources, and the institutional framework all bear upon the size of the market, each reflecting a different dimension of the size of the economy.

Efficiency

It is not easy to define economic efficiency. A number of yardsticks can be used, but each renders a different result. For example, either the consumption or production of goods and services might be used. If production is used, an additional question intrudes. To what should total production be related to make it meaningful? Should it be compared to total population, to get per capita figures, or to the labor force, to express the productivity of the productive age groups of the society, or to those actively employed in production? Would any or all in combination be synonymous with the efficiency of the business system as a whole? How about the value of leisure? How about the differences in working conditions, differences among industries, among countries, among cities, among occupations?

An additional shortcoming in using production per person is that it measures efficiency as a function of labor time; the unit of measurement is the time people spend at work. How different would the results be if efficiency were measured by the ratio of product to the inputs of services of all productive agencies and resources? Is this not the more inclusive and, therefore, more appropriate measure of overall efficiency?

This list of questions is by no means exhaustive. It points up, however, the necessity of adopting a compromise criterion that can be used as a standard point of reference. No such criterion has so far been agreed upon. However, the writer assumes that the best way to measure the overall efficiency of a business system is by the quantity of goods and services it provides per capita. For particular purposes, this general measure can be supplemented by the product of an hour's or a year's work.

ASPECTS OF INTEGRATION

It should be evident that no simple explanation of the relationship between the size and the efficiency of the economy is possible. Instead of any single, direct link, we must search for a multitude of links, each of a different kind. These four seem particularly significant: production cost and the size of production units, economic organization, international trade, and the cost of government.

Cost of Production

Economies of scale and mass production are a basic axiom in economic theory. The central point of this axiom is that as the size of a production unit grows, specialization of equipment and skills develops, thus increasing efficiency and decreasing costs. However, economic theory has nothing to say about the cost-size relationship of the economy as a whole. International integration has posed the question, Is the cost-size axiom valid for the entire business system? Does the economy as a whole have an average cost curve with an optimum such as that which a firm is postulated to have? If it does, then there must also be an optimum size for an economy, one that determines how many countries should integrate their economies to produce the greatest economic benefits for the society.

How to determine the optimal size of an economy remains yet to be discovered. The experience of the EC lends strong support to the view that the integrated supranational system, due to its greater size and dynamism, can make businesses more efficient. The increased efficiencies derive from a causal chain that runs from (1) integration of national economies, to (2) a supranational economy, to (3) larger markets, to (4) larger production plants, to (5) lower unit cost of production.

This causation presupposes first that an increase in the size of the country leads to an increase in the size of the market and, second, that an increase in the size of the market must lead to an increase in the size of the production unit. It is difficult to agree that all these relationships hold in all cases. If it were so, the size of the firm should parallel the size of the nation. But some large countries have only small firms and some small countries do have some large firms. If allowance is made for the level of industrial development, however, there seems to be a rather good correlation between the reasoning and the reality. This may be explained in part by the fact that a large country enjoys increasing returns that arise from the indivisibilities (administrative, economic, and political overheads), which it can utilize more efficiently, and in part from the windfall advantages that occur when the market and the economy grow. This would suggest at least that an analogy exists between the optimum of a firm and the optimum of an economy.

Economic Organization

The size of a firm may be expressed in terms of number of people employed, value of output, total sales, or total assets. Each of these is a measure of a different dimension, yet none or even all in combination truly reflect the size of the production unit as such. This is true because the statistical data are based upon a legal *rather than an economic concept*. Methods of business organization long ago outgrew the conceptual apparatus of economics. A business enterprise is no longer necessarily a single legal entity, operating a single factory, producing a single product, and distributing it in a single market. One entity may control several factories, and a factory may produce a number of products. Such diversification opens a gap between the unit of technical efficiency and the unit of managerial control. An enterprise such as the MNC may organize itself in the form of several corporate bodies bound together by ownership, contractual arrangements, and common management.

Production Optimality and Company Size The discrepancies between the size of the production unit and the size of the legal entity tend to be the greatest in large companies because of their complex structures, which often include scores of subsidiaries and other affiliates. If each subsidiary makes a product unrelated to the products of others, each can represent a suboptimal entity.

In small countries, the market limits the size of a production unit, such as a factory, if market demand is smaller than the output of an optimal factory. The options are either to build a suboptimal factory or to operate an optimal one below capacity. But the small market does not limit the size of the company, which can grow through conglomerating, that is, by adding new product lines. The only way a specialized firm in a small country can grow is by becoming international. Thus, the size of the country imposes at least two significant constraints upon an enterprise: it delimits the size of the technical production unit, and it requires a company either to diversify or to become multinational in order to avoid stagnation.

The large conglomerate remains subject to the first constraint, its technical production units being limited by the size of the market, but it can gain through a wider distribution of administrative overhead and especially through its relative power over transactions with other firms, which in small countries would generally have to be smaller by necessity. Thus, a diversified large firm in a small country possesses a strategic power position in that it buys from and sells to mostly smaller and weaker companies. Since such a situation is conductive neither to effective competition nor to optimal allocation of resources, it can be argued that small countries with very few large diversified companies lack the internal competitive balance necessary for efficiency and innovation.

Multinationalization   That leaves the companies that chose the alternative of expanding beyond the boundaries of a small country. For the MNC the domestic segment shrinks to a fraction of its overall size, and objectives and strategies are refocused from a national to a multinational perspective. The MNC cannot permit itself to be dominated by the considerations or conditions of any single country but must have strategies and policies appropriate to its total position. The main rivals of the MNC are other MNCs. Therefore, the behavior of the MNC may or may not conform to the requirements of effective competition in any particular country. It will compete if competition is consistent with its overall strategy and expectations regarding the reactions of its multinational rivals, but it will not compete in a particular country if that competition jeopardizes its other markets by provoking retaliatory actions of other MNCs or by disrupting orderly development of its corporate goals.

Cartels   When international cartels develop, their effect is likely to be greater on the small countries, for two reasons: if there is only one producing company, the cartel will allocate the entire national market to it and permit no outside competition; if there are a few producing companies, the cartel may force them to merge and thus produce a single-enterprise country. In addition, there is a built-in inclination for small economies to develop cartels. The preliminary to any international cartel is a national cartel. In a larger country the members of the domestic industry are more numerous and have much greater difficulty reaching a cartel agreement. Even when they do, the agreement tends to be unstable and vulnerable to diverse reactions of its members to new business situations. In a small country the internal framework is already cartelistic as far as any large company is concerned. All that is needed is to come to terms with the foreign competitors.

Organizational Efficiency   The organizational characteristics of business enterprises in reference to competition and cartels are quite different in small economies than in large ones. Effective competition, diversity, and change are more likely to be associated with the latter than with the former. Technological progress and international adjustment are more probable in large economies because of (a) the possibility of escaping from restrictions of vested interests, (b) the greater variety of resources in which to invest, and (c) more opportunities for marketing outside the established channels of conventional practice.

In sum, the organizational aspects of a small country tend to be even more constrictive than the technological aspects. Technologically, an economy is suboptimal if its markets cannot absorb the output of the most efficient plant in a particular industry; and it is optimal if its markets are large enough to provide adequate outlets for such a plant. Organizationally, an economy is suboptimal if it lacks the necessary number of competitors to spur efficiency and to compel the construction of the technically most efficient facilities. In other words, an economy large enough to absorb the output of at least one optimum sized plant may still be too small to provide the incentive for its construction. This means that the technological optimum size of an economy is much smaller than the organizationally optimum size, the technological optimum being a necessary but insufficient precondition for the organizational optimum.

International Trade

Can international trade offset smallness of the domestic market? It has been stressed elsewhere that the theory that international trade can have the same effect as domestic trade has been proven fallacious by experience, mainly because efficient production in the modern world is often mass production, with highly mechanized and automated plants. Mass production facilites, to be justified, require mass markets, which are not only large but also reasonably homogenous and stable over time. Export markets seldom meet these requirements. They are subject to sudden political interference, to monetary restrictions, and to constantly changing local conditions, all of which make forecasting, planning, and stable operation highly precarious. Mass production, therefore, is seriously constrained if the internal market is too small to absorb most of the output.

A large economy possesses some clear advantages over its smaller counterparts from the foreign trade standpoint. Because of the size of its internal consumption, it can absorb the bulk of its production at home and thus be less sensitive to foreign influences. For the same reason, it can fully utilize the economies of scale, and its size and influence enable it to be dominant in international transactions.

Are these advantages accessible to small economies? Not readily. A small nation may be dominant over still weaker ones, especially if it holds a monopoly position or if its own products are in great demand, but it usually does not possess any significant influence over larger economies. The same can be said about international fluctuations. A small economy depends on foreign countries for both sales and supplies and is thus inseparably tied to the international markets. If it tries to insulate itself from world economic fluctuations, it has to curtail its exports, which provide the only means it possesses for achieving an optimum scale of production and for procuring the necessary imports.

From the international trade standpoint, then, a small nation gains significantly from merging its economy with others through international integration. Conventional trade liberalization measures such as those attempted under the GATT program cannot produce the same advantage for smaller nations. Will this argument still hold after the small nations have combined into large integrated entities that equal or exceed in size the present giants such as the United States? Probably not. However, a more conclusive answer must wait for the integration movement to run its course.

Cost of Government

An important cost in any economy is the cost of government, which is analogous to overhead cost of a firm. How the cost of government varies with the change of the size of the economy is not well understood. Since international integration converts several smaller economies into a large supranational economy, its impact on the cost of government may be significant. Can this supranational economy be governed more efficiently than the smaller national economies? Are there any cost savings resulting from the increased scale of governance?

It is probably true that the cost of government in any economy varies with the type or system of government that a country has. But given a particular system, the cost of government depends in a variety of ways on the size of the economy. In internal affairs, both a small and a large nation need more or less similar central institutions for the legislative, executive, and judicial functions. On regional and local levels they differ. In a large nation, where the central institutions of government are farther removed from the individual communities, industries, and citizens, the need for various subinstitutions and agencies is also greater, but not in proportion to the size differences. As in business, certain functions can be performed centrally, regardless of the size of the country, with little or no change in cost.

Social Services   For the cost of social services the available data are inconclusive. Both educational and health services, however, tend to be more expensive in small than in large countries. A more decisive factor than size is the density of the population. Low density areas may require suboptimal hospitals and schools and thus lead to higher operating costs. This point holds only for government services where mass production economies exist. These include housing, electrical power, social insurance, judicial and legal services, and public safety. In other areas, mass production economies are negligible in a technical sense but may be very significant in a human sense. This is especially true for the professional and educational services, whose practitioners' qualifications and proficiencies depend to a high degree upon participation in the intellectual life of their respective specialties. A small country may lack the opportunities for such participation. Often a professional in a small country must spend a great deal of effort to become multilingual in order to be able to communicate with his peers in larger countries. Thus, again, the weight of the argument tips the scales against the small economy. On a per capita basis its government appears to be more costly if the same services are rendered.

Foreign Service   In foreign affairs, the disadvantage is even greater. The need for a diplomatic service is determined mainly by the number of contacts with the outside world—how many countries and how many foreign service posts in each. The size of the country itself and the prevailing international problems are contributory factors. A small nation needs the same number of embassies, consulates, and attachés as a large nation. A small country is actually more dependent on foreign markets and sources of supply. This is true not only for business but also for social, political, and military needs. Also, a small country is more internationally exposed: as a geographic fact, it has longer frontier per capita, and as a defense unit, it is less able to repulse foreign aggression. For all these reasons, a small nation must spend a higher percentage of its national income, both aggregate and per capita, on international relations.

SUMMARY

International integration is a long-term process. The nation state must pass through five distinctive phases before a completely integrated supranational system is achieved.

On all four accounts, technological efficiency, organizational optimality, international trade, and cost of government services, international integration offers significant theoretical advantages to small nations. Although in certain areas the advantages are offset in various degrees by disadvantages, there is little doubt that without integration small economies are deprived of optimal production and effective competition, that internal stability and progress are dependent upon the vicissitudes of international markets and foreign political actions, and that government and professional services are restrained more than in a larger integrated economy.

How large the integrated entities should become and if there is a size beyond which further expansion of the integrated group of countries will lead to negative results remain unknown. It seems quite clear, however, that the average cost behaves not too differently from the costs of a firm, in that it declines with the increase of the economy. Whether the curve will have a general optimum and whether it will then start rising has yet to be proven; both are plausible propositions.

Until such evidence is produced, we have no theoretical foundation for estimating at what point an integration scheme will reach its optimum. Oratorical rhetoric about small countries being better off by avoiding international integration rests on nationalistic and ideological biases, not on rational analysis.

FOR REVIEW AND DISCUSSION

1. How useful for understanding world business environments is a good grasp of the stages of integration? Can you cite concrete situations in which such a grasp would be of practical value?

2. Can you find any evidence that there is a causal relationship between the size of an economy and its efficiency? If not, does that mean no such relationship exists?

3. How would you choose from among all the different ways that efficiency can be measured? What criteria would guide your choice?

4. Large firms of small countries are subject to different environmental stimuli (positive or negative) than their counterparts in large countries. Justify or refute.

5. Do financial statements of companies give us good insights into how large or efficient their physical production is? Explain.

6. Drawing on your study of Chapters 9 through 16, elaborate on the point that the behavior of MNCs may or may not conform to the requirements of competition in any particular country.

7. Why is it important to distinguish between technical suboptimality and organizational suboptimality?

8. Would free trade obviate the advantages of international integration?

9. If we want to compare the costs of government in the United States, Japan, and Finland, what problems would complicate our task?

10. Of what relevance is it to business managers whether a nation has an extensive foreign service or relies on a very limited number of diplomatic posts supplemented by honorary consuls and similar token representations?

SUGGESTED READINGS FOR PART EIGHT

The European Community After Twenty Years. Annuals of the American Academy of Political and Social Sciences. Special Issue. 440: November, 1978.

Clough, S. *European Economic History.* New York: McGraw-Hill, 1975.

European Economic Community. *Treaty Establishing the European Economic Community* (English language edition). Brussels: EEC, 1957.

European Free Trade Association. *Convention Establishing the European Free Trade Association.* London: H. M. Stationery Office, 1960.

Green, R. H., and Krishna, K. G. W. *Economic Cooperation in Africa: Retrospect and Prospect.* Nairobi: Oxford University Press, 1967.

Gruhn, I. *Regionalism Reconsidered: The Economic Commission for Africa.* Boulder: Westernview Press, 1979.

Jenkins, D. *Job Power: Blue and White Collar Democracy.* New York: Simon and Schuster, 1976.

Katzman, M. T. *Cities and Frontiers in Brazil.* Cambridge: Harvard University Press, 1977.

Kerr, A. *The Common Market and How It Works.* Oxford: Pergamon Press, 1977.

MacArthur, J. *Industrial Planning in France.* Cambridge: Harvard University Press, 1969.

Robson, P. *Economic Integration in Africa.* Evanston: Northwestern University Press, 1968.

Shaw, T. *Alternative Futures for Africa.* Boulder: Westernview Press, 1981.

Epilogue

The Need for International Business Competence

*I*nternational business has become a vital necessity for the contemporary world. Increasingly it is a part of how we live and how we make our living. This applies to nations, to enterprises, and to individuals.

BENEFITS FROM INTERNATIONAL BUSINESS

The Nation

The growing linkages and interdependencies among national economies create new options and opportunities from which nations can benefit according to their specific needs and preferences. Access to natural resources, to technologies, to human resources, to capital, to markets, and to other essential elements that are scarce or unavailable at home is but one indicator of the important contributions of international business to a nation's economy.

But these benefits are not autogenous; they must be uncovered and harnessed, under the specific conditions that prevail, to the particular purposes that the nation's needs dictate. This requires knowledge and sophistication in international business. Ignorance and misapplications can turn the potential benefits from international options into gateways for counterproductive, or even destructive, foreign dependencies.

Ignorance and ineptitude in international business have both economic and political costs. Economically, they deny the public the gains in productivity and the enrichment of consumption that results from well-informed and competently executed activities. Politically, failure to benefit from the opportunities exposes the country to the risks of economic stagnation and political unrest, which tend to undermine government stability and social order.

The Company

For business firms the stakes are even higher. International successes have become decisive for profits and corporate growth in many sectors; international

473

setbacks, either the failure to penetrate foreign markets or the failure to withstand foreign penetration of the domestic market, threaten the survival of other industries. Thus, the spectra of success and failure have widened and diversified for business firms everywhere.

Though the nature and intensity of the international influences may vary from company to company, none can altogether escape their impact. Management no longer has the choice to deal or not to deal with the international factors; its only choice is how to deal with them most effectively, that is, how to identify, predict, adapt to, and use relevant international variables. This can be done only if a firm's management cadre contains people with a proficiency in international business commensurate with the proficiency of the cadres in other aspects of business administration.

BEYOND THE HORIZON

The push for internationalization of business has been a permanent dynamic of recent decades. Informed scenarios for its future course range from the continuation of recent trends to substantial enlargement of both its scope and intensity. The expansionary scenarios envisage the rise of a global industrial system in which MNCs of different types constitute the central core of internationally integrated industrial, commercial, and financial activities. Important avenues for multinationalization of business firms are indicated by the appearance of new kinds of coalitions among enterprises of different nations, notably, joint undertakings between privately owned and publicly owned firms, between firms of rich nations and poor nations, and between firms on different sides of ideological divides such as capitalism and communism.

Such an evolutionary process imposes its own imperatives. The MNCs will have to shed their ethnocentric as well as functional parochialisms and grow not only in scope but more importantly in quality and adaptiveness; decision making strategies and policies will, thus, shift from country to regional and world frames of reference; the geocentralization of management will require a grasp of worldwide markets, resources, peoples, and cultures; business must learn to reach for ideas from any part of the globe, deploy organization and technological skills in all environments, and tap resources and markets across national, ideological, and cultural divides.

While geocentralizing themselves, the MNCs will act as geocentralizers of other business organizations as well as of the economic and social infrastructures of nation states. Accusations of antinational and irresponsible propensities will continue, but, as we have discussed in Parts Four and Five, the superior economic performances of MNCs, particularly if their increasing sophistication continues to eliminate past mistakes, can be expected to prevail. The transformations of the infrastructures will depend upon mechanisms by which individual nations and supranational economic communities can objectively assess and effect an equitable distribution of the economic contribution

Table 1   Ignorance in World Affairs

In 1980, a federally funded study, based on a random sample of more than 3,000 students at 185 colleges and universities, showed that less than 15 percent could answer two-thirds of the 101 questions about world events and history correctly.

Seniors correctly answered only half the 101 questions about world affairs, compared with 41 percent by freshmen and 40 percent by junior-college students.

Getting two-thirds of the answers right on the test is worth a D in most grading systems.

Source: The Council of Learning.

of MNCs. Systematic rules of transfer pricing, monetary movements, and technology transfers should greatly reduce government fears of MNCs' powers. This will enhance the political viability and social legitimacy of the MNCs as business institutions and accelerate the geocentralization processes in related spheres. Among other things, these projections have far-reaching implications for national education systems in general, and for the quantity and quality of international education in particular.

CAREERS IN INTERNATIONAL BUSINESS

Business Careers

In business organizations, the need for expertise in international business pervades all functions and hierarchical levels. In some aspects it provides the primary criteria, in others the supporting criteria, and in still others the contextual criteria for a decision process.

In accounting, competent treatment of both cost and revenue data is necessary to obtain comparability and consistency of records. This requires an intimate knowledge not only of the laws and accepted standards of the accounting profession in different host countries, but also of the concepts employed in valuation of different business assets as well as tax laws and liabilities.

In finance, interaffiliate transfers of assets of any kind create the necessity for understanding foreign exchange, inflation and interest rate differentials, and currency controls. To raise capital and to manage liquid assets properly, financial executives must be well versed in money and capital markets in both home and host countries.

In marketing, MNC managers must handle interaffiliate trade in components and serve as exporters of their own goods and importers of other affiliates' goods. Often company policy calls for an integrated marketing program in which all affiliates participate. Thus, the entire marketing mix—product design and assortment, advertising and promotion, pricing, and channel selection—becomes dependent on the managers' ability to understand and to use the different value systems and other motivational forces at work in different host country cultures.

In production operations management, the significance of international expertise may be less obvious than in the other functional areas, yet it is no less real. The fact that factories require engineering, machinery, physical layouts, and time schedules creates the false image of a purely mechanistic setting. Though technologies do play the paramount role in production systems as such, managers of these systems cannot disregard the human element. Without workers, all technologies are of little value. Productivity depends on the attitudes and actions of the employees, their unions, and their sociopolitical support systems.

In intracompany international relations, expertise in international business is paramount for executives who are planning and managing operation relations among the MNC entities in different countries; theirs is primarily an international relations job. As indicated above, although such interentity problems are intrinsic to a degree to most, if not all functional activities, of MNCs, this burden weighs heaviest on strategic planners, company-wide policy makers, and operating executives directly involved with cross-boundary coordination and integration of specific programs.

Nonbusiness Careers

In government and social agencies the need for international business knowledge has also risen sharply.

For some government agencies this growth is a direct function of the multinationalization of business, since these agencies exercise surveillance over some aspect of business activity. Such is the case with tax authorities, central banks, national treasuries, and the ministries of commerce and labor. The agencies required to trace the international flows of strategic goods and technologies and assure compliance with laws and regulation of export destinations, capital transfers, securities dealings, and other regulated international business arrangements, all need considerable knowledge of international business.

Other government agencies have been confronted with international problems due to some shared jurisdiction with the first group of agencies (for example, the U.S. Department of Agriculture) or because foreign-based MNCs have entered their previously domestic realms of responsibilities (for example, U.S. Department of Interior). Thus, the multinationalization of business tends to generate a corresponding multinationalization of government agencies. To perform their expanded responsibilities, these agencies must acquire a knowledge in international business as sophisticated as that which the MNCs under their surveillance employ.

In addition, religious orders, sports associations, and associations devoted to arts and avocations all have acquired multinational scope and composition. From this stem needs and problems that are closely akin to those in business.

Thus, their administrative knowledge base requires the addition of international business competence.

Recruitment

Since business and government are inextricably entangled with international factors, simple logic would dictate that both would rate high on their want list jobseekers with education credentials in international business. This has not been true. Recognition of expertise in international business comes grudgingly. Ignorance and bureaucratic resistance for change have long blocked the path. In the last few years, however, these barriers have started to fall and managerial positions explicitly specifying competence in international business have increased rapidly.

For the entrants to entry-level positions, the new trend has meant very little; the system seems to work from the top down. International competence figures prominently in the required qualifications of corporate directors and high level operating executives; it fades rapidly as one descends to the lower echelons of the management hierarchy.

The rationale of this from-top-down trend of specifying international business knowledge as a job prerequisite has not been fully explained. One factor has been the lack of sufficient collegiate programs in international business to justify setting up recruitment and entry-level training programs. The few recruits with such background are more economically trained, along with the majority who have domestically oriented business degrees. As more and more universities are adding international business courses, at least some relief from this shortage can be predicted.

Another factor has been what might be called the parochial politics of organizational bureaucracies; namely, the resistance of existing managerial cadres to recognize as essential knowledge and skills other than those they themselves possess. Such resistance is strongest on the lower levels of an organization, where the battle for identity and promotion is all consuming.

In this respect college graduates with a degree in international business face the same kinds of hurdles as the computer experts faced a generation ago. The computer people were materially aided by the hardware, which imposed concretely demonstrable sets of efficiencies and skill requirements. International business training, lacking such hardware support, must demonstrate its usefulness in other ways.

The lack of a sufficient supply of entry-level jobseekers, combined with the absence of generally recognized educational standards for international business graduates, has forced corporations to rely on internal recruitment for international jobs. That is, people hired for noninternational assignments are later reassigned to an international responsibility. The preparation such domestic managers typically get is a brief survey of the firm's international activities. In some cases, he or she may also be sent to an intensive seminar of a few weeks' duration offered by the American Management Association, the New York World Trade Center, or some similar trade association.

When looking for outside talent for their international managerial requirements, U.S. firms have chosen to recruit non-U.S. citizens with U.S. business
education or U.S. citizens with foreign degrees. Apparently the biculturalism
that one inevitably develops when completing an academic degree in another
country, especially in a country with a different language, equips individuals
with an increased ability to cope with international complexities.[1]

This is not to say that study abroad and bilingualism are a satisfactory
substitute for systematic education in international business. If knowledge of
language and culture were all that was needed to make competent executives,
the need for schools of business administration would never have arisen.
Rather, bilingualism and experiential exposure to some form of foreign culture
are important facilitators that, if incorporated, significantly strengthen an individual's preparation for international business reponsibilities. A systematic
study of the core areas of business administration—accounting finance, marketing, human resource management, and business policy—is necessary as the
substantive body of concepts, relationships, and facts that all managers—domestic or international—must master.

---

1. Recent discoveries in linguistics and brain neurology strongly imply that this may indeed be
true. Mappings of electrical stimuli caused by word tests on the brain have shown that the different
languages of a bilingual or multilingual individual occupy some of the brain space that a monolingual
uses for language. In addition, the second and third languages possess some brain space of their own.
This added brain space serves an intricate series of functions which are not required from the brain
of a monolingual individual: distinguishing between the vocabularies, syntaxes, and other processes
of each language; retrieving the right word and sentence structure from duplicate sets for each meaning;
and structuring and positioning specific events in the different systems of each language. This latter
point is clarified by the finding that the grammatical and semantic features of a particular language
determine not only how one communicates reality, but also how one perceives and structures it. Thus,
bilingualism fosters biculturalism in a fundamental sense.

Appendix

Assignments Abroad

*T*he expatriate members of an enterprise face various manifestations of culture conflict that prevent their integration and assimilation into the host society. As detached aliens, neither the managers nor the corporate units they control can be fully effective. Both must, therefore, acquire the capacity to adapt to the alien social setting.

The use of expatriate personnel creates a two-edged identity conflict. The executive who is transferred abroad leaves behind the cultural system that defined and supported his place in the home society. He is literally cast adrift in the strange seas of the host society, whose ways, institutions, and values constitute his new reality. To the host society, the expatriate is similarly strange. It is imperative that the expatriate manager actively endeavor to adapt his behavior to the indigenous society; it is equally imperative that the parent company assist him to achieve this objective, for it underlies the ability of the entire affiliate structure to achieve accommodation and assimilation in its various home environments throughout the world.

THE EXECUTIVE AND FORMAL GROUPS

By definition, a formal group is one to whom the responsibility for a specific function has been assigned. To the executive, the formal group will normally be the organizational layers and functional divisions of his company. Again by definition, a formal hierarchy exists and, by implication, there is acceptance by the group of the legitimacy of this hierarchy. An individual joining a formal group can be assured of overt acceptance by this group. For example, a comptroller, by virtue of his appointment, receives overt acceptance by the executive

479

and accounting staff with whom he interacts. This acceptance is, however, not necessarily either complete or final. Not infrequently, the situation described by Edward T. Hall applies: "The stranger enters and behaves differently from the local norm, he often quite unintentionally insults, annoys, or amuses the native with whom he attempts to do business."[1] Each apparent deviation from the norm may effectively undermine the legitimacy of his position. The formal group recognizes hierarchical patterns, satisfactions, and shared purpose. Acceptance rests on establishing common norms of behavior.

The ideal executive would appear to be one who was completely aware of each and every trait and in fact not a stranger at all. No expatriate can hope to be in this position. Even within one nation, significant differences occur. The Bavarian, the Swabian, the Hamburger, and the Berliner differ vastly, as do the Yorkshireman and the Londoner. In any multi-unit corporation, there coexist with the common, company-wide norms of executive behavior certain parochialisms of the different regional units of the firm. The greater the geographic separation of the units and the more decentralized the administration, the more pronounced and variegated will the parochial superstructure be.

In the multinational corporation, the superstructure adds a new layer, which consists of the different national norms that are interposed between the company-wide standards and the regional parochialisms of the individual operating units. Since contrasts within the national norm are not only often sharper but quite different in nature from the intranational ones, they are the source of problems for the expatriate executive. Along with the company-wide norms, which by definition must be multinational, the expatriate executive must adapt to the national norms of his host country. Contravention or even neglect of the nationally accepted standards can not only mean dissonance and friction for the organization, but also confront the newcomer with the total force of the host society.

How can adaptability of the expatriate executive be enhanced? One writer stresses selecting the executive by concentrating on four criteria:

1. Qualification for the position
2. Personal traits
3. Language facility
4. General health[2]

Certainly, the capability of performing the duties of a position should be the prime consideration. Under personal traits, adaptability, open-mindedness, lack of prejudice, and flexibility are important. These traits are not only parallel but can be assessed by careful investigation. Discreet inquiry, structured interviews, and investigations into spare-time hobbies, pursuits, and affiliations

1. Edward T. Hall, "The Silent Language in Overseas Business," *Harvard Business Review* (May–June 1960).

2. R. C. Zuelke, "How to Hire Employees for Foreign Assignments," *International Management* (January 1965).

are some of the machinery available to help determine these personal traits. Insofar as these traits can be found, then adjustment to different norms will be possible.

This adjustment can be furthered by preparatory instruction in the cultural values and characteristics of a country. It is important to recognize that the value derived from such instruction will probably be in cushioning the culture shock as it affects the executive rather than in delineating norms to observe. Certain obvious proscriptions can be taught, such as the Islamic attitude toward alcohol or women's protected role in many societies. Generally observed social usages and relative degrees of formality can be noted. However, generalizations on norms are like seeking the average family with 2.6 children. Not all Englishmen are phlegmatic and politely uncommunicative nor all Scots dour Calvinists. Nor is any country, company, or group a static entity.

THE EXECUTIVE AND INFORMAL GROUPS

Within most formal groups, and partially dependent on group size, are informal groups. These may be created by common interests, shared tasks, or many extraneous causes. Their composition may be well defined or frequently varied, depending on their nature. In a multinational company, the shared interest might be nationality or language. The group could share such a tenuous bond as an interest in soccer, or it could be a power-seeking alliance. Acceptance of the stranger within an informal group depends on the factors that gave rise to the group.

Organization theory suggests that these informal groups may be used to managerial advantage. Membership in them or their acceptance of the stranger is of lesser importance and indeed unlikely in that their purposes and satisfactions are not generally shared. They do provide a vehicle for greater acceptance within the formal group. In addition, informal groups have an identifiable leadership, which is most frequently an opinion leader. Personal interaction with such leaders on an informal basis can be expeditious.

Outside of the company there are informal and indeed formal groups by whom acceptance can be valuable to the executive. These should be distinguished from purely social groups. For example, in London, membership in certain clubs or luncheon patronage at certain restaurants is almost completely reserved to specific trades or professions. The virtual preemption of a golf course on a Thursday afternoon by the medical profession is another example. Here acceptance is a function of the degree of shared interest.

Acceptance in such groups does extend when a common purpose becomes identifiable. The threat of government action against an industry, an unwelcome market innovation, or similar external influences all tend to coalesce the informal group and define its purpose and rewards. Just as danger or peril may make strange bedfellows, so common interest against external forces welcomes the stranger.

THE EXECUTIVE AND SOCIAL GROUPS

The social groups available to the executive in the United States, centering on the corporation, are a rarity in most other areas of the world. They are almost nonexistent in countries with highly structured class systems or traditionally oriented societies. In addition, in certain countries wives are not normally included in any intracompany social groupings, which can be the case in the United States.

Medardo Rodriguez speaks of the separation of social and business life in Latin America,[3] and Granick notes that the top level French executive "fails to socialize with any of the department heads of his own firm."[4] In the main, acceptance of the expatriate executive by social groups is not a function of his hierarchal position. In some instances in fact, this may hinder acceptance. Harbison and Myers refer to this when they say, "in Chile, the landed and traditional commercial aristocracy tended in the past to regard new entrepreneurs as social upstarts."[5]

Common social prerequisites, education level, social competence, and the vouching of mutual acquaintances reduce the problems of acceptance in a social group. Essentially, these are the predominant conditions for social acceptance in any society. Social acceptance is significant in that in many societies it is tantamount to acceptance of the corporation the executive represents. This will most frequently be the case in countries in which there is a marked division between the hierarchy of the legal-political structure and that of the economic structure. Also, there are traditionally-oriented societies in which business is awarded on the basis of friendship.

THE ACCEPTANCE OF SPECIALISTS

The expatriate specialist encounters and seeks acceptance by similar groups. Here he carries a significant advantage in his specialized qualifications. Assuming his competence, his peer group (and this approximates the formal group he fits into in his organization) accepts him. The freemasonry of specialized skills closes its ranks to the stranger only when it is threatened economically.

It is in acceptance within the social groups of a different community that difficulties will be encountered. The value structure and the positioning therein of the technical skill of the expatriate may differ materially from that of his home country. If he is to be accepted outside the structures of his organization, he must learn and acknowledge the norms of his new society.

3. Medardo Rodriguez, "Doing Business in Latin America Today," *Management Review* (July 6, 1965), pp. 4–13.

4. David Granick, *The Red Executive: A Study of the Organization Man in Russia* (Garden City, NY: Doubleday, 1961), p.203

5. Frederick C. Harbison and Charles Myers, *Management in the Industrial World* (New York: McGraw-Hill, 1969), p. 123.

It is not improper to consider sales personnel as specialists, particularly those who impinge directly on a formal group in their approaches to a market. Two particular circumstances abroad affect their success. First, norms of behavior may proscribe action. In England, for example, to attempt to sell directly to a building contractor creates serious repercussions. The norm requires that this sale be made by an intermediary, who in turn buys from an importer, who places his order with an agent. These are the normal channels, which cannot be circumvented without consulting with all members, without an actual alienation of sales. This is not to say that innovation of business practices is to be avoided, only that they must be undertaken with full realization of their social context, which determines the approaches and methods to be used.

Second, in most companies outside of the United States, authority is placed much closer to the apex of the organization pyramid. To sales personnel this is both an aid and a difficulty. If accessible, the formal group that makes decisions to purchase is small and unquestioned. Their level suggests that sales personnel approaching them are better chosen from higher echelons of the selling company. One vice president of a U.S. firm indicated that in two months he was able to obtain more orders in Europe than in eight months at home, because decisions were made at higher levels and without equivocation.

Index